SEX-POL

Essays 1929–1934

SEX-POL

Essays 1929-1934

Wilhelm Reich

Edited by Lee Baxandall

Introduction by Bertell Ollman

Translated by Anna Bostock,
Tom DuBose and Lee Baxandall

Random House New York

Library of Congress Cataloging in Publication Data

Reich, Wilhelm, 1897–1957.
Sex-pol; essays, 1929–1934.

Includes bibliographical references.
1. Sex (Psychology)—Addresses, essays, lectures.
2. Alienation (Social psychology)—Addresses, essays, lectures.
3. Communism and society—Addresses, essays, lectures.
I. Title.

BF692.R35 1972   301.41   72–2735
ISBN 0–394–47921–1

Manufactured in the United States of America
by American Book–Stratford Press, Inc.

9 8 7 6 5 4 3 2

First Edition

Foreword

"Love . . . first really teaches man to be-
lieve in the objective world outside him-
self. [It] not only makes man an object,
but the object a man!"

—*Karl Marx*, THE HOLY FAMILY

Wilhelm Reich died in 1957 at the age of sixty. He was in the Lewisburg federal penitentiary. He had been jailed as a result of charges brought by the U.S. Food and Drug Administration, which had also impounded or burned Reich's books. He seemed at the time an improbable candidate for the wave of enthusiasm which his works have since caused world-wide.

An ignominious death was but the ultimate humiliation for a man who had only wanted to relieve mankind of some of its miseries—and whose transgression was that he tirelessly and utterly without compromise pursued that goal wherever it might lead.

Reich's truth-seeking and courage led him, while still in medical school, to the still-experimental and then-suspect discipline of psychoanalysis. He became a major pupil of Freud. And almost as early, these same qualities led to an interest in the ideas of Marx and of socialism and communism. For once a pathway forward was indicated he stepped immediately onto it. The logic of Reich's personal decisions was utterly impersonal in this sense. That he might encounter disapproval and even great hardships from any quarter whatever could not deter him from bringing his life wholeheartedly into line with his thought.

The same disregard for opportunism led to Reich's expulsion from the Communist Party in 1933, and from the International Psychoanalytical Association in 1934.

Thus Reich was cut off (and in one sense, he cut himself off) at the peak of his work from his professional and political colleagues of long standing.

That this severance from the psychoanalytical and socialist movements was not to be irrevocable, however, should have been evident even in the mid-1930s from the obvious fact that both movements were in profound crisis and the expulsions of Reich were one (very significant) token of these crises. His principled and polite but unbending critiques of his co-workers—especially of those Creons who represented the administrative wisdom of the two institutionalizations of basically revolutionary conceptions, and of those who bowed to the Creons—were more than they could tolerate.

But during the 1960s in the New Left youth movements the antagonist of Creon, Antigone, was reborn. And with this development the fallen but hardly decomposed figure of Wilhelm Reich has risen again, borne into view by the fresh generation of radical youth—whose own limitations of courage and vision, we should add, remain to be demonstrated.

The careful Creons whose concern is to preserve the status quo of psychoanalysis or of the political left are undoubtedly apprehensive that this troublesome specter is once more abroad.

From the Antigones of the same world, however, a fraternal response awaits. The integration of Reich's work with that of his peers and successors, and into the structures of our own lives and organizations and thought, is a process that can be said to have begun but has no ending in prospect.

The introductory essay which follows is remarkably concise and totalizing and suggestive. It provides, I believe, a notable contribution to the interpretation equally of Reich and of Marx. The discriminations offered by Bertell Ollman should enter the mainstream of our discussions.

As concerns the texts in this volume: they are the *first* straightforward, unrevised English translations of any of the writings of Wilhelm Reich from his Marxist years.

This statement may come as a surprise and shock. The reader may be familiar with such English-language titles as *The Mass Psychology of Fascism* and *The Sexual Revolution*—weren't

these first published in German no later than 1936? Yes, books
with these titles were first brought out then. However, the
contents of the German texts differ, often greatly, from the
same titles in English.

Reich never hid this revising. In the years following his extreme disillusionment with Stalinist Russia and no less with the
uncritical backers of Stalinism, Reich stressed that politics
seemed to him no longer an effective means by which to heal the
suffering human animal. Accordingly, in the English editions of
books and articles he now chose to bring before a new audience,
Reich largely removed the terminology and analysis of social
class; he expunged the political guidelines and horizons.

In consequence, to read even what have seemed the most
Marxist of Reich's books in English prior to the present volume
is to read texts from the European period which were diluted and
altered by a welter of terminological changes and substantial
omissions and substitutions.

We needed a collection of unrevised European-period Reich
writings in English. In particular, we needed a selection of the
sex-political investigations and guideline papers which Reich,
once he had grown intransigent toward Stalinistic socialism and
labor organizations, no longer felt he had any reason to reissue.

This volume contains the first collection of such texts.

It is to be hoped that English translations of all the original
writings of Reich from 1927–36 may shortly follow.

Lee Baxandall

Contents

Contents   x

The social revolution is only a prerequisite (and not a sufficient condition) for the sexual revolution, but Reich believed that recognition of their close relationship, particularly among the young, helped to develop consciusness of the need for both revolutions. With the exception of *Character Analysis* (1934), which psychoanalysts still regard as a classic in their field, and a few related articles, Reich's early work was devoted almost entirely to the attainment of such a consciousness.

Not content to debate his ideas, in 1929 Reich organized the Socialist Society for Sexual Advice and Sexual Research. A half dozen clinics were set up in poor sections of Vienna, where working-class people were not only helped with their emotional problems but urged to draw the political lessons which come from recognizing the social roots of these problems. Moving to Berlin in 1930, Reich joined the German Communist Party and persuaded its leadership to unite several sexual-reform movements into a sex-political organization under the aegis of the party. With Reich, the chief spokesman on sexual questions, lecturing to working-class and student audiences throughout the country, membership in the new organization grew quickly to about forty thousand.

By the end of 1932, however, the Communist Party decided —whether to placate potential allies against fascism or because of the general reaction that was then overtaking the Soviet Union —that Reich's attempt to link sexual and political revolution was a political liability. Interpretations which were previously considered "sufficiently" Marxist were now declared un-Marxist, and party organs were prohibited from distributing Reich's books. In February 1933, despite the support of his co-workers in Sex-Pol, Reich was formally expelled from the party.

If the Communist leaders found Reich's stress on sexuality intolerable, his psychoanalytic colleagues were no more appreciative of his Communist politics. Badly frightened by the import of Reich's *Mass Psychology of Fascism* (1933)—and, as difficult as it is to believe today, still hoping to make their peace with fascism—the International Psychoanalytic Association expelled Reich the following year.

First from Denmark, then from Sweden and Norway, Reich

continued his efforts to influence the course of working-class protest against fascism. Most of his writings of this time appear in the *Zeitschrift für politische Psychologie und Sexualökonomie,* a journal he edited from 1934 to 1938. From about 1935 on, however, Reich's interest in politics was gradually giving way to a growing interest in biology, spurred by the belief that he had discovered the physical basis of sexual energy (libido). From being a psychoanalyst and Marxist social philosopher, Reich became a natural scientist, a metamorphosis that was to have drastic effects on both his psychoanalysis and social philosophy. Reich emigrated to America in 1939. Each year added to his spiritual distance from Marx and Freud. After a new round of persecution by the authorities, this time in connection with his scientific research, he died in an American prison in 1957.[2]

Reich's later work, as fascinating and controversial as it is, lies outside the bounds of this Introduction, which is concerned solely with his Marxist period. What does concern us is that the break with his Marxist past led him to dilute much of the class analysis and politically radical content of whatever works of this period he chose to republish. Consequently, *The Sexual Revolution* (1945) and *The Mass Psychology of Fascism* (1946), until recently the only "Marxist" works available in English, give a very misleading picture of Reich's Marxism. Two recent pirate editions of *The Mass Psychology of Fascism,* both taken from the 1946 English version, and a new translation of the third German edition, exhibit the same fault, as does *The Invasion of Compulsory Sex Morality* (Farrar, Straus & Giroux, 1971), which takes account of textual revisions Reich undertook in 1952. Only "Dialectical Materialism and Psychoanalysis" (*Studies on the Left,* July–August 1966) and "What Is Class Consciousness?" (*Liberation,* October 1971) are exempt from this criticism, but besides being difficult to obtain, these essays in themselves are hardly adequate as an introduction to Reich's Marxism. The present volume, then, offers the English-speaking reader his first real opportunity to become acquainted with Reich's contribution to Marxist theory.

As indicated above, I believe Reich's main efforts as a Marxist were directed to filling in the theory of alienation as it applies to the sexual realm. Reich himself would have been surprised by such a judgment, since he was only partially familiar with this theory and seldom employed the vocabulary associated with it. *The German Ideology* and *1844 Manuscripts,* which contain Marx's clearest treatment of alienation, became available only in 1928 and 1931 respectively, and it seems as if Reich never read the latter work. Still, fitting rather neatly into this Marxian matrix is his discussion of the split between the individual and his natural sexual activity, reflected in part by the split between spiritual and physical love (likewise between tenderness and eroticism); the fact that sexuality comes under the control of another (repression and manipulation); of its objectification in repressive structures (symptoms as well as social forms); of the reification (neurotic attachment) connected with each; of people's treatment of one another as sexual objects and the dissatisfaction this breeds; of the role money plays in purchasing sexual favors (which is only possible because they are no longer an integral part of the personality); and of the incipient conflict between repressors and repressed. Moreover, by using the theory of alienation Marx tried to show—in keeping with his dialectical conception—that people were not only prisoners of their conditions but of themselves, of what they had been made by their conditions. It is perhaps in marking the toll of sexual repression on people's ability to come to grips with their life situation (and, in particular, on the working class's ability to recognize its interests and become class-conscious) that Reich makes his most important contribution to Marx's theory of alienation.[3]

In his investigation of sexual alienation, Reich was greatly aided by Freud's four major discoveries: 1) man's psychic life is largely under the control of his unconscious (this shows itself in dreams, slips of the tongue, forgetting and misplacing things—all have a "meaning"); 2) small children have a lively sexuality (sex and procreation are not identical); 3) when repressed, infantile sexuality is forgotten but doesn't lose its strength, its energy (this only gets diverted into various psychic disturbances which are beyond conscious control); 4) human morality is not of supernatural origins but is the result of repressive measures taken against children, particularly against expressions of natural sexuality.

To these basic discoveries Reich soon added two of his own. Psychoanalysts of the time were puzzled by the fact that many severely disturbed people had a "healthy" sex life, i.e., in the case of men, had erections and experienced orgasm. Reich began to question his patients more closely about the quality of their sexual activity, and found that none of them had great pleasure in the sexual act and that none experienced a complete release of tension in orgasm. Reich concluded that erective and ejaculative potency (the only types then recognized by psychoanalysis) did not necessarily lead to "orgastic potency" which he defined as "the capacity for complete surrender to the flow of biological energy without any inhibition, the capacity for complete discharge of all dammed-up sexual excitation."[4] Without orgastic potency much of the sexual energy generated by the body remains blocked and available for neuroses and other kinds of irrational behavior.

Reich also noted that orgastic impotence in his patients was always coupled with distinctive ways—including both beliefs and bodily attitudes—of warding off instinctual impulses. He labeled these defensive behavior patterns "character structure." Reich believed that character structure originates in the conflicts of the oedipal period as ways of responding to external pressures and threats. Both its form and strength reflect the repression to which the individual was subjected at this time. The motive for developing such mechanisms is conscious or unconscious fear of punishment.

While protection against the outside world is the chief objective in the formation of character structure, this is not its main function in the adult individual. After maturation, it is mainly against internal dangers, against unruly impulses, that character mechanisms guard. In this case, character structure blocks the impulse and redirects the energy, acting both as repressing agent and controller of the resulting anxiety.

Achieving impulse control in this manner, however, has serious side effects on a person's overall motility and sensibility. According to Reich, it makes "an orderly sexual life and full sexual experience impossible."[5] All the manifestations of character structure—the inhibition and the fears, the tense and awkward mannerisms, the stiffness and the deadness—work against the capacity to surrender in the sexual act, and thus limit both the pleasure and the discharge of tension attained in orgasm. Character structure also deadens people sufficiently for them to do the boring, mechanical work which is the lot of most people in capitalist society. The same dulling insulates people from outside stimuli, reducing the impact on them of further education and of life itself. Finally, the increased sexual blockage which results from damming up the libido is responsible for various reaction formations, chief of which is an ascetic ideology, which in turn increases the blockage.

Drawing upon his clinical experience, Freud had already noted a number of disturbing personality traits and problems that result from sexual repression. Among these are the "actual" neuroses, tension and anxiety ("modern nervousness"), attenuated curiosity, increased guilt and hypocrisy, and reduced sexual potency and pleasure. On one occasion, he goes so far as to claim that repressed people are "good weaklings who later become lost in the crowd that tends to follow painfully the initiative of strong characters."[6] This provocative remark is never developed. Reich, on the other hand, emphasizes those aspects of submissiveness and irrationality that we now associate with the notion of the authoritarian personality. For him, the most important effect of sexual repression is that it "paralyzes the rebellious forces because any rebellion is laden with anxiety" and "produces, by inhibiting sexual curiosity and thinking in the child, a general inhibition of thinking and critical faculties."[7] And Reich is unique in rooting these qualities in the very defense mechanisms (character structure) responsible for self-repression.

But if the human cost of repression is so great, the question arises: Why does society repress sexuality? Freud's answer is that it is the *sine qua non* of civilized life. Reich replies that sexual repression's chief social function is to secure the *existing* class structure. The criticism which is curtailed by such repression is criticism of *today's* society, just as the rebellion which is inhibited is rebellion against the status quo.

Closely following Marx, Reich declares, "every social order creates those character forms which it needs for its preservation. In class society, the ruling class secures its position with the aid of education and the institution of the family, by making its ideology the ruling ideology of all members of the society." To this Reich adds the following: "it is not merely a matter of imposing ideologies, attitudes and concepts . . . Rather it is a matter of a deep-reaching process in each new generation, of the formation of a psychic structure which corresponds to the existing social order in all strata of the population."[8]

In short, life in capitalism is not only responsible for our beliefs, the ideas of which we are conscious, but also for related unconscious attitudes, for all those spontaneous reactions which proceed from our character structure. Reich can be viewed as adding a psychological dimension to Marx's notion of ideology: emotions as well as ideas are socially determined. By helping to consolidate the economic situation responsible for their formation, each serves equally the interests of the ruling class.

Within the theory of alienation, character structure stands forth as the major product of alienated sexual activity. It is an objectification of human existence that has acquired power over the individual through its formation in inhuman conditions. Its various forms, the precise attitudes taken, are reified as moral sense, strength of character, sense of duty, etc., further disguising its true nature. Under the control of the ruling class and its agents in the family, church and school who use the fears created to manipulate the individual, character structure provides the necessary psychological support within the oppressed for those very external practices and institutions (themselves products of alienated activity in other spheres) which daily oppress them. In light of the socially reactionary role of character structure, Reich's political strategy aims at weakening its influence in adults and obstructing its formation in the young, where the contradiction between self-assertiveness and social restraint is most volatile. The repressive features of family, church and school join economic exploitation as major targets of his criticism.

To avoid the kind of misunderstanding that has bedeviled most discussion of Reich's ideas, I would like to emphasize that

Reich's strategy is not a matter of "advocating" sexual intercourse. Rather, by exhibiting the devastating effects of sexual repression on the personality and on society generally, he wants people to overturn those conditions which make a satisfactory love life (and—through its connection to character structure—happiness and fulfillment) impossible. In a similar vein, Reich never held that a full orgasm is the *summum bonum* of human existence. Rather, because of the psychological ills associated with orgastic impotence, the full orgasm serves as an important criterion by which emotional well-being can be judged. Furthermore, with the relaxation of repression, Reich does not expect everybody to be "screwing" everybody all the time (a fear Freud shares with the Pope), though such relaxation would undoubtedly lead—as it already has in part—to people making love more frequently with others whom they find attractive.

Many of Reich's critics make it a point of honor never to engage him in intelligent debate, simply assuming that any position which is so "extreme" must be erroneous. Among those from whom we deserve better are Herbert Marcuse, who remarks, "sexual liberation *per se* becomes for Reich a panacea for individual and social ills," and Norman Brown who says of Reich, "This appearance of finding the solution to the world's problems in the genital has done much to discredit psychoanalysis; mankind, from history and from personal experience, knows better."[9] Reich's masterly analysis of the social function of sexual repression is duly lost sight of behind these unsupported caricatures.

Another related misinterpretation, which is widespread among Marxists and must be taken more seriously, holds that Reich replaces "economic determinism" with "sexual determinism." At the time of his expulsion from the Communist Party, a spokesman for the party declared, "You begin with consumption, we with production; you are no Marxist."[10] It is only fitting in an Introduction to a collection of Reich's Marxist essays that special attention be given to an objection which calls into question his entire enterprise.

Marxist theory offers Reich two complementary ways of responding: either the notion of production can be differently de-

fined to include sexuality (which his Communist Party critic
restricted to a form of consumption), or the interaction between
the "base" and such elements of the "superstructure" as sexuality
can be emphasized to bring out the hitherto neglected importance
of the latter. Reich's strategy, as found in several of his works,
takes advantage of both possibilities. On the one hand, he points
out that Marx's materialism logically precedes his stress on economic factors, such as production, and that sex is a "material
want." On the other hand, while willingly declaring even for
sexual practices the primacy "in the last instance" of economic
factors (work, housing, leisure, etc.), he argues that the social
effects of sexual repression are far greater than have previously
been recognized.

Marx's materialism is first and foremost a matter of beginning his study of society with the "real individual," who may be
viewed strictly as a producer but is just as often seen as both
producer and consumer.[11] In his only methodological essay,
Marx is at pains to show that production and consumption are
internally related as aspects of the individual's material existence
and that information which generally appears under one heading
may be shifted—in order to satisfy some requirement of inquiry
or exposition—to the other with no loss of meaning.[12] Likewise,
the "real individual" has both subjective and objective aspects—
he feels as well as does—and again, because of this interrelated-
ness his life situation can be brought into focus by emphasizing
either feelings or actions. Based essentially on methodological
considerations, this choice simply subsumes those aspects not
directly named under those which are.

Perfectly in keeping with this broader notion of materialism
is Reich's claim that "Mankind exists with two basic psychological needs, the need for nourishment and the sexual need,
which, for purposes of gratification, exist in a state of mutual
interaction."[13] Stressing the active component, Engels had said
as much: "According to the materialist conception, the determining factor in history is, in the final instance, the production
and reproduction of the immediate essentials of life. This, again,
is of a twofold character. On the one side, the production of the
means of existence . . . on the other side, the production of

human beings themselves, the propagation of the species."[14] The social organization of each epoch, according to Engels, is determined by both kinds of "production."

So little is this dual basis of Marx's conception of history appreciated—not least by Marx's followers—that the editor of the Moscow edition of *Origins of the Family, Private Property and the State,* where this remark appears, accuses Engels of "inexactitude," a serious admission for any Communist editor to make in 1948.[15]

Reich, too, is not altogether satisfied with Engels' formulation. The parallel Engels draws between production and procreation as determining forces in history requires some emendation. For if people produce in order to satisfy the need for food, shelter, etc., they do not engage in sex in order to propagate the species. Goods are not only the result of production but its aim. Sex, however, is almost always engaged in for pleasure or to relieve bodily tension. For the greater part of human history the link between sexual intercourse and paternity was not even known. Beyond this, sexual desire, which makes its appearance in early childhood, precedes the possibility of procreation in the life of everyone. Consequently, as a material need, as a subjective aspect of the "real individual," sex is essentially the drive for sexual pleasure. It is, therefore, how society responds to the individual's attempt to satisfy his hunger and obtain sexual pleasure that determines the social organization of each epoch.[16]

Besides accepting Marx's notion of "material forces" (however extended), Reich, as I have indicated, also accepted the primacy "in the last instance" of economic factors (narrowly understood). To grasp the latter admission in the proper perspective one must replace the causal model into which it is often forced with a dialectical one. On the basis of the dialectic, mutual interaction (or reciprocal effect) exists between all elements in reality. This basic assumption does not rule out the possibility that some elements exert a proportionately greater effect on others or on the whole as such. As Marx discovered, this was generally the case for economic factors. His claim regarding the primacy of economic factors is an empirical generalization based on a study of real societies, and not an a priori truth about the

world. Consequently, Marx himself could call attention to the
predominant role that war and conquest seem to have played in
the development of ancient societies, and Engels could say that
before the division of labor reached a certain point, kinship
groups bore the chief responsibility for determining social
forms.[17] Reich, who made a special study of primitive societies,
concurs with Engels' judgment, though his qualification shows
him to be even more of an "economic determinist" in this matter
than Engels. Basing himself primarily on the anthropology of
Malinowski, Reich emphasizes the importance of the marriage
dowry (arranged as a form of tribute between previously warring
primal hordes) in establishing both clan exogamy and the incest
taboo; whereas Engels, under the influence of Morgan and
Darwin, attributes both developments to natural selection.[18]

If Reich's research into the social origins of neuroses, beginning with his work in the free psychoanalytic clinic of Vienna,
led him to accept the primacy in the last instance of economic
factors, the same research made him want to alter the weight
Marx attached to at least one of the elements in this interaction.
Marx had mentioned sex as a natural and human power, as a
way of relating to nature, along with eating, seeing, working and
many other human conditions and functions. He did declare, as
we saw, that the quality of the sexual relationship offers the
clearest insight into the degree to which man the animal has
become a human being. Yet, the only power whose influence is
examined in any detail is work.

Reich does not by any means seek to belittle the importance
Marx attributes to work, but he does wish to accord greater
importance to sexuality, particularly in affecting people's capacity
for rational action. For very different reasons, Marx and Freud
had underestimated the influence on character and social development of the area of life investigated by the other. The result
was that "In Marx's system, the sexual process led a Cinderella
existence under the misnomer 'development of the family.' The
work process, on the other hand, suffered the same fate in
Freud's psychology under such misnomers as 'sublimation,'
'hunger instinct' or 'ego instincts.' "[19] For Reich, synthesizing
Marx and Freud meant breaking out of the prison imposed by

such categories to redistribute causal influence in line with the basic discoveries of both men.

Sartre has recently remarked that most Marxists treat man as if he were born at the time of applying for his first job.[20] Writing as a Marxist psychoanalyst, it is chiefly this distortion that Reich sought to correct.

The attack on Reich as a sexual determinist has led most Marxist critics to overlook the real differences that exist between Marx's materialist conception of history and Reich's. The chief of these has to do with the different time periods brought into focus. Whereas Marx concentrated on the social-economic forms that have come into existence in the West in the last two to three thousand years (slavery, feudalism, capitalism), Reich—while accepting Marx's divisions—generally operates with a periodization based on social-sexual developments, whose three main stages are matriarchy, patriarchy (covering the whole of recorded history) and communism. Though they overlap, these two ways of dividing time are not fully integrated, either conceptually—so that one is forced to think of one or the other—or practically— so that followers of Marx and Reich often dismiss economic or psychological factors (depending on the school) in accounting for social change.

This contrast between the two thinkers is nowhere so clearly drawn as in their treatment of contradictions. At the core of Marx's materialist conception of history, insofar as it passes beyond methodology (how best to study social change) to a set of generalizations on how such changes occur, is his stress on the reproduction of the conditions of social existence which at a certain point begins to transform the old order into a qualitatively new one. So it is that attracting more and more workers into towns to reproduce the conditions necessary for the production of capital results eventually, through social activity and combination, in the abolition of competition between workers which is a necessary condition for the production of capital. For Marx, the content of contradictions is always provided by the particular society in which their resolution takes place.

As a kindred thinker to Marx, Reich too is particularly attuned to contradictory tendencies in the material he examines.

Yet, with few exceptions, the contradictions he believes will be resolved in capitalism possess a content that is derived from patriarchal society as such. This is the case with the contradiction between repression strengthening marriage and the family and, in virtue of the sexual misery caused, undermining them; and likewise of the contradiction he sees between repression producing a character structure which inclines youth to accept parental authority (and by extension all forms of authority) and simultaneously provoking sexual rebellion against parents (and by extension all forms of authority).

Without roots in the particular society in which they are found (capitalism), it is not altogether clear how these contradictions contribute to the demise of this society, nor why its demise will necessarily lead to the resolution of these contradictions. And adding that repression is greater in the capitalist era does not solve the problem. Even sexual alienation is affected, for to the extent that its peculiarly capitalist features are overshadowed by patriarchal ones it becomes, for the time span with which Marx is concerned, an ahistorical phenomenon. Thus, a form of sexual alienation, as Reich was forced to admit, could exist even in the Soviet Union, still a patriarchal society.[21]

Reich's error—for all the use he made of Marx's analysis— lies in conceptualizing his findings apart from the findings of Marxist sociology, rather than integrating the two within the same social contradictions. He himself offers a good example of the alternative when he speaks of the capitalist economy fostering family ideology while simultaneously undermining it through inner family tensions caused by unemployment and forcing women to go to work. In this way, that is, through the operation of typical capitalist trends, the family whose ideological function is necessary to capitalism is rendered increasingly dysfunctional.[22] Such examples in Reich's work, however, remain the exception.

Marxists have always managed better to explain the transition from slavery to feudalism and from feudalism to capitalism than to explain the onset of class society and, as events show, its eventual replacement by communism. It is just such developments, however, that Reich's work does most to illuminate. Yet, while Reich's contradictions occur in patriarchal times and the main contradictions Marx uncovered take place in capitalism, Reich's contribution to Marx's analysis can only be peripheral and suggestive. If Reich's "sexual economy" is ever to become an integral part of Marxism, the peculiarly capitalist qualities of sexual repression, including its distinctive forms and results within each social class (making allowances for racial, national and religious differences), must be brought out in greater detail. And, conceptually, from a patriarchal social relation, sexual repression must be broken down into slave, feudal, capitalist and even "socialist" social relations, in order to capture its special contribution to each period as well as the opportunities available in each period for its transcendence. Most of this research and work of reformulation is still to be done.[23]

Aside from the accusation that Reich's theory is of sexual determinism, another potentially telling criticism raised by many radicals today has to do with the relevance of his ideas in light of all the changes in sexual behavior that have occurred since he wrote. Have Reich's teachings missed their revolutionary moment? Reimut Reiche, in his book *Sexuality and the Class Struggle,* argues that the spread of sexual education, the availability of birth control pills and abortions, the easy access to cars (if not rooms) in which to make love, etc., have made it impossible to link the denial of a satisfactory sex life with the requirements of the capitalist system. The market has been able to absorb even these needs, turning their satisfaction into a profitable business venture for some section of the capitalist class. For him, the focus of interest has changed from finding out why sexuality is being denied to discovering how in the very means of its satisfaction it is being manipulated to serve the ends of the capitalist system.[24]

Neither Reimut Reiche's optimism regarding the extent to which repression has diminished nor his pessimism as to the extent capitalism is able to exploit whatever new freedom exists seems fully justified. A recent poll of eighteen-year-old college students in the United States, for example, shows that 44 percent of the women and 23 percent of the men are still virgins, and one expects that a far greater percentage have known only one or a few encounters.[25] Radicals tend to believe that on sexual matters, at least, their generally liberated attitudes and practices are shared by most of their age peers. This is a serious mistake.

As for capitalist reforms blunting the revolutionary edge of sexual protest, it must be admitted that this can happen. What remains to be seen, however, is whether the new contradictions embodied in these reforms simply make the old situation more explosive. How long can the pill be easily obtainable, venereal diseases curable, etc., and youth still frightened by the dangers of sexual intercourse? At what point in making marriage unnecessary for sex will young people stop getting married in order to have sex? When will the rebellion that has known some success in sexual matters be directed against intolerable conditions elsewhere? Put in Reichian terms, how long could capitalism survive with a working class whose authoritarian character structures have been eroded through modifications in their sexual lives?

The revolutionary potential of Reich's teachings is as great as ever—perhaps greater, now that sex is accepted as a subject for serious discussion and complaint virtually everywhere. The origins of the March Twenty-second Movement in France illustrate this point well. In February 1967, the French Trotskyist, Boris Frankel, spoke on Reich and the social function of sexual repression to a crowd of several hundred students at the Nanterre branch of the University of Paris. I can personally attest to the enthusiastic response of the audience, for I was there. In the week following the talk, Reich's booklet, *The Sexual Struggle of Youth,* was sold door to door in all the residence halls. This led to a widespread sex-educational campaign based—as Danny Cohn-Bendit tells us—on Reich's revolutionary ideas, and resulted in the occupation by men and women students of the women's dorms to protest against their restrictive rules.[26] Other struggles over other issues followed, but the consciousness which culminated in the events of May 1968 was first awakened in a great number of Nanterre students in the struggle against their sexual repression.

The same struggle is being repeated with local variations at universities and even high schools throughout the capitalist world. Generally lacking, however, is the clear consciousness of the link between restrictions on sexual liberty and the capitalist order that one found at Nanterre. Reich's teachings, whatever their shortcomings, are the indispensable critical arm in forging these links.

NOTES

1. Karl Marx, *Economic and Philosophic Manuscripts of 1844,* trans. by Martin Milligan (Moscow, 1959), p. 101.
2. There is no good biography of Reich available. The only English-language account of Reich's life to which I can in good conscience refer readers is Paul Edwards' brief essay, "Wilhelm Reich," in *The Encyclopedia of Philosophy,* VII, Paul Edwards, ed. (New York, 1967), 104–15. A more detailed study by Constantine Sinelnikoff, *L'Oeuvre de Wilhelm Reich,* which also contains a good bibliography of Reich's Marxist writings, will soon be brought out in English.
3. For a fuller treatment of the theory of alienation, see my book, *Alienation: Marx's Conception of Man in Capitalist Society* (Cambridge, 1971).
4. Wilhelm Reich, *The Function of the Orgasm,* trans. by T. P. Wolfe (New York, 1961), p. 79. First published in 1948, this book contains a very useful account of the development of Reich's psychology and particularly of his changing relationship to Freud.
5. Wilhelm Reich, *Character Analysis,* trans. by T. P. Wolfe (New York, 1970), pp. 148–9.
6. Sigmund Freud, " 'Civilized' Sexual Morality and Modern Nervousness," *Collected Papers,* II, trans. by J. Riviere (London, 1948), p. 92.
7. Wilhelm Reich, *Mass Psychology of Fascism,* trans. by T. P. Wolfe (New York, 1946), p. 25.
8. *Character Analysis,* XXLL.
9. Herbert Marcuse, *Eros and Civilization* (New York, 1962), p. 218; Norman Brown, *Life against Death* (New York, 1961), p. 29.
10. Wilhelm Reich, "What Is Class Consciousness?"
11. Karl Marx and Friedrich Engels, *The German Ideology,* trans. by R. Pascal (London, 1942), p. 7.
12. Karl Marx, *A Contribution to the Critique of Political Economy,* trans. by N. I. Stone (Chicago, 1904), pp. 274–92. Marx also says that the forces of production have their subjective side, which is the "qualities of the individuals," and refers to the "communal domestic economy" which replaces the family in communist society as a "new productive force." Karl Marx, *Pre-Capitalist Economic Formations,* ed. by E. J. Hobsbawm and trans. by Jack Cohen (New York, 1965), p. 95; and *German Ideology,* p. 18.
13. Wilhelm Reich, "The Imposition of Sexual Morality."

14. Friedrich Engels, "Origins of the Family, Private Property and the State," *Marx/Engels Selected Writings*, II (Moscow, 1951), 155–6.
15. *Ibid.*, p. 156.
16. "The Imposition of Sexual Morality."
17. Marx, *Pre-Capitalist Economic Formations*, p. 83; Engels, *Selected Writings*, II, p. 156.
18. "The Imposition of Sexual Morality."
19. Wilhelm Reich, *People in Trouble* (Rangely, Maine, 1953), p. 45.
20. Jean Paul Sartre, *Critique de la raison dialectique* (Paris, 1960), p. 47.
21. For Reich's account of the sexual reforms and subsequent reaction in the Soviet Union, see his book *The Sexual Revolution,* trans. by T. P. Wolfe (New York, 1951).
22. Wilhelm Reich, "The Sexual Struggle of Youth."
23. For further discussion of the conceptual difficulties involved in integrating Reich's theories into Marxism, see my article, "The Marxism of Wilhelm Reich: or the Social Function of Sexual Repression," in *European Marxism since Lenin: the Unknown Dimension,* Karl Klare and Dick Howard, eds. (New York, 1972), particularly the final section.
24. Reimut Reiche, *Sexualité et lutte de classes,* trans. by C. Parrenin and F. J. Rutten (Paris, 1971).
25. Quoted in "The International Herald Tribune" (Paris, August 13, 1971).
26. Daniel Cohn-Bendit, *Obsolete Communism and the Left Wing Alternative,* trans. by A. Pomerans (London, 1969), p. 29. Reich's *Sexual Struggle of Youth* is now banned in some French high schools.

DIALECTICAL MATERIALISM AND PSYCHOANALYSIS

(*1929; second edition, 1934*)

Dialectical Materialism and Psychoanalysis was first published in 1929 in both the Russian and German language editions of the Moscow theoretical journal *Under the Banner of Marxism*. Reich revised and reissued it as a pamphlet in 1934 during his Danish exile. The integral 1929 text may be consulted in English in *Studies on the Left* for July–August 1966; this translation of the 1934 edition is based on it. Reich indeed dropped almost nothing of the 1929 text. All of the footnotes added in 1934 are so annotated by Reich himself; and the final section, a response to left-wing critics, such as Sapir and Fromm, and to the pattern of the experience gained since 1929, was added in 1934.—*L.B.*

Foreword
to the 1934 Edition

This first comprehensive view of the connections between dialectical materialism and psychoanalysis, written in 1927–28, was published in 1929 by the journal *Under the Banner of Marxism* in the Russian and German languages. A French-language version is included in my book *La crise sexuelle* (Paris, 1933). The Sex-Pol Press has now arranged republication of the treatise as a separate brochure, due to the considerable interest shown in it.

The decision had to be made whether to undertake a new version stemming from my thought today or to bring the treatise back before the public in its former condition. I took the second course. The fundamental aspects seem to me in need of no changes. A significant expansion of the insights has of course become possible with the passing of six years, and corrections or greater clarity have been supplied here and there. Yet in general, the concrete elaboration of the domain of Sexual Economy as presented here finds itself in the fullest flux of development and beset with problematic new difficulties. Accordingly the treatise is reissued in the old form while special footnotes indicate where passages were reworked, corrections had to be made and subsequent problems and new solutions have arisen.* The treatise can only provide then an introductory orientation in regarding psychoanalysis from the Marxist standpoint.

* These are designated by "(1934)."

It is my obligation to point out that all of the involved principals dissociate themselves from the interrelations presented here. The connections between Marxism and psychoanalysis were fundamentally rejected by Freud, who said that the two disciplines were opposed to each other. The identical stand is asserted by the Comintern official representatives. I was given the same alternative in both camps of a choice between psychoanalysis and revolutionary Marxism. Who has been right? The answer must be left for the public to judge and for the future to decide. I hope I shall perhaps find occasion to explore the causes which have led to the taking of those positions.

Finally I must touch on the numerous other attempts which seek to formulate the elusive connections between Marxism and psychology. I will not offer individual evaluations of them here. Yet I must note the most overriding issue that separates us. They one and all miss the central matter—that is, the sexual needs of the masses of the world's peoples—and accordingly they overlook the opportunity for the sex-political perspective and the praxis that I have represented. In the accommodating of sociology and psychology they are academically-theoretically timid or they are generously open-minded to a fault. The complexity of the facts, and their significance for the cultural politics of the revolution, demand from us only the most precise distinctions and sharpest presentation of views, which, if wrapped in cloudy vagueness when first contemplated, now and more and more form the ideological and cultural process of our existence. Therefore, I must also reject responsibility for all the output in the domains of dialectical-materialist psychology and sexology which is not by myself or my students. This disavowal must also apply to works which may adopt some of my basic views and yet leave out the most essential elements, so that they say little; moreover, the authors of these works neglect to acknowledge the origin of their borrowed ideas, because, I suppose, they regard this mention as dangerous or sure to lessen their own fame.

Wilhelm Reich
October 1934

1) Introductory Note

The purpose of this paper is to investigate whether, and to what extent, Freudian psychoanalysis is compatible with the historical materialism of Marx and Engels. Whether or not psychoanalysis is compatible with the proletarian revolution and the class struggle will depend on our answer to the first question. The few contributions so far published on the subject of psychoanalysis and socialism suffer from the fact that their authors lack the necessary insight into either psychoanalysis or Marxism. Among the Marxists, criticism of the way psychoanalytic discoveries have been applied to social theory has been in part justified. The few contributions by psychoanalysts have lacked the necessary familiarity with the fundamental problems of dialectical materialism and have, moreover, completely overlooked the central issue of Marxist sociology—the class struggle. They were thus useless to the Marxist sociologist, just as a treatise on psychological problems becomes useless to the psychoanalyst if it fails to mention the theory of the libido.

The most unsatisfactory of these works is Kolnai's paper entitled "Psychoanalysis and Sociology."[1] Kolnai is an author who has now, without ever having really been an analyst, ended up by being an adherent of Scheler's and has officially (though not, un-

[1] Internationaler Psychoanalytischer Verlag, 1923.

fortunately, before the publication of his pamphlet on sociology) announced that he has given up psychoanalysis because, as he says, it no longer corresponds to his views. The paper bristles with incorrect metaphysical and idealistic interpretations of the discoveries of psychoanalysis and does not deserve to be considered in connection with the present discussion. Jurinetz, who makes Kolnai's paper the starting point of a criticism of psychoanalysis, mistakenly describes him as "one of Freud's most zealous disciples."[2]

We cannot here discuss Jurinetz's article in detail, but we must make clear from the start that negative criticism of psychoanalysis by Marxists can be justified in two respects.

1) As soon as we leave the sphere of psychoanalysis proper, and especially if we attempt to apply psychoanalytic theory to social problems, there is an immediate tendency to build it up into a world philosophy; it is then set against the Marxist view of the world as a psychological one which preaches the rule of reason and claims to lay the basis for a better social life by the rational adjustment of human relations and by education toward a conscious control of the instinctual life. This utopian rationalism, distorted by an overindividualistic view of the social process, is neither original nor revolutionary and goes outside the proper scope of psychoanalysis, which, according to the definition of its founder, is nothing more than a psychological method using the means of natural science for describing and explaining man's inner life as a specific part of nature. Psychoanalysis, then, is not a world philosophy, nor can it develop such a philosophy; consequently it can neither replace nor supplement the materialist conception of history. As a natural science it is quite disparate from the Marxian view of history.[3]

---

[2] "Psychoanalyse und Marxismus" (Psychoanalysis and Marxism), *Unter dem Banner des Marxismus,* Vol. I, No. 1, p. 93.

[3] *(1934)* This certainly does not mean that no social *consequences* can be drawn from analytical findings. Every science is the outcome of a practical position taken up vis-à-vis certain questions of existence; psychoanalysis, for example, is an attempt to come to terms with the question of understanding and healing psychological disorders. That being so, all scientific research has to be based on practical needs. A natural scientist can do useful research without drawing any philosophical conclusions

2) The proper study of psychoanalysis is the psychological life of man in society. The psychological life of the masses is of interest to it only insofar as individual phenomena occur in the mass (e.g., the phenomenon of a leader), or insofar as it can explain phenomena of the "mass soul" such as fear, panic, obedience, etc., from its experience of the individual. It would seem, however, that the phenomenon of class consciousness is not accessible to psychoanalysis, nor can problems which belong to sociology—such as mass movements, politics, strikes—be taken as objects of the psychoanalytic method. And so it cannot replace a sociological doctrine, nor can a sociological doctrine develop out of it. It can, however, become an auxiliary science to sociology, say in the form of social psychology. For instance, it can explore the irrational motives which have led a certain type of leader to join the socialist or the national-socialist movement;[4] or it can trace the effect of social ideologies on the psychological development of an individual.[5] Thus the Marxist critics are right when they reproach certain representatives of the psychoanalytic school with attempting to explain what cannot be explained by that method. But they are wrong when they identify the method with those who apply it, and when they blame the method for their mistakes.

These two points lead on to a necessary distinction, not always clearly defined in Marxist literature, between Marxism

---

himself; but the quality of his research will normally be impaired if his world view, acquired elsewhere, contradicts his scientific work. If he then prevents others, whose work is the practice of philosophy, from drawing conclusions from his own research which he has failed to recognize or has rejected, then he enters into conflict with himself—a fate which has overtaken some of our greatest researchers. Thus it was not Freud's duty as a scientist to draw social conclusions from his studies; this was left to the practical sociologists. It goes without saying that this divorce between research and its consequences is merely a peculiarity of bourgeois society and will disappear under socialism.

[4] Cf. E. Kohn, *Lassalle der Führer* (Lassalle the Leader), Int. Psychoanalytischer Verlag, 1926.

[5] *(1934)* These formulations came under fierce attack by psychoanalytical sociologists. In this regard see my study "The Use of Psychoanalysis in Historical Research," 1934, reprinted at the back of this revised text. As for application of psychoanalytical findings to questions of class consciousness, see my "What Is Class Consciousness?"

as a sociological doctrine—that is to say as scientific method—and Marxism as the philosophical practice of the proletariat.[6] Marxist social theory is the result of the application of the Marxist method to problems of social existence. As a science, psychoanalysis is equal to Marxian sociological doctrine: the former treats of psychological phenomena and the latter of social phenomena. And only insofar as social facts are to be examined in psychological life or, conversely, psychological facts in the life of society, can the two act mutually as auxiliary sciences to one another. Marxism cannot illuminate neurotic phenomena, disturbances in a man's working capacity or in his sexual performance. The situation is quite different in the case of dialectical materialism. Here there are only two possibilities: either psychoanalysis is contradictory to it as a method, i.e., it is idealistic and undialectical, or else it can be proved that psychoanalysis—if only unconsciously, like so many natural sciences—has actually stumbled upon a materialist dialectic in its own sphere and developed certain theories accordingly. As far as method is concerned, psychoanalysis can only correspond to Marxism or contradict it. In the latter case—that is, if the findings of psychoanalysis are not dialectical-materialist—the Marxist must reject it; in the former case, he will know that he is dealing with a science which is not contrary to socialism.[7]

[6] Method and science cannot, of course, be separated in practice; they are closely interwoven. The distinction is made in order to clarify the concepts.

[7] On the concept of "proletarian" and "bourgeois" science, cf. Wittfogel, *Die Wissenschaft in der bürgerlichen Gesellschaft* (Science in Bourgeois Society), Malik Verlag.

(*1934*) But it would not only have to be recognizable as such but it should then be reconstructed in the structure of the dialectical-materialist view of the world. This in turn would certainly have its impact on current theories and attitudes. Marx and Engels always emphasized that every new discovery in the natural sciences would change and develop the dialectical-materialist view of the world. When narrow-minded Marxists oppose the acceptance of new sciences, as they so often do, they are undoubtedly motivated by a sincere wish to preserve the "purity" of Marxism, but they commit the serious error of confusing the general dialectical-materialist world view and method with Marxist theory on specific facts. The former is much more comprehensive and durable than the latter, which, like any theoretical construct concerning matters of fact, is subject to change. For example, a theory concerning the middle classes

Marxists have raised two objections against psychoanalysis as a scientific discipline having a right to exist within socialism.

1) Marxists claim that it is a phenomenon of the decadence of the decaying bourgeoisie. This objection suggests an inconsistency in dialectical thinking. Is not Marxism itself a "phenomenon of the decadence of the bourgeoisie"? It could never have come into being without the contradiction between productive forces and capitalist production conditions; but it represented the discovery and hence also the ideological germ of the new economic order taking shape in the womb of the old one. Later we shall discuss the sociological position of psychoanalysis in greater detail; as for the objection referred to, we can best refute it by quoting the words of the Marxist Wittfogel.[8]

2) Marxists also say that it is an idealist science. A little more knowledge of the subject would have saved the critics from this judgment, and a modicum of objectivity toward psychoanalysis would have prevented them from forgetting that every science, however firmly rooted in materialism, must inevitably have its idealist deviations in a bourgeois society. In theory formation, if it is—however slightly—removed from empiricism, an idealist deviation is understandable and signifies nothing so far as the real nature of science is concerned. Jurinetz has taken a great deal of trouble to point out and emphasize the idealist deviations in psychoanalysis; certainly such deviations exist— they are even numerous—but what matters are the elements of

---

established in 1849 cannot possibly be completely valid for the middle classes of 1934; yet the method whereby we arrive at correct conclusions about the middle classes then and now remains the same. The method of investigation is always more important than any particular theory.

8 "Certain Marxist critics—the 'iconoclasts'—have discovered a very easy way of judging the sciences of today. They murmur with a comprehensive gesture: 'Science, science!' and the whole of science is thereby disposed of so far as they are concerned; the problem is settled. Such a method (or pseudo-method) is barbarian. As an attitude, it owes nothing to Marx and his dialectical manner of thinking except, alas, the name. The dialectical materialist knows that a culture is not uniform like a bushel of peas: that every social order has its contradictions, and that the beginnings of a new social era germinate in the womb of the old. For the dialectical materialist, therefore, by no means everything that has been created by bourgeois hands in the bourgeois period is of inferior value and useless to the society of the future."—op. cit., p. 18.

the theory, the fundamental concepts of psychological processes.

Psychoanalysis is very often said to be connected with reformist movements in politics (Thalheimer, Deborin). The implication is that reformist philosophers are fond of appealing to psychoanalysis; and indeed it is true that de Man has actually tried to play off psychoanalysis against Marxism in a reactionary manner. I maintain, however—and here I am thinking of some Left Marxists—that one can if one wants to, play Marxism itself off against Marxism, likewise for reactionary purposes. Anyone who really understood psychoanalysis would never dream of equating de Man's "psychology" with Freud's, as Deborin has done.[9] What has de Man's sentimental "socialism of opinion" got to do with the theory of the libido, even if he does make references to psychoanalysis (which he has never understood)?

In the last section of this essay I shall try to demonstrate that psychoanalysis suffers the same fate at the hands of reformism[10] as does orthodox Marxism—that is to say, it is emasculated and made trivial. Meanwhile, let us consider, in order, the following questions: the materialist basis of psychoanalytic theory, dialectics in the life of the psyche and the sociological position of psychoanalysis.

[9] Deborin, "Ein neuer Feldzug gegen den Marxismus" (A New Campaign Against Marxism), *Unter dem Banner des Marxismus,* Year 2, No. 1/2.
[10] *(1934)* and of economism.

2) The Materialist Discoveries of Psychoanalysis and Some Idealist Deviations

Before we demonstrate the great advance in the direction of materialism which psychoanalysis represents compared with the predominantly idealist and formalist psychology which existed before it, we must make clear that we do not accept a certain "materialist" conception of psychology widespread in Marxist circles and in some others. It is the concept of mechanistic materialism first put forward by the French eighteenth-century materialists and Büchner and kept alive in the vulgarized Marxism of our own day.[11] According to this view, psychological phenomena as such do not exist: the life of the soul is simply a physical process. To such materialists the very concept of the soul, or psyche, is an idealistic and dualistic error. Undoubtedly

---

[11] "The materialism of the last century was predominantly mechanistic, because at that time, of all natural sciences, only mechanics . . . had come to any definite close. Chemistry at that time existed only in its infantile, phlogistic form. Biology still lay in swaddling-clothes; vegetable and animal organisms were explained as the result of purely mechanical causes. What the animal was to Descartes, man was to the materialist of the eighteenth century—a machine. This exclusive application of the standards of mechanics to processes of a chemical and organic nature—in which processes the laws of mechanics are, indeed, valid, but are pushed into the background by other, higher laws—constitutes the first specific but at that time inevitable limitation of classical French materialism."— Engels, "Feuerbach," in Karl Marx and Friedrich Engels, *Selected Works* (2 vols.), Vol. II, Moscow, Foreign Languages Publishing House, 1951.

this is an extreme reaction to the Platonic idealism which continues to this day to dominate bourgeois philosophy. Such materialists maintain that only the body—and not the soul—is real: that only the objective facts which can be measured and weighed are true, not the subjective ones. The mechanistic error consists in the fact that measurable, ponderable and palpable matter is identified with matter as such.

Marx wrote: "The chief defect of all hitherto existing materialism . . . is that the thing (*Gegenstand*), reality, sensuousness, is conceived only in the form of the object (*Objekt*) or of contemplation (*Anschauung*), but not as *human sensuous activity,* practice, not subjectively. Hence it happened that the *active* side, in contradistinction to materialism, was developed by idealism—but only abstractly, since, of course, idealism does not know real, sensuous activity as such. Feuerbach wants sensuous objects, really differentiated from the thought objects, but he does not conceive human activity itself as objective (*gegenständliche*) activity."[12]

Marx considered that the question of objectivity, that is to say, of the material reality of psychological activity ("of human thought"), was a purely scholastic question if isolated from practice. But he wrote: The materialist doctrine that men are products of circumstances and upbringing, and that, therefore, changed men are products of other circumstances and changed upbringing, forgets that it is men that change circumstance and that the educator himself needs educating.[13]

There is no question in Marx of the material reality of psychological activity being denied. And if in practice the material reality of the phenomena of the life of the human psyche is recognized, then in principle the possibility of a materialistic psychology must be admitted, even if it does not explain the activity of the soul in terms of organic processes. Unless one holds this view, there can be no basis for a Marxist discussion of any purely psychological method. But in that case, if one is

[12] Karl Marx, "Theses on Feuerbach," in Karl Marx and Friedrich Engels, *Selected Works* (2 vols.), Vol. II, Moscow, Foreign Languages Publishing House, 1951.
[13] *Ibid.,* p. 365.

logical, one should not speak of class consciousness, revolutionary will, religious ideology, etc., but should wait until chemistry has supplied the necessary formulae for the physical processes concerned, or until the science of reflexes has discovered the appropriate reflexes. And even then—because such psychology must necessarily remain rooted in causal formalism and cannot penetrate the actual content of feelings and ideas—our understanding of what pleasure (or sorrow, or class consciousness) actually is will not have advanced a jot. This line of thought suggests the necessity, within the framework of Marxism, of a psychology which deals with psychological phenomena by a psychological rather than an organic method.

Of course, such a psychology must do more than merely concern itself with the material facts of the life of the psyche if it is to deserve the right to be called a materialistic psychology. It has to be clear about whether psychological activity can be viewed as a metaphysical fact—i.e., a fact outside the organic world—or as a secondary function bound up with and developing out of the organic world.[14] According to Engels,[15] the princi-

---

[14] *(1934)* This formulation corresponded to the state of psychoanalytical knowledge at the time when the present paper was written. In the meantime it has become possible to sum up the situation in more precise terms. Psychoanalysis first discovered certain laws specifically characteristic of the life of the psyche, e.g., projection. Freud always assumed that the psyche is based on the organic, but he did not deduce the laws of the psyche from those of the organic. Sexual economy, if it wants to become a proper scientific discipline, must study the sexual process in all its functions, psychical as well as physiological, biological as well as social, and must equally investigate all the functions of the basic law of sexuality; thus it is faced with the difficult task of deducing sexual-psychical functions from sexual-biological functions. In this task it is assisted by the dialectical method which it consciously employs. We may put forward the following principle: it is certainly true that the psychical is the product of the organic and must consequently follow the same laws as the organic; but at the same time, it is the opposite of the organic, and in that function, it develops a set of laws which are its own and peculiar to itself. Only the study of these latter laws has been the task of psychoanalysis; and in the main, this task has been completed. Sexual economy may be expected to solve the problem of the relationship between physical and psychological functions; whether it does so depends on conditions outside our control. Cf. "Der Urgegensatz des vegetativen Lebens" (The Fundamental contradition of Vegetable Life), *Ztsch. f. pol. Psych. u. Sexualök.*, No. 2–4, 1934.

[15] *Op. cit.*, p. 335.

pal distinction between materialism and idealism is that the latter regards the "spirit" and the former regards (organic) matter —nature—as the origin of things, and he emphasizes that he uses the two terms in that sense and in no other. Lenin in *Materialism and Empirio-Criticism*[16] makes another distinction the theme of his critical study of epistemology, namely, one's answer to the epistemological question whether the world really exists outside the mind and independently from it (materialism) or whether it exists only in the mind as idea, sensation or perception (idealism). A third distinction, connected with the first, is whether one believes that the body builds the soul or vice versa.

Instead of replying to these questions on behalf of psychoanalysis in general, let us begin by recalling its fundamental theories. Whether the facts on which psychoanalysis is based are true or false can never be a matter for methodological criticism but only for empirical criticism. Among the Marxists, Thalheimer[17] made the mistake of criticizing psychoanalytical theory empirically and of contesting its findings without sufficient knowledge of the subject, while Jurinetz applied only methodological criticism, again without adequate knowledge of the empirical facts of psychoanalysis. We shall not attempt to prove the theories of psychoanalysis; such an attempt would surely go beyond the framework of this essay and would, moreover, be fruitless. The proofs are to be found only in our own empirical experience.

The Psychoanalytical Theory of Instincts

The basic structure of psychoanalytic theory is the theory of instincts. Of this, the most solidly founded part is the theory of the libido—the doctrine of the dynamics of the sexual instinct.[18]

[16] Lenin, *Collected Works,* Vol. XIV, Moscow, Foreign Languages Publishing House.
[17] "Die Auflösung des Austromarxismus" (The Disintegration of Austro-Marxism), *Unter dem Banner des Marxismus,* Vol. I, No. 3, pp. 517 ff.
[18] *(1934)* Dialectical-materialist reexamination and clinical-empirical elaboration of Freud's theory of instincts have yielded a concept of the

The instinct is a "borderline concept between the psychic and the somatic." By the term "libido" Freud understands the energy of the sexual instinct.[19] According to Freud the source of the libido is a chemical process, not yet fully understood, in the organism and especially in the sexual apparatus and the so-called "erogenous zones": that is to say, in parts of the body which are particularly excitable and therefore represent points of concentration of physical sexual excitation.[20] Above these sources of sexual excitation rises the powerful superstructure of the libido, a superstructure which always remains connected with its base, changes together with it both quantitatively and qualitatively (as for instance in puberty), and begins to die with it, as after the climacteric. The libido is reflected in consciousness as a physical and psychic urge for sexual gratification. Freud expressed the definite hope that psychoanalysis would one day be placed firmly on its organic foundations; the concept of sexual chemistry plays an important part as an auxiliary concept in his theory of the libido. However, psychoanalysis cannot methodically deal with concrete processes in the organic sphere, that being the proper concern of physiology.[21] The material nature of Freud's concept of the libido is very clearly seen in the fact that his doctrine of infantile sexuality was confirmed by physiologists when they eventually discovered that even the newborn registered evolutive processes in their sexual apparatus.

Freud completely disposed of the view that the sexual urge

---

dynamics of instincts which may already be regarded as a more or less satisfactory development of Freud's original view. Cf. *Charakteranalyse* (Character Analysis), last chapter, Verl. f. Sex.-Pol., 1933.

[19] *Drei Abhandlungen zur Sexualtheorie* (Three Essays on the Theory of Sexuality), London, Hogarth Press, 1962.

[20] *(1934)* Recent clinical observations in conjunction with the latest research in organ physiology have modified these ideas. It is now thought that electrophysiological processes of charge and discharge in the organism are at play. Cf. "Der Organismus als elektrophysiologische Entladung" (The Organism as Electro-Physiological Discharge), *Z.f.p.P.u.S.*, No. 1, 1934, and the passages in "Der Urgegensatz" dealing with Fr. Kraus's work. So-called sexual chemism would appear to be only a function of a more general organic energy system; but very little is as yet known about this entire subject.

[21] *(1934)* See the correction of this formulation in footnote 14.

does not awaken until puberty; he demonstrated that the libido goes through certain stages of development from birth onward before it reaches the stage of genital sexuality. He expanded the concept of sexuality by including in it those pleasure functions which are not connected with the genitals but are nevertheless unambiguously erotic in character, such as oral eroticism, anal eroticism, etc. These "pre-genital," infantile forms of sexual activity later become subordinated to the primacy of the genitals.

Every phase of development of the libido, of whose dialectical character we shall speak later, is related to the actual life of the child; for example, the oral stage is formed in connection with the taking of nourishment and the anal stage in connection with toilet training. Pre-Freudian science, caught up in bourgeois morality, had completely overlooked these facts and had merely confirmed the popular idea of the "purity" of the child. Social repression of sexuality had become an obstacle to research.

Freud distinguished between two main groups of instincts, not further reducible in psychological terms, namely the self-preservation instinct and the sexual instinct. These are linked to some extent with the popular distinction between hunger and love. All other instincts—will for power, ambition, greed for profit—he regards as secondary formations, offspring of these two fundamental needs. Freud's dictum that the sexual instinct first appears in connection with the instinct for nourishment should be of great importance in social psychology if a relationship can be established between it and Marx's not dissimilar thesis that in social existence the need for food is also the basis for the sexual functions of society.[22]

[22] *(1934)* Sexual-economic studies have somewhat advanced our knowledge of the relationship between the need for food and the sexual instinct. The need for food corresponds to a lessening of tension (or energy) in the organism, the sexual instinct to an increase in tension (energy); hence the former can be satisfied only by an additional supply of energy and the latter only by a withdrawal or expenditure of energy. This explains why hunger plays no role, or at least no direct role, in building up the psychical apparatus, whereas sexual energy is *the* essentially constructive, positive and productive force in the psyche. A more detailed study of these matters is in preparation. It will be readily understood that findings of this kind are of decisive importance as regards the question of energy in the formation of structure and ideology.

Later in his career Freud counterposed the destructive instinct to the sexual instinct, and classified the self-preservation instinct under the erotic instinct as a function of the instinct of self-love (self-preservation narcissism).[23] The relationship of this later classification of instincts to the earlier theory has not yet been completely worked out. The later classification, opposing the sexual or erotic instinct to the destructive or death instinct, was developed on the basis of the two fundamental functions of organic substances, assimilation (composition) and dissimilation (decomposition). Eros includes all those urges of the psychic organism which construct, combine and drive forward: the destructive instinct includes all those which decompose, destroy and drive back to the initial condition. Thus psychic development is seen as the product of a struggle between these two opposing tendencies—and this corresponds to a wholly dialectical view of development.[24] The difficulty lies elsewhere. Whereas the physical basis of the sexual and self-preservation instincts is perfectly clear, the concept of the death instinct has no such obvious material foundation. To refer to the organic processes of decomposition is, for the present, a matter of formal analogy only; it can establish no association of content. Only if there is a real relationship between the death instinct and the self-destructive processes in the organism can this view be considered materialist. Nor can it be denied that the unclear content of this instinct and its refusal to be defined (as the libido can be defined) make it an easy loophole for idealistic and metaphysical speculations on the life of the psyche. It has already caused many misunderstandings in psychoanalysis and has led to finalist theory formations and to exaggerations of the moral functions, which we must regard as idealist deviations. According to Freud himself, the "death wish" is a hypothesis beyond the clinical sphere, but it cannot be by chance that it is so readily seized upon and that it has opened the door to so many futile speculations in psychoanalysis.

[23] *Beyond the Pleasure Principle* and *The Ego and the Id,* London, Hogarth Press.
[24] *(1934)* This view requires correction. See the last two chapters of *Charakteranalyse,* Verl. f. Sex.-Pol., 1933.

In opposition to the idealist tendencies which have developed along with the new hypothesis concerning instincts, the present author has suggested that the destructive instinct may also be dependent upon the libido, i.e., he has attempted to classify it within the materialist theory of the libido.[25] This attempt is based on clinical observations. It seems that a man's readiness to hate and his guilt feelings are dependent, at least so far as their intensity is concerned, upon the state of his libido economy, and that sexual dissatisfaction increases aggression while gratification reduces it. According to this view, the destructive instinct is psychologically a reaction against the failure of an instinct to be satisfied, while physically it consists of a displacement of libidinous excitement to the muscular system.

Clearly, however, the aggressive instinct is also related to the self-preservation instinct; it increases most markedly when the need for nourishment is not sufficiently satisfied. The destructive instinct, in my view, is a later, secondary formation of the organism, determined by the conditions under which the self-preservation and sexual instincts are satisfied.

The regulator of instinctual life is the "pleasure-unpleasure principle." Everything instinctual is a reaching out for pleasure and an attempt to avoid unpleasure. An unpleasurable tension arising from a need can be removed only by satisfying the need. The aim of the instinct is therefore to get rid of instinctual tension by removing an irritation at the source of the instinct. This satisfaction is pleasurable. For example, physical excitation in the genital zone causes an irritation which produces a need (an instinct) to remove this tension. Organic tension in the alimentary organs causes hunger and produces an urge to eat.[26] This causal explanation also deals with the question of aim, since the aim of an instinct is determined by the source of irritation. Here psychoanalysis is entirely opposed to Alfred Adler's individual psychology, which is exclusively concerned with aims.

Since everything that gives pleasure attracts and everything

---

[25] Reich, "Dependence of the Destructive Instinct on Libido Damming," in *Die Funktion des Orgasmus* (The Function of the Orgasm), Psychoanalytischer Verlag, 1927.
[26] (*1934*) Cf. footnote 22.

that gives unpleasure repels, the pleasure principle is a form of movement and change. Its source is the organic instinctual apparatus, and, particularly, sexual chemistry. After each satisfaction of a need, followed by a short period of rest, the instinctual apparatus tenses itself like a spring again and again. Metabolic processes are possibly at the root of this tension.[27]

Yet the working of the two fundamental needs of man is finally given form by the social existence of the individual, which limits the satisfaction of his instincts. Freud brackets all limitations and social necessities which diminish these fundamental needs or defer their satisfaction under the concept of the "reality principle." The reality principle is, in part, directly opposed to the pleasure principle insofar as it completely prohibits certain satisfactions, and, in part, it modifies the pleasure principle insofar as it forces the individual to accept substitute satisfactions or to defer satisfaction. For example, an infant may only receive food at certain hours; a girl during the years of puberty may not, in the society of today, immediately satisfy her natural sexual needs. Economic interests (the bourgeois would say "cultural interests") force her to keep her virginity until marriage, unless she wants to risk the disapproval of society and reduce her chances of finding a husband. Similarly, the stopping of direct anal-erotic satisfaction as practiced by infants is also an effect of the reality principle.

But the definition of the reality principle as a social demand remains formalistic unless it makes full allowance for the fact that the reality principle as it exists today is only the principle of *our* society. There exist many idealist deviations in psychoanalysis concerning the concept of the reality principle. For example, it is often presented as absolute. Adaptation to reality is interpreted simply as adaptation to society, which, applied in pedagogy or in the therapy of neuroses, is unquestionably a conservative view. To be concrete, the reality principle of the capitalist era imposes upon the proletarian a maximum limitation of his needs while appealing to religious values, such as modesty and humility. It also imposes a monogamous form of sexuality,

27 *(1934)* Cf. footnote 20.

etc. All this is founded on economic conditions; the ruling class has a reality principle which serves the perpetuation of its power. If the proletariat is brought up to accept this reality principle—if it is presented to him as absolutely valid, e.g., in the name of culture—this means an affirmation of the proletarian's exploitation and of capitalist society as a whole. It must be clearly realized that the concept of the reality principle as it is in fact understood by many psychoanalysts today corresponds to a conservative attitude (if only unconsciously) and is therefore opposed to the objectively revolutionary character of psychoanalysis. The reality principle has had different contents in the past and it will change again to the extent that the social order changes.

The concrete contents of the pleasure principle are, of course, not absolute either; they also change together with social existence. For example, anal satisfaction in an age when so much emphasis is laid on cleanliness must be different (i.e., less) and the desire for such satisfaction must be greater than, say, in a primitive society, and this finds qualitative expression in the formation of certain character traits. One need only think of aestheticism, which is based on anal eroticism, and of the difference between its significance in the bourgeois era and, say, in primitive society or in the Middle Ages. Class, of course, also helps to determine which contents of the pleasure urge will be more strongly or less strongly emphasized. For example, anal urges seem to be much more strongly marked in the middle classes than in the working class, whereas, conversely, genital urges are more intense in the working class. This also depends on upbringing and on housing conditions.

Biologically the difference should not, of course, be very great, or at least not decisive. But social environment begins to mold the content of the pleasure principle at birth. And whether or not differences in nourishment affect a child's instinctual constitution even in the germinal phase, influencing the quality and intensity of its urges, is a question for future research.[28]

[28] *(1934)* These hints require very far-reaching elaboration. The way in which a social system reproduces itself structurally in human beings can only be grasped concretely, whether in theory or in practice, if we under-

The Doctrine of the Unconscious
and of Repression

Freud distinguished between three systems in the psychological apparatus: the conscious, comprising the perceptive function of the sensory apparatus and all feelings and ideas that are actually conscious; the pre-conscious, including all those ideas and attitudes which are not within the conscious at a particular moment but which can become conscious at any time (both these systems were well known to pre-analytical psychology; what non-psychoanalytical researchers call the "unconscious," or subconscious, belongs wholly to what in the Freudian classification is described as the pre-conscious); and the unconscious, Freud's real discovery, which is characterized by the fact that its contents cannot become conscious because a "pre-conscious" censorship prohibits it. This censorship is nothing mystical but includes rules and prohibitions taken over from the outside world, which themselves have become unconscious.[29]

The unconscious includes not only all the forbidden wishes and ideas which cannot become conscious, but also (probably)

---

stand the way in which social institutions, ideologies, life-forms, etc., mold the instinctual apparatus. The thought structure of the mass individual, which is dependent on the instinctual structure, in turn determines the reproduction of the social ideology and the extent to which it is firmly anchored in the psyche—in brief, the effect of ideology on the social and economic structure of society, the power of "tradition," etc. This subject is discussed, with examples drawn from history, in *Der Einbruch der Sexualmoral* (The Imposition of Sexual Morality), Verl. f. Sex-Pol., 1934, 2nd ed., and in *Massenpsychologie des Faschismus* (Mass Psychology of Fascism), 2nd ed., 1934.
[29] The extent to which Jurinetz has misunderstood the meaning of psychoanalysis can be judged from the following sentence in his article "Psychoanalysis and Marxism" (*Unter dem Banner des Marxismus,* No. 1, p. 98): "How is it possible to discuss the content of the unconscious if one is unable to analyze it, since it never crosses the threshold of consciousness?" A curiously naïve question! It was precisely through his method of free association, by excluding censorship, that Freud discovered the unconscious. The whole of analytic theory consists in making conscious that which was hitherto unconscious. It is incapable of becoming conscious only under ordinary circumstances.

inherited images corresponding to symbols. That the unconscious, too, changes with time, is shown, however, by the interesting clinical fact that with the development of technology
the unconscious acquires new symbols; for example, many
patients at the time when Zeppelins were in the news dreamt of
airships as representations of the male sexual organ.

As it became clear in the course of research that the unconscious contains much else besides actually repressed material,
Freud decided that it was necessary to supplement his theory of
the structure of the psychological apparatus. He proceeded to
draw a distinction between the id, the ego and the superego.

The id, again, is not anything supernatural but is an expression of the biological sector of the personality. A part of it
is the unconscious in the sense just described, that is to say it
belongs to what has actually been repressed.

But what is repression? It is a process taking place between
the ego and the urges of the id. Every child is born with instincts
and acquires wishes during its childhood which it cannot satisfy
because society in both the broader and narrower sense—the
family—will not tolerate it (incest wish, anal eroticism, exhibitionism, sadism, etc.). Social life, in the person of educators,
demands that the child should suppress these instincts. The
child—which has only a weak ego and chiefly obeys the pleasure
principle—often succeeds in doing this only by banishing the
wish from his consciousness and refusing to know anything more
about it. Thus the wish becomes unconscious by repression. Another, more social way of dealing with unfulfillable wishes is
sublimation, which is the counterpart of repression: instead of
being repressed, the instinct is diverted into a socially acceptable
activity.[30]

---

[30] Freud never, as Jurinetz asserts, replaced the theory of suppression by
that of "condemnation." Jurinetz has misunderstood what Freud meant
when he said that an instinct, once it has become conscious as a result of
analysis, can be condemned by the ego. Condemnation is one of the antith-
eses of suppression. It is not true that, as Jurinetz claims (*op. cit.,* p.
110), "the Freudians progressively destroyed their theory of the unconscious." This idea comes from the confusion which the more recent
theory of the id, the ego and the superego has sown in Jurinetz's mind.
That theory does not negate the doctrine of the unconscious but in-
corporates it.

Thus we see that psychoanalysis cannot conceive of the child without society. The child exists for it only as a being in society. Social existence exercises a continuous effect on the primitive instincts, limiting, reshaping or encouraging them. The two fundamental instincts react differently to this effect. Hunger is more stringent, more inexorable and demands immediate satisfaction more violently than the sexual instinct; in no case can it be suppressed like the latter. The sexual instinct is modifiable, plastic, capable of sublimation; its partial tendencies can be reversed into their very opposites, but cannot completely forgo satisfaction. The energy used for social performance—including the performance of those acts which satisfy the hunger instinct—derives from the libido. It is the driving force of psychological development as soon as it comes under the influence of society.

The motive force of suppression is the self-preservation instinct of the ego. It gains control of the ego, and psychological development is the product of the conflict between them. If we do not think of suppression as a mechanism and agree for a moment to ignore its effect, we may say that suppression is a social problem because the contents and forms of suppression depend on the social existence of the individual. This social existence is ideologically concentrated in a sum of rules, prescriptions and prohibitions—that is to say in the superego, large portions of which are themselves unconscious.

Psychoanalysis traces all morals back to the influences of education, and therefore rejects the assumption that morality is metaphysical in character, e.g., in the sense of Kant's conception of morality. It provides a materialist solution to the concept of morals by tracing it back to experience, to the self-preservation instinct and to fear of punishment. All morals in a child are the result either of fear of punishment or of love of those who bring him up. If Freud speaks of "an unconscious morality" and "unconscious guilt feelings," he means only that, together with forbidden wishes, certain elements of guilt are also suppressed, as for instance with the ban on incest. Jurinetz has completely misunderstood the concept of unconscious guilt when he says that the assumption of an initially moral quality of the ego, in the sense of metaphysical guilt, has crept into that concept. Some individual analysts may, for one reason or another, and despite the psychoanalytic method which they practice, believe in an original moral or divine principle in man. That is not part of analytic theory: the exact opposite is true. Psychoanalysis finally and scientifically destroys such beliefs by withdrawing the discussion of morals from the sphere of philosophy. We must leave it to the individual analyst to settle the conflict which arises when he tries to combine a belief in God and metaphysical morality with his psychoanalytical convictions. There would be every reason to worry about psychoanalysis if it began reconciling itself with the metaphysical view.[31] But the theory of unconscious guilt does not in the least, as Jurinetz fears, cancel out the theory of the unconscious: on the contrary, it demonstrates that the acquisition of a moral sense comes from a material source.

We have shown that both the id and the superego, far from being metaphysical constructions, can be traced back wholly, so far as their content goes, to needs or real acquisitions from the outside world. I cannot understand where Jurinetz gets the idea that "as in Schopenhauer, so also . . . in Freud the world is a product of the individual ego, created with the object of regulating our needs."[32] The exact opposite is stated by Freud in countless passages—some of which, by the way, Jurinetz himself quotes: namely, that the ego is a result of the effect of the real outside world on the instinctual organism, and is formed as a protection against irritation. Even in *Beyond the Pleasure Principle,* Freud's deliberately speculative work which Jurinetz takes as the principal basis for his critique, there is not a word to imply that the real world is created by the ego. Jurinetz totally fails to

[31] *(1934)* The anxiety expressed here has since proved to be well founded. Today, the entire psychoanalytical movement—in large measure because of the political reaction, which has grown so much stronger in recent years—is in a situation of acute crisis; the crisis can be described as an expression of the contradiction between the revolutionary ideas of psychoanalytical sexual theory and the bourgeois-religious-ethical world view of many leading analysts. The principal areas of theoretical disagreement between the scientific (Marxist) and bourgeois lines within the psychoanalytical movement relate to the origin of sexual repression, the role of genital sexual life in mental health, the existence of a biological self-destructive instinct, and certain technical and therapeutic problems.
[32] Jurinetz, *op. cit.,* p. 103.

come to terms with the concept of projection, which is not discussed in detail in that work; had he read Freud's clinical writings he would be clearer on the subject. The ego believes that ideas which it has suppressed within itself and whose pressure it feels are in the outside world. That and nothing else is projection. It was precisely with the help of this materialist theory that Freud was able to discover the true nature of hallucinations in the mentally ill. The voices they hear are in fact only unconscious wishes or pangs of conscience, but that does not make them objectively real.

Beyond the Pleasure Principle was, of course, apt to allow incorrect interpretations to crop up in psychoanalysis. But Freud himself has expressed a critical attitude to this work, both within the text itself and on many occasions verbally. He has said that it is outside clinical psychoanalysis. That it can nevertheless offer a point of departure for absolutely unfounded speculations regarding the hypothesis of the death wish is probably due to the libido theory: a delicate issue which the bourgeois is only too ready to exchange for a less dangerous hypothesis.

The material nature of the ego is unassailable, if only because the ego is linked with the perception system of the sensory organs. Furthermore, as already stated, Freud derives the ego from the effect of material irritations or stimuli upon the instinct apparatus. According to Freud the ego is no more than a specially differentiated part of the id, a buffer or protective organ between the id and the real world. The ego is not free in its actions: it is dependent on the id and the superego, i.e., on biological and social factors. In other words, psychoanalysis challenges free will, its conception of the latter being identical with that of Engels: "Free will is nothing other than the ability to decide with full knowledge of the facts." The agreement is so complete that it even finds expression in the fundamental concept of therapy of neuroses: by obtaining insight into the repressed matter within himself—i.e., by the unconscious being made conscious—the patient gains the ability to decide with better "knowledge of the facts" than would be possible so long as his most essential urges remained unconscious. This is certainly not free will in the sense of the metaphysicians;

it is always limited by the patient's natural needs and demands. For example, if a man's sexual wishes have become conscious, he cannot decide to repress them again, nor can he decide to practice chastity permanently; he can, however, decide to live chastely for a certain time. After successful analysis the ego remains no less dependent on the id and on society than before: it is merely better equipped to cope with conflicts.

It follows from the conditions of formation of the ego and the superego that questions related to social life account for one half of the concrete content of the former and the entire concrete content of the latter. Religious and ethical demands change with the social order. The superego of a woman in the age of Plato was fundamentally different from that of a woman in capitalist society; and to the extent that a new society is ideologically foreshadowed within the existing one, the contents of the superego naturally change also. This applies to sexual morality, say, as much as to the ideology of the inviolability of the ownership of the means of production; it also changes, of course, with the position of the individual in the production process.

But in what way does social ideology affect the individual? The Marxian doctrine of society was obliged to leave this question open as being outside its proper sphere; psychoanalysis can answer it. For the child, the family—which is saturated with the ideologies of society, and which, indeed, is the ideological nucleus of society—is temporarily, even before he becomes engaged in the production process, the representative of society as a whole. The Oedipus relationship not only comprises instinctual attitudes: the manner in which a child experiences and overcomes his Oedipus complex is indirectly conditioned both by the general social ideology and by the parents' position in the production process; furthermore, the Oedipus complex itself, like everything else, depends ultimately on the economic structure of society. More, the fact itself that an Oedipus complex occurs at all must be ascribed to the socially determined structure of the family. The question of the historical nature not only of the forms but of the very existence of the Oedipus complex is discussed in the next chapter.

3) The Dialectic of the Psyche

We now pass to the question whether the materialist discoveries of psychoanalysis have also revealed the dialectic of psychological processes. First, however, let us recall the fundamental principles of the dialectical method as established by Marx and Engels and taken up by their followers.

Marx's materialist dialectic formed a contrast to the idealist dialectic of Hegel, the real founder of the dialectical method. Whereas Hegel regarded the dialectic of concepts as the initial motive force of historical development, and the real world merely as a mirror image of dialectically developing ideas or concepts, Marx reversed this view and made it materialist: in his own words, he put Hegel's construction "on its feet" by recognizing that material events were at the origin of all things and that ideas were dependent upon them. He took over the dialectical view of events from Hegel, but he rejected Hegel's metaphysical idealism, just as he also rejected the mechanistic materialism of the eighteenth century.

The fundamental principles of dialectical materialism are as follows:

1) The dialectic is not only a form of thought; it is also a fact given in matter independently from thought, i.e., the motion of matter is dialectical in an objective way. The materialist dialectician does not, therefore, endow matter with what exists

only in his thought; on the contrary, he directly apprehends, through his sensory organs and through his thought (which itself is subject to the law of dialectics), the material happenings of objective reality. It is clear that this attitude is diametrically opposed to Kant's idealistic doctrine.[33]

2) The development, not only of society but also of all other phenomena, including natural ones, does not—as every kind of metaphysic, whether idealist or materialist, maintains—occur as a result of a "development principle" or a "tendency towards development inherent in matter," but out of an inner contradiction, out of contrasts which are present in matter and out of a conflict between these contrasts which cannot be solved within the given mode of existence, so that the contrasts break down the current mode of existence and create a new one, in which new contradictions must eventually occur, and so on.

3) Everything that results from dialectical development is objectively neither good nor bad but unavoidable and necessary. However, something that was at first beneficial in a particular period of development can later become an impediment. Thus the capitalist method of production was at first immensely favorable to the development of technical productive forces, but later, owing to the contradictions inherent in it, it began to inhibit those forces. The liberation from this inhibition must come from the socialist method of production.

4) Because of this dialectical development out of contradictions, nothing is constant; everything that comes into being already carries the seed of its own decay. Marx has shown that a class which wants to consolidate its rule cannot accept the dialectical view because by doing so it would be pronouncing the death sentence upon itself. He explained that the rising capitalist bourgeoisie created a new class—the proletariat—which, as a result of its conditions of existence, spells the downfall of the bourgeoisie. Hence, only the proletarian class can fully and in practice accept the dialectic, whereas the bourgeoisie must, of necessity, continue to cling to absolute idealism.

5) Every development is an expression and a consequence

[33] Cf. Lenin, *Materialism and Empirio-Criticism.*

of a double negation: the negation of a negation. To illustrate this, let us once again consider an example from the development of society. Commodity production was a negation of primitive communism, in which there existed only production of consumer values. Socialist economy is the negation of the first negation; it denies commodity production and thus arrives spirally at an affirmation of that which was at first denied—the production of consumer values, and communism.[34]

6) Contradictions are not absolute: they interpenetrate each other. At a certain point quantity changes into quality. Every cause of an effect is at the same time the effect of that effect, which is also a cause. And this involves not merely the reciprocal effect of strictly separate phenomena, but rather a whole process of mutual interpenetration and reciprocal action. Moreover, an element can, under given conditions, change into its opposite.[35]

---

[34] *(1934)* The same applies, as has been discovered in the meanwhile, to the development of sex forms and sex ideology. In primitive societies, with a primitive communist economy, sexual life is approved and provided for. With the development toward a commodity and private economy, the affirmation of sexuality turns into its denial, both in society as a whole and in the individual human structure. Given the dialectical law of development we must now assume that the denial of sexuality will, at a higher level of development, once again be transformed into social and structural approval. The present period is a period of two conflicts: one concerns the abandonment or preservation of the commodity economy; the second sees an increasingly acute conflict between a social tendency toward a more stringent suppression of sexuality, and an opposing tendency toward a restoration of natural sexual economy in place of moral regulation and suppression. In the first years of the existence of the Soviet Union the two progressive tendencies were very clearly marked; so far as sexuality is concerned, the progress was interrupted and a retrograde development set in, the causes and nature of which have not yet been properly investigated. (Cf. *Der Einbruch der Sexualmoral.*) The theory of a social economy of sexuality can be viewed as the subjective recognition, the theoretical realization, of this social contradiction. The leaders of the proletarian movement today are ignorant of this contradiction, and efforts to reveal it have met with violent resistance on the part of important sections of the leadership. Cf. "Die Geschichte der Sex.-Pol." (The History of the Sex-Political Movement) *Z.f.p.P.u.S.,* starting with No. 3/4.

[35] *(1934)* The fascist mass movement makes this process almost palpably evident. The anticapitalist rebellion of the mass of the German people, which is in acute contradiction with the objective function of fascism,

7) Dialectical development takes place gradually, but at certain points it becomes sudden. When water is continuously cooled, it does not gradually turn into ice: the quality "water" suddenly, at a certain point, becomes the quality "ice." That does not mean, however, that the sudden change comes out of the blue; it has developed gradually, dialectically, up to the point of sudden transformation. In this way the dialectic also resolves, without denying it, the contrast between evolution and revolution. A change in the social order is at first prepared by evolution (labor becoming a social process, the majority becoming proletarian, etc.) and then actually brought about by revolution.

Let us now, using a few typical processes in human psychological life, try to show the dialectical nature of these processes: a nature which, we maintain, could not have been discovered without the psychoanalytical method.

First, as an example of dialectical development, the formation of symptoms in neurosis as first discovered and described by Freud: Freud maintains that a neurotic symptom is created because the socially restrained ego at first resists and eventually

---

has become interwoven with that function and so has transformed itself, for a time, into its opposite—namely, a reinforcement of the rule of German capital.

At this point I should like to refer in passing to a problem which will be discussed in detail elsewhere. The special nature of Marxist politics consists in foreseeing the trends of possible development in any situation and in encouraging those processes which are favorable to social revolution. The theoretical thinking of the Comintern leaders, in whose hands lies the fate of world revolution, has degenerated, becoming economist and mechanical; as a result, the Comintern has been regularly overtaken by events. It has proved incapable of foreseeing anything; for example, it overlooked the revolutionary tendencies in the fascist mass movement and was therefore unable to turn them to advantage. Both revolutionary and reactionary tendencies were temporarily combined in fascism. The mass slaughter of the storm troop leaders on June 30, 1934, has shown that the rift between the two has once again become acute; it remains to be seen whether the break will be final. All this could have been foreseen as a possibility. A way of learning from the past exists. If we can recognize at an early stage the inner contradictions in any important social phenomenon, then we can calculate in advance its possible trends of development. In this connection, cf. *Massenpsychologie des Faschismus* (Mass Psychology of Fascism), Verl. f. Sex.-Pol., 2nd ed., 1934, where an attempt is made to analyze the ideological contradictions of fascism.

represses an instinctual urge. However, the repression of an instinctual urge does not, in itself, create a symptom: the repressed urge must break through the repression and reappear in disguised form. According to Freud, the symptom contains both the rejected urge and the rejection itself: the symptom allows for both diametrically opposed tendencies. What, then, does the dialectical nature of symptom formation consist of? On the one hand, there are the demands of instinct, and on the other hand, there is reality which prohibits or punishes its gratification; this contradictory situation calls for a solution. The ego is too weak to resist reality, but also too weak to control the urge. This weakness of the ego, which is itself the result of a previous development in which the symptom formation is only a phase, is the framework within which the conflict takes place. It is now dealt with in such a way that the ego, ostensibly serving the dictates of society, but really acting in order not to be punished or destroyed —i.e., following the instinct of self-preservation—represses the urge.[36] Thus repression is the consequence of a contradiction which cannot be resolved under conditions of consciousness. The becoming-unconscious of the urge is a temporary, albeit pathological, solution of the conflict. Second phase: after the repression of the wish, which has been both denied and affirmed by the ego, the ego itself is now changed; its conscious is poorer by one component (instinct) and richer by another (temporary peace). The instinct, however, can no more relinquish its urge for gratification when it is suppressed than when it is conscious—if anything, less, because it is now no longer subject to the controls of consciousness. Repression posits its own destruction, since as a result of repression, instinctual energy is powerfully dammed up until it finally breaks through the repression. The new process of breaking through the repression is a result of the contradic-

[36] *(1934)* The English psychoanalytical school overlooked the fact that this weakness of the ego is an artificial expression resulting from the inhibition of urges. If there were no conflict between the ego and sexual demands, and if the ego could obtain the satisfaction corresponding to whatever stage of development it happens to have reached, then it would not fear the urge. Yet the resulting weakness is regarded by the English and many other analysts as biologically founded. From their position it would follow that sexual repression is a biological necessity.

tion between suppression and the increased strength of the dammed-up instinct; just as repression itself was a result of the contradiction between the instinctual wish and its denial by the outside world (given the condition that the ego is weak). Thus there is no such thing as a tendency toward symptom formation; we have seen how the development arises from the contradictions of psychological conflict. As soon as there is repression there are also the conditions for its breakthrough on account of the increased energy of the dammed-up unsatisfied instinct. Does the breakthrough of the repression in the second phase restore the initial situation? Yes and no. Yes, insofar as the instinct once again dominates the ego; no, insofar as it reappears in the conscious as a symptom, that is to say, in changed or disguised form. This symptom contains the old element—the instinct—but also, at the same time, its opposite, the resistance of the ego. In the second phase (symptom) the original contradictions are therefore united in the same phenomenon. That phenomenon itself is a negation (breakthrough) of a negation (repression). Let us stop here for a moment to demonstrate this by a concrete example from psychoanalytic experience.

We will take the case of a married woman who has a fear of burglars and imagines that they are going to attack her with knives. Let us assume that she cannot stay in a room by herself and suspects a violent burglar in every corner. Analysis of this working-class wife yields the following facts:

Phase I: psychological conflict and repression. Before she was married, this woman met a man who pursued her with propositions which she would have liked to accept had she not been morally inhibited. She was able to put off the solution of this conflict by comforting herself with thoughts of eventual marriage. The man gave her up and she married another, without, however, being able to forget the first. The memory of this first man disturbed her incessantly. Meeting him again on some occasion, she again fell into an acute conflict between her desire for him and the demands of conjugal fidelity. Under these conditions the conflict became intolerable and insoluble, the desire for the other man being as strong as her moral sense. She now began to avoid him (resistance) and, finally, seemed to forget him. It was, however, not a real forgetting but a repression. She thought she was cured and consciously never gave him another thought.

Phase 2: breakthrough of the repression. Some time afterward she had a violent quarrel with her husband because he had been flirting with another woman. In the course of this quarrel, as was discovered much later, she thought: If you can do this, then I'm a fool if I stop myself from doing the same. In thinking this she momentarily saw the image of her first lover before her. The thought, however, was too dangerous, since it could conjure up the whole ancient conflict, and so it did not occupy her further: she had once again repressed it. But that night a fear overcame her; she suddenly had the idea that a strange man was creeping toward her bed wanting to rape her. The instinct had reentered the conscious in disguised form, or even as its own direct opposite: fear of the stranger had replaced desire. This disguise (phase 3) provided the basis for symptom formation.

If we now analyze the symptom itself, we shall see that the fantasy image of a strange man creeping into her bed at night satisfies a repressed wish to commit adultery (analysis showed in detail that the man imagined in the fantasy resembled her first lover in build, hair coloring, etc., without her realizing it). The same symptom, however, also contains an element of defense, of fear of the urge, which appears as fear of the strange man. Later, the element of "being raped" disappeared from the fear and was replaced by "being murdered," thus corresponding to a further displacement of the hitherto excessively obvious content of the symptom.

In this example we see not only the joining of initially separate contradictions in a single phenomenon, but also the transformation of a phenomenon into its opposite—the transformation of desire into fear. In such a case the transformation of sexual energy into fear—and this was one of Freud's first and most fundamental discoveries—the same energy produces under one set of conditions the exact opposite of what it has already produced under another set of conditions.

There is yet another dialectical principle to be found in our example. The new element—the symptom—contains the old one (the libido), and yet the old element is no longer itself, but at the same time something entirely new, namely fear. The dialectical contradiction of libido and fear can be resolved in another way, that is to say, out of the contradiction between the ego and the outside world.[37] But before we consider this, we should think of some further, less detailed example of the dialectic of psychology. For example, the transformation of quantity into quality: the repression of an instinctual urge from the conscious, or even its mere repression, is, to a certain extent, pleasurable for the ego because it removes a conflict; but beyond a certain point this pleasure is transformed into unpleasure. Slight irritation of an erogenous zone incapable of final satisfaction is pleasurable; if it continues too long, the pleasure is again transformed into unpleasure.

Tension and relaxation are dialectical concepts or processes. This fact is best seen in the sexual instinct. Tension of a sexual

---

[37] *(1934)* At the present stage of knowledge, the difference between this view of the duality of urges (which today may be described as the "sexual economy" view) and Freud's can be summed up as follows: Freud posited, on the one hand, a conflict between the ego and the outside world, and then, independently from this, the inner dualism of two basic urges. He discovered the dual character of the psychical process, an idea which he never abandoned. Sexual economy takes another view of the inner dualism of urges, which is not absolute but dialectical; moreover, we believe that inner conflicts between urges follow from the fundamental conflict between the ego and the outside world. It would take us too far to discuss these complicated matters in detail in this paper, and, in particular, to describe how the sexual economy theory of urges grew out of the Freudian theory, which of the specific elements it took over in their entirety and which it replaced or developed, etc. Some friends of sexual economy are inclined to ascribe views to Freud which he himself rejects. Since sexual economy is, among other things, the most consistent continuation of psychoanalytical science, it goes without saying that many of its fundamental views were prefigured or hinted at—or were already present in latent form—in psychoanalytical research; hence the difficulty of separating the two disciplines from one another. Yet today a glance at the literature is enough to show how the sexual economy doctrine of sexuality and instincts is irreconcilable with that of the psychoanalytical school. Unlike very well-intentioned friends of both disciplines, I should like to avoid trying to reconcile the irreconcilable. The fundamental principles of the sexual-economy doctrine of instincts are explained in the last chapter of *Charakteranalyse* and in the "Urgegensatz des vegetativen Lebens," *Z.f.p.P.u.S.*, 1934.

urge increases desire; at the same time it reduces tension (i.e., reduces itself) by satisfaction through irritation, so that it is simultaneously tension and relaxation. But tension also prepares for the coming of relaxation, just as, for instance, the winding of a clock prepares for its running down. Conversely, relaxation is connected with maximum tension—e.g., in the sexual act or in the dénouement of an exciting play—but is also the basis for the renewal of tension.

The principle of the identity of opposites is to be found in the concepts of the narcissistic libido and the object libido. Freud maintains that love of self and love of another ("object love") are not only opposites: object love comes out of the narcissistic libido and can be transformed back into it at any point; insofar as both are love tendencies, they are identical, not least because both derive from a common source—the somatic sexual apparatus and "original narcissism." As for the concepts of the "conscious" and "unconscious," these are opposites, but the example of compulsive neurosis shows that they can be contradictory and identical at the same time. Patients suffering from compulsive neuroses banish ideas from their conscious by merely withdrawing attention or affective engagement from them; the "repressed" idea is at all times conscious and yet unconscious, i.e., the patient can produce it but does not know its significance. Likewise, the concepts "id" and "ego" express identical opposites: the ego, on the one hand, is only a specially differentiated part of the id, but under special conditions it becomes its opponent or functional counterpart.

The concept of identification not only corresponds to a dialectical process but also to the identity of opposites. According to Freud, identification comes about in such a way that, say, the person who brings up a child and who is simultaneously loved and hated by the child is "absorbed" by it: the child "identifies" with the teacher, i.e., makes the teacher's attitudes or precepts its own. This usually means the end of the object relationship. Identification takes the place of the object relationship and is therefore its opposite or negation; at the same time it maintains the object relationship in another form, so that it is also an affirmation. This is based on the following contradiction or conflict: "I love X; because he is my teacher, he forbids me to do many things, and for that reason I hate him; I would like to destroy or eliminate him, but I also love him and for that reason I want him to stay." From this contradictory situation, which cannot continue as such if the conflicting urges reach a certain intensity, there is the following way out: "I absorb him, I identify myself with him, I destroy him (i.e., my relationship with him) in the outside world, but I keep him within myself in an altered form: I have destroyed him and yet he stays."

In such situations, which in psychoanalysis are covered by the concept of ambivalence, of Yes and No simultaneously, there exist many other dialectical phenomena, of which we emphasize only the most striking, the transformation of love into hate and vice versa. Hate may, in reality, mean love, and love may mean hate. They are identical insofar as both make possible an intensive relationship with another person. Transformation into the opposite is a property which, Freud says, all the instincts in general possess. In such reversal the original instinct is not destroyed but is fully maintained in its opposite.

The opposites "perversion" and "neurosis," too, should be seen dialectically, in that every neurosis is a negated perversion and vice versa.

A very good example of dialectical development is found in the history of sexual repression over the centuries. Among primitive races there is a sharp contrast between the incest taboo in respect of the sister (and mother) and sexual freedom in respect of all other women. But the sexual restriction gradually spreads further and further, at first affecting cousins and later all women of the same *gens,* until, finally, as a result of further extension it is transformed into a qualitatively different attitude to sexuality in general, as for instance under the patriarchal system and especially in the age of Christianity. Yet the increased repression of sexuality as a whole produces its opposite, with the result that, today, the taboo on relationships between brother and sister has in fact been broken so far as children are concerned. Adults, because of their excessively powerful sexual repression, have absolutely lost all knowledge of infantile sexuality, so that sexual play between brother and sister is today not regarded as sexual at all and forms part of the accepted pattern of life in the most "refined" nurseries. Primitive man may not so much as look at his sister, but in all other respects he is sexually free; civilized man lives out his infantile sexuality with his sister, but is otherwise bound by the most stringent moral precepts.[38]

Let us now examine the extent to which psychoanalysis has uncovered the dialectic of those psychological processes which concern the individual's general development in society. Two basic questions have to be considered: first, the question as to whether the dialectic of psychological processes can be traced back to the (fundamental but resolvable) contradictions between the ego (instinct) and the outside world; second, the manner in which rational and irrational interpretations of the same facts contradict one another and yet merge into one another.

In the first section of this article we have explained that according to Freud's psychoanalytic theory, the individual comes into the world, psychologically speaking, as a bundle of needs and corresponding instincts. Being a social creature, the individual with all his needs is immediately placed in the midst of society—not only the close society of the family but also, indirectly, through the economic conditions of family life, of society at large. Reduced to the most simple formula, the economic structure of society—through many intermediary links such as the class association of the parents, the economic conditions of the family, its ideology, the parents' relationship to one another, etc.—enters into a reciprocal relation with the instincts, or ego, of the newborn. Just as his ego changes his environment, so the changed environment reacts back upon his ego. The needs are partially satisfied, and to that extent there is harmony. To a major extent, however, there arises a contradiction between the instinctual needs and the social order, of which the family (and

[38] *(1934)* This paragraph needs correcting. When I first wrote it I was influenced by the bourgeois theory that the patriarchal family was the sexual unit of primitive society—a theory which coincided with Freud's as put forward in *Totem and Taboo*. I have since learned something about the crucial development processes which transformed matriarchy into patriarchy, and am now forced to recognize that not only sisters but all girls of the same clan are subject to taboo. For comments on the contradiction between family and clan, cf. *Der Einbruch der Sexualmoral.*

later the school) act as the representative. This contradiction produces a conflict which leads to a change, and as the individual is the weaker opponent, the change occurs within his psychological structure. Such conflicts, resulting from contradictions which, if the child's psychological structure remained constant, would be insoluble, arise daily and hourly and create the energy for development. True, psychoanalysis does speak of predisposition, of development tendencies and so forth, but the facts which have so far been discovered by experience concerning psychological development in early childhood suggest only the dialectical development as described above—progressive movement by means of contradictions from step to step. A distinction is made between different stages of development in the libido. It is said that the libido passes through these stages, but observation shows that no stage is really reached unless there has been a refusal of instinctual satisfaction in the preceding stage. Thus the refusal of instinctual satisfaction becomes, through the conflict which it causes within the child, the motive force of its development. We neglect that share of this development which is due to heredity because it is difficult to represent it purely as such, as for instance, with the disposition of erogenous zones and of the perception apparatus. This is still a more or less uncharted area of biological research, and the question as to the nature of its dialectic does not belong within this essay. We have taken it into account, but we must be satisfied with Freud's formula, according to which instinctual disposition and experience account for more or less equal parts in development.[39]

[39] (*1934*) This passage, too, needs to be carefully corrected. In place of the absolute view of instinctual predisposition, sexual economy holds that in the first place, a predisposition can exist only as regards differences of biological and physiological energy production, and secondly, that these differences appear as a "hereditary predisposition" only when the necessary conditions are present. In other words, the same make-up may be conducive to neurosis in one case and not in another. Our incomplete concrete knowledge of these processes means that theoretical formulations, too, have to be very tentative. A first attempt is to be found in the postscript to *Einbruch der Sexualmoral*. It is unlikely that the dialectical-materialist science of the future will take over much from today's science of genetics, which is one of the strongholds of bourgeois culture, based mainly on moral value judgments and containing very few scientific ele-

Thus, side by side with the satisfaction of instinctual wishes, the refusal of these wishes plays a dominant role as a motive force of psychological development. The contrast between the ego and the outside world eventually becomes an inner contradiction in that an inhibiting force—the superego—begins to form within the psychological apparatus under the influence of the outside world. What was originally a fear of punishment becomes a moral inhibition. The conflict between instinct and outside world becomes a conflict between the instinct-ego and the superego. We must not forget, however, that both are materially based, the former fed directly from an organic source, the latter created within the ego in the interests of the self-preservation instinct (narcissism), which limits the sexual instinct and aggressivity. In that way two fundamental needs, which at first—in the infant stage and in many situations later in childhood—formed a unity, enter into contradiction to one another and drive the development forward from conflict to conflict, not only occasioned but actually caused by social limitations.[40] And although inner and outer conflicts usually determine development, here social existence gives both to the aims of the instinctual wish and to the moral inhibitions which restrain it their time-conditioned ideas and contents. Thus psychoanalysis fully confirms Marx's dictum that social being determines "consciousness," that is to say ideas, aspirations and wishes, moral ideologies, etc., rather than vice versa. Furthermore, it adds a concrete content to this dictum as regards the development of children. This is not to

---

ments. Its culmination to date has been Hitler's megalomaniac "theory of race."

[40] (*1934*) The question here is how the inner contradictions which produce the inner psychical conflict develop out of the basic conflict between ego and the outside world and how they later assume independent existence. This fundamental question as to the nature of the "dialectical law of development" arose for the first time quite recently in connection with a discussion on character formation. I cannot at present judge to what extent it is already dealt with in Hegel or Marx; anyway, I would prefer to approach the new field—that of the dialectics of the psyche—entirely unprejudiced. When I was studying Marx, it seemed to me that Marx does not answer the question of the origin of man's inner contradictions, but it may be that at that time I was not specially concerned with this problem, and Marx's comments therefore escaped my attention.

deny, however, that both the intensity of needs—which is somatically determined—and qualitative differences in development can be caused by the instinct apparatus. Many Marxists have said to me in discussion that this is an "idealist deviation"; on the contrary, it entirely agrees with the Marxian principle that man himself makes his history, though only under given specific conditions and prerequisites of a social nature.[41] Engels in one of his letters expressly rejects the idea that the production and reproduction of reality is the only determining element in the development of ideologies; it is, he says, the determining element only in the final instance.[42]

Translated into the language of sociology, Freud's central thesis concerning the importance of the Oedipus complex in the development of the individual means precisely that social being determines that development. The child's instincts and disposition—empty molds ready to receive their social contents—go through the (social) processes of relationships with father,

[41] *(1934)* Since the economist Marxists of today attack sexual economy in the name of Karl Marx, let me quote a famous statement which proves that Marx believed human needs to be the basis of production and society. In doing so I fully realize that scientific debates today tend to be decided by prestige politics rather than by objective argument, so that quotations are of little use. Marx said that "individuals have always built on themselves" (*The German Ideology*, R. Pascal, ed., New York, International Publishers, New World Paperback, 1963, p. 76). By this he did not mean that individuals do not need relationships with one another; on the contrary—because the needs of individuals, that is to say their nature, and their way of satisfying those needs, bring them into association with one another (sexual intercourse, trade, division of labor), they have to establish relations among themselves. Since, further, they enter into these relations not as pure egos but as individuals at a certain stage of development of their productive forces and needs, and since their relations, in turn, determine their production and their needs, it is the personal, individual behavior of individuals to one another which has created the existing relations and re-creates them anew every day. Individuals entered into relations with one another as what they were, they "built on themselves" as they were, regardless of their "ideology"; this "ideology," whatever it was, even the distorted ideology of the philosophers, could only be determined by their real life.

[42] Engels, letter to J. Bloch: "Hence if somebody twists this into saying that the economic element is the *only* determining one, he transforms that proposition into a meaningless, abstract, senseless phrase." Karl Marx and Friedrich Engels, *Selected Works* (2 vols.), Vol. II, Moscow, Foreign Languages Publishing House, 1951.

mother and teacher, and only then acquire their final form and content.

The dialectic of psychological development shows itself not only in the fact that contrasting results can arise out of any situation of conflict depending on the ratio of forces of the opposing sides; clinical experience has proved that character traits can, given appropriate conflict situations, change into their exact opposites which were already present in germinal form when the first solution of the conflict occurred. A cruel child can become the most sympathetic of adults, in whose compassion it would be impossible, without detailed analysis, to find a trace of the old cruelty. A dirty child can later become a fiend for cleanliness; a curious child can become scrupulously discreet. Sensuality easily changes into asceticism. In fact, the more intensively a character trait has developed, the more readily it will change into its opposite, given the appropriate circumstances (reaction formation).

However, as development progresses the old element is not entirely lost through transformation. While a part of the trait develops into its opposite, another continues to exist unchanged, not without undergoing formal modifications as a result of changes in the personality as a whole. The Freudian concept of recurrence plays a great part in developmental psychology, and close examination shows it to be wholly dialectical.[43] That which is repeated is always both the old thing and an entirely new one, the old thing clad in new clothing or performing a new function. When a child which once liked to play with excrement later enjoys building sand castles and eventually, as an adult, develops a great interest in building, this means that the old element is

[43] *(1934)* The theory of compulsive repetition which goes beyond the pleasure principle has since proved itself to be a hypothesis which might have been specially invented in order to de-sexualize the psychical process. A detailed clinical refutation of this theory is to be found in the chapter entitled "Der masochistische Charakter" in *Charakteranalyse,* 1933. Within the meaning of my text, repetition is dialectical only if it occurs within the pleasure–unpleasure principle; this principle—if only for heuristic reasons—must not be limited unless one wishes to fling the doors wide open to the metaphysics we have driven out with so much effort.

contained in all three phases, but in a different form and serving a different function. Another example is the story of the surgeon or gynecologist, the former is satisfying his sadism (cutting open), the latter his infantile pleasure in looking and touching. To judge whether or not these findings are correct is not a matter for methodological but only for empirical criticism. No one who has not analyzed a surgeon can challenge this theory. Methodologically, however, he can raise a serious objection, that of the dependence of any human activity on economic living conditions. But psychoanalysis claims no more than that certain particular forces can have an effect on activity.[44] Side by side with the subjective urge, the form which sublimation takes is, of course, economically conditioned; it is above all a man's social position which decides whether he will sublimate his sadism as butcher, surgeon or policeman. Sublimation may also, for social reasons, prove to be impossible; this then leads to dissatisfaction with the occupation forced upon the individual by social conditions. Methodology can further raise the question of how the undeniably rational character of an activity is compatible with its equally undeniably irrational meaning. After all, the painter paints, the engineer constructs, the surgeon cuts open and the gynecologist examines in order to make a living, i.e., for economic, rational reasons. Moreover, work is a social, that is to say a wholly rational activity. How can this be reconciled with the explanation offered by psychoanalysis that man sublimates an instinct in his chosen activity and so satisfies it? Many analysts

[44] (1934) My judgment of the attitude of psychoanalysis toward its own fundamental precepts was too favorable at the time. No analyst who is not a Marxist will admit that the contents of psychical activity are rational constructs of the outside world, and that only the energy ratios involved are the product of the individual's inner world. This is confirmed, for example, by the suggestion, offered in all seriousness, that capitalism is a matter of the instincts. We are not, however, overlooking the as yet unsolved problem of how the psychical energy apparatus sets about transforming the stimuli it receives from the outside world into notions concerning the outside world which can later reproduce themselves independently from any outward stimuli. This problem is of the same order as that of the origin of inner contradictions. It is, unquestionably, also the problem of the origin of consciousness as a whole. In this field not even the first steps have been made toward a workable solution.

fail to appreciate sufficiently the rational character of work. They see in the products of human activity nothing but projections and satisfactions of instincts.[45] However, a certain analyst did once jokingly admit that while it was true that an airplane was a penis symbol, all the same it got you from Berlin to Vienna.

The problematic nature of the relationship between the rational and the irrational[46] can be seen again in the following example. The cultivation of the earth with tools and the sowing of seeds serves, socially and individually, the purpose of producing food. But it also has the symbolic meaning of incest with the mother (Mother Earth). The rational attracts the symbolic and becomes filled with symbolic meaning. The link between the rational activity and its irrational, symbolic meaning is to be found in the sequence of actions: the plunging of the tool into a material, the implanting of a seed and the production of fruit through such treatment of the material. Hence the symbolism is justified. We can see that the apparently meaningless has a meaningful core and that the symbolism has a background of reality— the mother, like the earth, after treatment with a tool (penis symbol), bears fruit. The setting up of artificial phalluses on cultivated fields as fertility charms, an objectively useless action of a magic kind practiced by many primitive races, illuminates a particular aspect of the relationship between the rational and the irrational; it represents a magical attempt to achieve a certain end more easily and effectively by irrational means. But it does not mean that rational activity—in this case, ploughing and cultivating the field—is neglected. And what in agriculture appears as an irrational, symbolic element—namely sexual intercourse— is in itself also a thing of meaning and purpose; it serves the satisfaction of the sexual need, just as sowing serves the satisfaction of the self-preservation instinct. And so we see again that there

---

[45] *(1934)* In Freud himself we find only vague hints of such an approach, as, for example, in his remarks about the invention of fire; these faint suggestions of an idealist world view—which, in Freud, are quite negligible compared with his materialist discoveries and theories—have been exaggerated in a grotesque way by metaphysically and ethically minded analysts.

[46] The term "rational" is used throughout in the sense of "having meaning and purpose," and "irrational" as its opposite.

are no absolute opposites and that the contradiction between rational and irrational can also be solved dialectically.

The dialectical fact that the rational contains the irrational, and vice versa, requires closer examination. Psychoanalytical experience of clinical cases supplies certain answers. It seems that socially purposeful activities may acquire symbolic meaning, but, equally, that they need not acquire such meaning. When, say, a person dreams of a knife or a tree, this may be a penis symbol or it may stand for a real knife or a real tree. And if it does appear in the dream as a symbol, this by no means excludes the rational meaning, for if we analytically pursue the question why the penis is represented by a tree or a knife and not, say, by a stick, we will in many cases find a rational explanation. For example, a nymphomaniac patient used to masturbate with a knife, which unquestionably represented a penis. But the choice of a knife was based on the fact that her mother had once thrown a knife at her and in so doing had injured her; and now, in her onanism, the idea predominated that she must destroy herself with a knife. This behavior, which seemed irrational in its later stage, had once been wholly rational in that it served sexual gratification. Such examples show, and many others could be quoted to show, that everything which appears irrational at the moment of examination once possessed a rational meaning. Every symptom, irrational in itself, has meaning and purpose if it is analytically traced back to its origin. The conclusion to be drawn is that all infantile-instinctual actions serving the rational urge for pleasure turn into irrational actions when they have undergone repression or some similar fate. Thus the rational always comes first.

If, for example, we consider the activity of engineering, we find in it certain irrational elements, e.g., the symbolic satisfaction of an unconscious wish. In sublimation, a driving force which once—in childhood—was rationally directed toward satisfaction is diverted from its original purpose by education and is directed toward a different aim. But at the very moment when the original aim has been given up in reality but retained in fantasy, the striving for it becomes irrational. If the urge finds a new aim in sublimation, then the old striving, which has become irrational, mingles with the new rational activity, appearing now as the irrational causation of that activity. This can be demonstrated schematically by taking the example of a child's desire for sexual knowledge later working itself out by the adult becoming a doctor.

Phase 1: the wish for sexual knowledge is rationally aimed at the contemplation of the naked body and the sexual organs. Rational aim: satisfaction of the wish.

Phase 2: refusal of direct satisfaction; the wish loses the possibility of satisfaction, the urge becomes irrational in relation to the person's actual sexual life.

Phase 3: the wish finds a new activity having a substantive connection with the first. The person concerned becomes a doctor and is once more free to look at naked bodies and sexual organs as he did as a child. He is doing the same thing and yet something else; insofar as it is the same—insofar as his activity relates to the situation of his childhood—it is now without meaning or purpose; but insofar as it relates to his present social function, it is entirely rational and useful.

It is, then, the social function of an activity which decides whether it is rational or irrational. The transformation of the character of an activity from rational to irrational and vice versa also depends on the social position of the individual at a given moment. An action of the doctor's which is without meaning in his consulting room becomes meaningful in his private life—when, for instance, he is making love: another action, meaningful in his professional work, will lose its rational character if repeated in his personal life.

These considerations can lead us to realize that psychoanalysis, by virtue of its method, can reveal the instinctual roots of the individual's social activity, and by virtue of its dialectical theory of instincts can clarify, in detail, the psychological effects of production conditions upon the individual; can clarify, that is to say, the way that ideologies are formed "inside the head." Between the two terminal points—the economic structure of society at the one end, the ideological superstructure at the other: terminal points whose causal connections have been more or less explored by the materialist view of history—the psychoanalyst sees a number of intermediate stages. Psychoanalysis proves that the economic structure of society does not directly transform itself into ideologies "inside the head." Instead it shows that the instinct for nourishment (self-preservation instinct), the manifestations of which are dependent upon given economic conditions, affects and changes the workings of the sexual instinct, which is far more plastic (i.e., malleable). In limiting the aims of sexual needs, this constantly creates new productive forces within the social work process by means of the sublimated libido. Directly, the sublimated libido yields working capacity; indirectly, it leads to more highly developed forms of sexual sublimation, e.g., religion, morality in general and sexual morality in particular, etc. This means that psychoanalysis has its proper place within the materialist view of history at a very specific point: at that point where psychological questions arise as a result of the Marxian thesis that material existence transforms itself into "ideas inside the head." The libido process is secondary to social development and dependent upon it, but it intervenes decisively in it insofar as the sublimated libido is turned into working capacity and hence into a productive force.[47]

If, however, we recognize the libido process[48] as secondary, we are still left with the question of the historical significance of the Oedipus complex. We have seen that psychoanalysis deals dialectically (even if unconsciously so) with all psychological processes; only the Oedipus complex seems to be a static exception. There may be two reasons for this. It could be that the

[47] (1934) The above paragraph remains valid in its essentials, but recent knowledge shows the ideas it contains to be very primitive and imprecise. That "working capacity" forms, in its energetic core, part of the individual's sexual economy, i.e., of what happened to his libido in the course of development, is no longer open to doubt. That the economist Marxists seem to see this as an insult to labor, that they violently reject this possibility, and that in so doing they cease to be Marxists is equally certain. But we must add that little is known as yet about the structural and dynamic make-up of working capacity, although this question is the central problem of the socialist cultural revolution and of so-called "human planning," which must follow economic planning if the latter is to become structurally anchored in human life.

[48] (1934) The emphasis here is on "process." The fact that sexual life energy is present as a vital driving force before any production is taken for granted.

Oedipus complex is interpreted unhistorically as an unchanged and unchangeable fact, a fact given as part of the nature of man. Or, secondly, it could be that the family form which is the basis of the Oedipus complex of today has in fact existed more or less unchanged for thousands of years. Jones[49] seems to represent the first view when, in a discussion with Malinowski[50] on the Oedipus complex in a matriarchal society, he says that the Oedipus complex is *"fons et origo"* of all things. This viewpoint is unquestionably idealist, for to represent the recently discovered relationship between a child and its father and mother as eternal and unchangeable, whatever the society in which the child is living, is reconcilable only with the view that social existence itself is unchangeable. To eternalize the Oedipus complex is to regard the family form which has given rise to it as absolute and eternal, which would be tantamount to thinking that the nature of mankind has always been as it appears to us today. The Oedipus complex can be assumed to apply to all forms of patriarchal society, but the relationship of children to their parents in a matriarchal society is, according to Malinowski, so different that it can hardly be called by the same name. Malinowski says that the Oedipus complex is a sociologically conditioned fact which changes its form with the structure of society. The Oedipus complex must disappear in a socialist society because its social basis—the patriarchal family—will itself disappear, having lost its raison d'être. Communal upbringing, which forms part of the socialist program, will be so unfavorable to the forming of psychological attitudes as they exist within the family today— the relationship of children to one another and to the persons who bring them up will be so much more many-sided, complex and dynamic—that the Oedipus complex with its specific content of desiring the mother and wishing to destroy the father as a rival will lose its meaning. All that is left is a question of definitions: Do we describe real incest as it existed in primeval times in terms of the Oedipus complex, or do we reserve the term for the forbidden incest wish and rivalry with the father? This not

[49] Ernest Jones, writing in *Imago,* 1928.
[50] *Sex and Repression in Savage Society,* London, Kegan Paul.

only means that the validity of a fundamental psychoanalytical thesis is limited to certain definite social forms. It also means that the Oedipus complex is regarded as a fact which in the last analysis is economically determined and, at least in the form which it assumes, socially determined. Given the lack of agreement among ethnologists, the question of the origins of sexual repression cannot as yet be solved.[51] Freud in *Totem and Taboo* relies upon Darwin's theory of the primeval horde and interprets the Oedipus complex as the *cause* of sexual repression. But obviously this does not give sufficient consideration to matriarchal society. Conversely, from the viewpoint of the Bachofen-Morgan-Engels school of research, we can see a possibility of interpreting the Oedipus complex, or, rather, the family form out of which it arose, as a *consequence* of sexual repression, which had already set in. Whatever the answer, psychoanalysis would surely be the poorer in possibilities of research in the social and pedagogical fields if it chose, so far as the Oedipus complex is concerned, to deny the dialectic which it has itself discovered in all other spheres of the life of the psyche.[52]

[51] *(1934)* A workable theory of the social origins of sexual repression has been established in the meantime. See my book *The Imposition of Sexual Morality.*

[52] *(1934)* This apprehension has since proved justified. The development of psychoanalytical pedagogy is inhibited by two ideological limitations of the bourgeois analysts: first, by their refusal to cope with the contradiction between the removal of sexual repression and bourgeois sexual inhibitions in children and adolescents; and secondly by their biological view of the child–parents conflict.

4) The Sociological Position of Psychoanalysis

If we now consider psychoanalysis from the viewpoint of sociology, the following questions arise: 1) What were the sociological facts which gave rise to psychoanalysis, and what is its sociological significance, 2) what is its position in the society of today, and 3) what will be its mission under socialism?

1) Like every other social phenomenon, psychoanalysis is bound up with a particular stage of social development; its conditions of existence are connected with a certain level of relations of production. Like Marxism, it is a product of the capitalist era, except that its connection with the economic basis of society is less direct. The indirect relations, however, can be clearly traced. It is a reaction to the ideological superstructure—the cultural and moral conditions of modern man in society. The conditions particularly involved are the sexual ones which developed out of ecclesiastic ideologies concerning sex. The bourgeois revolution of the nineteenth century swept away almost all feudal methods of production and created its own liberal ideas in opposition to religion and its moral laws. The break with religious morality, however, had already begun, as for instance in France at the time of the French Revolution; the bourgeoisie seemed to be carrying within it the seeds of a new morality, opposed to the morality of the Church in general and particularly in the sexual sphere. But just as the bourgeoisie, once its power and capitalist

economics were established, became reactionary and re-allied it-self with the Church because it needed the help of the Church to control the newly created proletariat, so also it took over in a slightly different form, but fundamentally unchanged, the sexual morality of the Church. The damming up of sensuality, monoga-mous marriage, the chastity of young girls and hence also the fragmentation of male sexuality, all acquired a new meaning—this time a capitalist one. The bourgeoisie, having overthrown the feudal system, took over to a large extent the ways of life and the cultural needs of the feudal world; it had to barricade itself against "the people" by moral laws of its own, and thus imposed increasingly greater limitations on the primitive sexual needs of man. Sexual freedom in the middle class is completely denied—except in marriage—for economic reasons; the young males of the bourgeoisie look to the young women and girls of the proletariat for their sexual satisfaction. The insistence on chastity for girls of the bourgeoisie is therefore further intensified —because of the ideological opposition of the classes—and a double standard of sexual morality arises on a capitalist basis. As in a vicious circle, this double standard of sexual morality has a disintegrating effect on the sexuality of the men and an annihi-lating one on that of the women, who, as a result of their early development, remain "chaste"—i.e., frigid, repellent, unattrac-tive—in marriage itself; this again reinforces the double standard, because the man goes on looking for satisfaction among working-class women whom his class consciousness tells him to despise; he is forced to make an outward show of respectable morality while inwardly he resents his wife. This whole ideology is then inevitably transferred to his sons and daughters. Yet the con-tinuing repression and debasement of sexuality is dialectically transformed into a force which destroys the institution of mar-riage and the ideology of sexual morality. The first stage of the breakdown of bourgeois morals is revealed in the sudden over-whelming prevalence of psychological illness. Official science, itself caught up in sexual repression, despises sexuality as a subject for research and looks with contempt upon the writers and poets who become more and more preoccupied with this burning question. It dismisses the continued increase of psychological illness, of hysteria and a general nervousness as imaginary, or ascribes them to overwork. At the end of the nineteenth century, as a reaction against science being the servant of morality and as a portent of the second, scientific phase of the downfall of bourgeois morality, a scientist appears within the bourgeois class itself who claims that the highly nervous state of modern man is a consequence of cultural sexual morality[53] and that, generally speaking, neuroses are by their specific nature sexual illnesses resulting from excessive restriction of sexual freedom. This scientist, Freud, is ridiculed and outlawed by official science; he is presented to the outside world as a charlatan. He maintains his position quite alone and remains unheard for several decades. During this time psychoanalysis is born. The theory horrifies and outrages the whole bourgeois world—not only its scientists—because it strikes at the very roots of sexual repression, upon which so many conservative ideologies are based (religion, morality, etc.).[54] Its appearance coincides with other signs of a revolt against bourgeois ideology within the bourgeoisie itself. Bourgeois youth begins to protest against the parental home and creates a "youth movement" of its own. Because it has no connection with the working-class struggle, this movement soon disintegrates; but not until it has, at least in part, achieved its purpose. Voices are raised in the liberal bourgeois

[53] Freud, *Die "Kulturelle" Sexualmoral und die moderne Nervosität* ("Civilized" Sexual Ethics and Modern Nervous Sickness), English Standard Edition, Vol. 9, London, Hogarth Press, 1953.

[54] *(1934)* Freud himself accepted this view only as regards religion but not as regards morality. Freud ascribed the resistance he encountered to the infantile complexes and repressions of those offering it. That is correct, but it is the least significant aspect. Those who offered and still offer the most stringent opposition to Freud's theories of the unconscious, infantile sexuality, etc., are acting—quite unconsciously—as executive organs of socially reactionary interests, even when they are Marxists. Sexual oppression serves class rule; ideologically and structurally reproduced in the ruled, sexual oppression represents the most powerful and as yet unrecognized force of oppression in general. Bourgeois society resisted Freud because he appeared to present a mortal threat to the continuing existence of its ideological apparatus. Freud himself never admitted this causal connection; indeed, he was displeased when others pointed it out. Sexual economy takes up the social function of psychoanalysis at the point where the representatives of psychoanalysis put it down.

press against the tutelage of the Church. Bourgeois literature adopts an increasingly free position on moral questions. But all these phenomena, some of which accompanied the birth of psychoanalysis and some of which preceded it, die out as soon as matters become really serious; nobody dares to pursue the ideas to their conclusions or to draw logical consequences; economic interest still has the upper hand, and in fact brings about an alliance between bourgeois liberalism and the churches.

Just as Marxism was sociologically the expression of man *becoming conscious* of the laws of economics and the exploitation of a majority by a minority, so psychoanalysis is the expression of man *becoming conscious* of the social repression of sex. Such is the principal social meaning of Freudian psychoanalysis. But whereas one class exploits and another is exploited, sexual repression extends over all classes. Seen from the viewpoint of the history of man, sexual repression is even older than the exploitation of one class by another. But it is not quantitatively equal in all classes. At the time of the earliest formation of the proletariat, at the beginning of capitalism, there was—to judge by Marx's account in *Capital* and Engels' in *The Condition of the Working Class in England*—practically no restriction or repression of sexuality among the proletariat.[55] The sexual habits of the working class were distinguished and influenced only by its wretched social conditions, in the way that still applies to the *Lumpenproletariat* today. As capitalism developed, however, and as the ruling class, in the interests of its own continued profit and existence, began to take social policy measures and to practice so-called "welfare," the ideological bourgeoisification of the working class set in; and this process is still becoming more intense day by day. Thus the effects of sexual repression spread to the proletariat, but without ever becoming as extreme as they

[55] *(1934)* A correction here. Sexual repression was not absent in the proletariat; because of a different social situation it was present in a different form. This is another subject about which we know too little. A proletarian child enjoys great sexual freedom and at the same time suffers extremely severe sexual oppression. This creates a special structure which is fundamentally different from that, say, of the petty-bourgeois structure.

are in the lower-middle class, which is "more Catholic than the Pope" and follows the moral ideals of its model—the upper-middle class—more closely than that class does itself. The upper-middle class began long ago to liquidate its own standards of morality for its own members.

The history of psychoanalysis in bourgeois society, then, is connected with the attitude of the bourgeoisie to sexual repression, or, to put it another way, to the removal of sexual repression.

2) Can the bourgeoisie live side by side with psychoanalysis for any length of time without damage to itself? (Assuming, of course, that the discoveries and formulations of psychoanalysis are not watered down and that it does not gradually, without its apologists realizing what is happening, lose its meaning.)

The founder of psychoanalysis has had nothing good to prophesy for its future. He believed from the start that the world would, in one way or another, suppress his discoveries because it could not tolerate them. Clearly he must have been thinking only of the bourgeois half of the world, for the proletariat as yet knew nothing of psychoanalysis and did not know that it existed. Today we cannot yet tell what the proletariat's attitude to psychoanalysis will be, but there are sufficient symptoms on hand for us to be able to study the reactions of the bourgeois world.[56]

The rejection of psychoanalysis is directly connected with the social significance of sexual repression. But what does the bourgeois world make of psychoanalysis when it does not condemn it out of hand? On the one hand there are the sciences, in particular psychology and psychiatry, on the other hand the lay public. A remark of Freud's made almost as a joke, applies equally to both: "I wonder," he said, "whether people accept psychoanalysis in order to preserve it or destroy it."

[56] (1934) Experience has now shown beyond any doubt that workers who have not suffered bourgeois deformation, as is the case with some party officials who have "come up in the world," display a natural understanding of the discoveries of psychoanalysis; one must simply avoid using psychoanalytical jargon and speak in clear language about facts drawn from the sexual life of the masses. The Sex-Pol movement in Germany proved by its rapid success the political strength of the scientific theory of sexuality. Cf. the history of the Sex-Pol movement in Z.f.p.P.u.S., 1934.

If we encounter psychoanalysis in the hands (or rather, the heads) of scientific people who have not been properly trained in psychoanalytic method, we hardly recognize it as the work of Freud. All that about sex is true, of course, but oh, those exaggerations . . . and what about ethics? Analysis is an excellent thing, certainly, but . . . synthesis, after all, is just as necessary. When Freud began to construct his psychology of the ego on the basis of his sexual theory, you could almost hear the sigh of relief being heaved all over the scientific world: at last the man was beginning to set a limit to his absurdities, at last the "higher force" in man was coming into its own, and, when all is said and done, morality. . . . After that, it was not long before people were talking only about "ego ideals" and sexuality was forgotten—the stereotype excuse being that it "went without saying." They spoke of a new era of psychoanalysis, of a renaissance. In short, psychoanalysis had become socially respectable.[57]

The attitude of the lay public is no less hopeless and, if anything, even more repellent. Under the pressure of bourgeois sex morality, psychoanalysis has been seized upon as a fashionable craze for the superficial satisfaction of lascivious desires. People analyze each other's complexes, chatter about dream symbols over cups of tea in the salons, argue for and against analysis without knowing the least thing about it, only because it deals with sex. Mr. A. is enthusiastic about the "magnificent hypothesis"; Mrs. B., no less ignorant than he, is convinced that Freud is a charlatan and his theory a soap bubble; both deplore the "one-sided exaggeration of sexuality, as if there was nothing else, nothing higher in life," yet, while deploring it, they talk about sex and nothing but sex. Special societies and discussion clubs for psychoanalysis are being formed in America; the market is good and must be exploited; the public indulges its unsatisfied sexuality; and at the same time this craze which they dare to call psychoanalysis is an excellent source of income.

[57] *(1934)* This has been tragically confirmed by the progressive abandonment of the sexual theory (Adler, Jung); the situation in this respect deserves to be discussed in detail. Within psychoanalysis itself the sexual theory has been repudiated.

So-called psychoanalysis has become good business. That is how things stand outside the psychoanalytical world.

And inside? One splinter movement follows another; the pressure of sexual repression is too great for the analysts themselves. Jung stands the whole of analytic theory on its head and turns it into a religion in which there is no longer any mention of sex.[58] Adler, likewise a victim of sexual repression, produces the thesis that sexuality is only a form of the will for power; once again, psychoanalysis is discarded and an ethical community is formed. Rank, once one of Freud's most gifted disciples, seizes upon ego psychology as an excuse for watering down the concept of the libido, develops his theory of the womb and the birth trauma, and finally denies the most fundamental psychoanalytical discoveries. Again and again, sexual repression fights psychoanalysis—and wins. In other respects, too, the marks of social and economic pressure can be seen in psychoanalytic circles. The work done becomes milder, gentler, more inclined to compromise. After the publication of *The Ego and the Id,* the libido is hardly mentioned for a number of years; attempts are made to recast the whole theory of neuroses in terms of ego psychology; it is announced that the discovery of unconscious guilt was Freud's real achievement, and that only now the real and essential heart of the matter has been reached.

In neurosis therapy, which is a matter of the practical application of a wholly revolutionary theory to man in capitalist society, the tendency toward compromise and capitulation in the face of bourgeois sexual morality can be seen at its most obvious. The analyst's social existence forbids him, indeed makes it impossible for him, to proclaim publicly the incompatibility

[58] *(1934)* Jung has appeared of late as the spokesman for fascism within psychoanalysis. The International Psychoanalytical Association is completely unaware of the social-cultural significance and origins of these developments; rather it resists their exposure. All the breakaway movements within psychoanalysis have the demonstrable common feature of being rooted in the contradiction between the analytical theory of sexuality and the analyst's bourgeois way of life, whether the point at issue is analytical therapy (Rank, Stekel) or theory (Adler, Jung). This situation requires thoroughgoing discussion because it reveals nothing more nor less than the social significance of psychoanalysis.

of the sexual morality of our day—marriage, the bourgeois family, bourgeois education—with any radical psychoanalytic therapy of neuroses. Although on the one hand it is admitted that family conditions are deplorable and that the patient's environment is usually the greatest obstacle to his cure, there is—understandably—a reluctance to draw the right conclusions from this fact. Thus it comes about that the reality principle and adjustment to reality are interpreted as meaning, not efficient functioning in relation to reality, but—in many cases—total subjugation to the self-same social pressures that created the neurosis. It need hardly be pointed out that this is disastrous for the practical application of psychoanalysis to the treatment of neuroses.

And so the capitalist mode of existence of our time is strangling psychoanalysis from the outside and the inside. Freud is right: his science is being destroyed, but we add—in bourgeois society. If psychoanalysis refuses to adapt itself to that society, it will be destroyed for certain; if it does adapt itself, it will suffer the same fate as Marxism suffers at the hands of reformist socialists, that is to say death by exhaustion of meaning: in the case of psychoanalysis, above all by neglect of the theory of the libido. Official science will continue to have nothing to do with psychoanalysis because its class limitations prevent it from ever accepting it. Those analysts who are optimistic about the popular propagation of psychoanalytical ideas are making a big mistake. It is precisely this popularization which is a symptom of the decline of psychoanalysis.

Because psychoanalysis, unless it is watered down, undermines bourgeois ideology, and because, furthermore, only a socialist economy can provide a basis for the free development of intellect and sexuality alike, psychoanalysis has a future only under socialism.[59]

---

[59] *(1934)* In the Soviet Union, psychoanalysis has been unable to develop. It met with the same difficulties there as in the capitalist countries, with the single striking difference that analysts as individuals occupy important posts. Socially, however, it has remained undeveloped. This is probably due to the fact that the Soviet leaders have not recognized (or anyway not yet) the contradictory situation of the sexual and cultural revolution in their country. This whole field is so wide and so full of problems that nothing further can be said about it here, although the question is a

3) We have seen that psychoanalysis cannot develop a world philosophy out of itself, and cannot therefore replace a world philosophy; but it can mean a reassessment of values, and in its practical application to the individual, it can destroy religion and bourgeois sexual ideology and can liberate sexuality. These, too, are precisely the ideological functions of Marxism. Marxism overthrows the old values by economic revolution and the materialist philosophy; psychoanalysis does the same, or could do the same, in the sphere of the psyche. But since, in bourgeois society, it must remain socially ineffective, its purpose can only be achieved *after the social revolution*. Some analysts believe that psychoanalysis can reshape the world by a process of evolution and so replace social revolution. That is a utopian dream founded on total ignorance of economic and political reality.[60]

The future social significance of psychoanalysis would appear to lie in three areas:

1) The area of research into the early history of mankind, as an auxiliary science within the framework of historical materialism. Early history, condensed in the myths, folk rites and customs of primitive races still extant, is methodologically not accessible to Marxist social theory. But work in this sphere can only be successful when the social and economic training of analysts is extremely thorough and when individualist and idealist views of social development have been abandoned.

---

burning one. If, as I have been told, Stalin has admitted that human planning in the Soviet Union, in contrast to economic planning, cannot be described as successful, this must, according to all our discoveries and findings, be ascribed to the absence of sexual restructuring. I know what indignation this statement will provoke, but can do no more at this stage than to promise a thorough examination of this problem which I hope to be able to put before the public in the not too distant future.

[60] *(1934)* The view that psychoanalysis could become effective as a social force only after the completion of the revolution was a short-sighted concession to ultra-left economist Marxism. Experience in Germany, especially the prompt reaction of young people of all classes to the first attempts to politicize personal life through sexual politics, has shown that the loosening of contradictions between sexual needs and moral inhibitions by mass-psychological means can become an important lever in revolutionary work—indeed the crucial lever so far as cultural policy is concerned. Cf. the description of the sexual-political problematic in *Massenpsychologie des Faschismus*.

2) The area of mental health, which can only be developed on the basis of a socialist society. The claim for an ordered libido economy within the psyche can only hope to be satisfied on the basis of an ordered economic life. This, in the bourgeois world, is out of the question so far as the masses are concerned, and can happen only in the case of a few privileged individuals. Only under socialism would individual therapy of neuroses find its proper range of effectiveness.[61]

3) The area of child education as a psychological basis for socialist education. In this field, because of its discoveries concerning the psychological development of children, psychoanalysis must be recognized as irreplaceable. In bourgeois society it is condemned to sterility, if to nothing worse, as an auxiliary science to the science of education in general. Since, in bourgeois society, we can only educate children for living in that society—because education for any other society must, for practical reasons, remain illusory—psychoanalytical education methods before the social revolution can only be applied within the rationale of bourgeois society. Those psychoanalytical educators who hope to alter this world while living and working within it must, in time, suffer the same fate as the priest who visited an unbelieving insurance agent on his deathbed, hoping to convert him, and in the end went home with an insurance policy. Society is stronger than the endeavors of its individual members.

---

[61] (1934) The investigation of human structure formation has acquired ever-increasing significance in recent years. Without it, it is impossible to obtain a serious scientific grasp of the prophylaxy of neuroses, the eradication of religious feeling, and planned development of working capacity as a productive force, or to achieve the conscious integration of a socialist economic system in the structure of society.

5) The Use of Psychoanalysis in Historical Research

The following chapter did not appear in the first edition of the present essay. It was added by Reich to the second edition of 1934.—*L.B.*

The task of scientific psychology is the investigation of psychical structure formation. Only a psychology which possesses the necessary methods for comprehending and representing the dynamism and economy of the psychical process can be regarded as scientific. In my work on the relationship of psychoanalysis to dialectical materialism[62] I have attempted to show that psychoanalysis is the germ from which a dialectical-materialist psychology can be developed. Since the bourgeois outlook of most scientists leads to distortions and false fundamental theories entering into their work, any attempt at a dialectical-materialist psychology must be preceded by careful methodological scrutiny. In my study of the matter I rejected the possibility of developing a sociological theory out of psychoanalysis because the method of psychology when applied to the facts of the social process must inexorably lead to metaphysical and idealist results and has, indeed, done so. For this view I was severely attacked by the "amateur sociologists" of the psychoanalytical school. At that

[62] I refer here to the preceding chapters of "Dialectical Materialism and Psychoanalysis," published in *Under the Banner of Marxism* in German and in Russian in 1929.

time it was clear to me that no psychological method can properly be applied to sociological problems, but it was equally clear that sociology cannot do without psychology as soon as questions of so-called "subjective activity" or ideology occur. When I finally arrived at a provisional formula which attempted to define the place of psychoanalysis in sociology, Sapir[63] reproached me with contradicting myself; such a reproach was not difficult to make, since I had previously denied the use of psychoanalysis in sociology, and now allotted it a specific place within that discipline. It is true that my critics had an easier time of it than I. Some of them continued undisturbed to brew their own special brand of "psychoanalytical sociology," whose latest triumph is the thesis that the existence of the police can be explained by the masses' desire for punishment.[64] Others dismissed the whole complex problem with the simple assertion that psychoanalysis is an "idealist" discipline which it is best not to worry too much about. An attitude which evades a serious problem. Some critics, such as Sapir, contradicted themselves because, while advancing this thesis, they had to admit that psychoanalysis had made a number of fundamental discoveries, had established the soundest theory of sexuality, and by discovering sexual repression and the unconscious had uncovered the entire psychical process, etc. To my question, How is it possible for an idealist discipline to make important discoveries? no answer was forthcoming.

Discussion to date concerning the sociological significance of psychoanalysis has been characterized by the opposition of two views: one, that psychoanalysis is individual psychology and therefore cannot explain social matters, and the other that it is not only individual psychology but also social psychology and consequently perfectly applicable to social questions. This discussion has remained entirely verbal without anyone making the attempt to check the various assertions against real facts. When in 1929 I declared that the psychoanalytical method is not ap-

[63] Sapir, "Freudism, Sociology, Psychology," *Under the Banner of Marxism*, 1929, 1930.
[64] S. Laforgue, "The Psychoanalysis of Politics," *Psychoanalytische Bewegung*, 1931. This work has been subjected to a critique of its methodology and content by Fenichel in *Psychoanalytische Bewegung*, 1932.

plicable to social matters, I based my view on applications of the psychoanalytical method to sociology made by psychoanalysts which were completely in contradiction with Marxism and proved to be false. The fact that psychoanalysis has something important to say in sociology was perfectly clear; the question was only how to avoid the previous absurdities and how to extract the latent value which, although visible, had until then proved inaccessible. It is true that I had denied in the *Banner* that the psychoanalytical method can be applied in sociology, but at the same time, I proposed a provisional application of it. This was why Sapir was able to accuse me of inconsistency. I wrote:

> These considerations can lead us to realize that psychoanalysis, by virtue of its method, can reveal the instinctual roots of the individual's social activity, and by virtue of its dialectical theory of instincts can clarify, in detail, the psychological effects of production conditions upon the individual; can clarify, that is to say, the way that ideologies are formed "inside the head." Between the two terminal points—the economic structure of society at the one end, the ideological superstructure at the other: terminal points whose causal connections have been more or less explored by the materialist view of history—the psychoanalyst sees a number of intermediate stages. Psychoanalysis proves that the economic structure of society does not directly transform itself into ideologies "inside the head." Instead it shows that the instinct for nourishment (self-preservation instinct), the manifestations of which are dependent upon given economic conditions, affects and changes the workings of the sexual instinct, which is far more plastic (i.e., malleable). In limiting the aims of sexual needs, this constantly creates new productive forces within the social work process by means of the sublimated libido. Directly, the sublimated libido yields working capacity; indirectly, it leads to more highly developed forms of sexual sublimation, e.g., religion, morality in general and sexual morality in particular, etc. This means that psychoanalysis has its proper place within the materialist view of history at a very specific point: at that point where

psychological questions arise as a result of the Marxian thesis that material existence transforms itself into "ideas inside the head." The libido process is secondary to social development and dependent upon it, but it intervenes decisively in it insofar as the sublimated libido is turned into working capacity and hence into a productive force.

Today I would word many of the above statements more clearly, and would not subsume religion and morality under the sublimation of instincts. At that time I was only dimly aware of the simple fact—which I have since come to appreciate to a much greater degree—that the psychical structure of, say, a Christian working-class woman who supports the centrist party or the fascists and cannot be talked out of her political convictions by normal means of persuasion, has a specific structure which is different from that of the psychical structure of a Communist working-class woman; for example, her material and authoritarian dependence on her parents in childhood and, later, on her husband, have forced her to repress her sexual demands, as a result of which she has fallen into a character-state of timidity and sexual reticence which has rendered her incapable even of understanding the Communist slogan of self-determination for women. Further, sexual repression, when it exceeds a certain measure or is produced in a certain manner, creates a strong bond with the church and the bourgeois social system and makes its victim incapable of a critical attitude. The significance of this question lies not only in the fact that there are millions of such women, but more important still, that such thinking cannot be ascribed to their being "fooled" or "befogged"; it is the product of a fundamental modification of the human psychical structure to the benefit of the dominant system. Given the practical scope of this and similar questions of mass psychology I was unable to satisfy the demands of Marxist friends who wanted an immediate theoretical reply to Sapir's criticism. Theoretical discussions tend to become sterile[65] unless they are firmly based on concrete

---

[65] Meanwhile, Sapir, I have heard, is no longer judged competent in the Soviet Union, since he was a student of Deborin and for that reason an idealist.

practical questioning. The question as to the role of psycho-analysis in the class struggle had to be determined on the basis of specific problems of the political movement. Such a method proved in fact fruitful both as regards the critique of metaphysical theories in psychoanalysis and of the theoretical integration of psychoanalysis in Marxist historical research.[66]

This integration had to proceed from the clear recognition that sociological questions cannot be approached by psychological methods. But at the same time, it revealed a possibility of making Marxist research in history and politics more fruitful in certain areas, such as those concerning the formation and the effects of ideology, by making use of the discoveries (not the method) of psychoanalysis. Having arrived at such a recognition, the sociologically untrained psychoanalyst will refrain from the practice of sociology, and will learn the method of historical research; at the same time, the economist will be forced to recognize the contradiction within himself when he speaks of class consciousness.

If, therefore, I am told by psychoanalysts today that I have modified my strict viewpoint according to which psychoanalysis has no place in sociological research, because I myself am now considering mass phenomena from a psychoanalytical angle, my answer is that a rereading of my text of 1929 will convince them that this is not the case. I wrote:

> The proper study of psychoanalysis is the psychological life of man in society. The psychological life of the masses is of interest to it only insofar as individual phenomena occur in the mass (e.g., the phenomenon of a leader), or insofar as it can explain phenomena of the "mass soul" such as fear, panic, obedience, etc., from its experience of the individual. It would seem, however, that the phenomenon of class consciousness is not accessible to psychoanalysis, nor can problems which belong to sociology—such as mass movements, politics, strikes—be taken as objects of the psycho-

[66] In this matter see *Massenpsychologie des Faschismus,* 1933.

analytic method. And so it cannot replace a sociological doctrine, nor can a sociological doctrine develop out of it.

It will be clear from what has been said thus far that the above remarks are still entirely valid and have merely been made a little more precise. We still cannot give a psychoanalytical interpretation to social problems, i.e., social problems cannot be an object of the psychoanalytical method. The question of class consciousness was not yet clarified when the text was first written, and so I was obliged to say "It would seem that . . ."; today it is possible to speak in more definite terms.

Experience has confirmed what was merely hinted at in the *Banner* text, namely that the first precondition of a psychological approach to the problem of class consciousness is a clear differentiation between the subjective and objective aspects of that problem. It also showed that the positive elements and driving forces of class consciousness cannot be psychoanalytically interpreted, whereas the forces inhibiting the development of class consciousness can *only* be understood psychologically because they spring from irrational sources.

My critics have often been and are still too rash in their judgments; when science enters a new field it must first get rid of many old ideas before it can unconditionally view the problems in a new light, and mistakes are sure to be made in the formulation or presentation of certain points. Thus, in order to develop a correct Marxist psychology it was first necessary to stop trying to apply the psychoanalytical interpretation technique to sociological questions; only then did it become possible to judge what is rational and what is irrational in the problematic of class consciousness, i.e., to decide how much room should be given to the interpretation of irrational phenomena. To quote an example: if I interpret the revolutionary will as rebellion against the father wherever it occurs, including the sociological sphere, I subscribe to the ideology of political reaction; but if I make a concrete investigation of how far the revolutionary will corresponds to a real situation, to what extent the *lack* of such a will is irrational, the point at which the revolutionary will really does correspond to an unconscious rebellion against the father, etc., then I have carried the bourgeois "preconditionless" science *ad absurdum,* have done authentic scientific work of my own and have thereby done a service to the working-class movement and not to political reaction; for Marxist science is nothing other than the incorruptible exposure of relations and connections as they really are.

A clear understanding of methodology in allocating a place to psychoanalysis in historical research is of decisive importance for the outcome of every investigation. It is important therefore to dwell in some detail on the criticism of my views as expressed in "Dialectical Materialism and Psychoanalysis" which Erich Fromm advances in his paper "Über Methode und Aufgaben einer analytischen Sozialpsychologie" (On the Method and Tasks of an Analytical Social Psychology).[67] Fromm writes:

An attempt must be made to find the secret meaning and
cause of irrational ways of behavior in social life as they so
strikingly occur, not only in religion and popular custom,
but also in politics and education . . . If it [psychoanalysis]
has found the clue to an understanding of human behavior
in the life of the instincts, in the unconscious, then it must
also be entitled and able to impart essential knowledge about
the background causes of social behavior. For "society," too,
consists of separate individuals who cannot be subject to any
other psychological laws than those which psychoanalysis
has discovered in the individual. It seems incorrect to us,
therefore, when W. Reich prescribes for psychoanalysis only
the sphere of personal psychology and contests, as a matter of
principle, its applicability to social phenomena such as
politics, class consciousness, etc. The fact that a phenomenon
is dealt with by sociology certainly does not mean that it
cannot be the object of psychoanalysis (just as it is wrong to
believe that a subject which is examined from the viewpoint
of physics cannot also be examined from that of chemistry).
It merely means that this phenomenon is an object for psychology—and, in particular, for social psychology, whose

task consists in determining the social background causes
and functions of psychical phenomena—only insofar as
psychical facts are involved.

It is unfortunate that Fromm quotes only what I said psychoanalysis could *not* do and not what I very clearly stated
about the role it should, and alone can, perform in sociological
research—namely, that of showing how material facts are transformed into ideas inside the human head. That psychoanalysis
and it alone can explain irrational ways of behavior (such as
every kind of religiosity and mysticism) is clear, because psychoanalysis alone is capable of investigating the instinctual reactions of the unconscious. But it can do this in the right way only
if it does not merely "take account of the economic factors," but
is clearly aware that the unconscious structures which are thus
reacting irrationally are themselves the product of historical
socio-economic processes, and that, therefore, they cannot be
ascribed to unconscious mechanisms as opposed to economic
causes, but only viewed as forces mediating between social being
and human modes of reaction. But when Fromm goes further
and asserts that psychoanalysis has something "essential" to impart about the "background causes of social behavior" because
society is composed of separate individuals, this is a wrong use
of words which opens the way to abuses of psychology which
Fromm himself would condemn. Insofar as we understand
"social behavior" to mean the behavior of human beings in
social life, to oppose personal to social behavior has no meaning,
since there exists no behavior other than social behavior. Even
behavior in a daydream is social behavior, conditioned by social
realities as well as characterized by fantasy relations to objects.
To make the point finally clear (we hope), we must take up
Fromm's criticism in conjunction with the official psychoanalytical sociology. We are not talking about fine points but about
quite crude issues. There are plenty of instances of human social
behavior in which the unconscious instinctual mechanisms in-
terposed in human action, which psychoanalysis has described
and which are of decisive importance in other phenomena, play
virtually no part at all. The point I want to make is that, say, the
behavior of people with small savings after a bank failure or a

peasants' uprising after a sudden drop in wheat prices cannot be explained by unconscious libidinous motives or as a case of rebellion against the father. It is important to realize that in such cases psychology can indeed have something to say about the effects of the behavior, but not about its causes or background. The essential point is that capitalism cannot be explained by the anal-sadistic structure of man, but that this structure can be explained by the sexual order of the patriarchal system. And society consists not only of separate individuals (that would be a crowd, not society) but of a multiplicity of individuals whose life and thoughts are determined by production relations which act between and upon them and which are totally independent of both their will and their instincts—with the important rider that production relations, precisely, can modify the instinctual structure at certain essential points, e.g., in the ideological and structural reproduction of the economic system. When we say, therefore, that we can throw light on background causes, we must be very clear which background causes we mean. The essential point, the point on which we differ from the trends in current "social psychology," is that we are aware of the limitations of psychology and of the areas in which it is dependent on other disciplines; we know we can only clarify the mediating, connecting links between basis and superstructure, only the "metabolism" taking place between nature and man as represented in the psyche. The fact that in so doing we can also elucidate the way in which ideology reacts back upon the basis through production relations which have become transformed into structure is purely a side benefit—though a decisively important one. Why is it so extraordinarily important to draw such precise boundaries? Because this is the borderline between the idealist and dialectical-materialist use of psychology in the social sphere. The fruits which the latter promises to yield merit the most painstaking and careful precision in formulating our approach. This approach can be summed up as follows: we cannot say anything about the background causes of human behavior in the extra-psychical sphere—about the economic laws which determine the social process and the laws of physiology which govern the instinctual apparatus—without immediately embracing metaphysics.

There is one further point on which I am obliged to contradict Fromm and others who approve of my views on other matters. Fromm considers that I am wrong to deny that the psychoanalytical method can be applied to social phenomena, such as strikes, etc. Other Marxist friends have argued that the psychoanalytical method *can* be applied to social phenomena because in its fundamental features it is a dialectical-materialist method. Fromm himself says that my attitude as expressed in my sociological-empirical works has undergone a "welcome" change. This is not the case. I avoid applying the psychoanalytical method to social phenomena as much as I ever did, and for the following reason, which I can now for the first time formulate with precision. It is true that we use the method of dialectical materialism to examine social phenomena; it is true that psychoanalysis is a dialectical-materialist method of examination; therefore, the abstract logician might conclude, the psychoanalytical method can "logically" be applied to social phenomena, and no harm done. At this point my friends unconsciously fall into abstract idealist-logical thinking. They are right, according to the laws of abstract logic; they are seriously mistaken, according to the laws of dialectics. A quibble? No, a very simple matter of fact. The method of dialectical materialism is the same wherever we apply it; that much is true. The principles of the unity of opposites, the transformation of quantity into quality, etc., remain the same everywhere. And yet, materialist dialectics is one thing in chemistry and another thing in sociology and again in psychology. For the method of examination is not suspended in air; it is determined in its specific nature by the subject to which it is applied. It is here that the truth of the principle of the unity of consciousness and being is fully revealed. And so the special case of the materialist dialectic of the sociological method is not exchangeable against the other special case of the psychological method. Anyone who argues that sociological questions can be correctly dealt with by the psychoanalytical method is saying at the same time, whether he means to or not, that capitalism could be explained by the methods of chemical analysis. The arguments for this would be the same as those advanced for the validity of the psychoanalytical method applied to social situations; for the social process, unquestionably, involves matter as well as man. Consequently, if it lends itself so directly to psychological investigation, why not to chemical investigation too? The example shows where Fromm's attitude would lead if consistently pursued. Fromm is mistaken when he says that the psychoanalysts have come to wrong conclusions in the sociological sphere because, in sociology, they diverged from the analytical method. No, they were completely consistent in applying to social phenomena, such as capitalism or monogamy, the method of interpretation of meaningful psychical content, and the method of tracing psychical phenomena to unconscious instinct mechanisms. And that is precisely why they failed, because society has no psyche, no instinct, no superego, as Freud assumes in *Civilization and Its Discontents*; the real facts, which must serve as the basis for any special application of materialist dialectics, were thus transferred into processes of another kind, in which they do not objectively occur, and the result was nonsense. Nor is it correct to assume, as Fromm does, that the same subject can be examined simultaneously from the point of view of chemistry and physics. Physics cannot determine chemical composition any more than chemistry can determine the speed of fall; what happens is that two different methods, both of which are dialectical-materialist, are used to examine two different properties or functions of the same object. Exactly the same applies to sociology. Only scientific jugglers of a certain well-known type can explain the same social phenomenon by means of psychology *and* by means of sociology and economics. That is eclecticism of the worst kind. To examine different functions of the same phenomenon by the appropriate methods and, in the process, to elucidate the mutual coordination and interdependence of these functions—that is dialectical materialism properly applied. Fromm is wrong when he says that social psychology "determines the social background causes and functions of psychical phenomena." An example: the social background and function of religion, morality, etc., are sociological-economic functions of a class relationship, the production relation between worker and capitalist; this production relation is determined by private ownership of the means of production, by differences between the use value and the exchange value of labor power as a commodity, i.e., by sociological categories. As a result of the economic measures adopted by the ruling class, this production relation becomes anchored in the psychical structures of members of society and, in particular, of the ruled class. Special institutions such as family, school, church, etc., modify the structure and mold it into an organism which will always react in a typical manner. We now face a social-psychological phenomenon, say, the father-son relationship in its duality: subjection plus rebellion against authority, based primarily on the economic relationship and secondarily on an irrational emotional attitude. According to the official psychoanalytical view it is the emotional relationship which actually creates the father-son relationship, that is to say, the phenomenon of an authoritarian relationship between, for example, capitalist and worker; whereas in fact the authoritarian relationship exists before the emotional one, and is based on the class relationship. Examination of the problem by means of the sociological-economic method leads to the exposure of the class relationship. Examination by the methods of psychoanalysis leads to the exposure of the *derivative* of the class relationship, i.e., to an elucidation not of the social functions but of the way they anchored in the psyche. But if one proceeds the other way around—if one treats the relationship between various individuals belonging to two different classes as though it were a matter of two psychical instances within the same person—then, although one may not be a congenital villain, one is bound to arrive at the conclusion (which a leading analyst once divulged to me) that the bourgeoisie is the superego and the proletariat the id of the social organism, and the bourgeoisie is simply fulfilling the superego's function of keeping the id under control. I am convinced that Laforgue has a heart of gold, and yet he was obliged to conclude that the existence of the police is due to the masses' desire for punishment: because, with the methods of psychology, he examined the police as a social institution instead of examining the psychology of the police and its effect on the ruled classes.

In a number of empirical-sociological studies I have applied the findings of psychoanalysis to sociology without explicitly commenting upon the questions dealt with by that method. Let me explain by quoting an example.

The strike is a sociological phenomenon in the capitalist phase of social development. Marxist sociology examines the processes leading to a strike by studying, say, the production relations between workers and capitalists and the law of capitalist economy according to which the commodity of "labor power" is bought and used like any other commodity by the owner of the means of production; it discovers other economic laws, according to which competition forces the entrepreneur to reduce wages in order to raise the rate of profit, etc. But the strike is carried out by the will and consciousness of the workers concerned, that is to say, the sociological fact is psychically represented in a certain specific way. Therefore psychology must have something to say about the matter, but how? For on the "how" depends what it will have to say. It will be seen at once that a psychoanalytical study of one or several workers who are on strike can say nothing about the strike as a social phenomenon, nor about its "background causes," nor even very much about the motives which lead workers to participate in a strike. Even if we analyze what these workers have in common, i.e., if we practice social psychology, we shall have nothing at all to say as to why strikes occur; in other words, social psychology does not explain the strike either. Uncovering the infantile conflicts between workers and their fathers or mothers has nothing to do with the particular strike in question; it only has something to do (and it is precisely this that ought to interest us) with the common historical-economic soil (the capitalist or private-economy structure of society) which produces both strikes and conflicts between parents and children. But if one insists upon using the results obtained by psychoanalyzing individual workers to explain the phenomenon of the strike, then the conclusion is inescapable that a strike is a revolt against the father. The fact that in reaching this conclusion one identifies "strike" with "psychical behavior in a strike" passes unnoticed; yet the difference is decisive. It passes unnoticed either because of methodological confusion or for conscious or unconscious reactionary motives, for the conclusions to be drawn from the sociological interpretation are not the same as those to be drawn from the psychological interpretation. The former leads to recognizing the laws of class society, the latter to obscuring those laws.

The strike may play a part in the psychical work of the unconscious, say, in the form of a dream, where it has the effect of a day residue; curiously, this is much less frequently the case than with other phenomena deriving from the sexual sphere. But to explain a strike by such a fact is as absurd as what Geza Roheim, the official spokesman on culture among the psychoanalysts, does when he makes assertions about primitive cultures on the basis of the dreams of primitives, instead of explaining the conflictual content of these dreams by the primitive cultures concerned.

Thus the function of psychology is to investigate the behavior of the workers in a strike, not the strike itself. But insofar as the behavior of workers in part determines the outcome of the strike, "psychical factors" play a role. The case is different when the sociological-economic situation is such that it should really produce a strike, yet no strike occurs. In this case the sociological-economic method will fail if it sets out to discover an immediate (direct) historical-economic reason, because the sociological process is here disturbed in its development by a third factor. This third factor is a psychological (social-psychological or mass-psychological) one, e.g., the workers' lack of trust in the leaders of the strike, the influence of reformist trade union leaders who sabotage the strike, or fear of the entrepreneur. In other cases the decisive cause may be a fear of material difficulties resulting from the strike. But this behavior, too, while it has a determining effect on the progress of the class struggle, should not be explained only in immediate psychological terms but also—and this is very important—indirectly in terms of sociology. The influence of reformist trade union leaders is itself the result of a specific relationship which, in the last analysis, is sociological; in one case it may be explained by superficial fear of dismissal, by the deeper fear of rebelling against authority, which, in turn, is rooted in the infantile relationship with the father. But what causes infantile father-bondage and fear of authority? Only the family setup, which is based on sociological and economic factors. And so, when we apply the methods of psychology, we should aim only at elucidating the more or less numerous intermediate links between the economic process and the actions of men within it. The more rational the behavior of men, the narrower is the area occupied by the psychology of the unconscious; the more irrational it is, the more sociology requires the help of psychology. This is true especially of the behavior of the oppressed classes in the class struggle. The fact that an industrial worker, or the industrial workers as a body, aspires to appropriate the means of production requires no comment other than that they are following the simple laws of the pleasure–unpleasure principle.

The fact, however, that large strata of the oppressed class accept or even support exploitation in one form or another must be interpreted directly in terms of psychology and only indirectly in terms of sociology. The reason why analytical sociology to date has gone about the task in the opposite way, trying to explain rebellion in psychological terms and taking obedience for granted, lies in the psychoanalytical notion of the reality principle, according to which the pleasure principle is replaced in the adult by adaptation to the demands of reality. But reality includes not only the capitalist law of exploitation but also man's consciousness of it, which is a consciousness of suffering and therefore leads to a refusal to adapt. The official view is that nonadaptation constitutes infantile, irrational behavior. Here one view of the world confronts another. Unlike our opponents, we do not deny that our standpoint is a political one. But we point out that the difference between these two standpoints consists in the fact that the one interprets psychologically, as a fundamental predisposition of human nature, what should be explained in terms of sociology and economics, and ignores what psychology really could explain, namely the causes inhibiting the development of social processes, thus—in both cases—creating a diversion from reality; whereas the other standpoint excludes nothing—nothing at all—from the scope of man's capacity for knowledge; indeed it aims at bringing everything into the sphere of science, arriving at a scientific view of the world by the systematic application of the method of dialectical materialism in all fields, and in this way making philosophy—insofar as it is the science of the unknown—redundant.

To sum up: conscious or unconscious application of dialectical materialism in the sphere of psychology has given us the findings of clinical psychoanalysis; the application of these findings to sociology and politics leads to a Marxist social psychology. Conversely, the application of the psychoanalytical method to problems of sociology and politics must result in a metaphysical, psychologizing and ultimately reactionary sociology.

PSYCHOANALYSIS IN THE SOVIET UNION

(1929)

"Psychoanalysis in the Soviet Union" was published by Reich in the journal *Psychoanalytische Bewegung* for 1929, following a first visit to Russia in August and September of that year. It is particularly valuable to read these earliest firsthand impressions of sexual policy under the Bolshevik government in view of the increasingly more critical response aroused in Reich by Stalinist policies of the years immediately following.—*L.B.*

It is impossible to speak of a "psychoanalytic movement" existing in the Soviet Union as it exists in Western Europe and the
United States. There does exist in Moscow a society which is
concerned with the theories of psychoanalysis and under whose
auspices regular meetings of a high scientific level are held, but
there are very few doctors who practice the psychoanalytical
method. The first impression one gets in the Soviet Union is one
of outright rejection. It is true that in 1925, on the occasion of
a discussion on the problem of sex, the People's Commissar for
Health, Semashko, spoke of the unconscious and publicly supported the theory of sublimation. But many influential public
personalities are against psychoanalysis, while others, such as
Bukharin and Radek, are interested in it without doing a great
deal to defend it. From time to time lively discussions take place
on the question whether psychoanalysis should or should not be
recognized. Its opponents reject it on the grounds that it is an
idealist science. It is said that in the years 1922 and 1923 Soviet
communist youth were strongly interested in psychoanalysis. The
party then intervened because discussions on psychoanalysis
interfered with political work. Does all this mean that there is
no room for psychoanalysis in the workers' and peasants' state?
Is psychoanalysis rejected there as a matter of principle, as, for
instance, it is rejected by official science in the bourgeois coun-

tries? The first impression certainly suggests that this is so. But if we go beyond superficial opinions and declarations, if we seriously try to discuss and analyze the nature of this rejection—if, in particular, we take the trouble to study Marx, Lenin and the history of the Russian Revolution—we shall find that the attitude toward psychoanalysis in the Soviet Union has a very special character. In essence, it can be understood only within the context of the overall structure of Soviet Russia on the one hand and of the general world situation of psychoanalysis on the other.

In order to understand the position of psychoanalysis in the Soviet Union, we must ask: What is it, in psychoanalysis, that is rejected, and why? To answer these questions we must briefly describe the present situation in the Soviet Union.

March 1917 marked the overthrow of Tsarism; and October of the same year, that of bourgeois government. The councils of workers and peasants seized all power. The revolution was led by the Bolsheviks—old, orthodox, well-trained Marxists—with Lenin at their head. Marxism, the doctrine of laws governing social history, was not only the theory which, in its consistent and practical application by Lenin, led the revolution to victory: after the revolution it became the official and solely recognized pattern for the reshaping of society in accordance with planned economic ideas. Because Marxism had acted so powerfully as a lever of social revolution, it is understandable that proletarian leaders today want to preserve it from any contamination by other theories and doctrines. They want to keep Marxism pure.

But Marxism is more than a social theory. It is at the same time a philosophic method of thinking in general, and Marxist social theory is the result of the application of dialectical materialism to human society. Since, moreover, its findings correspond to the class interests of the proletariat rather than those of the bourgeoisie, its method of thinking has become the world philosophy of the class-conscious proletariat. Thus Marxist political, economic and social theory, the Marxist method and the Marxist world view form a unified system, but a system which, unlike others, never becomes rigid, but as a result of its dialectical method, is always dynamic within itself, always mobile and adapted to the constant movement and change taking place in nature and society. It is a system which does not admit of a psychological explanation of social history or even of social phenomena, because a psychological explanation of, say, capitalism must of necessity be abstract and idealist, since it replaces the economic motive forces of social history by psychological ones, and more particularly as they appear in single individuals. Hence any psychological explanation of history is inevitably, and without any possibility of compromise, in conflict with Marx's materialist interpretation of history, which teaches that the individual's will and actions—so far as their concrete content is concerned—must be seen only as products of a given social structure, and not vice versa. Yet Marx himself stated explicitly that men (not as individuals but as a collective) make their own history, albeit only under given and requisite economic conditions. Anyone who, for example, views the history of France at the turn of the eighteenth century as a result of Napoleon's personality, or tries to explain the World War of 1914–1918 in terms of the megalomania and greed for power of Wilhelm II, is sharply contradicting the teachings of historical materialism because he is trying to replace a materialist method of thinking with an idealist one. From the historical-materialist point of view, the individual of genius is only the executive organ of social trends: from the bourgeois-idealist point of view he is the very driving force of history. The former view is sociological-materialist, the latter psychological-idealist.

Let us now briefly consider the political and economic situation of the Soviet Union today. The process of social transformation began after the October Revolution with an economy shattered by the World War. During this process of transformation, Russia was not only isolated but actually had to fight for her very life against the intervention of the capitalist powers and the White armies in a civil war lasting three years (1919–1922). As a result, production dropped catastrophically, and the period of economic reconstruction began only after the victorious conclusion of the civil war.

By 1927, in the most important branches of the economy, the prewar level of production had already been exceeded. In

1928, a plan of the Supreme People's Economic Soviet, the Five-Year Plan, came into force. The central object of this plan is to free the Soviet Union from economic encirclement, i.e., to transform the economy within five years in such a way that the Soviet Union will become entirely independent of other countries. Industrial production is to be many times greater than prewar production, and agriculture is to be industrialized.

The fulfillment of the Five-Year Plan, which is to bring the Soviet Union into line with the modern capitalist countries (and which, judging by the results of the first year of the plan [1928–1929], will achieve its purpose unless a war intervenes), demands the straining of Russia's available forces to the very limit. The hostility of the surrounding countries requires the strictest discipline within; but that is not the only thing that matters. It is also important to preserve and rigorously apply the scientific method with whose help alone, as the Communists see it, the construction of socialism can be achieved. It is not so much that the Russians have no time to discuss a modern psychology which also claims to have something to say on the subject of social development: rather, they see no necessity for it, and indeed certain experiences have taught the Russian Marxists that the psychological interpretation of social problems carries reactionary dangers within it. And so the science as a whole is rejected, even though it contains only the germ of a threat to the success of the great cause.

It might be argued that psychoanalysis does not make claims such as I have described—that it is content to be a psychological method or system, as the founder of psychoanalysis himself has emphasized. But the situation is not as simple as that. Psychoanalysis, as represented by many of its spokesmen, has gone beyond its specific sphere, and the statements and actions of these spokesmen have gone unchallenged within the psychoanalytic world. The Russians, who are forced to struggle incessantly against a world of enemies in order to secure and complete the success of their revolution, are not inclined to treat such matters lightly. They take psychoanalysis seriously, not only as a modern science, but also because the bourgeoisie likes to play it off against Marxism.

Attempts are not lacking in the bourgeois countries to "psychologize" the science of sociology. For example, Hendrik de Man, a former Marxist, attacks Marxism with badly understood psychoanalytical terms in his book *The Psychology of Socialism*. And even certain representatives of psychoanalysis itself have repeatedly attempted a psychoanalytic explanation of sociological facts and phenomena. Thus, for instance, Kolnai, who for a time was considered to be a psychoanalyst, explains the communist revolution and communism in general in terms of a neurotic regression to the mother. In other quarters the German revolution of 1918 has been interpreted as a rising of sons against their father (the Kaiser), and so forth. The discussion following a lecture on "Psychoanalysis as a Natural Science" which I delivered at the Communist Academy in Moscow last September made it clear that the Russians have nothing against psychoanalysis as a psychological discipline, but are opposed only to so-called "Freudism," by which they mean a "psychoanalytical view of the world." This distinction is important. For the reasons described, *Totem and Taboo* (insofar as it explains the origins of culture in terms of the Oedipus complex) and *Group Psychology and the Analysis of the Ego*[1] are rejected as "un-Marxist," idealist works. On the other hand, Sapir, an official spokesman of the academy, has explicitly referred to the theories of the unconscious, of repression, infantile sexuality, etc., as important and valuable. People in Russia talk a great deal about *perekluchenie,* that is to say conversion of sexual energy into work. Freud's theory of sublimation is fully recognized.

The campaign against psychoanalysis is often the result of methodological confusion on the part of the Marxists, e.g., when they accuse psychoanalysis of being an individualist psychology unconcerned with social psychology. The obvious answer to such an accusation is that any form of psychology can only, of necessity, be a psychology of the individual. Social phenomena, such as class consciousness, the will to strike, etc., are not acces-

[1] Psychoanalysis denies the existence of a collective psyche or a collective unconscious; hence it can offer no explanations which presuppose these concepts. It can, however—as Freud has done—throw light on the relationship of individuals in a mass to their leader and to one another.

sible to it. But the critics of psychoanalysis, when they make this charge, often mean that it leaves out of account the class situation of the individual.

Another reproach is that psychoanalytic theory overemphasizes the biological aspect of personality to the detriment of the social aspect; as a result, social performance—for instance, creative or productive work—is ascribed entirely to instinct.

This objection is based on the argument that no attempt has so far been made by psychologists to define the influence of social factors as against that of biological factors. And it is true that in psychoanalytical literature one encounters attitudes which suggest that instinct, independent of any molding influences from the outside world, is all that matters. Yet this view does not form part of Freudian psychology, which states very clearly that psychological development is due to the molding of instincts by influences from the outside world. Even the Oedipus relationship is not a biological but a social phenomenon, determined by the patriarchal structure of the family. Surely neither the Marxist nor the psychoanalyst can have any objection to the view that psychological development results from the conflict between individual needs and social limitations (which also includes the conflicts of the Oedipus age).

Another area of controversy concerns the respective spheres of competence in the explanation of ideologies. For instance, should religion be explained sociologically or psychologically? The Marxist says: Religion is a social phenomenon whose origins are demonstrably to be found in concrete conditions of production. The Freudian maintains that religion can be explained by the child's attitude to its father; the idea of God is unequivocally a father idea, and analogies can be found between religious dogma and certain compulsive notions. On this point there exists practically no possibility of compromise, but only of methodological clarification. Psychoanalysis cannot do more than explain how, and by what motives, a child absorbs those religious concepts and ideas which it finds in a certain form in its environment. It cannot explain why a particular religion arises and gains ground as a social phenomenon in a particular historical period. And psychoanalysis has never claimed to be able to explain religion as a whole. Where, however, the majority of individuals in the same social situation practice similar rites, psychoanalysis can uncover the meaning of those rites as it appears typically among all those who practice them. Undoubtedly Marxism alone is capable of showing why the Jewish religion is different in character from the Christian, and these again from the Buddhist; it can find connections with the social and economic mode of existence of the Jews (or Christians or Indians) to explain the specific nature of each religion. Likewise, psychoanalysis cannot explain the disappearance of religion under socialism or the phenomenon of the religious inquisition in the Middle Ages unless it applies Marxist viewpoints when interpreting these phenomena, but, in that case, it is no longer functioning purely as a theory of psychology.

The handling of the problem of symbolism by some authors —which, even from the purely psychoanalytical point of view, is incorrect or at least extremely one-sided—has done much harm to the cause of psychoanalysis in Soviet Russia. For instance, certain psychoanalytical writings on the agriculture of primitive races convey the impression that land cultivation is only a symbolic action and nothing more. Symbolic speculations of this kind must discredit psychoanalysis in the eyes of even the most well-disposed Marxist, for the outsider cannot be expected to distinguish between psychoanalysis and pseudo-psychoanalysis. Marxist thinking, being absolutely materialist-orientated, resists not symbolism as such but its misuse; but then, so does the thinking of a clinical psychoanalyst. Every object and every activity has its rational meaning; it may become a symbol, but does not by any means have to become one. Objects and activities owe their existence, not to their symbolic meaning, but to their value as utility articles or commodities—or, in the case of activities, as productive work. Airplanes and railways are not made because they are symbols of instinctual ideas, but because certain production conditions lead to their being invented and made. What goes on in the designer's unconscious as he designs them is of importance only if he comes to us as a patient. And even if the airplane he has invented has some phallic significance for him, that does not mean that the symbol was the motive for making the airplane. In the fifth century, when phallic ideas were no different from what they are today, the same man could certainly not have designed an airplane. We have to admit that this argument, often advanced by Marxists, is objectively faultless.

This is not the place to show in detail that such cases—cases where psychoanalysis goes beyond its proper sphere and is methodologically misapplied—do occasionally take place, leading to completely mistaken views concerning the real nature of psychoanalysis among orthodox Marxists. When, once in a while, psychoanalysis *is* correctly represented, Marxists refuse to recognize it as "Freudian." In a paper entitled "Dialectical Materialism and Psychoanalysis," I tried to set out the fundamental principles of psychoanalytic theory, placing the emphasis on purely Freudian—that is to say, clinical—psychoanalysis. The editorial board of the Moscow journal *Pod Znameniem Marxisma,* where the Russian text of this paper was published, felt itself obliged to add an editorial note to the effect that it did not agree with my account of psychoanalysis. And two Communists expressed the view that what I said in my article was very convincing, but was not Freudian psychoanalysis as they knew it.

This means two things: first, that the development of psychoanalytic theory over the last few years has blurred the pure, empirical and scientifically unassailable features of psychoanalysis, so that today we can almost speak of two kinds of psychoanalysis; second, that the Marxists have no objection to scientific psychoanalysis. In the article by Sapir[2] published in reply to mine, the theories of the unconscious, of repression, of the instincts and other cardinal elements of psychoanalysis are recognized. Sapir's attacks are directed in part against theses which psychoanalysis has never advanced and, in part, against excessive claims of competence, such as we have described in various psychological interpretations of social processes.

My overall impression in Moscow was that the Marxist theoreticians will accept psychoanalysis if they are presented

[2] Sapir: "Freudism, Sociology, Psychology," *Pod Znameniem Marxisma,* No. 7/8, 1929.

with its pure scientific core, i.e., the materialist-dialectical foundations of psychoanalysis, and if a clear division is drawn between these and various idealist theories and applications of psychoanalysis. Here is the difference between the position of psychoanalysis in bourgeois countries and in the Soviet Union: in Germany and America psychoanalysis only began to be recognized when it became nonmaterialist, that is to say idealist, in some of its most important aspects (deviation from the theory of the libido, emergence of the death-wish theory, the incorrect —in my opinion—application of psychology to sociology and cultural history, etc.). In the Soviet Union it is precisely these aspects of psychoanalysis which are objected to, while the core of psychoanalytic theory could readily be accepted. Jurinetz, in his critique of psychoanalytic theory, actually speaks of a "decay" of original, scientific psychoanalysis.

I must add that many Marxists—partly because their knowledge of psychoanalysis is poor, and partly for reasons of personal resistance—show a lack of objectivity in their criticisms. To some extent these criticisms come from medical men of the older generation who can neither think in psychological terms nor are trained in methodology. Their uninformed attitude is greatly confirmed by the lack of unity on theoretical issues among psychoanalysts today. The true Marxist, however, is so objectively oriented by his general attitude to life and society, he is so immune from every form of mysticism or idealist thought, that the plain facts about psychoanalysis are bound to achieve recognition in the end. Salkind, trying to attack my lecture at the Communist Academy, could finally find nothing more to say than that I had taken a very diplomatic line: I had spoken about psychoanalysis as a science, but not about so-called Freudism. In my final contribution I was able to quote Freud himself, who has spoken against the interpretation of psychoanalysis as a world philosophy, i.e., implicitly against the so-called Freudism attacked by the Marxists.

For the Marxist, a theory is of great interest only if it also has practical significance. The question has been asked again and again: What is the practical significance of psychoanalysis for socialism? The first answer is, obviously, psychotherapy. But all psychoanalysts must surely be agreed that psychoanalysis cannot be a mass therapy, and by reason of its nature, can never become one. True, at Professor Rosenstein's neuropsychological institute in Moscow, psychoanalytical therapy is practiced, among other methods. Dr. Friedmann, a member of the Moscow psychoanalytical society, is the institute's official psychoanalyst. Psychoanalysis is used there side by side with other forms of therapy. Dr. Rosenstein showed us the "psychotherapy room," where a picture of Freud hangs on the wall. We were also able to note with satisfaction that many young doctors, both at the venerological dispensary and in the psychoneurological institute, have an attitude of complete understanding and appreciation vis-à-vis psychoanalysis and apply it in practice when assessing cases. Professor Rosenstein, the chief of the institute, is a declared friend of psychoanalysis. But the main practical importance of psychoanalysis does not reside in therapy.

It is characteristic of Soviet medicine as a whole that it is paying more and more attention to mass prophylaxis. Extensive and interesting statistical and other research is being carried out at all institutes with a view to developing this field of study. Some statistics concerning the sexual life of the masses have already been obtained, the questions being formulated in a manner which could not even be dreamt of in Western countries, where they would be considered "shocking." It must be emphasized that this work is being done by official bodies and not privately. Hence the interest in prophylaxis of neuroses is very great, and concrete questions are being addressed to psychoanalysis in connection with this subject. Intensive collaboration with Russian institutes is urgently needed in this field. In our countries, because of the concentration on individual therapy, the question of prophylaxis has not yet been broached. The statement that only a theory of neuroses which proceeds by causal investigation can furnish the fundamentals of prophylaxis of neuroses was received with great attention,[3] but concrete results are still awaited.

At the venerological dispensary (director, Dr. Batkis) great

[3] The question was discussed at a lecture on "Psychotherapy or Prophylaxis of Neuroses," to which I was invited by the psychoneurological institute.

interest was also shown in the practical application of psycho-analysis at the Sexual Advice Bureau for Industrial and Office Workers in Vienna.

At the Marx-Lenin Institute in Kharkov psychoanalytical research is being carried out, but owing to lack of personal contact I cannot say anything about its value or content. The fact, however, that in response to my sending in a psychoanalytic paper, the institute invited me to continue as its regular con-tributor on psychoanalysis and appointed me a corresponding member shows considerable active interest.

In contrast, confusion reigns in matters of sexual psychology. In this respect we were unable to note any difference from conditions in Western Europe. (It should be mentioned here that the children's home run by the psychoanalyst Vera Schmidt was not officially banned, as was reported in the West; the director of the home closed it down herself because, as she personally told me, she realized that the requisite conditions for that type of work were not yet available.)

It has also been rumored here that Freud's *The Future of an Illusion* was banned in Soviet Russia. In this field, as in many others, I have found that political animosity toward the workers' state (particularly on the part of Russian émigrés of more or less White persuasion) has led to the dissemination of conscious untruths. Freud's book on religion has not only not been banned but was actually translated into Russian in 1928. The Psychoanalytical Association in Moscow has decided to send Professor Freud a copy of the translation as concrete proof of the fact that the report is untrue.

All in all, the contradictory impressions of the tour led to the conclusion that psychoanalysis in its pure empirical form will eventually be accepted as a theory of psychology, but only on the condition that it is freed from all idealist and extraclinical excrescences. Such acceptance, however—and this emerges clearly from the overall structure of the Soviet Union—will not remain a private one but will become official once the economic pressure has slackened, the hostile encirclement by capitalist countries has ended and the leaders of the socialist state become aware of neurosis as an urgent mass problem.

It is then that psychoanalysis will come into its own as a practical psychology, particularly in the prophylaxis of neuroses.

Today there is a neutral zone, fifteen kilometers in width, between the Soviet Union on the one hand and Poland and Rumania on the other. With Rumania there are no railway communications whatever, and at the Polish frontier we passed barbed-wire entanglements and trenches. The Soviet Union is a besieged fortress, and those who hold this fortress are keeping a close check on all imports, including scientific ideas. They want to know for certain what their country stands to gain or lose from a science which a part of the bourgeoisie regards as a new cultural philosophy. Only by bearing this in mind can we hope to understand the position of psychoanalysis in the Soviet Union.

THE IMPOSITION
OF SEXUAL
MORALITY

(1932; second edition, 1935)

The Imposition of Sexual Morality was completed in September 1931 and appeared in 1932. The following is a translation of the 1935 Copenhagen reissue of the book which was prepared by Reich in 1934 and to which he added a few footnotes and appended a review—omitted here—of Geza Roheim's *Psychoanalyse primitiver Kulturen*.

NB: There is another translation of *Der Einbruch der Sexualmoral*. Made at Reich's prompting, it was titled *The Invasion of Compulsory Sex-Morality* when finally published in 1971. The English-language reader, then, has a unique opportunity to compare two versions of a major text. The version here is a faithful translation of the book in its original conception, with the sex-political vocabulary and methodology intact. The 1971 text—"based on a draft translation by Werner and Doreen Grossmann"—reflects the changes in Reich's thought two decades after the writing of this work.—*L.B.*

Foreword
to the First Edition

The following work is the analysis of an era in the history of sexual economy. As such it is intended to contribute to a present-day sexual politics. It is necessary to start, however, by providing an overview to explain how the method of inquiry arose on which this work is based.

I moved from studies of sexology to psychiatry and psychoanalysis; I did this because I was profoundly impressed by the potential offered by psychoanalytical therapy for treatment of mental disturbances which would look for causes and thus be theoretically well founded. The old-school approaches to therapy seemed ineffective by comparison—oriented to sheer intuition, or to a superficial persuasion, at best. Even if psychoanalytical therapy still lagged far behind its theory of neurosis, there was nonetheless an abundance of possibilities for the unification of psychological theory with psychotherapeutic practice, as I perceived in becoming familiar with the material. In any case it was clear that to be able to cure a neurosis one had to understand neurosis, and this was so even if everyday therapeutic experience more often than not resulted in failure. Especially as therapeutic problems aroused more and more interest in theoretical matters, one estimated that no better access could be had into understanding the myriad unsolved questions of neurosis formation than through a comprehensive working-through of the question: How can an ill psychic apparatus be made healthy? As one observed the living processes of change in psychic mechanisms during the course of treatment, the question would continually arise as to how mental health is to be distinguished from mental illness; and from this, too, further insights emerged into the dynamic of the psychic apparatus.

To start with Freud's original formula: the neurosis is a product of an unsuccessful sexual repression; accordingly, the first condition for its cure consists of the removal of the sexual repression and the freeing of the repressed sexual demands. This leads to the question: What is to be done with the liberated drives? On the whole, the literature of psychoanalysis has given two replies: (1) the sexual desires having been made conscious, they must be controlled or subjected to condemnation; (2) the sublimation of the instincts is an important therapeutic resource. The need for direct sexual gratification of the patient has never been accorded serious consideration. I was convinced by a fund of experience over several years that the vast majority of ill persons could not gain the capacity for sublimation that the cure of a disturbance required. Thus the control and condemnation of the liberated infantile drives would have to be but a pious wish—assuming the patient's sexual life could not be properly ordered, that is, assuming the treatment had not given the patient the ability to engage in gratifying and regular sexual intercourse. Soon it became clear that not only does neurosis never occur except in relation to genital disorders and the gross blockage of sexual energies, but also, a mental disturbance due to fixation on infantile sexual goals will interdict a normal genital organization and accordingly an ordered sexual regimen. The achievement of full genital organization and of *genital gratification* thus proved here, too, the fundamental, indispensable curative factor. Indeed, genital gratification is alone capable, as against the non-genital sexual drives, of removing a sexual blockage and thus of withdrawing the source of energy from neurotic symptoms. Having arrived at this confidence that the key had been found to sexual economy and thus to the therapy of neurosis, I was later instructed by experience that even though one might achieve a viable sexual organization in a number of very difficult cases, the environment in which the ill and recuperating patient lived could undo the cure. Many and varied examples could be given. An unmarried seventeen- or eighteen-year-old girl from a bourgeois household had the strictest watch set over her chastity; the life of a proletarian girl offered such grim social circumstances (the housing question, the problem of contraception, the frequently expressed severely moral attitude of proletarian parents, too) that faced with obstacles set by society to a sex life, the patient who had laboriously struggled to overcome neurosis might retreat into the conveniences of the neurosis. The patient shattered by the sex prohibitions in childhood was to be cured later only with great difficulty, or not at all, due to the sex prohibitions enforced from without. And for the unhappily married woman dependent financially on her husband, or with children to think of, the case scarcely differed. One came to see, moreover, how difficult it might prove for the neurotic person intent upon a cure to find a suitable partner. Trouble stemmed from the unsure potency or the erotic grossness among the men, and the sexual incapacities or character deformations among the women, who, the neurotics hoped, were to be the sexual partners contributing to a cure. The same social conditions which initially produced childhood neurosis militated in a somewhat different form against the recuperation of the adult patient. In this respect, the first, curiously revelatory critiques from my colleagues began to emerge in regard to my claim that without the achievement of a gratifying sex life there could be no recovery from a neurosis. Against my finding, they gave their votes either to sublimation or to a need for renunciation of sexual happiness. That is to say, the social obstacles became ever more apparent in their words. Additionally, the previous specialized literature's neglect for this group of problems seemed to point to the identical motivation, since the clinical data could only urge that *for the causal and comprehensive therapy of neuroses, the socially instilled morality of the patients had nearly always to be banished*. Thus the alarmed reaction. And the results of repeated testing of the therapeutic prescription were unvarying: a neurosis is a product of sexual repression and the blockage of sexual energy, while its cure requires the removal of repression and a healthy sex life; wherever one turned in social life one encountered opposition to the practical realization of this exacting prescription.

Nor is it to be forgotten that the great majority in our culture are disturbed, sexually and neurotically; but psychoanalysis, the single causally coherent therapy, takes a great deal of time. The hope for a prevention of neuroses is, then, self-evident. There would be little or no point in vesting our efforts undividedly in individual therapy. Indeed, one has to be astonished that up to now the prophylaxis of neuroses was not even broached, or if it came up, was passed over with generalities. Our work, however, impelled us to inquire: How may neurosis be prevented? Official psychopathology maintained, contrary to Freud, that a hereditary etiology was the decisive factor. This false and barren doctrine responds to a need evinced by bourgeois science, and the heredity specialists particularly, to misdirect attention from the external conditioning factors. Study of Marxist sociology later set their puzzling doctrine in a clear light.

A direct road was opened leading toward Marx just as soon as the sexual environment of a person's existence was recognized as the determinant of neuroses in childhood and the later obstacle to a cure. This problem could be divided into several distinct aspects. Freud glimpsed the key aspect of the etiology of neuroses in the conflict of the child with its parents, crucially in the sexual domain and most sharply around the Oedipus complex. Why should life in the family have this result? The neurosis is produced in the conflict of sexuality with a surrounding world that wants to suppress it. Sexual repression stems, then, from the society. The family and entire system of education operate together to impose sexual repression by all means. Yet why should this ever happen? *What is the social function that is gained by a family upbringing and the sexual repression that it instills?*

Freud held that the most important prerequisite for cultural development was sexual repression. Civilization, then, was built on repressed sexuality. For a time this estimate was credible. But in the long run it was impossible not to observe that the sex-disturbed person or the neurotic just did not compare, culturally, with the sexually free and healthy and satisfied human being. At this point the aspects of the problem based in class relations had by no means been integrated. On the one hand, in the act of bringing mobile psychoanalytic clinics to factory and office workers for their treatment, the very different world of the proletariat was acknowledged to have existence. Their sexual and material lives were strikingly unlike the lives one had come to know through the treatment of well-paying private patients. On the other hand, along with the unfamiliar attitudes toward sex, one noticed attitudes very much like those in the middle class. Especially, the nature of the family-organized process of education was remarkable. Sexually and otherwise it reduced and shattered the working person just as it did the middle-class person. Yet, up till that point, psychoanalysis had ventured very little in the way of criticism of these training policies. And when it did criticize them, its criticism was mild and insufficient. Nonetheless one saw in daily experience that psychoanalysis was indeed the keenest critical instrument to employ against the prevalent culture of sex. Why wasn't it being used? An enormous bulk of social phenomena—schools, the stifling of sex in childhood, the misery of the puberty years, the oppression which was sex within marriage—brought repression to individuals and spread a plague among the people. How could these phenomena also provide the vehicle of cultural achievements! With the mobile psychoanalytic clinic, as with the customary psychiatric practice, it grew impossible not to observe the mental disturbances en masse. Had the limits of one's profession led to a one-sided impression? There were reasons enough now to study the distant as well as the near reaches of the environment one lived in. And, with but few exceptions, you would see these distortions of sexual life, this same neurotic plague everywhere, if in amazingly varied forms: in one person, as a block set against the exercise of a strong talent; in others, as fierce marital struggle; elsewhere, as character distortion. Even in persons of whom one least expected it one might glimpse the same sexual disturbances: the same symptom neuroses and character neuroses. When Freud said he had the whole of humanity for patients he was right. He taught how to understand neuroses clinically. Yet he had failed to draw the necessary conclusions. What then were the social circumstances which caused human beings to become neurotic? Had these circumstances always prevailed?

After one had rejected the Freudian principle that repression is intrinsic to the cultural development of a society, it was only a matter of time until the principle of sexual repression as a social product was carried over to the next question: *"What is society's interest in sexual repression?"* No answer was provided by the established sociology, except for the stereotypical "Civilization requires morality." Finally a study of Marx and Engels produced a store of insight into the functions of material existence. It came as a shock, at first, to waken to the fact that one might pass through high school and university without ever being told of Marx or Engels. Soon one understood why.

Without any doubt, the questions of class interest and class struggle determine our present ways of existence, extending even so far as the realms of philosophy and science. Behind the façade of "objectivity," class interest is at work. Morality is a social product which, according to the period, can come into being or cease to exist. In a class society, morality stands in the service of the dominating class. Engels' *Origin of the Family* provided the stimulus for studies in ethnology—the anthropological approach to diverse socio-economic systems and the factors influencing cultural change and growth. One learned that moral principles developed from certain other forms and that the family had not existed, as some maintained, from the dawn of civilization. Morgan's historical discoveries were welcome. However, his discoveries and the whole theoretical conception of Marx and Engels in their understanding of social processes basically contradicted *Totem and Taboo*. Marx argued that the direction taken by moral views is constantly determined by the conditions of material existence. Everyday experience verifies this. Yet, according to Freud, the unique occurrence of archetypal parricide produced morality; it was this one event which brought feelings of guilt into being and which supposedly adequately explains the fact of sexual repression. Thus, while Freud's explanation of sexual repression referred to an event occurring in society, this event was not discoverable in humanity's material conditions of existence; it was presumed to descend rather from violent jealousy of an archetypal father. This proved to be the crucial point of the whole inquiry. It related closely to the practical questions of preventing neurosis. If Freud proved to be right with his belief that sexual repression and the restriction of instincts were needed in the development of civilization and culture, and further (a point on which there can be no doubt), if the sexual repression created neuroses en masse, then there is no hope for an effective prophylaxis of neurosis. But if Marxist sociology is correct, when it maintains that changes in the moral order accompany changes in the economic order, and if Morgan and Engels did accurately portray the history of the family, then moral principles could change once again and grant the possibility of neurosis prevention, affording a solution to this problem of sexual immiseration. The moral principles *could* change, but that still leaves unanswered the question whether a following era of morality would prove responsive to the evolved claims of sexual economy.

One had to examine the sexual behavior of primitive peoples so as to be aware of the sociology of perversions, sexual disorders and antisocial behavior. The literature of sexology and ethnology was more than replete with commentary. You could read that numerous primitive peoples adopted completely alien moral views. Yet others were said to manifest codes quite like those of our own culture, particularly in regard to marriage. There was no possibility of negotiating the conflicts between these reports. Some were distorted by hostile moralistic interpolation, others by the desire to find confirmed the authors' moral principles. For instance, Westermarck tried to prove the eternal nature of the family and marital institutions. Others, such as Ploss, have praised our "progress" as against the "savagery" and "licentiousness" of primitive man. However, in a period in which scholarly and ethical literature mourned over the decline of morality, there could also be read lyrical reports of a primitive sexual paradise. This chaos of commentaries was at first confusing. One could be sure of only one thing. Most of the ethnological literature was moralistically biased. Yet one saw that primitive societies, at least some of them, had attitudes different from ours and they experienced their sexuality differently. One could compare this with the way the proletariat produced its own viewpoints alongside the different ones of the bourgeoisie.

It also seemed important to gain a precise understanding of the upheaval of sex ideologies that had taken place in Soviet Russia. The organs of the bourgeois press all raged against the decline of civilization and morals that the social revolution had caused. In point of fact, the Soviet legislation on sexual matters was astonishing for its sobriety and directness. It totally disdained bourgeois sex legislation and was not at all in awe of the sacrosanct "accomplishments of civilization" and "moral nature" of man. Abortion was allowed, and even established in law. The government promoted birth control programs and adolescent sex education. The idea of "the unwed" was abolished and marriage was treated in practice as superseded. So, too, the punishment of incest. Prostitution was fought back and genuine equality for women fostered, together with much else which clearly argued that *morality was in the process of change, and in the direction of sexual affirmation,* thus completely reversing what had been. Nonetheless, bourgeois journalism and scholarship continued to fume at the "decline of civilization." Well, but perhaps Freud's thesis was being proved correct? A journey to the Soviet Union dispelled at once any talk of a decline of culture. It also gave evidence, strangely enough, of an almost ascetic moral climate. On the streets, there was no blatancy at all in sex; rather, everything was reserved and serious. Prostitution was still to be noticed, but now it was not forthright. One occasionally found couples on park benches in the evening but much less often than in Vienna or Berlin. And there was an absence of the sexual allusions and ribaldry that are so common among us in social gatherings. Some instances may illustrate. If a man dares to pat a woman's buttocks or pinch her cheek there, as is habitual in our part of Europe, he may very likely be summoned before a party hearing, if he is a Communist. On the other hand, there was often an unprecedented candor and directness about the selection of sexual partners, with an unequivocating communality in sex and the sexuality of the woman accepted as being natural. One acquaintance was in her eighth month of pregnancy and nobody ever inquired into the father's identity. A family offered lodging to a guest, and when this produced a space problem the sixteen-year-old daughter declared openly and spontaneously to her parents, "Well, I will leave and sleep with X [a boyfriend]." Two members of the Young Communist League go down to the alimony bureau and both request to be put on the list to make payments, for both of them had slept with the girl and either might be the father. At the obstetrical clinics, there is official cooperation if a termination of pregnancy is desired. At the Parks of Culture, where young people congregate, graphs and charts publicly display information about conception, birth, contraception, venereal disease.

It is nonetheless a fact that old bourgeois physicians still cling to their timid notions regarding sex, as do ours. And too often sexology has remained in the hands of urologists and physiologists who have moralizing attitudes and lack training in sexual psychology. Contradictions, yes. But the overall situation had changed. Affirmation was the direction, with many key matters simply taken for granted from their positive side, even though the academics and older state officials in numerous spheres still carried old ways to the point of revering marital morality. A strong departure, if far short of the ultimate forms: in the immense effort to build the productive forces and to raise all the members of society to a high cultural plane through increased wages and a shortened work week—combined with mass education and a fight against religion—one could discern the economic groundwork being laid for the future sexual hygiene of the masses.* But despite the change in the objective mode of sexual existence, there has been no corresponding development of sexual theory. The incorrect sociological forays of psychoanalysis, and also the reactionary statements made by many of its practitioners, have discouraged such a development. Besides, psychoanalysis took not the least interest in the vast upheavals

---

* (1934) The process later ran into severe difficulties and it reverted in part to a plane where bourgeois governing policies were applied. I have to reserve my discussion of this Soviet sexual economy for another occasion, when it will be treated in detail.

under way in Russia. And in recent years psychoanalysis as a profession has clearly retreated from the stern and revolutionary theory of the libido. A barrage of efforts to de-sexualize the theory of neurosis, and to translate it into the terminology of the death-instinct, was fired from the moment when Freud's first papers on the ego and the instinct to destruction were published. Theories emerged about the cause of suffering being a biological "will to suffer," a veritable need for punishment and extinction, instead of seeing misery as a result of the objective conditions of existence. I found it impossible as a veteran psychoanalytical clinician to go along with this shift. The clinical data pronounced otherwise, and the sociology of Marx provided an explanation for the shift. Psychoanalysis, once a revolutionary sexual theory and a psychology of the unconscious, had begun to adapt itself in its aspect of sexual theory to the claims made by bourgeois society, thus to assure its viability among the bourgeoisie.

It would be false to make an assertion that the revolutionary character of the psychoanalytical theory of sex had been recognized in the Soviet Union. Equally untrue would be the assertion that because of bourgeoisification of the theory it had been rejected, although that process had at least the effect of impeding recognition. The various Marxist critics of psychoanalysis, who usually lacked real familiarity with it, in general did prove unaware of that turning point in the formation of psychoanalytical theory where it changed from a discipline irreconcilable to the bourgeois class into one the bourgeoisie might find safely intriguing. And just as Marxist opponents threw out the clinical psychology of psychoanalysis in rejecting its sociological excursions, so some Marxist friends acclaimed the so-called psychoanalytical sociology, merely because its clinical psychology was so persuasive. But in sum, when psychoanalysis is rejected, the only satisfactory theory of sexuality is abandoned. The changing sexual life in the Soviet Union develops in consequence in a more unconscious fashion, guided to a far lesser degree by the will of its subjects than is true of other aspects of Soviet life. For instance, the steps to eradicate religion are lucid and purposeful by comparison, based as they are on scientific enlightenment of the masses combined with a flourishing technology turned directly over to the laboring operatives. Medical experience can abundantly predict the pitfalls awaiting sexual education programs for children and teen-agers that ignore the analytically discoverable facts. Even with this said, it is striking to see how the more sexually free climate in the Soviet Union opened the eyes of many who held influence to numerous facts that psychoanalysis had discovered: for instance, the direction of sexual energy toward an interest in work (sublimation, *perekluchenie*), and also the acknowledgment of infant sexuality in some quarters, even if psychoanalysis as a conception was turned down. Following a lecture I gave at the Neuro-Psychological Institute of Moscow, a high official in the Public Health Service remarked on the need for a practical theory to prevent neurosis. I had to reply that this theory unfortunately did not yet exist. They were agreed, however, that it had to be worked out, not only sociologically but medically as well.

I returned from the Soviet Union with these encouraging and very useful impressions. I then took up the task of ascertaining the present political role of sexual repression in capitalism. This was best done by concrete work in close contact with the proletarian movement. Quite soon it became clear that the marriage-and-family institution is the axis around which the class struggle revolves in the sexual domain (however little seen this still is). Bourgeois sexual science and sexual reform continually run against this function of the institution as though against a blank wall. I sketched this problem and its solution in *Geschlechtsreife, Enthaltsamkeit, Ehemoral; Eine Kritik der bürgerlichen Sexualreform* (Münsterverlag, 1930). Perhaps the most important finding to come from this political work for future research in the sociology of sex is the discovery that sexual oppression is among the ruling class's key ideological resources in holding down the working population. Moreover, the sexual suffering among the masses is only to be resolved by means of the proletarian mass movement—to be precise, through the context of revolutionary struggle against economic exploitation. One can find little solace in this reflection. Yet the conclusion seemed inescapable that the effects of thousands of years of sexual oppression were only to be superseded, and a gratifying sexual life to eliminate the plague of neuroses from the masses was only to be established, when the socialist economy had been put together and consolidated and the material prerequisites of the populace guaranteed.

If the context for continued work was thus defined, there remained a difficult stretch of theory to be developed in regard to the foundations of sexual economy. The contact with clinical activity and with the proletarian movement could not for an instant be lost. Otherwise one risked the limbo of vacant theorization. One also had to worry about the possibly deep roots of sexual oppression among the oppressed masses themselves. As yet, one had no real concept of how the various strata of the populace would react to the posing of the sexual question, with its barbs touching marriage and the family and the sexual life of children and teen-agers. Years of dealing with sex-political issues and of operating sexual advisory stations for that purpose offered assurance that the masses are as eager to find solutions in this area as they are in matters bearing directly on material conditions. A young, determined sex-political movement under revolutionary leadership is at the present moment spreading through Germany.

The work of defining a historical context for the problems of sexual disorder and neurosis was nearly prevented by the lack of concern shown in previous ethnological literature for the inner character of experience, the nature of sex gratification and questions of neurosis. One expected something of such books as R. Schmidt's *The Indian Art of Love*. It became clear they had nothing to offer—nostrums only, and no description of the sexual patterns of foreign peoples, and absolutely no regard for the links between the sex life and the economy. The part of the literature which did try to look at these connections—Cunow, Müller-Lyer, for example—stopped with a treatment of the external forms of marriage and family, failing to dig into the root functionality of sex and the actual sex experience. One concluded at last, moreover, that the only theory to offer any possible assistance was that of Morgan and Engels. At this point the research of Malinowski, the English ethnologist, claimed my attention. It traced connections between the sexual forms and the economy and the sexual life among primitive peoples who adhered to the mother-right. It yielded material long sought on the real sexual experience and with reference to neurosis. His discoveries exceeded all expectations.

On the basis of this new material—which may be considered the direct continuation of the Morgan and Engels studies—one may venture to deal with ethnological aspects of the problem of sexual economy. The findings are in the subsequent paper. I hope I have not been guilty of gross ethnological errors in the details. If I have committed any, I will plead that I had no recourse but to base myself on the available ethnological literature, since an opportunity for personal ethnological research has not presented itself, to date at least. I would gladly accept an opportunity. In addition, I cannot conceal the fact that I believe a few errors of detail will not be tragic, assuming that my historical conception of sexual economy is correct. Study of the ethnological literature has convinced me that specialized knowledge does not at all save one from gross errors in regard to the questions of sexual life.

Wilhelm Reich
Berlin
September 1931

The Origin of
Sexual Repression

1) The Sexual Economy in Matriarchal Society

Recently, after having spent several years in the study of the matriarchal structure of society among the Trobriand Islanders of northwestern Melanesia, the English professor of ethnology Bronislaw Malinowski published an extensive report on the sexual life of this primitive people. He has written not only the first description of its kind, but also the most complete description of sexual relationships in conjunction with their economic and social foundations—a treatment which we shall restate here in the second chapter. Where Malinowski has not been expressly quoted, I have provided the results of my own analysis based upon his research. This has enabled us to extricate the ethnological evidence for certain laws of sexual economy.

The sexual suffering in the private-enterprise/patriarchal society results from an innate pattern of sexual denial and oppression which produces a blockage of sexual energies in all individuals subject to it, and accordingly, neuroses, perversions and sexual criminality. But in a society which lacks any incentive for sexual oppression—or historically considered, as long as, and as far as, a society has no such interest—that society will be free of sexual misery. We could say, then, that the members of that society experience a life which is *sexually economical*—a statement which implies no value judgment but, rather, refers to the fact that there is a *well-ordered patterning of their sexual energy*.

We shall have to devote our inquiry, then, to the modes of ordering sexual life, with the assumption that regulation stems *from the satisfaction of sexual drives* rather than flowing from moral norms. In this regard we expect to locate in the sexual mores of the Trobrianders more or less the direct opposite of those mores prevalent among members of our society: among the children and adolescents, an untroubled sexual activity; a complete capacity for gratification among the genitally matured —in other words, an orgastic potency among the mass of individuals.

THE SEXUAL ACTIVITY
OF TROBRIAND CHILDREN

We shall start with the children and hear from Malinowski himself. The natives begin their sexual experiences at a very early age.

> The unregulated and, as it were, capricious intercourse of these early years becomes systematized in adolescence into more or less permanent liaisons. (p. 51)*
>
> The child's freedom and independence extend also to sexual matters. To begin with, children hear of and witness much in the sexual life of their elders. Within the house where the parents have no possibility of finding privacy, a child has opportunities of acquiring practical information concerning the sexual act. I was told that no special precautions are taken to prevent children from witnessing the parent's sexual enjoyment. The child would merely be scolded and told to cover its head with a mat. (p. 54)

This admonition has nothing in common with sexual denial; rather, it represents simply a measure to ensure that those having intercourse will be undisturbed. The children are permitted to examine one another and to otherwise engage in sexual play as

* All references, unless otherwise noted, are to Bronislaw Malinowski, *The Sexual Life of Savages* (1929), the Harvest Book paperback edition of 1969.

much as they desire. To be noted here is that despite or, better, just because of this sexual freedom in childhood, the voyeuristic perversion does not occur. From this the anxiety-ridden may learn, if psychoanalytical research into the genesis of perversions has been unable to persuade them, that the freedom of sexual secondary drives in childhood leads to perversion not of itself but only when sexual repression is otherwise inflicted. To continue:

There are plenty of opportunities for both boys and girls to receive instruction in erotic matters from their companions. The children initiate each other into the mysteries of sexual life at a very early age. A premature amorous existence begins among them long before they are able really to carry out the act of sex. They indulge in plays and pastimes in which they satisfy their curiosity concerning the appearance and function of the organs of generation, and incidentally receive, it would seem, a certain amount of positive pleasure. Genital manipulation and such minor perversions as oral stimulation of the organs are typical forms of this amusement. Small boys and girls are said to be frequently initiated by their somewhat older companions, who allow them to witness their own amorous dalliance. As they are untrammeled by the authority of their elders and unrestrained by any moral code, except that of specific tribal taboo, there is nothing but their degree of ripeness, of curiosity, and of "temperament" or sensuality, to determine how much or how little they shall engage in sexual pastimes.

The attitude of the grown-ups and even of the parents towards such infantile indulgence is either that of complete indifference or of complacency—they find it natural, and do not see why they should scold or interfere. Usually they show a kind of tolerant and amused interest, and discuss the love affairs of their children with easy jocularity. I often heard some such benevolent gossip as this: "So and so [a little girl] has already slept with a little boy." And if such were the case, it would be added that it was her first experience. An exchange of lovers or some small love drama in the little ones would be half seriously, half jokingly discussed. The infantile sexual act, or its substitute, is regarded as an innocent amusement. "It is their play to *kayta* (to have intercourse)." They give each other a coconut, a small piece of betel nut, a few beads or some fruit from the bush, and then they go and hide and *kayta*." But it is not considered proper for the children to carry on their affairs in the house. It has always to be done in the bush. (pp. 55–56)

All sorts of round games, which are played by the children of both sexes on the central place of the village, have a more or less strongly marked flavor of sex. (p. 57)

Now, it is not very important to our theme that the Trobriand children have sexual play, for that is true also for most children in our culture, especially those of the exploited classes (if we except those already severely neurotic). However, just as in sexual intercourse what figures as important is not that it is *done* but rather with what inner attitude and in what social circumstances it is done, so, too, we especially note here how educators and parents relate to the children, their sexual play and natural spontaneity. The way that they relate will ultimately determine the sex-economic value of the sexual activities. We stress this, because nowhere else in the literature of sexology is this aspect remarked on; rather, the mere fact of the transpiring play is registered—or overlooked. Only the psychoanalytic perspective regarding the economy of the sexual function instructs us that the act as such has less significance than the accompanying conscious and unconscious psychic attitude.* And considered from the biological side of the sexual function, the attitude in its triggering of pleasure is basically, unequivocally positive; thus it will be decided by the reaction in the social environment whether this originally positive attitude can be sustained or whether it will be displaced by guilt feelings and sexual anxiety introduced into the amatory activity by society in diverse ways.

Among the Trobrianders it is now confirmed that the parents not only have no disruptive attitude but rather a benevolently

* On this point, see my discussion of orgastic potency in *The Function of the Orgasm.*

friendly viewpoint, so that we may state: with the exception of a narrow sphere where the incest taboo is operative, there occurs no morality that denies sexuality; instead, an unambiguously positive formation of the ego occurs, and, as we shall also see later, a sex-affirmative ego ideal.* Because the sexuality is free, we cannot look upon the incest prohibition as a sexual restraint. From a sex-economic standpoint more than sufficient avenues remain for the gratification of sexuality. One similarly could not speak of a restraint upon the satisfaction of the need for nourishment simply because green beans and mutton were restricted while all other meats and vegetables were available without restriction for his enjoyment. We stress this against the frequent claims that the instinctual life of primitives is severely restrained. The restraints that occur are of no economic-dynamic importance. And where economic and dynamic overvaluation is accorded to the incest wish, or to any other urging of instinct, this occurs as the result of an inordinate preoccupation with one single interest where in fact a general restraint upon instinct has somewhere occurred. This explains why the incest prohibition is

* (1934) The distinction between mere tolerance and active affirmation of sexual activity in childhood and puberty may seem an unimportant one; yet it is decisive in the structural formation of the psyches of early-school-age children. There is a kind of permissiveness common today among educators in certain circles which one must see as a total sexual denial. Not only does the child sense that this tolerance is the nonpunishment of something that is actually prohibited; additionally, to merely permit or "put up with" sexual play offers no countermeasure of substance against the overpowering pressures of the social environment. On the other hand, the articulated and definite affirmation by the educator of childhood sex may become part of the basis for a sexually affirmative ego structure, though it cannot fully counter the environmental influences. This perspective ought to be taken as critical of those psychoanalysts who do not dare take the important step from mere tolerance to affirmation in their patient relations. The advice that such things must be left for the children to work out is a plain avoidance of responsibility. If one applies no sufficient measures to counterweight the social influences in analyzing children, teen-agers and adults, then the removal of the sexual repression remains merely theoretical. It is true that no course of action should be thrust upon people that is not organically wanted; all the same, it is indispensable that sustenance be given to the tendencies of the child or the patient that help in the direction of sexual economy. Falling between the toleration of sexual behavior and its affirmation is the barrier of the society to sex. To encourage sexuality means to step over the sexual barrier.

an entirely conscious matter for the primitive and need not be repressed, for so long as the other desires can readily be satisfied the desire for incest will not be exaggerated beyond its proportion.

Every Trobriand boy knows that he must not regard his sister as a sexual being. The conscious avoidance of any closer contact is testimony to his consciousness of sexual urges toward the sister. Were the other aspects of his sex life restricted, his eagerness for incest would heighten to such a degree, owing to her proximity, that a deep repression of the desire would become necessary, inevitably becoming resolved pathologically. These circumstances ought to explicate the intensity of the incest wish found in our children. It is carried to an exorbitant degree in the context of the natural bond with parents and siblings and is the result of the wholesale denial of other sexual contacts. One contributing factor is the parents' sexual involvement with their children; this, in turn, is the concomitant of the sexual frustration of the adults.

A characteristic of the Trobriand upbringing is that the conduct of the parents toward children is in every respect devoid of the authoritarian note which pervades our pedagogical measures. We can fully understand the inner ties between sexual denial and oppression and the patriarchal instruction when we have heard about its opposite among the Trobrianders described:

> Children in the Trobriand Islands enjoy considerable free-
> dom and independence. They soon become emancipated
> from a parental tutelage which has never been very strict.
> Some of them obey their parents willingly, but this is
> entirely a matter of the personal character of both parties:
> there is no idea of a regular discipline, no system of
> domestic coercion. Often as I sat among them, observing
> some family incident or listening to a quarrel between
> parent and child, I would hear a youngster told to do this
> or that, and generally the thing, whatever it was, would be
> asked as a favor, though sometimes the request might
> be backed up by the threat of violence. The parents would

either coax or scold or ask as from one equal to another. A simple command, implying the expectation of natural obedience, is never heard from parent to child in the Trobriands.

People will sometimes grow angry with their children and beat them in an outburst of rage; but I have quite as often seen a child rush furiously at his parent and strike him. This attack might be angrily returned, but the idea of definite retribution, or of coercive punishment, is not only foreign, but distinctly repugnant to the native. Several times, when I suggested, after some flagrant infantile misdeed, that it would mend matters for the future if the child were beaten or otherwise punished in cold blood, the idea appeared unnatural and immoral to my friends, and was rejected with some resentment.

Such freedom gives scope for the formation of the children's own little community, an independent group, into which they drop naturally from the age of four or five and continue till puberty. As the mood prompts them, they remain with their parents during the day, or else join their playmates for a time in their small republic. And this community within a community acts very much as its own members determine, standing often in a sort of collective opposition to its elders. If the children make up their minds to do a certain thing, to go for a day's expedition, for instance, the grown-ups and even the chief himself, as I often observed, will not be able to stop them. In my ethnographic work I was able and indeed forced to collect my information about children and their concerns directly from them. Their spiritual ownership in games and childish activities was acknowledged, and they were also quite capable of instructing me and explaining the intricacies of their play or enterprise. (pp. 52–53)

We see in patriarchal society (feudal and bourgeois) how the authoritarian oppression of the child promotes the genesis of a structure of subordination, which conforms to the organization of the society at large, which for its part continually reproduces itself in the patterning of childhood. The parents act as executors of the dominant order, while the family instills its ideology. In sharp contrast, the matriarchal society reproduces its ideology—insofar as one may speak of a distinct ideology—through granting liberty of development to the child's psychic formation, nourished in turn by the social ideologies of this society starting with the children's communes. And where the sexual oppression in private-enterprise society prepares the way to the all-round inhibition of the psyche, in matriarchal and communistic society the sexual freedom becomes the groundwork for that freedom of character which will guarantee libidinally close and solid connections with other members of society. Here is demonstrated the possibility of the self-government of sexually communal life based upon gratification of the instincts (in contrast to moral regulation).

THE SEXUAL ACTIVITY OF ADOLESCENTS

Let us turn now to the sexual activity of Trobriand adolescents. To be sure, we shall note sexual conflicts and, up to a point, a sexual suffering that results from the difficulties of numerous love relationships, but we shall not find any kind of external constraint, we shall remark the absence of "pubertal neurosis," of suicide, and of abnegation which "marks one as cultured."

As the boy or girl enters upon adolescence the nature of his or her sexual activity becomes more serious. It ceases to be mere child's play and assumes a prominent place among life's interests. What was before an unstable relation culminating in an exchange of erotic manipulation or an immature sexual act now becomes an absorbing passion, and a matter for serious endeavour. An adolescent gets definitely attached to a given person, wishes to possess her, works purposefully toward this goal, plans to reach the fulfillment of his desires by magical and other means, and finally rejoices in achievement. I have seen young people of this age grow positively miserable through ill-success in love. This stage, in fact, differs from the one before in that personal preference has now come into play and with it a tendency toward greater permanence in intrigue. The boy develops a desire to retain the fidelity and exclusive affection of the loved one, at least for a time. But this tendency is not associated so far with any idea of settling down to one exclusive relationship, nor do adolescents yet begin to think of marriage. A boy or girl wishes to pass through many more experiences; he or she still enjoys the prospect of complete freedom and has no desire to accept obligations. Though pleased to imagine that his partner is faithful, the youthful lover does not feel obliged to reciprocate this fidelity . . .

This group leads a happy, free, arcadian existence, devoted to amusement and the pursuit of pleasure . . .

Many of the taboos are not yet quite binding on them, the burden of magic has not yet fallen on their shoulders . . .

Young people of this age, besides conducting their love affairs more seriously and intensely, widen and give a greater variety to the setting of their amours. Both sexes arrange picnics and excursions and thus their indulgence in intercourse becomes associated with an enjoyment of novel experiences and fine scenery. They also form sexual connections outside the village community to which they belong. Whenever there occurs in some other locality one of the ceremonial occasions on which custom permits of licence, thither they repair, usually in bands either of boys or of girls, since on such occasions opportunity of indulgence offers for one sex alone. (pp. 63, 64, 65)

It has been contended by some ethnologists acquainted with psychoanalysis that the puberty rites of many primitive organizations constitute a kind of punishment for pubertal sex activity just as we penalize the activity—the only difference being that here the punishment precedes the commencement of coitus. Our reader will understand that the study of ethnological literature makes one skeptical of any interpretation too obviously imbued with the hope of providing anthropological justification for our own conduct. Likewise one is wary of interpolations of criteria out of our own sphere of productive relations into other circumstances created by a different social organization. I do not point this out to impugn the above hypothesis, which possibly is correct. However, it will gain importance for us if those who assert it show which economic interests are involved, and how the whole of sexual life has a corresponding pattern. It seems highly improbable that such penalization of adolescent sexuality can be rooted in the structure of human instincts (e.g., ambivalence, hatred, jealousy), if one considers sexual economy historically. For then organizations come to light, like the Trobriandic one, which not only exhibit no punishments but afford quite striking provision for the sexual welfare (the *bukumatula,* adolescent coming-out and festivals, etc.), and which shift the burden to the advocates and defenders of lopsided biological and psychological notions to explain why, in these organizational models, pathological jealousy and other negative traits—supposedly intrinsic to human nature—are absent. We say such phenomena are the result of an encroachment of economic interests upon a purely natural sexual gratification; and we expect shortly to prove it.

Let us return to our theme. The sexual affirmation reaches the plane of institutional provisions:

> To meet this need, tribal custom and etiquette has provided accommodation and privacy in the form of the *bukumatula,* the bachelors' and unmarried girls' house, of which mention has already been made. In this a limited number of couples, some two, three, or four, live for longer or shorter periods together in a temporary community. It also and incidentally offers shelter for younger couples if they want amorous privacy for an hour or two . . . At present there are five bachelor establishments in Omarakana, and four in the adjoining village of Kasana'i. Their number has greatly diminished owing to missionary influence. Indeed, for fear of being singled out, admonished, and preached at, the owners of some *bukumatula* now erect them in the outer ring, where they are less conspicuous. Some ten years ago my informants

could count as many as fifteen bachelors' homes in both villages, and my oldest acquaintances remember the time when there were some thirty. This dwindling in number is due, of course, partly to the enormous decrease of population, and only partly to the fact that nowadays some bachelors live with their parents, some in widowers' houses, and some in the missionary compounds. But whatever the reason, it is needless to say that this state of affairs does not enhance true sex morality . . . I was told that sometimes a man would build a house as a *bukumatula* for his daughter, and that in olden days there used to be unmarried people's houses owned and tenanted by girls. I never met, however, any actual instance of such an arrangement. (pp. 70–72)

The *ulatile* (adolescent) has either a couch of his own in a bachelor's house, or the use of a hut belonging to one of his unmarried relatives. In a certain type of yam-house, too, there is an empty closed-in space in which boys sometimes arrange little "cosy-corners," affording room for two. In these, they make a bed of dry leaves and mats, and thus obtain a comfortable *garçonnière,* where they can meet and spend a happy hour or two with their lover. Such arrangements are, of course, necessary now that amorous intercourse has become a passion instead of a game.

But a couple will not yet regularly cohabit in a bachelor's house (*bukumatula*), living together and sharing the same bed night after night. Both girl and boy prefer to adopt more furtive and less conventionally binding methods, to avoid lapsing into a permanent relationship which might put unnecessary burdens on their liberty by becoming generally known. That is why they usually prefer a small nest in the *sokwaypa* (converted yam-house) or the temporary hospitality of a bachelors' house. (p. 66)

The Trobrianders' provision for the need of privacy is the best evidence of a social affirmation of sex which goes far beyond a mere laissez-faire. In parallel fashion the efforts of bourgeois society either to actively hinder or to ignore the needs of adolescents, among them the need for a place to have coitus, fully bespeak the sexual denial with which it is imbued. As the institutional concern has a basic influence upon the sexual health of the primitive adolescents, so the hindrance conduces to a crippled and brutalized sex life, not really defeated by the hindering measures, but rather transferred from quiet and hygienic locations and into dark corners and hallways, where the sex is done in haste and anxiety. And as to the "cultural level" to which our distraught critics constantly return our attention? It will be helpful to compare the bordello conduct of our petty-bourgeois youth with the following facts:

> To call this institution "Group Concubinage" would lead to misunderstanding; for it must be remembered that we have to deal with a number of couples who sleep in a common house, each in exclusive liaison, and not with a group of people all living promiscuously together; there is never an exchange of partners, nor any poaching nor "complaisance." In fact, a special code of honor is observed within the *bukumatula,* which makes an inmate much more careful to respect sexual rights within the house than outside it. The word *kaylasi,* indicating sexual trespass, would be used of one who offended against this code.
>
> Within the *bukumatula* a strict decorum obtains. The inmates never indulge in orgiastic pastimes, and it is considered bad form to watch another couple during their lovemaking. I was told by my young friends that the rule is either to wait till all the others are asleep, or else for all the pairs of a house to undertake to pay no attention to the rest. I could find no trace of any "voyeur" interest taken by the average boy, nor any tendency to exhibitionism. Indeed, when I was discussing the positions and technique of the sexual act, the statement was volunteered that there are specially unobtrusive ways of doing it "so as not to wake up the other people in the *bukumatula.*" (p. 73)

There is no sanction or custom that binds an adolescent couple to one another; they are held together solely by their personal inclination and the strength of their sexual desire and are able to separate whenever they wish. We have seen that their relationship is completely void of possessiveness. Each person is free to enter into erotic relationships with other partners, particularly during the harvest and lunar festivals. Occasionally there are manifestations of jealousy, but under certain circumstances even the display of jealousy is considered "indecent," as for example, in a case of mourning where young girls console the sorrowing men with sexual intercourse. In spite of everything—or from the viewpoint of sexual economy, just because of all this —the relationships are often (without external or internal coercion) longer-lasting, more intense, and more gratifying than the ones which our sexually crippled youth are able to put together.

The young couple's community of interest is solely one of sexuality. They would never share a common meal, which, as we shall later see, is a direct symbol of marriage proper.

It is clear that ambitious scientific categories, such as "monogamy," "polygamy," "polyandry," or "promiscuity," have little application to sexual relations which are begun and sustained solely for the gratification of sexual need. Trobriand couples are just as much "monogamous" as they are polygamous, and at feasts even promiscuous. These classifications are senseless in regard to Trobriand society, and *have meaning and content only as they evince our attempts to give a scientific sheen to moral regulation.* Even in our society they do not refer to the facts. In our society, too, we have volatile sexual relationships. The real distinction between our society and the primitive one—and we particularly stress this point, since it sets the viewpoint of sex-economy apart from all others, in every respect— is not that the primitive one is polygamous or promiscuous and we are monogamous (the monogamous life located among some primitive societies by many sexologists and ethnologists can likewise never justify the claims of monogamy); the distinction is rather represented solely in the *social ordering of the sex life* and the *different modes of having sex* that stem from each. The physiological side of the sex activity, with everything determined by that, is quite the same here as there, apart from racial differences and the phylogenetic engraining of thousands of years of sexual repression (a weakening of the somatic sexual response?). The frustrations of our sexologists confronted with primitive society arise precisely because the latter know nothing of the various "-gamy" categories and their goal is simply sexual gratification. Therefore, the basic question is simply whether a given social organization wishes to or is able to acknowledge this goal. And that is a matter which sociology will know how to explore.

With advancing years the Trobriand Islanders' sexual relationships become more firm and durable, a fact to be ascribed, as we have elsewhere noticed in detail,* to a gradual abatement of sensual needs after puberty which allows the affectionate tendencies to grow more prominent. Were there no institution of marriage, these relationships, too, would not last forever, they would in the course of time be exchanged for others. But given this institution, the more durable relationships develop toward it. There is first a "trial period" which gives the young couple opportunity for testing their desire and constancy, and the parents opportunity to accomplish their task of economic preparations.

At this point, sexual needs reach a conjuncture with some definite economic interests.

SEXUAL FESTIVITIES

The high sexual culture of the Trobriand Islanders is especially to be noted in the various celebrations which have as their sole purpose sexual play and the subsequent gratification of genitality. They are demarcated from similar social occasions among the youth of bourgeois society, first, because their actual purpose is no longer veiled; second, because there is an absence of attitudes which deny or reject the purpose and of external constraints upon ultimate gratification; and, third, because there are no anxiety and guilt feelings about sex which impair the sexual fulfillment of our youth, insofar as they do contrive to experience that goal. "The Trobriand boy has not to stumble upon the final fulfillment of erotic desire, he immediately antici-

* *Geschlechtsreife, Enthaltsamkeit, Ehemoral,* Vienna, 1930.

pates it. All the customs, arrangements, and codes of behavior dictate a simple, direct approach." (p. 311)

A further basic distinction is that every kind of sentimentality is absent from the sex liaisons, even though the sexual activities of the Trobriand Islanders do not lack a certain romance. This certainly puts a spotlight on the nature of the sentimentalization of sex so high-flown in the bourgeois commercial novel and so exploitable by the publishers; the sentimentalism depends upon obstacles constraining gratification, setting in its place an orgastic contentment postponed into the indefinite future, and a continual pursuit of fulfillment, whose feeble substitute is provided by the novel. "There is nothing roundabout in a Trobriand wooing; nor do they seek full personal relations with sexual possession only as a consequence. Simply and directly a meeting is asked for with the avowed intention of sexual gratification. If the invitation is accepted, the satisfaction of the boy's desire eliminates the romantic frame of mind, the craving for the unattainable and mysterious. If he is rejected, there is not much room for personal tragedy, for he is accustomed from childhood to having his sexual impulses thwarted by some girls, and he knows that another kind of intrigue cures this type of ill surely and swiftly." (p. 313)

We see therefore that the inclination to protracted, frustrating erotic involvement is side-stepped by fully developed genitality, and we understand better now that this tendency, frequently seen among our youth, arises from overestimation of a sexual object that results from the limited possibility of final gratification. Nonetheless, our renowned experts on adolescence offer "statistical" proofs that sexual sentimentality and bad poems belong to the "nature of puberty." Certainly they characterize the puberty of *our* youth, who grow up in a most hostile milieu.

Circumstances decide differently, among the Trobrianders and others who have in some degree eluded sacrifice to the furtherance of private property and the activities of white missionaries: "The facts described here have shown us that, subject to certain restrictions, everyone has a great deal of freedom and many opportunities for sexual experience. Not only need no one live with impulses unsatisfied, but there is also a wide range of choice and opportunity." (p. 236)

The woman's role in sexual life is comparable with that of the man: "In matters of love the Trobriand woman does not consider herself man's inferior, nor does she lag behind him in initiative and self-assertion. The *ulatile* have their counterpart in the *katuyausi,* amorous expeditions of village girls to other communities." (p. 269)

We shall speak later of the *ulatile* in another connection and reproduce here the report on the *katuyausi:*

> The *katuyausi* party have remained seated, nonchalant and detached. The youths and older men stand facing them, pursuing their own conversations with apparent unconcern. Then banter and jokes begin to pass from one side to the other; the boys come nearer the girls and the ceremony of choice begins. According to custom, the initiative in pairing off should come from the hosts, and each guest has to accept any offer made to her as a matter of etiquette. But, of course, definite preferences between the outstanding individuals of each group exists and are known. An unimportant boy would not dare interfere with the pleasure of his stronger, elder and more influential comrade, so that in reality, the choice is largely based on anterior intrigues and attachments. Each boy then ceremonially offers a small gift to the girl of his choice—a comb, a necklace, a nose stick, a bunch of betel nut. If she accepts the gift, she accepts the boy for that night as her lover. When the boy knows the girl well, he presents the gift himself. If he does not, or if he feels too shy, he will ask of an older man, who hands over the offering with the words, *"Kam va otu"* (*va otu*—visiting present, present of inducement). "So and so gives it to you, you are his sweetheart." Very rarely does a girl refuse or ignore such a present; if she did, she would offend and mortify the man.
>
> After the boys and girls have thus been allotted in pairs, they all, as a rule, go to some spot in the jungle, where they spend the best part of the night chewing, smoking, and singing, each couple keeping to themselves. At times a boy

and a girl will leave the main group without any attention being paid to them. Some of the boys may invite their sweethearts to spend the rest of the night in a *bukumatula* of the village, but usually this presents difficulties. All the arrangements associated with the *katuyausi,* as well as with the *ulatile,* are distinguished by complete decorum, and by the absence of all orgiastic elements. They are carried out, no doubt, in a less delicate manner in the southern villages than in the north, but even in the south they essentially differ from such orgiastic customs as the *kamali,* the *bi'u,* and the custom of the *yausa.* (p. 270)

In addition to the *ulatile* of the boys and the *katuyausi* of the girls, there is yet another custom, not researched by Malinowski, called *kayasa* in the communities to the north and south. In this,

the relaxation of all control was complete. Sexual acts would be carried out in public on the central place; married people would participate in the orgy, man and wife behaving without restraint, even though within hail of each other. This license would be carried so far that copulation would take place within sight of the *luleta* (sister, man speaking; brother, woman speaking): the person with regard to whom the strictest sexual taboos are always observed. The trust-worthiness of these statements is confirmed by the fact that I was told several times, when discussing other forms of *kayasa* in the north, that all of them were carried out in a much more orgiastic manner in the south. Thus at a tug-of-war *kayasa* in the south, men and women would always be on opposite sides. The winning side would ceremonially deride the vanquished with the typical ululating scream (*katugogova*), and then assail their prostrate opponents, and the sexual act would be carried out in public. On one occasion when I discussed this matter with a mixed crowd from the north and the south, both sides categorically confirmed the correctness of this statement. (p. 259)

The reason for the decline of this custom is not discoverable in Malinowski's reports. Is it to be traced to the advancement of the ownership interests of the nascent patriarchy? Or are there other historical causes? We don't know. Reports have it, how-ever, that not so long ago when the only outsiders to visit the Trobriand Islands were the so-called *Tula* expeditions (inter-island traders), the custom was for girls of the villages to go to the strangers on the beach following the barter. It was deemed a proper right for the girls to sleep with the outsiders; their regular lovers had no call to reproach them or evince jealousy. Whatever we may make of this custom, whether it is a survival of the theft of women by foreign tribes or a tentative version of exogamy, what matters to our theme is the regulation of the community life despite the lack of sexual morality.

ORGASTIC POTENCY
AMONG PRIMITIVE PEOPLES

To hear of such customs as the *ulatile* and *katuyausi* is to be brushed by the breath of the exotic, by customs that are irrecon-cilable with culture and civilization, that perhaps even exclude the latter. All the same, our collaborators in civilization develop a peculiar curiosity about such customs, and a "desire for the original condition in Paradise" becomes apparent. We can easily show how much of this is illusory, that what is longed for is not the *ulatile* expeditions as such, but rather the capacities of the primitive peoples for sexual experience. Indeed, we are not lacking in *ulatile* expeditions and *katuyausi* in our culture. The student flings in whorehouses, the travels of young people which lead to sexual adventure, the masquerade affairs and the retreats of the big and petty bourgeoisie, the barnyard dances and the "windowsill-shinnying" of the peasants—up to a point all these do not differ in principle from the festivities of primitive peoples; but that point is essential and decisive. Our celebrations of sex end in cruel disappointment, for the prickling hope of sexual gratification will be unmet, and in addition, in many cases, they are veiled and hedged with bourgeois banter and "respect-ability." These customs of primitive peoples have carried over into our own time, if in altered format; what they have lost is their sex-economical function, so that, instead of satisfying, they simply heighten the sexual tension. We have even retained the rites of adolescent initiation, but only through totally effacing their original sense and turning them into their negation; instead of initiating the sexual maturity of youth, the rites are "confirmation" of the Church's heightened influence on oppression.

Surely our culture does not have less sexual intercourse than do primitive peoples. Promiscuity among young males is more pronounced. Marital infidelity without doubt occurs more frequently than among the "savages," due to the greater economic and moral frictions as well as sexual disorders. On the one hand, the moralistic hypocrites assure us that we are set apart from the "savage" due to our ethical acquisitions, on which we have a monopoly, and on the other hand, everyone—from the Pope to the Swastika Honor students to bourgeois sexologists—rage against the "moral decline into savagery." And yet, one simple fact stands out: *the primitive peoples are in full possession of the capacity for sexual experience, and "civilized" peoples cannot obtain satisfaction in sex, since their sexual structures are deformed with neurosis due to moral constraints imposed in their upbringing.* Statistical samples have indicated that on the average about 90 percent of women and 60 percent of men are mentally ill, sexually disordered and incapable of gratification.* Even if we thus understand the underlying function of disordered sexuality among members of our society, it remains to be proven whether in fact the primitive peoples experience no disturbance of sexual functioning, and orgastic fulfillment in the sex act is the rule.

We are especially indebted to Malinowski for first bringing the facts about the sexual life of primitives to light which in the entire earlier literature were lost behind the cataloging of the externalities of sex-act variants.

On the basis of his report, we are able to adduce the evidence that follows as to the orgastic potency of the Trobriand males and females:

* See my study "Die seelischen Erkrankungen als soziales Problem" in *Der sozialistische Arzt,* 1931.

It is of some weight that the Trobrianders are convinced that "white men do not know how to carry out intercourse effectively" (p. 338), i.e., they do not know how to bring a woman to orgasm; "indeed, to the native idea the white man achieves orgasm far too quickly." (p. 338) In this last is confirmation that the Trobrianders know very well what *genuine* gratification is, where they deem the white man comes to climax in haste in comparison to the primitive male unencumbered by moral restrictions (I have elsewhere described the syndrome of the bourgeois male as "physiological ejaculatio praecox"). No mere racial difference is involved, either, as we can learn from the fact that the premature release of sperm, when chronic but not pathological, can be prevented through the psychoanalytical removal of the sexual constraints in effect. The overwhelming majority of males in our culture find that premature sperm release brings with it a notable lessening of satisfaction in sex, since full gratification requires a longer period of friction to concentrate all the suffused libido in the genital system.*

Another evidence for the orgastic potency of the female is the fact that the Trobrianders make no terminological distinction between her orgasm and the male's: they both are designated as *ipipisi momona,* that is. "the seminal fluid discharges. The word *momona* signifies both the male and the female discharge." (p. 339) Naturally, it is understood that the man should wait until the woman attains gratification.

The personal testimonies of this primitive people also unequivocally express their sexual functionalism. As in this testimony:

When I sleep with Dabugera I embrace her, I hug her with my whole body, I rub noses with her. We suck each other's lower lip, so that we are stirred to passion. We suck each other's tongues, we bite each other's noses, we bite each other's chins, we bite cheeks and caress the armpits and the groin. Then she will say "O my lover, it itches very much . . . push on again, my whole body melts with pleasure

* See the chapter on orgastic potency in *Die Funktion des Orgasmus,* 1927.

. . . do it vigourously, be quick, so that the fluid may be discharged . . . tread on again, my body feels so pleasant." (p. 341)

One should compare this wisdom from primitive peoples with the theories of many of our sex researchers who hold that gratification does not necessarily pertain to the feminine organism, or that nature has decreed that women will have insensitive vaginas so as to be spared pain in childbirth, or other such "scientific" gushings from morally deformed brains.

The majority of women in our culture are incapable of a certain type of rhythmic pelvic movement in coitus which helps induce a woman's own orgasm and intensifies male gratification; a movement coldly and consciously carried out by prostitutes in order to at least feign excitement to a man. The better to carry out this movement, and so obtain greater gratification, the primitive couple practices intercourse in a squatting position and mocks the European coital position which makes the movement of the woman so difficult. "The natives regard the squatting position as more advantageous, both because the man is freer to move than when kneeling, and because the woman is less hampered in her responsive movements. . . . Many a white informant has spoken to me about perhaps the only word in the native language he ever learned, *kubilabala* ('move on horizontally'), repeated to him with some intensity during the sexual act." (p. 338)

Malinowski gets his knowledge from the natives directly; and of how much greater value it is for estimating the sexual activity of primitive women than is, say, the notion conveyed by missionaries or ethnologists with closed minds, or the word of the white men who say native women are difficult to excite. It is customary in our culture to attribute frigidity in women not to masculine impotence and the sexual oppression in society, but to the "natural coldness of the sex or the weak sexual impulse of women"; on the basis of just such reports by white men whose sexuality is malformed, even "ethnological evidences" may readily be concocted.

Orgastic potency is achieved in part through appropriate

sexual instruction. Among Trobrianders there is a preparation of the body and the psychic system from early years in the natural techniques for obtaining pleasure in the sex act, as we have already been told, which obviates the later need to study an artificial "love" technique. But there are also primitive peoples among whom the women function importantly as instructors in coitus. It would be valuable to discover whether this deliberate instruction imparted by the adults does not represent *an initial response to the damage already done to the sexual structure* of these primitive peoples through a patriarchal oppression intruding upon childhood sexuality, or whether perhaps it is a coaching which corresponds to the first stages of patriarchy and which fosters the chastity of young girls but neglects the sexual well-being of the grown women. Thus Angus reports of the *chensan-wali* ceremony among the Azimba of central Africa (*Zeitschrift für Ethnologie,* 1898, p. 479):

> At the first sign of menstruation the young girl is led by her mother to an outlying grass hut, where she is initiated by the women into the facts of sexual intercourse and the different positions in which cohabitation takes place. A horn is inserted into the vagina to widen it, and secured with a bandage. At the end of the menstruation the women perform a dance before the girl. The girl sits on the ground in the circle of dancers; no man may observe. The girl must then mimic the act of coitus; she is instructed through songs in the sexual act and the obligations of a married woman; she also learns that she must be taboo during the menstrual period, and wear a tuft of grass over her vulva. The songs include teaching about the obligation of *marital fidelity,* pregnancy, the arts of attracting her man and exerting power over him. This instruction is deemed perfectly natural, in no way improper: the women of this tribe are mostly chaste. . . .
>
> In Abyssinia and Zanzibar the young girls are instructed in pelvic movements which are said to heighten the pleasure in coitus; to be ignorant of the so-called *duk-duk* is thought shameful. Similarly the Swahilis cultivate an exercise in hip

and buttock movement. The exercise is taken in groups of fifty to sixty women, naked, sometimes for eight hours a day. No one is allowed to watch. A description of this dance is given by Zache. (*ibid.*, 1899, p. 72) This training of the young girls lasts about three months, whereupon they return home in ceremonial regalia. Similar customs are said to occur in the Dutch East Indian colonies and elsewhere.

No doubt there are overstatements in this report, but we need not doubt the fact of the sexual instruction. That these women should live in chastity or strict marital fidelity points to the advances of patriarchy. Our suspicion that there is an effort here to restore the women's impaired sexuality gains in probability.

NO NEUROSES—NO PERVERSIONS

Where the overwhelming majority of a society experiences sex-economical activity, neuroses cannot exist—as the psychoanalytical theory of sex and doctrine on neurosis teach us, if we take them really seriously—since neuroses are the result of an impaired genitality.* And we know from our sociological inquiries into the genesis and effects of sex-denying morality, that it is the cause of repression, and thus of the blockage of sexual energy, which contributes to transforming everyday psychic conflicts into neurotic ones. Similarly, we have learned from psychoanalytical research into the origins of perversions that they are ultimately the result of the diversion of sexual energy from its normal genital outlets; when genitality is thus constrained then all the pre-genital desires are so surcharged with energy that under

* *(1934)* I alone bear the responsibility for this interpretation; Freud and his school reject and resist it; they do not wish to see it advanced in the name of psychoanalysis. In this, I must agree with Freud: the basic conception of sexual economy was worked out only after the orgastic functionalism of genitality was perceived and added to the psychoanalytical edifice. That step, however, basically altered the explanation of the economy of psychic illness. It led to the present rift that divides the sex-economic theory from what is today the psychoanalytical doctrine of neurosis.

certain conditions they can emerge as perversions. And the fixation on an infantile goal or instinct, which psychoanalysis considers the essence of perversion, is the direct result of the constraint of the natural genital eroticism among children and adolescents caused by a sex-denying sexual governance, whose administrative organ is the parents.

A moralistic type of sex instruction is linked in human history to the interest in private property. The two develop together. Neuroses must then be seen in relation to the patriarchal social order of private property.

From Malinowski's observations and comparative inquiries, we can bring irrefutable evidence of these interconnections which is just as clearly persuasive as his material establishing the possibility of self-regulation in sexual activity through attaining gratification in sex.

In addition to the predominantly matriarchal Trobriand society, Malinowski had opportunity to observe another primitive society that lay south of the Trobriand Islands in the Amphlett chain. This people were very similar to the Trobrianders in race, customs and language, writes Malinowski, but they differed considerably in their social organization; they already manifested a strict sexual morality in regard to premarital intercourse, which they condemned, and they lacked any such institutions as found among the Trobrianders for fostering sex activity; characteristically, the family life was much more privatized. Even though maternal authority still prevailed, a much stronger role for patriarchal influence had emerged, and "this, combined with the sexual repressiveness, establishes a picture of childhood sexuality more similar to our own." Malinowski states: "In the Trobriands, though I knew scores of natives intimately and had a nodding acquaintance with many more, I could not name a single man or woman who was hysterical or even neurasthenic. Nervous tics, compulsory actions, or obsessive ideas were not to be found." There were occasional occurrences of cretinism, mental retardation and speech difficulties; also infrequent outbreaks of anger and violence. The natives ascribed all this to black magic. The Trobrianders discerned a different sort of black magic at work in the Amphlett Islands, which accounted for different forms of compulsory actions, ideas and nervous symptoms: "During my stay in the Amphletts, my first and strongest impression was that this was a community of neurasthenics. Coming from the open, hearty, gay, accessible Trobrianders it was astonishing to find oneself among a community of people distrustful of the newcomer, impatient in work, arrogant in their claims, though easily cowed, and extremely nervous when tackled more energetically. The women ran away as I landed in their villages and kept in hiding the whole of my stay . . . I at once found a number of people affected with nervousness."*

Even more interesting, and the key to our concept of the connections between social organization, sexual economy and neuroses, is what Malinowski reports about the Mailu, a tribe indigenous to the southern coast of New Guinea, and already fully patriarchal in organization: ". . . they have a pronounced paternal authority in the family, and a fairly strict code of repressive sexual morals. Among these natives, I had noted a number of people whom I had classified as neurasthenics, and therefore useless as ethnographic informants." (*op. cit.,* p. 89) And further:

It was fully confirmed in the Trobriands that free development of infantile sexuality shows a minimum of perversions. Homosexuality cropped up in the Trobriands only with the influence of the white man, more especially of white man's morality. The boys and girls on a mission station, penned in separate and strictly isolated houses, had to help themselves as best they could, since that which every Trobriand looks upon as his due and right was denied to them. According to very careful inquiries made of non-missionary as well as missionary natives, homosexuality is the rule among those upon whom white man's morality has been forced in such an irrational and unscientific manner.

Effective here is the economic expansion of capitalism, with the missionaries as its advance men who prepare the natives by

* Malinowski, *Sex and Repression in Savage Society,* London, Kegan, 1927, pp. 86 ff.

plying them with morality, alcohol, religion and other "attainments of civilization," in whose name and defense the bourgeoisie will shortly assign the labors of the best and most gifted of its scientists. Yet we must be cognizant that the internal development of matriarchal society, too, leads to qualitatively similar phenomena of sexual morality, if at an incomparably less rapid and cruel pitch. The pace merely is accelerated by the missionaries and their white thieving associates, who imbue it with all the horrors that can be conceived by impotent and rapacious "bringers of civilization."

We should add to this Malinowski's reports in regard to perversions among the Trobrianders: "misconduct contrary to nature" does not occur. Such phenomena as sodomy, homosexuality, fetishism, exhibitionism and masturbation are ridiculed by the natives as silly substitutes for the natural sex act, therefore as paltry and fit only for fools. The Trobriander would be deeply wounded in his vanity were it presumed he could not enjoyably satisfy his drives in the natural way and so turned to second-best. The Trobriander holds perversions in contempt, just as he would a person who consumes inferior or impure nourishments instead of the best.

> The following are typical remarks on the subject of perversions: "No man or woman in our village does it." "No one likes to penetrate excrement." "No one likes a dog better than a woman." "Only a *tonagawa* (idiot) could do it." "Only a *tonagawa* masturbates. It is a great shame; we know then that no woman wants to copulate with him; a man who does it, we know, cannot get hold of a woman." In all native statements the unsatisfactory nature of a substitute or makeshift is emphasized, and the implication is of poverty as well as of mental and sexual deficiency. The natives would also quote instances such as that of Orato'u, the village clown of Omarakana, deformed and defective in speech; the several albinos and a few especially ugly women, and say that such people, but not an ordinary man or woman, might practice one perversion or another . . . If inversion is defined as a relationship in which detumescence is regularly achieved by

contact with a body of the same sex, then the male friend-
ships in the Trobriands are not homosexual, nor is inversion
extensively practiced in the islands. For, as we know, the
practice is really felt to be bad and unclean because it is
associated with excreta, for which the natives feel a genuine
disgust. And while the ordinary caresses of affection are
approved as between members of the same sex, any erotic
caresses, scratching, nibbling at eyelashes, or labial contact
would be regarded as revolting. (pp. 470, 472)

The Trobriander therefore develops a genital pride and
sexually affirmative ego ideal which allow him to appropriately
evaluate the genuine nature of perversion. The sex-denying
climate in our society has induced the best among our sexual
scientists to fail to recognize this simple connection between the
disordering of potency caused by the social order and the perversions as substitutes for genital gratification. "In some respects
his moral regulations are biologically sounder than our own, in
some more refined and subtle, in some a more efficient safeguard for marriage and the family," writes Malinowski (p. 440).

Only the first two of these observations are correct: the sex
life of this primitive people is natural, and sex-economically
regulated, and on this basis is erected a superior sexual culture.
But the putative safeguard of the marriage and family, which is
supposed to be the result, is a notion superimposed by Malinowski, who, despite his firsthand research, has still not entirely
shaken off a biological definition of the family unit.

Such forms of license as we find in the Trobriands fit so well
into the scheme of individual marriage, the family, the clan,
and the local group—and they fulfill certain functions so
adequately that there remains nothing serious or incomprehensible to explain away by reference to some hypothetical
earlier stage. They exist today because they work well side
by side with marriage and family; nay for the benefit of
marriage and family; and there is no need to assume any
other causes for their past than those which maintain them
at present. (p. 537)

Yet we shall be able to show from Malinowski's own reports that the "licentious," biologically regulated sex life of the Trobrianders really does coexist in contradiction with their marriage and family, and that if we really do want to come out for a "license" which eliminates neuroses and perversions, as against the marriage and family which bring perversions and neuroses and sexual suffering, then we really must forget about compromise.

Sadism and masochism—whether these complementary perversions play a large part in the sexual life of the natives I am unable to say. The cruel forms of caress—scratching, biting, spitting—to which a man has to submit to a greater extent even than the woman, show that, as elements in eroticism, they are not absent from native love-making. On the other hand, flagellation as an erotic practice is entirely unknown; and the idea that cruelty, actively given or passively accepted, could lead, of itself alone, to pleasant detumescence is incomprehensible, nay ludicrous, to the natives. I should say, therefore, that these perversions do not exist in a crystallized form.

Fellatio—this is probably practiced in the intimacy of love-making. Receiving my information exclusively from men, I was told that no male would touch the female genitals in this manner, but at the same time, I was assured that penilinctus was extensively practiced. I do not feel convinced, however, of the truth of this masculine version. The expression *ikanumwasi kalu momona,* "lapping up the sexual discharges," designates both forms of fellation.

Masturbation is a recognized practice often referred to in jokes. The natives maintain, however, that it would be done only by an idiot or one of the unfortunate albinos, or one defective in speech; in other words, only by those who cannot obtain favours from women. The practice is therefore regarded as undignified and unworthy of a man, but in a rather amused and entirely indulgent manner. Exactly the same attitude is adopted toward female masturbation . . .

Exhibitionism is regarded by the natives with genuine contempt and disgust . . .

In the treatment of these deviations of the sexual impulse, it is impossible to draw a rigid line between the use of certain practices—such as fellatio, passionate and exuberant caresses—when they are used as preliminary and preparatory sexual approaches on the one hand, and as definite perversions on the other. The best criterion is whether they function as a part of courting, leading up to normal copulation, or whether they are sufficient by themselves for the production of detumescence. It is well to remember in this context that the nervous excitability of the natives is much less than ours, and their sexual imagination is relatively very sluggish; that excitation and tumescence are usually achieved only by the direct visual, olfactory, or tactual stimulus of the sexual organs; and the orgasm, in man or woman, requires more bodily contact, erotic preliminaries, and, above all, direct friction of the mucous membranes for its production. It is, therefore, plausible to assume that preparatory erotic approaches with the natives would have less tendency to pass into autonomous acts, that is to develop into perversions, than is the case among nervously more excitable races. (p. 475) Scenes of frequent occurrence in any public park in Europe, after dark or even before, would never be seen in a Trobriand village. (p. 478) The whole attitude of the Trobriander towards sexual excess displays an appreciation of restraint and dignity, and admiration for success; not only for what it gives to a man, but because it means that he is above any need for active aggression. The moral command not to violate, solicit, or touch is founded on a strong conviction that it is shameful because real worth lies in being coveted, in conquering by charm, by beauty, and by magic. (p. 491)

We note here a basic distinction between Trobriand moral valuations and ours. Our own moral judgments stem from a generally negative attitude toward sexuality, while the judgments of the Trobriand Islanders are based on a positive attitude toward genital sexuality, together with an appropriate sense of the inadequacy of perversity. "When a woman has no men who come to her, and takes the initiative and goes herself to a man, we call her a wanton." As Malinowski correctly notes, "It is clear that the moral censure incurred by such women is founded on the shame that attaches to erotic unsuccess." (p. 488) Of course, that is also the case in our society, with the difference that here this valuation remains private and without official sanction. The bourgeois view of propriety and decency is not directed against ineffectuality; on the contrary, it is a condemnation of sexual drives outside the institution of marriage and, in certain social groups, even within it. The implications of these two value systems, the sex-economic and the moral, are enormously different: one impels the development of genital vigor, physical beauty, and attractiveness; the other leads in the opposite direction—toward a crippled sex life, false modesty, and even to physical disability (e.g., religious opposition to women's physical education).

Let us consider another example of the Trobriand sex-economic value system. They condemn sexual greed and lechery, typical products of repression. "Inability to master desire, leading to insistent and aggressive sexuality, is regarded with contempt both in man and in woman." (p. 488) Obviously this has not been stated with exactitude. A Trobriander would not reject the inability to control oneself as such, but rather the basis for pathological sexual aggressiveness—the disturbed powers of gratification. That follows unequivocally from the general attitude of the Trobrianders, who, as a matter of course, are able to have sexual relations daily, and who are innocent of any genital inhibitions.

We must take note of an important fact here: a person healed by psychoanalytic treatment—previously neurotically in need of sexual experience, aggressive, or unsatisfiable because of defective powers of gratification—begins to develop characteristics similar to those of man in the sex-economically regulated Trobriand society. He develops a natural discretion, chooses a partner according to sex-economic principles, rejects intercourse with prostitutes, masturbation, and obsessional perversity, insofar as his genitality has been liberated from moral pressure and he has advanced from attitudes of sexual denial to those of sexual affirmation. We may therefore assert that the abolition of moral inhibition leads to a sex-economic regulation of erotic needs, while the system of sexual morality can only bring about the polar opposite of a healthy sex life.

In the next section, we shall consider the transformations in the direction of European and American morality which developing patriarchy is forcing on this sex-economically regulated society. We shall see that the intrusion of sexual morality is closely accompanied by other phenomena of our cultural sphere, bound up with the institution of marriage in connection with its economic foundations.

2) Economic and Sexual Contradictions
Among the Trobrianders

MATRIARCHAL ORGANIZATION
AND THE EMERGING PATRIARCHY

The matriarchal organization of society studied by Malinowski among the Trobriand Islanders of northwestern Melanesia is well suited for shedding light on the dimly illuminated early history of prohibitory sexual morality, and its relation to the beginnings of class division.

At various points in his report, Malinowski stresses that there are remarkable contradictions among the Trobrianders in regard to the maternal line of hereditary succession and maternal clan arrangements, on the one hand, and the social role that the male assumes, whether as the mother's brother or as the husband. Let us assemble the relevant material, from which we shall draw our conclusions at a later moment. For the time being we shall merely anticipate that the basic question here is one of contradictions between the existing matriarchal society and the beginning patriarchy. Let us listen now to Malinowski's report on the economic and social organization of the Trobrianders, which he frequently and correctly designates as the basic institution determining sexual relationships.*

The Trobriand archipelago is located northeast of New Guinea and consists of a number of low-lying coral islands which surround a broad lagoon. The islands' surface is very fertile and the lagoons are well endowed with fish. The inhabitants of the several islands participate in trade with one another, as do the inhabitants of the coastal regions with those of the islands' interiors. Agriculture and fishing are the staples of the economy. There is a brisk barter trade in garden products and fish. Production is socially organized as is product distribution. Malinowski, with a false conception of communism, does not believe the Trobriand economy can be designated by the term "primitive communism," but his exact descriptions of, for example, the ownership relations in regard to the canoes, indicate an explicit communist character. For each canoe there is only one man who is the "rightful owner," to be sure, but usually all the men who are the crew of a canoe belong to the same sub-clan; they are bound to one another by certain obligations; if the community desires to fish, the owner cannot refuse the canoe. In various passages Malinowski speaks of an outright ownership and mentions the canoe as an example. However, the above-mentioned obligation indicates that this "ownership" has nothing in common with our ownership of the means of production and that, practically speaking, it is more a case of community property. If the property owner is not able to go along on a fishing expedition, he must either yield up the canoe or send a substitute in his place. Every man on a canoe team has an assigned place and function and is obligated to participate. Each then receives his share of the fish taken. Malinowski never says that "ownership" of a canoe implies special privileges. The designation *toli* (owner) has only one meaning, it merely distinguishes a certain function, "even when it does not give a claim to rights of exclusive use." (p. 24) "Thus the ownership and use of the canoe consists of a series of definite obligations and duties uniting a

---

* The following description is based on pp. 1–39 of *Crime and Custom in Savage Society*, New York, Humanities Press, 1926.

group of people into a working team." (*Crime and Custom,* p. 18)

The "owner" and the other team members are entitled to defer their rights to a relative or friend. This occurs often, and always accompanied by some sort of payment. Malinowski argues vigorously against considering these relationships communist, and asserts that, with the same justification, one might designate a modern joint-stock company as communism. He indicates a poor knowledge of capitalist economic relationships by not being able to distinguish between social and private appropriation of the products created by society. He has the typical bourgeois conception of communism as a social organization in which the individual has no rights at all, where there is a complete absence of self-interest. He views Trobriand society from such a standpoint, and therefore criticizes descriptions of this society involving terms such as "communism," "clan solidarity," etc. However, as he clearly establishes, Trobriand society is a system characterized by a division of labor and by mutual obligations, in which a binding sense of duty and the recognition of the necessity for cooperation exist side by side with self-interest and privileges. Malinowski's description of canoe ownership corresponds perfectly with Marxist descriptions of primitive communism. The "master of the canoe," who is at the same time leader of the canoe team, is responsible for financing a new canoe (natural economy prevails) when the old one becomes worn out, and must maintain it in good condition with the help of the other members of the canoe team. In this manner the members of the group remain in a continual state of mutual obligation. Every "joint owner" has a right to a certain place in the canoe and to the privileges which are associated with it. In exchange, he must fulfill his duties and receives a special title ("custodian," "fish observer," "net keeper," etc.). Hence, we discover community ownership, division of labor, socialization of labor, and product distribution according to the labor invested: in a word, *primitive communism.**

---

* *(1934)* Without going into the distinction between ownership and property at length, I wish to point out that they are not identical. Probably the "rightful owner" of the canoe can determine who may use his pipe

Normally, two villages maintain barter trade relations with one another. Part of the fish catch is kept, the surplus is exchanged for the surplus in garden products of the second village. Every fisherman is strictly obligated to settle his debt with his partner in the gardening village if he received fruits from him, and vice versa. Neither partner can refuse to trade, neither can postpone the debt.

The whole legal system, writes Malinowski (*Crime and Custom,* p. 25), is based on "the symmetry of all social transactions," on mutual service, so that the resulting system establishes sociological ties of an economic nature. The principle of mutuality replaces social sanction for every rule of conduct. Two parties, exchanging services and functions, determine mutually the exact amount of payment and the appropriate attitude regarding the exchange. This "well-assessed give and take" creates a free and easy style of negotiating business matters.

Our discussion of the economic foundations must be discontinued at this point. We have the task before us of considering economic and social structure in respect to the matter of dowry.

The most important factor in the Trobriand legal system is the belief that the mother is solely responsible for a child's physical being, and that the male has made no contribution to the child's creation. The child is made of the same substance as his mother and has no corporeal connection with his father; it is not known that the male has a role in conception. As a consequence, clan divisions and incest taboos follow only the maternal line of succession. All blood relations of the mother constitute a clan, which is further divided into sub-clans determined by closer or more distant blood relationship.

---

because his pipe is his personal property; that is not the case in regard to the canoe. It is not the intention of modern communism to abolish property in general; it aims, rather, at transferring the means of production from the sphere of private property to that of social ownership. In this sense, then, society, or whoever functions as society's representative, would not have the right to do as it pleases with the agricultural equipment in its keep. It would own it only in the sense that the canoe owner owns his canoe: they would have to care for the equipment and would be held responsible for it.

The sub-clans are at least as important as the clans, for the members of the same sub-clan regard themselves as real kindred, claim the same rank, and form the local unit in Trobriand society. Each local community is composed of people belonging to one sub-clan, and to one sub-clan only, who have joint rights to the village site, to the surrounding garden lands, and to a number of local privileges. Large villages are composed of several minor local units, but each unit has its own compact site within the village and owns a large contiguous area of garden land. (p. 495)

A very strict incest taboo prevails for the members of a sub-clan; the taboo is somewhat milder for members of a clan. The members of a given sub-clan consider themselves real blood relatives, while they regard members of other sub-clans, still in the same clan, as only superficially or figuratively related. On the whole, there are four clans according to totemistic divisions. In the native's opinion, belonging to a clan is just as much a matter of inheritance as one's physical characteristics.

In regard to the children the role of the mother's brother is entirely different from that of her husband, the actual father. The mother's brother is the real head of the family in matriarchal society. He is the "guardian" of the children of his sister. When they are growing up he teaches them the magical arts, as well as the ideals of the clan. He is respected by them and is the model to follow for the young boys who will later inherit his function. At the same time, he is obligated to take care of his sister and is the one who must deliver the marriage dowry. On the other hand, the woman's husband has the position of a treasured friend, who affectionately accepts the children of his girlfriend and assumes the role of a mature companion and partner in play with them. As a consequence of these relationships, children do not develop the same attitude toward their father (the concept of father can only be defined as a social function in Trobriand society) as in our society; they consider him as a friend and not as an authority. This role, as mentioned, is relegated to the uncle on the mother's side.

This purely matriarchal principle encounters another principle, which, at least in its social characteristics, already deserves to be considered patriarchal. The corresponding arrangements are as follows: first, marriage is patriarchal, that is, the wife follows her husband to his village. Only the son of the chief has a "matrilocal" marriage, which, as we shall later see, has a special economic motive. The male has already developed marked ownership interests, and the actual exercise of power is in his hands, even if it derives from the maternal line. It is here that the original maternal right comes into conflict with incipient paternal right. Even though Malinowski mentions arrangements "whereby tribal law, which enjoins matrilineal succession, and the promptings of paternal love, which incline the father to bestow all possible privileges on his son, find equitable adjustment and adequate satisfaction" (p. 95), it will soon become apparent that this "paternal love" in its promptings and privileges represents the first stages of a clearly economic paternal right. A village also has a chief, and a group of village communities has an even higher ranking chief who enjoys many more privileges. But woman is "barred from the exercise of power, land ownership, and many other public privileges; it follows that she has no place at tribal gatherings, and no voice in such public deliberations as are held in connection with gardening, fishing, hunting, oversea expeditions, war, ceremonial trade, festivities, and dances." (p. 36)

We see here such obvious manifestations of paternal right that we cannot agree with Malinowski's view that it is merely a question of the "promptings of paternal love." That it is a matter of encroaching patriarchal dominion is implicit in the economics of the custom of dowry. At first, however, we must examine the social position of the chief more closely.

> It is a very remarkable fact in the constitution of the tribe of which we are speaking, that the source of power is principally economic, and that the chief is able to carry out many of his executive functions and to claim certain of his privileges only because he is the wealthiest man in the community. A chief is entitled to receive tokens of high respect, to command observance and require services; he can insure the participation of his subjects in war, in any expedition, and in any festival; but he needs to pay heavily

for all these things. He has to give great feasts and finance all enterprises by feeding the participants and rewarding the chief actors. Power in the Trobriands is essentially pluto-cratic. And a no less remarkable and unexpected feature of this system of government is that, although the chief needs a large revenue, there is nothing of the sort directly attached to his office: no substantial tributes are paid him by the inhabitants as from subject to chief. The small annual offerings or tribute in certain dainties—the first fish caught, early vegetables, special nuts and fruits—are by no means a source of revenue; in fact, the chief has to repay them at full value. For his real income he has to rely entirely on his annual marriage contribution. This, however, in his case, is very large, for he has many wives, and each of them is far more richly endowed than if she had married a commoner. (p. 130)

Only the chief has the right to polygamy. We know that there two main directions in anthropological research stand-ing in opposition to one another. The first direction sees in matriarchy the original form of human society, from which, in the course of economic development, patriarchy and polygamy developed. The leading representatives of this view are Morgan and Engels. The other direction maintains that the present patri-archal familial organization was already present in prehistory in the form of a polygamous primal horde led by a strong chieftain. Freud himself was a supporter of this view. We do not wish to enter into a discussion of the pro and con of these views at the moment. We merely mention them here because the two forms of societal organization are closely interwoven in Trobriand society. It remains only to be said that supporters of the view that matriarchy represents the original societal form emphasize sociological and economic factors in the development of human society and familial institutions, while those who support the patriarchal view emphasize biological and psychological factors to a greater extent.

Malinowski's research now affords a clear insight into the process in which the Trobriand social, economic and ideological relationships are transformed as the society develops from matriarchy to patriarchy. We have an opportunity to directly observe a process which, under ordinary circumstances, could only be derived from a reasoned consideration and comparison of purely patriarchal and matriarchal social organizations.

Before we examine the transformation process itself, it is necessary to register the individual relocations that can be observed.

1. The transferral of power from the woman to the man. The power disproportion increases vertically according to rank. The chief has the most power in relation to the citizens; his women have the fewest rights.
2. The transition from sexual freedom to marital ties.
3. The transition from sexual affirmation to sexual negation; from affirmation of premarital sexual activity to the demand of premarital chastity.
4. Finally, the most important point: the progressive division of society into exploitative upper groups and exploited lower groups.

We witness here the process of power transference, and not the beginnings of the process. We are indeed able, however, to follow the incursions of sex negation and class division from the first moments on.

The central mechanism for the whole transformation process is the *ritual of marriage dowry*.

THE DESTRUCTIVE EFFECT OF THE DOWRY ON MATRIARCHAL SOCIETY

a) The Marriage Rites   The marriage rites themselves are completely unceremonial. If a lasting relationship has developed, it often suffices merely for the couple to jointly announce in public their intention of marrying. Divorce is equally uncomplicated; each partner has the right to leave the other if he or she no longer wishes to remain in the association. It is a loose "pairing marriage," as Morgan first described it, which represents an earlier stage of our institution of long-term monogamous marriage. But as we shall soon see, the male has a much greater interest in entering into marriage and in maintaining it than the female.

> The formalities of divorce are as simple as those by which marriage is contracted. The woman leaves her husband's house with all her personal belongings, and moves to her mother's hut, or to that of her nearest maternal kinswoman. There she remains, awaiting the course of events, and in the meantime enjoying full sexual freedom. Her husband, as likely as not, will try to get her back. He will send certain friends with "peace offerings" for the wife and for those with whom she is staying. Sometimes the gifts are rejected at first, and then the ambassadors are sent again and again. If the woman accepts them, she has to return to her husband, divorce is ended and marriage resumed. If she means business, and is determined not to go back to her wedded life, the presents are never accepted: then the husband has to adjust himself as best he may, which means that he begins to look for another girl. The dissolution of marriage entails in no case the restitution of any of the inaugural marriage gifts exchanged. (p. 146)

As long as the marriage lasts, the matrimonial ties are "firm and exclusive." Matrimonial ties are maintained by law, morality and custom, all of which clearly reflect economic interests.

In the Trobriand institution of marriage we encounter for the first time moral demands and phenomena as well as the typical consequences of marital morality. Instead of seeming strange or unusual to us, as is the case with Trobriand premarital relations, these phenomena have a familiar aura. The ties are firmer, marital fidelity is demanded, infidelity is punished. Jealousy and adultery have become serious problems in sexual life. "Any breach of marital fidelity is as severely condemned in the Trobriands as it is in Christian principle and European law; indeed the most puritanical public opinion among ourselves is not more strict." (p. 115) Doesn't that sound like a reference to a moral feeling which might perhaps be intrinsic to human nature? We shall not be led astray. A comparison with the policies of the Catholic Church, or with American puritanism, will lead to the discovery of qualitatively similar causes in each case.

We mention now a few of the characteristic symptoms of encroaching sexual negation. Mention of the couple's sexual relations or earlier erotic life is strictly forbidden, and a violation of this custom is considered disreputable. The first period after the marriage vows are exchanged is characterized by abstinence. "Although there is no definite sexual taboo at this time, the newly wedded couple probably think less of love-making during the stage which corresponds to our honeymoon than they have done for a long time previously. I have heard this statement volunteered: 'We feel ashamed in the house of our mother and father. In the *bukumatula* a man has intercourse with his sweetheart before they marry. Afterwards they sleep on the same bunk in the parental home but they do not take off their garments.' The young couple suffer from the embarrassment of new conditions. The earlier nights of marriage are a natural period of abstinence." (p. 111)

Where the sharing of meals was once an inconceivable, even disreputable act, it has now become the direct symbol of marriage; the intent to marry or the consummated marriage are now announced by this act. Strict codes of etiquette begin to develop. The marriage partners are not permitted to make any sort of gesture which might indicate affection between them. (p. 111) Married women are not permitted to take part in the hide-and-seek games of young people which afford an excellent opportunity for sexual intercourse. It is almost as if custom itself were conscious that marriage has no contribution to make to sexuality; that marriage is, in fact, opposed to sexuality.

There is an interesting, and, indeed, startling contrast between the free and easy manner which normally obtains between husband and wife, and their rigid propriety in matters of sex, their restraint of any gesture which might suggest the tender relationship between them. When they walk, they never take hands or put their arms about each other in the way called *kaypapa,* which is permitted to lovers and to friends of the same sex. Walking with a married couple one day, I suggested to the man that he might support his wife, who had a sore foot and was limping badly. Both smiled and looked on the ground in great embarrassment, evidently abashed by my improper suggestion. Ordinarily a married couple will walk one behind the other in single file. On public and festival occasions they usually separate, the wife joining a group of other women, the husband going with the men. You will never surprise an exchange of tender looks, loving smiles, or amorous banter between a husband and wife in the Trobriands. (p. 111) When the pair move on to their own hut, they may or may not share the same bunk; there seems to be no rule in this matter. Some of my native authorities specifically informed me that married couples always sleep in the same bed at first, but later on they separate and come together only for intercourse. I suspect, however, that this is rather a piece of cynical philosophy than a statement of accepted useage. (p. 110)

It is interesting in itself that this cynical point of view coincides with marriage.

. . . it is impossible to get direct information from any man concerning his own conjugal life; for in this matter a very strict etiquette has to be observed. In speaking to a husband the slightest allusion to this must be avoided. Nor is any reference allowed to their common past, nor to the woman's previous love adventures with other men. It would be an unpardonable breach of etiquette were you to mention, even unwittingly, and in passing, the good looks of a wife to her husband. The man would walk away and not come near you for a long time. The Trobriander's grossest and most unpardonable form of swearing or insult is *kwoy um kwawa* (copulate with thy wife). It leads to murder, sorcery, or suicide. (p. 111)

We witness the beginning of an etiquette here that appears to have the character of compulsive avoidance. When one considers the contradiction between the sexual freedom prior to marriage and the constrained sexuality within marriage, the only possible conclusion is that certain interests have begun to en-croach on sexual life and to restrict sexual freedom, and that, in support of these interests, internalized psychic defenses (re-pression) have also begun to develop. In some passages Mali-nowski attempts to portray Trobriand marital life as generally harmonious, but his reports of tragic suicides among married women, of marital strife, and of the secretive quality which envelops married life indicate that Trobriand matrimonial rela-tionships have already developed all the contradictions that exist in our society; those contradictions being between sexual inter-ests, which point to relationships of limited duration, and eco-nomic interests, which aim at permanent relationships.

Malinowski discusses at length the individual motives which are at play when marriage occurs. The native's prior sexual life was completely free and satisfactory. Marriage is the beginning of serious sexual inhibitions and sizable obligations. Malinowski lists several motives:

1. A Trobriand man does not attain a full social position in the community until he is married.
2. Custom considers marriage a moral obligation.
3. A man "who is beyond early youth has a natural desire for his own home and household"; the services that a woman provides for her husband are also attractive.
4. "A woman has no economic motive for marrying and obtains less convenience and social esteem than her hus-band; usually she is motivated by personal inclination and the desire for legitimately born children."

A number of moral and biological reasons for marrying are given here; however, none of them are sufficient to explain how the marriage institution evolved to function as it does. The ques-tion here is one of psychological interests and moral attitudes which have been called into existence by the institution of mar-riage so that it will then gain a necessary anchoring in the indi-vidual psychic structure. Certainly an esteemed and fully ac-knowledged social position is imaginable without the institution of marriage: the custom itself requires a sociological explana-tion. A woman could satisfy her personal inclinations without the institution of marriage; there are, after all, other forms of prolonged sexual relationships in Trobriand society outside of marriage. Finally, even an interest in legitimately born children presupposes an interest in the institution of marriage. We therefore believe, in opposition to Malinowski, that one should not attribute the same value to male economic interests as to the other enumerated motives. Male economic interests are ultimately the crucial factor, not only in the motives for marrying, but more profoundly in the creation and maintenance of the marriage institution itself since

> Another very important reason for marriage, from the man's point of view, is economic advantage. Marriage brings with it a considerable yearly tribute in staple food, given to the husband by the wife's family. This obligation is perhaps the most important factor in the whole social mechanism of Trobriand society. On it, through the institution of rank, and through his privilege of polygamy, rests the authority of the chief, and his power to finance all ceremonial enterprises and festivities. Thus a man, especially if he be of rank and importance, is compelled to marry, for, apart from the fact that his economic position is strengthened by the income received from his wife's family, he obtains his full social status only by entering the group of *tovavaygile*. (p. 81)

Let us further follow the "most important factor in the whole mechanism of Trobriand society." It will not only resolve many mysteries of Trobriand society, but also those regarding the origin of sexual repression and of class divisions in general.

b) The "Only Lawful" Marriage Through marriage, the husband gains the right to certain economic claims on his male in-laws, who, in exchange for their services, retain a legal authority over the wife and her children. In consideration of the process set into motion by the ritual of marriage dowry, it is more proper to say, "retain for a while." Let us compile the relevant facts.

Until she married, the girl's family showed no interest in her sexual relations. She was permitted to do, or not to do, whatever she wished. The marriage itself, "for the family a lasting source of considerable tension and tribulation," is zealously discussed by the relatives, although they are excluded from exercising any influence on the matrimonial plans. The center of their interest is the dowry.

The dowry custom is very complicated. The gift and return gift, which are at first exchanged by the parents of the matrimonial candidates, develop after the marriage into a regularly delivered annual tribute from the relatives, particularly from the wife's brother to the husband and his family. The tribute continues to be made for the duration of the marriage. The return gifts, which are given by the family of the husband to the family of the wife, are mere gestures of courtesy; they are not to be compared in value to the gifts of the wife's family. The dowry consists primarily of garden fruits. The amount of the gift is determined by the social rank of the family in question. In an average household it amounts to about half of the total consumption. Each person retains a part of the garden production for his own use, and the rest is given to the female relatives and their husbands. However, as Malinowski emphasizes, the dowry is "the primary and most presentable product of gardening." Ideologically, the marriage tribute is represented as "the greatest pride of the Trobriander, to be considered a master gardener." In order to attain this honor, the Trobriander invests his greatest efforts and cultivates the largest possible area of gardenland. It can be seen, writes Malinowski,

> . . . that it has very considerable effect, not only on the marriage institution itself, but on the whole economy and constitution of the tribe. Looked at from the point of view of the recipient, it is clear that every man has to guide his marital choice according to his needs, and to his prospective wife's endowment. For he will be dependent, not only on his own industry and capacity, but also on that of his relatives-in-law. A fortune hunter will lay siege to a girl who is the only sister of several brothers—the very existence of whom would cool the ardor of a European with a similar end in view. Only a man who could face destitution with equanimity would court a girl who had several sisters and but a single brother. As a man's wife bears sons and they grow up, he acquires, as it were, home-made relatives-in-law—for in a

matrilineal society children are naturally classed with relatives-in-law—and their first duty is to provide for the
parental household. Ordinarily the husband receives the
main part of his wife's endowment from relatives-in-law
only; but in the case of a chief or a man of importance,
though one man will nominally be responsible, many others
will cooperate with him to provide a suitable gift. Even a
commoner, however, receives, besides the *urigubu* from his
chief donor, a number of smaller girls named *kovisi* or
taytupeta from his wife's other relatives. They are all presented at harvest time and consist of several baskets of yams
and other vegetables.

A man also receives from his relatives-in-law various
services, given as occasion demands. They have to assist
him when he builds a house or canoe, arranges for a fishing
expedition, or takes part in one of the public festivals.
In illness, they must keep watch over him against sorcerers,
or carry him to some other place where he hopes to get
better. In feuds or in other emergencies, he may, given
certain circumstances, command their services. Finally, after
his death, the bulk of mortuary duties will fall upon them.
Only from time to time has the man to repay the annual
services of his relatives-in-law by a gift of valuables. (p. 125)

The taboo which prohibits the wife's brothers, on whom the
burden of the dowry falls, to concern themselves with the marital
affairs of the sister is merely a camouflage and a rationalization
for the actual material interests of the husband and his family.
The factual information can be briefly summarized as follows:
Since the brother of the young wife, as well as all of her relatives, in a word, the whole matrilineal clan are obligated to provide for the husband, the common assets of the wife's clan are
transferred to the husband's clan. Since he himself is a brother,
and must, for his part, provide for the husbands of his sisters, a
continuous relocation of the fruit production takes place from
one clan to another. Ordinarily, this would not be of further
significance, since women from the husband's clan marry men
from other clans, thus bringing the dowry back to the clan. The

situation is complicated, however, by the fact that the clans occupy different levels of social rank, and that the chief, who belongs to the highest ranking clan, has the right to polygamy. As a consequence, the circulation of marriage gifts, ordinarily balanced off by cross marriages between the various clans, is one-sidedly relocated in the direction of the clan chief and his family. This process of relocation of wealth is a rudimentary division of society into classes of profiteers and classes of the exploited. Before we can arrive at a fuller understanding of it, we shall have to see, with the aid of diagrams, how opinions concerning the "lawfulness" or "unlawfulness" of the different types of marriage are attributable to the various material advantages and disadvantages that these marriages may offer.

The sole form of marriage considered "truly lawful" is the so-called cross-cousin marriage, i.e., the marriage between a brother's son and the daughter of the brother's sister. Following Malinowski's discussion of the dowry, we shall demonstrate the arrangement in the case of the chief, where it is most clearly in evidence. First, a simple diagram of a cross-cousin marriage:

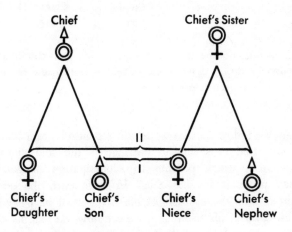

Fig. 1: Diagram of (I) the "lawful" cross-cousin marriage, and (II) the "unlawful" marriage according to Malinowski.

We see in the diagram that in contrast to the "lawful" marriage, marriage between a chief's daughter and the son of the chief's sister "is not highly regarded." In the diagram here and others that follow we have attempted to portray schematically the economic motives which underlie these judgments. They are based on Malinowski's discussion of the dowry ritual.

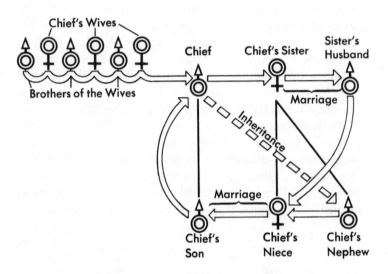

Fig. 2: Diagram of the chief's advantages in a cross-cousin marriage; it returns the dowry to him from his brother-in-law and consequently enables him to accumulate wealth.

As we follow the arrows in the second diagram it becomes apparent that cross-cousin marriage is the sole matrimonial combination which permits an accumulation of goods and garden products for the chief. In large part, the dowry he acquired from the brothers of his wives must be passed on to the husband of his sister. *If his niece now marries his son, the dowry returns to him,* since his nephew (sister's son and inheritor) as well as the parents of the niece (i.e., her father, the chief's brother-in-law) must provide for his son as long as the marriage lasts. But since the son must provide for the household of his mother, which, of course, is also that of his father, the chief shares in the economic rights of his son.

His actual lawful inheritor is his sister's son, to whom his fortune and office are transferred after his death. Between father and son the relations are no more than those of a friendship; as father, he has a right to obtain certain privileges for his son, but only as long as he lives. There is only one way for him to secure a lasting position in the village for his son with a guarantee of all rights for his son and descendants; that is to give his son the hand of his sister's daughter in marriage. The son then acquires the right to live wherever he wishes in the village, and to take part in clan affairs and magic. He thus acquires the same position after the death of the chief that he enjoyed during the chief's lifetime, but which he would have had to relinquish to the lawful inheritor, the chief's sister's son, if he had not married the niece of the chief.*

While living the chief can devote as much time to his son as he wishes, and is able to secure his son's lasting possession of privilege through marriage. The actual inheritor is forbidden to interfere in the matrimonial affairs of his sister by a strict taboo; as a consequence, he has no influence on developments that might work to his disadvantage. When Malinowski writes that a relationship is established between the chief's son and the lawful inheritor, the chief's nephew, which "suspends the frequent rivalry between them," we believe that he must have been in error—there is, after all, the tribute dependency on the chief's

---

* There is an analytical interpretation of the cross-cousin marriage; the incest prohibition between brother and sister is suspended by the marriage of their children by means of the identification of the brother with his son and of the sister with her daughter. The statements of the natives corroborate this interpretation rather temptingly.

"In order to further clarify the principle of exogamy, we remark that it is sometimes said, 'marriage between brother and sister is a bad thing' ['brother and sister' in an extrapolated sense; all matrilineally related individuals of different sex from the same generation.] 'It is proper to marry a *tabula* (cross-cousin); the real *tabula* is the proper wife for us [first cross-cousin].'" (p. 74) The economic interests are so unequivocal, however, that we cannot ascribe more than a secondary role to psychological factors.

son into which the lawful inheritor falls as a result of the marriage. Let us listen to Malinowski himself:

> The matrilineal principle is maintained by the more
> rigid rules of tribal law. These rules decree absolutely that a
> child must belong to the family, sub-clan, and clan of its
> mother. Less absolutely but still very strictly, they regulate
> the membership of a village community and the office of
> magician. They also arrange all inheritance of land,
> privileges, and material goods to the mother-line. But here
> a number of customs and usages allow, if not an evasion, at
> least a compromise and modification of tribal law. By these
> usages, a father can, for his own lifetime, grant the right of
> citizenship in his village to his son and bestow upon him the
> usufruct of canoes, lands, ceremonial privileges, and magic.
> By cross-cousin marriage, combined with matrilocal
> residence, he can even secure all these things to his son for
> life.
>
> Here we have to note one more important difference in
> the transmission of material goods and privileges, as from
> maternal uncle to a nephew on the one hand, and a father to
> a son on the other. A man is obligated to relinquish all
> possessions and offices to his younger brother or maternal
> nephew at death. But usually, the younger man wants to
> possess some of these things during his senior's lifetime; and
> it is customary for a maternal uncle to part with a portion of
> his gardens or some of his magic while he is still living. But
> in such cases he has to be paid for it, and the payment is
> often quite substantial. It is called by the special technical
> name *pokala*.
>
> When a man gives any of these things to his son, on the
> other hand, he does it of his own free will, and quite
> gratuitously. Thus, a maternal nephew, or younger brother,
> has the right to claim his share, and always receives it if he
> gives the first installment of the *pokala*. The son relies on
> his father's goodwill, which, as a rule, works very effectively
> on his behalf, and he receives all the gifts for nothing. The

man who has the right to the things has to pay for them, while the man who receives them without the sanction of tribal law gets them gratis. Of course he has to return them, at least in part, after his father's death; but the use and enjoyment he has had of material benefits remain his, while the magic he cannot return.

The natives explain this anomalous state of things by the father's partiality to his children which, in its turn, is accounted for by his relation to their mother. The natives say that his free gifts to the children are a reward for the free cohabitation which he enjoys with his wife. (p. 208)

We observe that the cross-cousin marriage is less "a compromise between the poorly balanced principles of matriarchy and paternal love," as Malinowski often asserts, than just the opposite: an arrangement which increasingly strengthens patriarchy. As the chief gains more and more power, there comes a point where the step of legislatively transferring hereditary rights from the maternal to the paternal side, from the sister's son to one's own son, would mean the fulfillment of the conditions of full patriarchy. Trobriand society still has a matriarchal organization in regard to the line of hereditary succession, yet we have already seen what privileges a chief can obtain for his son, and how he can secure the transferral of goods and power to his family by means of the cross-cousin marriage.

There is one passage where Malinowski indicates that the encroachment of aspects of patriarchy is not merely due to "paternal love"; he writes:

On the apparently unpropitious soil of strict matriliny, with its denial of the paternal bond through procreation and its declaration of the father's extraneousness to progeny, there spring up certain beliefs, ideas, and customary rules, which smuggle extreme patrilineal principles into the stronghold of mother-right. (p. 203)

We would like to illustrate with two more diagrams that the

motives underlying the natives' opinion that a marriage between the daughter of a chief and his sister's son is "not good" or "disreputable" are primarily economic in nature.

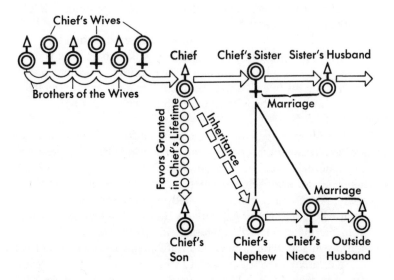

Fig. 3: Diagram of the economic disadvantages for the chief when his niece marries at random. (Arrows indicate movement of the marriage gift.)

In Figure 3 it is assumed that the niece marries a man at random. Following the arrows in the diagram, we see in this case that the chief is not able to accumulate goods because he must himself transfer possessions to the husband and family of his sister, and to the interloping husband of his niece via his nephew who receives the chief's inheritance. He has a great personal burden in his lifetime because of the first obligation, and after his death his wealth even leaves the clan when his nephew provides dowry for the man of an outside clan who married his niece.

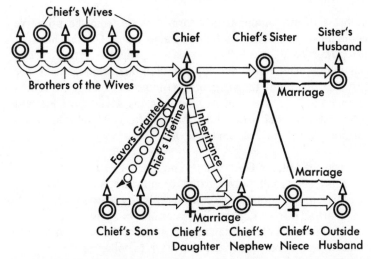

Fig. 4: The "bad" marriage (between the chief's daughter and the chief's nephew)—even the wealth of the chief's sons leaves the chief's line of succession.

In Figure 4 we see an even worse situation for the chief, when, besides the two aforementioned relocations of wealth, his sons, objects of his attention while he lived, are required to enrich the nephew who married his daughter. However, in contrast to his sons, a well-to-do nephew offers no advantages to him, since the nephew is not required to contribute to his household. This is also the explanation for the tense relationship between uncle and nephew, and the affectionate relationship between father and son, to which Malinowski often refers.

EXPLOITATION
AND ITS IDEOLOGICAL MOORINGS

We have observed how the institution of marriage dowry leads to a relocation of the power relationships to the benefit of the father and chief, and paternal right and its concomitant patriarchal and polygamous family form develop from the primitive communist matriarchy of blood-related clans. On the basis of his power (and as a result of his obligations) certain special possibilities and rights develop for the chief, among them, for instance, the right to polygamy, and the beginnings of feudal main force as a means of dealing with his wives' brothers and other relatives who owe him tribute. Here is Malinowski's description of the chief of Omarakana:

> The headman of Omarakana, and chief of Kiriwina, is supreme in rank, power, extent of influence, and renown. His tributary grasp, now considerably restricted by white men and crippled by the disappearance of some villages, used to reach all over the northern half of the island and comprise about five dozen communities, villages, or sub-divisions of villages, which yielded him up to sixty wives. Each of these brought him in a substantial yearly income in yams. His family had to fill one or two storehouses each year, containing roughly five to six tons of yams. The chief would receive from 300 to 350 tons of yams per annum. The quantity which he disposes of is certainly sufficient to provide enormous feasts, to pay craftsmen for making precious ornaments, to finance wars and overseas expeditions, to hire dangerous sorcerers and assassins—to do all, in short, which is expected of a person in power. (p. 132)
>
> Polygamy (*vilayawa*) is allowed by custom to people of higher rank or to those of great importance, such as, for instance, the sorcerers of renown. In certain cases, indeed, a man is obliged to have a great number of wives by virtue of his position. This is so for every chief, that is to say, every headman of high rank who exercises an over-rule in a more or less extended district. In order to wield his power and to fulfil the obligations of his position, he must possess wealth, and this in Trobriand social conditions is possible only through plurality of wives. (p. 130)

Maternal right is extinguished in this process by the necessarily resulting transference of hereditary succession from the maternal to the paternal side. In this society, the course of development to a system of feudalism and slavery can no longer be halted. Once wealth and power has been concentrated in the hands of the chief and his family, a certain modest development of the means of production will introduce the situation which Marx placed at the beginning of class society: a progressive division of labor leads to the production of exchangeable commodities, but the concentration of the means of production, or at least the power to appropriate them at any time, in the hands of the chief and his family, characterizes the birth of definitive classes divided into owners of the means of production and owners of labor power. In the legal structure of the Trobrianders we clearly observe the embryonic stages of such class structure. There exists a horizontal and a vertical "exploitative relationship": horizontally, the exploitation of the women's brothers by the husbands; vertically by the step-by-step accumulation of power in the "higher ranking" upper clans, i.e., the exploitation of the men by the chief through their wives. Parallel with these exploitative relationships, a relocation of power from the maternal side to the paternal side takes place.

Malinowski writes that

> if we examine the roundabout methods of native economy more closely, we see that they provide a powerful incentive to industrial efficiency. If he worked just to satisfy his own immediate wants, and had only the spur of directly economic considerations, the native, who has no means of capitalizing his surplus, would have no incentive to produce it. The deep-rooted motives of ambition, honor, and moral duty have raised him to a relatively high level of efficiency and organization which, at seasons of drought and scarcity, allows him to produce just enough to tide over the calamity. (p. 149)

The motive force continually at play here consists of primitive exploitative relationships maintained by the matrimonial system. Feelings of ambition, honor and moral duty are results of the relationships of production prevailing between brother and brother-in-law. They are the ideological moorings of an economic system that has already begun to exert pressure, and as it expands, continues to be maintained by the marriage system. We cannot understand how Malinowski could have come to the conclusion that the Trobriander is never motivated to act on the basis of purely economic considerations when he himself has written such detailed description of the function of economic institutions in Trobriand society.

Even the rites of mourning, which Malinowski closely described, indicate that the relationships of production prevailing between the maternal and the paternal clans have produced the ideological seeds of hatred between those who are exploited and their exploiters. If the husband dies, it is not, as one might expect, his blood relatives, but rather his wife's relatives, particularly her brothers, who are obligated to display extreme mourning. Malinowski says of the funeral rites:

> The ritual performances at his twice-opened grave and over his buried remains, and all that is done with his relics, are merely a social game, where the various groupings into which the community has re-crystallized at his death play against each other. (p. 108) The kindred must also not display any outward signs of mourning in costume and ornamentation, though they need not conceal their grief and may show it by weeping. Here the underlying idea is that the maternal kinsmen are hit in their own persons; that each one suffers because the whole sub-clan to which they belong has been maimed by the loss of one of its members. "As if a limb were cut off, or a branch lopped from a tree." Thus, though they need not hide their grief, they must not parade it. This abstention from outward mourning extends, not only to all the members of the sub-clan beyond the real kinsmen, but to all the members of the clan to which the dead man belonged. (p. 150) . . . Quite different in the native idea is the relation of the widow, and of the children and relatives-in-law, to the dead and to his corpse. They ought, according to the moral code, to suffer and to feel bereaved. But in feeling thus they are not suffering directly; they are

not grieving for a loss which affects their own sub-clan.
Their grief is not spontaneous like that of the *veyola*
(maternal kinsmen), but a duty almost artificial, springing
as it does from acquired obligations. Therefore they must
ostentatiously express their grief, display it, and bear witness
to it by outward signs. If they did not, they would offend the
surviving members of the dead man's sub-clan. Thus an
interesting situation develops, giving rise to a most strange
spectacle: a few hours after the death of a notable, the
village is thronged by people, with their heads shaven, the
whole body thickly smeared with soot, and howling like
demons in despair. And these are the non-kinsmen of the
dead man, the people not actually bereaved. In contrast to
these, a number of others are to be seen in their usual attire,
outwardly calm and behaving as if nothing had happened.
These represent the sub-clan and clan of the deceased, and
are the actually bereaved. Thus by a devious reasoning,
tradition and custom produce the reverse of what would
seem natural and obvious to us or any observer from almost
any other culture . . . In this group, and it may be in that
of the sons also, an observer well acquainted with these
natives would be able to distinguish an interesting interplay
of feigned and merely histrionic grief with real and heartfelt
sorrow. (p. 152) After the second exhumation the body is
buried, the wake is over, and the people disperse; but the
widow, who, during all this time, has not stirred from her
husband's side, nor eaten, nor drunk, nor stopped in her
wailing, is not yet released. Instead she moves into a small
cage, built within her house, where she will remain for
months together, observing the strictest taboos. She must not
leave the place; she may only speak in whispers; she must
not touch food or drink with her own hands, but wait till
they are put into her mouth; she remains closed up in the
dark, without fresh air or light; her body is thickly smeared
over with soot and grease, which will not be washed off for a
long time. She satisfies all the necessities of life indoors, and
the excreta have to be carried out by her relatives. Thus she
lives for months shut up in a low-roofed, stuffy, pitch-dark

space, so small that with outstretched hands she can almost
touch the walls on either side; it is often filled with people
who assist or comfort her, and pervaded by an incredible
atmosphere of human exhalations, accumulated bodily filth,
stale food, and smoke. Also she is under the more or less
active control and surveillance of her husband's matrilineal
relatives, who regard her mourning and its inherent
privations as their due. When the term of her widowhood
has almost run its course—its length depends upon the
status of her husband and varies from about six months to
two years—she is gradually released by the dead man's
kinsmen. Food is put into her mouth according to a ritual
which gives her permission to eat with her own hands. Then,
ceremonially, she is allowed to speak; finally she is released
from the taboo of confinement and, still with appropriate
ritual, requested to walk forth. At the ceremony of her
complete release by the female *veyola* of the dead man, the
widow is washed and anointed, and dressed in a new gaudy
grass skirt in three colors. This makes her marriageable
again. (p. 157) The idea that it is the imperative duty of the
widow and her relatives to show grief and perform all the
mortuary services, emphasizes the strength and the
permanence of marriage bonds as served by tradition (p.
159) In the first place, it is a duty towards the dead and
towards his sub-clan, a duty strongly enjoined by the code of
morals and guarded by public opinion, as well as by the
kinsmen. "Our tears—they are for the kinsmen of our father
to see," as one of the mourners simply and directly told me.
In the second place, it demonstrates to the world at large
that the wife and children were really good to the dead man
and that they took great care of him in his illness. Lastly,
and this is very important, it allays any suspicion of their
complicity in his murder by black magic. To understand the
last queer motive, one has to realize the extreme fear, the
ever-vigilant suspicion of sorcery, and the unusual lack of
trust in anyone at all with reference to it. The Trobrianders,
in common with all races at their culture level, regard every
death without exception as an act of sorcery, unless it is

caused by suicide or by a visible accident such as poisoning or a spear thrust. It is characteristic of their idea of *the bonds of marriage and fatherhood, which they regard as artificial and untrustworthy under any strain, that the principal suspicion of sorcery attaches always to the wife and children.* The real interest in a man's welfare, the real affection, the natural innocence of any attempt against him are, by the traditional systems of ideas, attributed to his maternal kinsmen. His wife and children are mere strangers, and custom persists in ignoring any real identity of interest between them. (p. 160)

One of the discoveries of psychoanalysis is that individuals who are given to a particularly ostentatious display of bereavement for a deceased person are, in reality, attempting to overcome and to conceal a forbidden and repressed hatred against this person by exhibiting the exact opposite of hatred. We observe that wherever an exploitative relationship exists between Trobrianders, distrust prevails. Trobrianders also manifest a proper awareness of the artificial nature of marriage. The fact that the wife's clan was exploited and then freed from its burden by the death of the husband should have been occasion for rejoicing. The members of her clan had developed a conscious or unconscious resentment for the tribute recipient, but instead of indicating that their burden had resulted in enmity, they must make a show of having discharged their obligations voluntarily and gladly while being scrutinized with suspicion by the husband's clan. For the blood relations of the deceased, material obligations did not exist, and, as a consequence, resentments requiring a compensatory toning down also did not develop. The relatives were permitted to express their grief in a natural fashion.

Here we observe moral custom arising directly from the relationships of production. In this process we may also recognize another of the functions of moral custom, namely, the *ideological consolidation of the economic situation* which produced it. This reciprocal action of ideology anchors into the psychic structure of the oppressed individuals, and works alterations in the instinctual pattern of activity; it then serves as a prop for the economic situation and its sociologically reactionary function, perpetuating material oppression and preventing rebellion—all this on an unconscious level. We may expect that this function of ideology can be regularly encountered in relation to an exploitative relationship. We shall deal with the question at further length in Part II.

At the Trobriand level of social organization the interests of the institution of marriage are already functioning as a central mechanism of exploitation. As one consequence, a widow is required to undergo the most terrible deprivations for an extended period of time. She is scrutinized suspiciously by the husband's relatives, whose task it is to determine how long she must endure the rites of mourning. The behavior of the relatives becomes comprehensible when one considers that the wife underwent a considerable restriction of her sexuality through her husband and must surely have developed resentments toward him. Before she is again permitted to enjoy her complete freedom she has to prove through suffering that she loved him and did not make use of black magic on him. *Tout comme chez nous.*

3) The Imposition of Antisexual Morality

PREMARITAL CHASTITY

From childhood on, the sex life of the Trobriand Islanders before marriage is completely free and is given social encouragement, as we have noted in Chapter I. There is one exception to this rule, and it has to do with those children who are destined for a cross-cousin marriage. For these children, social custom demands premarital chastity and an abstinence from the sexual activities which are otherwise customary and eagerly practiced. Malinowski merely registers this fact under the title "ceremonial customs for children's betrothal" without bringing it into any sort of perspective.

The relationships that exist among private property, the institution of marriage, and the demand for adolescent self-denial became evident as I studied the sociological function of sexual suppression in children and adolescents.* The findings of Malinowski have confirmed these relationships, and even furnished insight into their earliest beginnings. Here is a brief recapitulation of the results of my aforementioned study:

In its research into problems of adolescence, bourgeois scholarship has always maintained that asceticism for adolescents is a necessary requirement for "cultural development," that culture and civilization are inconceivable without continence on the part of young people. Now, Marxist training teaches us to phrase questions concretely rather than abstractly; as a consequence, I arrived at the obvious premise that it was not civilization in general, but rather a certain form of civilization, i.e., bourgeois civilization and perhaps the private enterprise system in general, in which adolescent asceticism, or at least the demand for it, was an integral component. The next question was to determine how the demand for asceticism fitted into the sociological reality.

At first it was only clear that there was a reason for capitalism's interest in the marital institution. It does constitute a social protection for the disenfranchised wife and her children, and economically it determines and protects the inheritance rights of the paternal line of succession, while in regard to its overwhelmingly *political* function in bourgeois society, marriage is the backbone of that bourgeois ideological workshop, the patriarchal family. As yet these remarks have no direct bearing on the demand for asceticism. After all, why shouldn't adolescents be permitted to live according to their psycho-physiological needs if only later, in marriage, they are to carry out the demands of the patriarchate? The psychoanalytic clinic indicated the solution of the problem: it became evident that people who had attained a full development of their genital needs, whether as a result of individual circumstance, or as a result of psychoanalytic

* *Geschlechtsreife, Enthaltsamkeit, Ehemoral: Eine Kritik der bürgerlichen Sexualreform,* Vienna, 1930. (This appears in a revised version as "The Fiasco of Sexual Moralism," Part I of *The Sexual Revolution,* New York, The Noonday Press, 1945, 1962.)

treatment, became unable to conform to the monogamous precept of private property: "one partner for a lifetime." One compared the orgastically fulfilled lives with the sexually-crippled and therefore decent petty-bourgeois housewives capable of following the dictates of morality and with the sexually disturbed men who, with relative ease, are able to suffer monogamy—and one was led to these conclusions:

1. *The impairment of genital sexuality creates the conditions for the acceptance of marriage.*

2. While fully developed sexuality and a satisfactory sex life before marriage do not eliminate the possibility of monogamy for a circumscribed period of time, they destroy the capacity to accept monogamy in the ecclesiastical and bourgeois sense. Disregarding for a moment subjective rationalizations and considering the problem from an objective sociological point of view, the meaning of demands for asceticism in adolescents and for sexual suppression in early childhood is the creation of the ability to accept marriage. This is even explicit in some of the anti-bolshevik publications of the the church and of the openly reactionary bourgeoisie.

We neglect here the contradictions which result for the institution of marriage,* to stay with this one fact: private ownership of the means of production has an interest in the institution of marriage; while to maintain itself this institution requires the demand for the strictest implementation of asceticism in its children and adolescents. This fact, and not considerations of "culture," as bourgeois sexual research maintains, is the real reason for the demand for continence. In contrast to the boringly repetitive assertions made by bourgeois sexual literature regarding health dangers putatively inherent in adolescent sexual intercourse, it was not difficult for us to prove in the clinic that, first of all, continence demands were practically never met in practice, and moreover that conflicts resulting from masturbation can impair sexual health to a far greater extent than sexual intercourse during puberty ever could. Feelings of

---

* See the chapter on the contradictions of the marital institution.

guilt and sexual anxiety were the sole hindrances standing in the way of adolescent sex life. And these emotions were responsible for impotence problems and gratification difficulties, thereby creating individuals with modest sexual needs. The sexual norm had not consciously intended that approximately 60 percent of men and 90 percent of women should fall ill with nervous and sexual disorders, but such was implicit in the system defended by bourgeois sexual research. Even psychoanalytic research into problems of adolescence has been liable to this error in spite of unequivocal facts speaking an unequivocal language.

Statistics compiled by Barasch in Moscow on the relationship between the chronological initiation of sexual intercourse and marital fidelity, resulted in a confirmation: among those who had begun sexual intercourse after the age of twenty-one, only 17.2 percent were unfaithful in marriage; among those who had had sexual intercourse between the ages of seventeen and twenty-one, the number had reached 47.6 percent; and finally, among those who had begun sexual intercourse before the age of seventeen, the level of marital infidelity had reached 61.6 percent.* Morally biased sexual research has brought a number of objections against these statistics and theoretical conclusions. However, the fact that the demand for childhood and adolescent continence in the otherwise sexually free Trobriand society begins just at the point where material interests are most clearly in evidence, i.e., in the cross-cousin marriage, constitutes an irrefutable proof of the economic motivation behind the demand for asceticism. It demolishes the cliché of cultural considerations, just as the actual sexual life of Trobriand youth refutes the empty phrase that sexual intercourse constitutes a health hazard. No one could maintain that the Trobriand Islanders haven't already attained a high level of agricultural development, or that they have been hindered in this process by the sexual activities of their young people. The discussion presented in *Geschlechts-reife* demonstrated in part that any damaging effects of sexual intercourse in puberty must be attributed to societal obstructions

* Barasch, "Sex Life of the Workers of Moscow," *Journal of Social Hygiene,* XII, iii (May 1926).

(crippling sex education, lack of living space, faulty home environment, etc.) and to contradictions between sexual and economic relations, and that they do not result from any natural factors.

Let us return to Malinowski's discussion of the imposition of ascetic demands in Trobriand society. The mother's brother, following his material interests, is always the one who takes the initiative in bringing about a cross-cousin marriage. As soon as a son is born to him he petitions his sister to choose a daughter or niece as future wife for his son. An age differential of two to three years is taken into consideration.

> Or the boy's father may wait, and if within ten years or so a girl is born to his sister, he may requisition her as a future daughter-in-law. His sister is not allowed to refuse his application. Soon after the preliminary agreement has been concluded, the man has to take a *vaygu'a* (valuable), a polished axe-blade or shell ornament, and give it to his sister's husband, the father (*tama*) of the infant bride. "This is the *katupwoyna kapo'ula* for your child," he says, and adds that it is given "so that she may not sleep with men, nor make *katuyausi* (licentious escapades), nor sleep in the *bukumatula* (bachelors' house). She must sleep in her mother's house only." Shortly after this, three gifts of food are offered by the girl's family to the boy's father. They are similar in nature to the three initial gifts in ordinary marriage, and are designated by the same names: *katuvila, pepe'i,* and *kaykaboma.* (p. 104)

> But before this stage is reached and the two are safely married, a somewhat difficult course has to be steered. Although nobody seriously expects the young people to be chaste and faithful to each other, appearances have to be kept up. A flagrant transgression of the obligation to the betrothed would be resented by the offended party, and with some exaggeration called "adultery." It is considered a great shame to the girl if her fiance openly has a liaison with someone else, and she on her side must not make a *bukumatula* her permanent abode either in the company of her betrothed

or of anyone else; nor may she go to other villages on those avowedly sexual expeditions called *katuyausi*. Both parties to the betrothal must carry on their amours discreetly and *sub rosa*. This, of course, is neither easy nor pleasant for them, and they tread the strait path of superficial decorum only under heavy pressure. The boy knows what he has to lose, so he is as careful as he can bring himself to be. Also, the father controls his son to some extent, and at the same time exercises some authority over his future daughter-in-law, through his status of maternal uncle. A man who had betrothed his son and niece to each other put the matter thus to me: "She is afraid that she might die (that is, by sorcery), or that I might hit her." And, of course, her mother is very careful and does what she can to conceal and make light of her daughter's delinquencies. (p. 106)

As we see, this clandestine activity accompanies the onset of sexual repression. In a society in which the striking of children is considered a disgrace the heavy pressures of the new morality, standing in such a crass contradiction to the otherwise free sexual organization, have brought about a situation where Trobriand girls develop a fear of being beaten for sexual transgressions, and their mothers begin to adopt the behavior of our mothers. In order that there be no misunderstanding on this point: "At the next harvest, the girl's father brings a *vilakuria* (substantial contribution of yam food) to the boy's parents. This fact is interesting, since it is a reversal, on account of the anticipated marriage, of what happened in the previous generation. The boy's father, who is the brother of the girl's mother, has to give a harvest gift year by year to the girl's parents; and this at the time of his sister's marriage he had inaugurated by a gift of *vilakuria*. Now he receives on behalf of his infant son a *vilakuria* from his sister's husband, who acts as the representative of his own son or sons, that is the brother or brothers of the future bride, who later on will annually bring substantial harvest offerings to the household, when it becomes such." (p. 105) As the sons have to nourish the household of their mother too, this ring of return of the harvest gift to its starting point is closed, and the way to sexual oppression is open. In the first chapter we have seen how, after a certain development of the patriarchal organization takes place, this repression acts as a factor in the creation of neurosis.

CRUEL RITES OF PUBERTY

Freud attempted to bring us a closer understanding of the pubertal rites of circumcision and genital mutilation. Practices common to many peoples, such as removal of the foreskin and excision of the clitoris and labial lips, are described by Bryk in his book *Negereros,* and have been compiled by Krische (whose collection includes Egyptians, Nubians, Abyssinians, Sudanese, Mandingo, the Masai and Watusi in east Africa). According to Krische, these practices are not only typical for a patriarchal organization as a symptom of the brutalization of sexuality, and in the Freudian sense as preventive punishment for sexual activity, they are supposedly also widespread among the Kamchatkanese, and among the matriarchally organized Malayans of the East Indian archipelago. According to Bachofen the custom also existed among the "matriarchally inclined Egyptians."* Bryk writes of the African Bantu tribes:

> The excision, limited to the clitoris, creates an impediment to the extravagant activity of the girls. Community property develops into private property [the African tribe described here is already completely patriarchal, Reich]. . . . The practical significance is found at first in the fact that the recuperating young girls are removed from contact with the importunity of young men for extended periods of time. The principal purpose, however, is to restrain her sexual desire by extirpating the organ which is most sensitive to the *libido sexualis* in order to force her, against her nature, into monogamy. (*Negereros,* p. 56)

* In Krische, *Das Rätsel der Mutterrechtsgesellschaft,* Munich, 1927, p. 231.

These genital ceremonies, in the form of pubertal rites, involving mutilation of the genitals and the inflicting of pain, signify obvious attempts of society to combat the sexuality of young people. However, it is still necessary to determine the meaning of the ritual in regard to socio-economic factors and to its historical place in the development of sexual morality and sexual repression. Presumably the ritual does not trace back to prehistoric times of free and unrestricted erotic life; hence, it must have undergone a process of development. It is more or less typical for all primitive patriarchal social organization. Krische's compilation indicates that it is also discoverable in matriarchal societies. How can this fact be reconciled with the sexually affirmative societal organization of matriarchy?

We must keep two things in mind: in the first place, the ritual does not occur very frequently in matriarchal society, and the Egyptians among whom the ritual was noted were merely [still] "matriarchally inclined"; in the second place, we should not imagine, in an unhistorical fashion, that matriarchy and patriarchy are sharply distinguished from one another in history. In the transition from matriarchy to patriarchy long periods of time elapse before all economic and social institutions and customs are completely transformed. And if we accept the sex-economic function of pubertal mutilation to be a primitive method of suppressing adolescent sexuality, we must conclude that the measure occurred during a period of transition and that it was created in the course of change from sexual affirmation to sexual suppression as an economically necessary step. But when and in what connection? Here we can only produce a conjecture, since the material is entirely inadequate—to be sure, a conjecture that fits with ease into our history of sexual morality and which is completely congruent with our psychoanalytic knowledge of the sexual apparatus.

As long as the economically all-important cross-cousin marriage was not fully developed and there was hence no general demand for chastity in adolescents, moral pressure alone was sufficient. As demands for chastity gained ground, young people were forced more and more to rebel sexually, and since the demand for chastity had to be implemented if the whole system of "lawful" marriage were not to be endangered by an inability to accept marriage brought about through premarital sexual freedom, harsher measures were deemed necessary. The excision of the clitoris in women has the function of violently reducing sexual excitability. Thus, circumcision ultimately has an economic function anchored and camouflaged in custom and tradition. The procedures endured by young people are not preemptive punishments for sexual activity, nor are they "acts of revenge" committed by adults; they are rationally validated measures taken by the dominant group for the purpose of violently suppressing pubertal sexuality detrimental to this stage of economic development. In the future when the patriarchate is more mature it becomes more sophisticated and more successful: it initiates a battle against childhood sexuality and harms sexual structure from the very beginning in the sense of orgastic impotence, not without coincidentally bringing down on themselves neurosis, perversion and sexual criminality. The fear of castration, which Freud discovered in bourgeois man, is historically rooted in the economic interests of the budding patriarchate. And the same motives which originally created the basis for the castration complex maintain this complex in capitalism today: the patriarchal private enterprise system's interest in monogamous permanent marriage—an interest in which parents, totally on an unconscious level, function as the executive organs.

4) Primitive Communism—Mother-Right Private Property—Father-Right

SUMMARY

In Trobriand society we have witnessed the growth of father-right from a system of mother-right, and we discovered in the ritual of marriage dowry the basic mechanism for the transformation of the one social organization into the other. We witnessed how the primitive communist matriarchal gens fell increasingly into an economic dependency, however ideologically camouflaged, on the chief and his family as the gens developed in a patriarchal direction. Is this process a general or at least frequently occurring type of primeval transformation into patriarchy and class division, or is the process unique for the Trobrianders and perhaps for a few other tribes? It is not at all easy to give a definitive answer to this question. Such exact and fruitful studies as that of Malinowski are not to be found elsewhere. Either the ethnologist lacks a psychoanalytic point of view which would sharpen his methodology in the study of sexual life, or else descriptions of the relationships between sexual and economic forms are missing, so that satisfactory conclusions are not possible. Many ethnologists even represent a point of view which insists on the priority of patriarchy, an outlook excluding the possibility of historical development from the very beginning. In most studies there is no indication whatsoever whether the tribes under observation are patriarchal or matriarchal, primitive communist or private-propertied in organization. One can count only a few ethnologists whose studies have permitted an insight into the historical development of primitive society. Among these authors, Lewis Morgan,* later followed by Engels in his book on *The Origin of the Family,* is preeminent as a representative of the point of view of original mother-right. Before them, Bachofen† had already demonstrated that mother-right was generally the original form of social organization, representing as it does actual natural law, while the patriarchate is preceded by complicated socio-historical influences.

The arguments of their opponents who maintain that earliest society was characterized by the paternal line of succession and by the patriarchate, are always inconsistent, lack the concise rigor of the maternal/natural rights theory, and do not constitute valid proofs even when father-right is discovered in very primitive tribes. A conclusive proof of the primacy of the present social order does not emerge from a mere observation of its presence in some primitive societies. For example, pygmies combine a very low level of development with a patriarchal social

---

* Morgan, *Ancient Society.*
† Bachofen, *Das Mutterrecht* (1861).

organization* yet their monogamous relationships and strong incest prohibition indicate a long period of historical development. Only a thorough study of their sagas and myths might afford an explanation of their particular historical development.

It is highly improbable that mother-right could have developed from a primal patriarchal organization. When we consider that mother-right is characterized by primitive communism and by the farthest-reaching sexual freedom, while father-right, wherever we encounter it, is characterized by private ownership, the enslavement of women, and sexual repression similar to our own, it is apparent that the first state is much closer to the natural state than the second one. Therefore, if one wished to derive matriarchy from patriarchy it would be necessary to assume a violent reversal in historical development, the transformation of a highly complicated organism into a more primitive, more natural one. Every principle of historical scholarship would have to be abandoned in such a view.

The third possibility, that alongside primal matriarchy a primal patriarchy existed, is not less improbable. While matriarchy is explainable as a result of the natural succession of one generation to the next and is entirely in accordance with the fact of incest and primitive communism in prehistory, the assumption of primal patriarchy requires a very complicated and forced hypothesis. Usually in the patriarchal assumption, much is made of the chief's strength, of his jealousy toward the other younger and weaker(?) rivals; and analogies from animal life are adduced, with descriptions of "patriarchal" lead hordes. We are then confronted with the following difficulties: the positing of jealousy excludes the irrefutable fact of incest in prehistoric times as well as the fact of primitive communist economy. If a strong and jealous male chief exists in a horde demanding all the women for himself and excluding or chasing away his rivals, then this state of affairs must always have existed, otherwise the totality is meaningless. The excluded men would continue to struggle and would not be able to contribute to the primitive economy, since that would entail their coming into close contact

* See Roheim's *Urformen und Wandlungen der Ehe.*

with the women. Similarly, they would also be excluded from the fruits of labor. The supposition that the primal father would be able to keep a group of men who are as strong as he permanently at bay seems entirely incredible. The sole hypothetical basis for this view is the supposed jealousy of the leading man and the occurrence (*nota bene,* infrequent) of animal groups (wild horses, deer, apes) among which a "leader" exists. These biological analogies, continually drawn from the animal world, vanish when confronted with the fact that millions of other animal species, with the exception of occasional pairings for the brooding period, have a demonstrably ungoverned sexual life. Nevertheless, such arguments are continually utilized in support of patriarchal ideology.

The patriarchal conception of prehistory has logically led to the assumption that monogamy (i.e., today's right of a man to several women), jealousy, the oppression of women, etc., have a biological basis. And when we note that this conception serves as a justification for our own patriarchal society and forms part of the foundation of fascist sexual ideology, while the matriarchal conception demonstrates that everything is in a state of flux and that other societal forms are possible, it scarcely behooves us to waver in deciding which conception we shall accept.

Above all, the matriarchal theory contributes greatly toward clarification of social realities and processes, while the patriarchal view merely places the stamp of eternity on that which is actually in a perpetual river of change. When we are on the firm ground of gradual transition from general matriarchy to patriarchy, we are then in harmony with a great number of observable facts, we are able to reject forced interpretations, and we have gained a great deal for the history of sexual forms and of sexual economy.

Recently Krische* completed a compilation of relevant ethnological material concerning the broad dispersion of historical and present-day matriarchy. We are left with the difficult task of showing the historical development of patriarchy from matriarchy in the case of several different primitive organizations

* *Das Rätsel der Mutterrechtsgesellschaft,* Munich, 1927.

as we have done in the case of Trobriand society. Matriarchy was discovered (1) among the agricultural Indians of North America, the Missouri tribes, Iroquois, Hurons, Algonquin tribes, Muskogees, Choctaws, Natchez, Pueblos, and among the primitive races of South America, the Tupi, Caribs, and Arawak; (2) in the East, among the Malayan tribes, the Nicobarians, the Palau Islanders, the Formosan tribes, and certain primitive tribes in China and in India (the Garos, the Pani-Kooch and the Kulu); and (3) among the ancient civilizations of Athens, Sparta, Megara, Crete, Lemnos, Lesbos, Samothrace, Elis, Mantinea, Lydia, Cyrenaica, etc., as well as in Rome, and among the Chinese, Arabs, Tibetans, Celts, Slavs, and others.

A fundamental theory concerning the relationship between primitive communist economy and matriarchy can only be found in the work of Morgan, who also was the first to prove that it is the generally occurring primitive social form. Roheim* compiled descriptions of tribes with a primitive communist organization, without, however, bringing economic forms into a perspective with sexual organization. The common elements of these societal forms are: community ownership of land and huts, common labor and product distribution, private property limited to tools, ornaments, articles of clothing, etc., as observed among the Kuli, the Lengua Indians, the Eskimos, the aborigines of Brazil, the Bakairi, Australia in general, Tasmania, and among the Comanches, the Sioux, Indo-Chinese peoples, natives of the Solomon Islands. However, the hunting areas of outside tribes are sometimes strictly partitioned; a border trespass can lead to war.

One of the discoveries of Roheim leads to our central problem, the mechanism of the marriage dowry. Roheim maintains that in many tribes property is analogous to an erotic relationship, and in support of this view, points out that in certain ceremonies, the wives make their appearance at the same place where landed property is located. If it is true that the dowry comes into the possession of the husband and his clan via the wife—since the clans here are still exogamous in character—

* Roheim, *Die Urformen und der Ursprung des Eigentums,* Archiv für Ethnographie, Vol. 29.

then we are able to comprehend this ritual of eroticized symbolism: *property is transferred with the assistance of sexual interests.* Roheim mentions several tribes in which primitive communism prevails and where the relationship of an owner to his "property" is more formal and ceremonial than practical. A similar situation was described by Malinowski in his remarks on private ownership of canoes among the Trobrianders.

These observations and similar ones compatible with the relationships among the Trobrianders and made by other ethnological scholars enable us to ascribe a more general significance to the marriage dowry. It is the basic mechanism in the transition from mother-right to father-right, from gentile primitive communism to the accumulation of wealth in one family, and thus from the original state of sexual affirmation to one of sexual repression. Future research dealing with other tribes and primitive races, and incorporating this view, will have to determine how widespread the ritual is and how far matriarchal organization has been transformed into patriarchal organization.

Should this be the general rule we would have before us a sociological mechanism in the institutions of marriage and dowry which, in primitive society at the very beginning of class division, creates an exploitative relationship between exploiter and exploited in the same way that the purchase of the commodity "labor power" forms the mechanism of capitalist accumulation in our society.

THE MARRIAGE DOWRY, TRANSITION TO THE COMMODITY

If sex-denying morality, which replaces the original sex-economic regulation of sexual life, is a result of certain economic interests, then it behooves us to consider further the nature of this economic transformation. It is a double transformation: first, there is the advance in production technology, which leads to larger and larger accumulations of wealth in society; and second, there is the division of labor, which introduces the creation of commodities in place of the creation of products for one's own use.

Division of labour in a society, and the corresponding tying down of individuals in a particular calling, develops itself, just as does the division of labour in manufacture, from opposite starting points. Within a family, and after further development within a tribe, there springs up naturally a division of labour, caused by differences of sex and age, a division that is consequently based on a purely physiological foundation, which division enlarges its materials by the expansion of the community, by the increase of population, and more especially, by the conflicts between different tribes, and the subjugation of one tribe by another. On the other hand, the exchange of products springs up at the points where different families, tribes, communities, come in contact; for, in the beginning of civilization, it is not private individuals but families, tribes, etc., that meet on an independent footing. Different communities find different means of production and different means of subsistence in their natural environment. Hence, their modes of production, and of living, and their products are different. It is this spontaneously developed difference which, when different communities come in contact, calls forth the mutual exchange of products, and the consequent conversion of those products into commodities. Exchange does not create the differences between the spheres of production, but brings what are already different into relation, and thus converts them into more or less interdependent branches of the collective production of an enlarged society. In the latter case, the social division of labour arises from the exchange between spheres of production that are originally distinct, and independent of one another. In the former where the physiological division of labour is the starting-point, the particular organs of a compact whole grow loose, and break off, principally owing to the exchange of commodities with foreign communities, and then isolate themselves so far that the sole bond, still connecting the various kinds of work, is the exchange of the products as commodities. In the one case, it is the making dependent what was before independent; in the other case, the making independent what was before dependent. (Marx, *Capital,* New World Paperbacks, p. 351)

We must, therefore, distinguish between exchange within a tribe and exchange between unrelated communities or tribes. Exchange within the tribe leading to the making dependent of what was independent and the making independent of what was dependent appears among the Trobrianders in the most primitive form as the exchange of marriage gifts in the form of garden fruits. It is not ascertainable from Malinowski's discussion whether different varieties of garden products are exchanged, a state of affairs which would indicate that genuine commodity exchange is already in existence. We observe its incipient form in the fact that part of a Trobriander's production is for his own use and the use of his family, while the other and larger part of his production is for the marriage dowry. This would mean that marriage dowry is an early phase of commodity, resulting from the very primitive relationship existing between the brother and the wife's husband. Later it will become clear that the Marxist assumption that exchange of commodities begins with the meeting of two unrelated clans is correct when we hear that exchange from clan to clan within a tribe is ultimately traceable to the clash of two primal clans. However, it is clear and should not be overlooked that we are not confronted with "commodity" in its fullest sense, but rather with an early phase, with the marriage dowry, which necessarily leads to an accumulation of wealth in one family and then to a fully developed system of commodity exchange.

THE FORMATION OF THE PATRIARCHAL FAMILY GROUP AND OF CLASSES

The next result of the marriage dowry mechanism is the formation of the patriarchal family group as it is described by Morgan, Engels, Cunow,* Lippert, Mueller-Lyer,† and others.

Cunow writes:

As the patriarchal family group becomes more and more

* Heinrich Cunow, *Zur Urgeschichte der Ehe und Familie,* supplement of *Neue Zeit,* Dietz Verlag, Nr. 14, 1912–13.
† Mueller-Lyer, *Die Familie,* 2nd ed., Munich, 1918.

clearly defined, its contrast to the totem confederation of the gens becomes more and more pronounced. *The house fathers take on one function after another to which the gentile confederation had formerly been entitled.* The landed property of the family group emerges as a special possession from the totem confederation's previous communal ownership of land, while the earlier claims of inheritance raised by the members of the gens on the property of a deceased person are increasingly restricted in favor of the household members, represented by the head man, the family patriarch. The patriarch also increasingly assumes the judicial functions formerly exercised by the confederation at large.

On the other hand the formation of an aristocratic caste from among the totem chiefs, the beginning division of those previously enjoying equal rights into groups of rich and poor (according to whether one belongs to a rich or to a poor family group), the formation of special professions, and the introduction of prisoners of war and slaves purchased from outside tribes, all lead increasingly to a disintegration and eventual breaking up of the old constitution based upon sexual confederation. *The old organization based upon consanguinity is replaced by a manoral or state organization based upon class distinction.*

The connection between the development of the sexual forms and of the economic forms which determine the former's nature was formulated by Engels for primitive society in the following manner:

The less labor is developed, the smaller the quantity of its products; and also the less the wealth of the society, the more the social order seems to be dominated by sexual ties. The productivity of labor develops more and more under this organization of society, based upon sexual ties; and concomitantly private property and exchange, distinctions in wealth, the use of outside labor power, and the basis of class contradiction develop also: new social elements which, in the course of generations, slave to adopt the old modes of

society to the new conditions, until the impossibility of the
two being united leads to a total restructuring. The old
society, based on sexual ties, is broken up in the clash with
the newly developed social classes; in its place, a new
society appears, consisting of the state, whose subdivisions
are no longer based upon sexual ties, but upon geographical
ties, a society in which family structure is completely dominated by the property structure, and in which the class
contradictions and class struggles freely develop, from
which the content of all previous written history derives.

When distinctions of wealth and the utilization of outside
labor develop along with labor productivity and exchange of
goods, the basis for class contradictions is established. The economic function of the marriage dowry indicates the character
which these transformations assume.

Among these authors the transferral of rights to the benefit
of the chief is usually accepted either without comment or with
some sort of hypothesis. Mueller-Lyer writes, for instance, that
with the developing of wealth by men who have functioned primarily as tradesmen, handcraftsmen, and technicians, the property they have acquired by work, trade or war is brought into
their private possession. Because of this, and also because of
the introduction of the advantageous custom of buying women
away from their clans, matriarchy was eventually undermined in
favor of patriarchy. The sequence would be as follows: wealth
was first created and came into the hands of the male; this led
to mercenary marriage, in which the female became the servant
of the male. The maternal line of succession was forced aside by
father-right. The maternal clan was replaced by the paternal
clan. This hypothesis, however, lacks a demonstration of the
process by which wealth finds its way into the hands of the male;
it does not indicate a mechanism of historical process.

Morgan writes:

As larger fortunes were produced, and the desire to transfer
these fortunes on to the children caused the hereditary
succession to bypass the maternal line in favor of the

paternal line; the material basis for paternal power was
created for the first time.

However, the desire to transfer the fortunes to the children
is itself in need of explanation. The process taking place among
the Trobrianders shows that the desire itself is explainable in
terms of the material interests of the chief or father who must
find recompense in some other relationship for the tribute he has
paid to the husband of his sister. And, as we have seen, he is
able to accomplish this only by means of the cross-cousin marriage, whereby the marriage tribute is brought back to him.
Morgan writes further that the increase in wealth and the desire
to transfer it to the children is the driving force which created
monogamy. The statement is perfectly true, but the desire for a
paternal hereditary succession is itself a product of the material
preponderance of the chief, steadily increasing as a result of his
right to polygamy and the cross-cousin marriage. The developing
enslavement of the lower-class citizenry is a consequence of this
preponderance.

The general increase in wealth is first of all attributable to
the advancing development of primitive technology. As yet it
does not explain the accumulation of wealth in one family and
the rise of two classes, one which becomes steadily poorer, and
the other which becomes steadily richer—the maternal clans on
the one hand and the chief's family on the other. If we agree for
a moment to ignore exogamy and the marriage mechanism, it is
apparent that primitive communist society could have produced
increasing wealth without the accumulation of these goods in
the hands of the chief and his family. The transferral of marriage
tribute in the form of the products of labor, and based on the
brother-husband relationship and the rank division within the
clan, is the crucial factor in bringing about this dichotomy.

The process does not occur immediately, but rather after
various transformations in the relationships of production have
taken place following the introduction of the tribute mechanism.
We shall consider these transformations in a later section. It
does not become an exchange value, a commodity, until pro-

duction has reached a certain level, until the use-object becomes "the quantum of use-value exceeding the immediate needs of its owner." (Marx, *Capital,* I)

> In themselves things are external to human beings and thus alienable. In order for the alienization to take place mutually, human beings need only silently confront these alienable things as private owners and thus as persons independent of one another. (Marx, *Capital,* I)

Among the Trobrianders all brothers are required to produce a surplus over and beyond the products necessary to their own existence, while for the most part the chief accumulates the surplus. He is the first one who begins to feel like a man of private property; and as such, he confronts, on the one hand, the other members of his clan, and on the other hand, other chiefs. Barter trade with outside tribes contributes a great deal to the whole process; it ultimately becomes one of the most important driving forces behind the desire to accumulate, which, for its part, increases interest in "lawful" marriage.

> However, such a relationship of mutual alienation does not exist for the members of a natural communal organization, whether it be in the form of a patriarchal family, of an ancient Indian community, or of an Inca nation, etc. Exchange of commodities begins where communal structure ceases to exist, at the points of conflict with outside communities, or with members of outside communities. (Marx, *Capital,* I)

Here is an apparent contradiction. Marx proceeded from the assumption that the communes in their original form were complete and spontaneously developed community systems. However, when very primitive relationships of exchange are already apparent in these tribes, one may conclude that the tribes were not spontaneous in origin, but rather the result of coalitions of other spontaneously arising communal organizations. This supposition is accurate. *The tribes are composite structures, and the early stage of commodity exchange, the marriage gift, originated from the time of their composition.* A certain amount of ethnological verification is necessary to clinch the argument. (See Chapter 6.)

It is already apparent that Engels had correctly surmised the nature of the relationships: he wrote that the origin of class division was to be found in the antithesis between man and woman. If a woman indeed belongs to the exploited clan, and the man to the clan of exploiters, then the marriage gift activates all processes which aim at enslaving woman, and at bringing the family of the woman, the maternal gens, into the power of the chief. Considered as groups, *the first classes are the maternal and the paternal clans, and, vertically, all maternal clans together, on the one hand, and on the other, the family of the chief.*

In the transitional phase between matriarchy and patriarchy the man is the recipient of the marriage gift. When the patriarchal system is fully developed, the marriage dowry given by the woman to the man loses its meaning, and the relationship turns into its converse: a man wishing to marry must buy his wife from her father through labor or the products of labor. In the patriarchal system woman herself becomes an object of value in the economic interests of her father, a fact which occasioned the custom of wife purchasing, typical of the primitive stage of patriarchy. Along with this custom the practice of marrying out of one's gens into the gens of the husband begins (*enuptio gentis* among the Romans). The marriage gift in the period of transition to the patriarchate returns in its higher stage among the bourgeoisie, in the form of the wife's "dowry." This change from the purchase of wives to the purchase of husbands requires a special explanation which cannot be given here. The carrying away of women by force, as it occurred in prehistory, is not the immediate stage preceding the purchasing of women, but belongs to a much earlier period of development, characterized by the random meeting of primal hordes, foreign to one another and still endogamous. (See the section called "The Origin of Clan Division and of the Incest Taboo.")

5) The Morgan–Engels Theory: Confirmation and Corrections

In outline terms we have already looked into the three basic ethnological conceptions of the history of primitive society: (1) father-right as evolution from mother-right, (2) mother-right as a late or accidental formation, (3) father-right and mother-right as originally coexistent. These considerations were necessary in establishing a basic viewpoint for the analysis of the developmental process among Trobriand Islanders. As we have observed, this process is solely compatible with the theory that father-right evolves from mother-right. We must now undertake a thorough investigation of the theory of Morgan and Engels, since not only are their discoveries and conceptions of the relations between mother-right, the patriarchate, and the development of the family and private property splendidly confirmed by Malinowski's researches (except for a few necessary corrections), but more than that, when supplemented by the discovery of the marriage dowry in the Trobriands, and its socially transforming economic function as described here, their theory becomes a complete conception of primitive history, against which the usual contradictory theories have even less chance of prevailing than at the time when Morgan's and Engels' theses were first established. Roheim, an ethnologist with psychoanalytic background, has made his own discovery of economic primitive communism; however, he bows to the untenable theory of the patriarchal primal horde maintained at any cost, and he does not examine the relationship to sexual forms. Similarly Malinowski overlooks the consequence of his discoveries and their compatibility with those of Morgan.

When we compare the results of Malinowski's research with those of Morgan and the theses of Engels, we encounter a great difficulty in the presence of an otherwise astonishing agreement: outside of a few exceptions which could be interpreted in this sense, we do not find in Morgan or in Engels a description or even a mention of the marriage dowry given by the mother's brother (of the wife's clan) to the sister's husband (the family of the husband). Now, since we have recognized in this institution the central economic mechanism in the transformation of society from mother-right to father-right, and since the transition from mother-right to father-right is otherwise amply described by Morgan, and is, in Engels's account, exactly analogous even to the smallest detail to the process as it occurs among the Trobrianders, there are only two possibilities: either this mechanism is valid only for the Trobriand society and does not otherwise occur, or it is generally valid and has been overlooked. The question is quite important. If marriage dowry as it appears among the Trobrianders represents the first germinal relationship of production leading to the formation of classes and to the creation of antisexual morality, then this fact is highly significant for the understanding of primitive history as well as for the final consolidation of the theory of mother-right.

SUMMARY OF THE MORGAN–ENGELS FINDINGS

Before we establish a relationship between the discoveries of Malinowski with our theses, and then with the Morgan–Engels theory, let us briefly summarize their basic conception.

Morgan, who spent the greater part of his life among the American Iroquois, was the first person to discover the development of the present form of familial institution from certain earlier stages of the family. He also confirmed the universal organization of primitive peoples in *gentes* (clans) with an original maternal line of hereditary succession (natural maternal succession, or mother-right). Before him in 1861 Bachofen had derived his theory of original mother-right from Greek and Roman mythology. The Bachofen theory postulated:

1. unlimited sexual intercourse in prehistoric times, the so-called hetaerism;
2. indeterminate paternity, with, as a result, a maternal line of succession;
3. the primacy of women (gyneocracy);

4. transition to individual marriage through a violation of a primitive religious law whereby all men had a right to the same woman; indulgence for this violation was attained by the surrender of the woman for a limited period of time ("holy prostitution").

Engels correctly noted that Bachofen's derivation of father-right from mother-right is historically accurate, but that it is false insofar as it attributes the transition to a development in religious beliefs.

In opposition to the English scholar MacLennan, whose *Studies in Ancient History,* published in 1886, distinguished between "exogamous" and "endogamous" tribes, two primitive forms of human organization, Morgan discovered that the Iroquois were organized in endogamous tribes which had been formed from exogamous gentes. In these matriarchally organized gentes, inside of which pairings were excluded, Morgan discerned the primitive form from which the patriarchally organized gentes of the Romans and Greeks were later developed. Wherever the gens was discovered, either matriarchal organization or its traces could be demonstrated. It was found, for example, among the Australian aborigines, of whom those from Mt. Gambier lived in one tribe consisting of two gentes or clans (Kroki and Kumite); among the Kamilaroi (originally two, later six clans) on the Darling River in New South Wales; among the Iroquois and all other North American Indians. MacLennan, not comprehending the difference between clan and tribe, discovered the gentile organization among the Kalmucks, Circassians, and the Samoyeds, in India among the Warelis, Magals, Munnipuris. Kovalewski found it among the Schavs, Shefzurs, Svanetians, and other Caucasian peoples, and also among the Celts, Germans (according to Caesar, organized *gentibus cognationibusque*) and in pre-eighteenth-century Scotland and Ireland. Along with Morgan, Arthur Wright discovered it among the Seneca Iroquois. The Greeks and Romans, however, make their historical appearance with patriarchally organized gentes (*gens* is Greek *genos*), later unified in phratries and tribes, and gradually making way for the Greek constitution and monogamous family. According to Bede, gentile organization existed among the Picts with a female line of hereditary succession. Engels derives the term *fora* (gens) of the Langobards and Burgundians from *faran* (wander), which is entirely compatible with the nomadlike way of life of the (natural law and consanguinity) primal horde.

In addition, let us take into account all the previously mentioned tribes where primitive communism has been established, as observed by Roheim, and consider that economic primitive communism tends to exclude a tightly knitted familial organization (indeed it invariably accompanies a gentile form of organization). If it is now shown that exogamy always occurs in relation to individual families, then we are presented with a conception of universal original gentile organization consisting of a maternal line of succession, primitive communism, exogamy in the gens, and endogamy in the tribe. These conclusions then make the conception of an individual family as original organization, whether monogamous or polygamous, completely untenable, even when we momentarily neglect other considerations.

Parallel to the development from the primal horde through the matriarchally organized gens to the patriarchal gens, and from the patriarchal communal family to the patriarchate, is the development described by Morgan from the family based on consanguinity (the parents' generation, the brother-sister generation, and their children, all engaging in sexual relations with one another), through the punaluan family (brother and sister excluded from sexual relations, but several sisters share several brothers of a different clan as husbands), and the pairing family, as still exists among the Trobrianders (single pairing for a limited period of time), and finally to the long-lasting monogamous family of the fully developed patriarchate.

Each of the stages of human development—savagery, barbarism, and civilization—distinguished by Morgan corresponds to a stage in familial development: consanguine family—savagery; the punaluan and pairing family—barbarism; monogamous family—patriarchate and civilization. When Bachofen speaks of "spontaneous generation in the slime" and when Caesar writes of the British, "They have their wives in common, ten or twelve of them, and usually brothers with brothers, and parents with children," "the explanation for this is best found," Engels writes, "in the punaluan family."

The polygamy of the chief, placed by bourgeois scholars at the beginning of human development, is thus a formation of an advanced phase of the matriarchate, when it is already in the process of transformation into the patriarchate. This phase is ascertainable among the Trobriand Islanders. The pairing family corresponds to this phase.

With the exception of the marriage dowry the following correspondences in structure were discovered wherever a thorough study of gentile social organization was made. They are entirely in accord with those of the Trobriand Islanders.

1. From two (Australian aborigines) to eight (Iroquois) gentes or clans united matriarchally or patriarchally (according to the level of development of the economic organization) into tribes.

2. The gens or tribe differentiated by language, customs, and mythology. (Only seldom are these distinctions within tribes. Among the Trobriand Islanders we hear: one clan, one hereditary line, one magic, one garden, one rank, etc.)

3. The chief's son is excluded from the line of hereditary succession; however, the sister's son or the younger brother (e.g., among the Seneca Indians according to Morgan) is the proper heir of the position and the property.

4. The chief of the tribe (sometimes, it is of the gens) is deposable in pure matriarchal organization. He has the right of polygamy; the custom of electing the chief by several gentes gradually becomes supplanted by the custom of electing within one gens and one alone, and finally evolves into hereditary usurpation of the chief's office (transition to patriarchal violence).

According to Morgan, after the chief's office among the Iroquois came to remain in the same gens, it eventually became the province of the sister's son or of the younger brother. Engels writes, "The fact that among the Greeks, under father-right, the office of *basileus* generally passed to the son, or one of the sons, only proves that the probabilities were in favor of the sons succeeding to the office by popular election: it is no proof at all of legal hereditary succession without popular election." (Engels, *Family*, p. 95) Engels believes, correctly, that in the gens of the Iroquois and Greek this constituted the first outlines of special aristocratic families, and that among the Greeks it was the outline of a future hereditarily determined caste of leaders, the monarchy. We are able to follow the course of this process among the Trobrianders exactly as Engels describes it. Through various means (benefits accruing to the son as long as he lives, matriarchal marriage for the son, the institution of cross-cousin marriage), the chief increasingly attempts to usurp the position of his legal heir, his sister's son, and to replace him with his own son. The motive here lies in the material advantages which the chief enjoys through the privileged position of his son. Since the son must care for the household of his mother, the dowry delivered by the chief to his sister returns to the chief himself.

At first the chief is merely a replaceable functionary; among the Greeks he merely fills the role of leadership and possesses no governing powers at all; according to a turn of phrase of Marx, it is merely a matter of a "military democracy." If, however, wealth and concomitant possibilities for the exercise of power have accumulated in his family, the next step is the actual transition to patriarchy through the paternal line of hereditary succession: chief to chief's son. Thus, when Engels writes that father-right first favors the accumulation of wealth in a family by transmission of property to the children and then leads to constitutional changes, in the sense of the first rudiments of hereditary aristocracy and enslavement of the other members of the tribe and gens, his conception is in need of a correction, one which can be derived from the situation among the Trobrianders. The obligation of the tribal brothers to deliver tribute to the chief exists prior to the institution of patriarchy; this leads to the accumulation of wealth in the family of the chief, and consequently to the creation of the patriarchate. The mechanism creating the obligation to render tribute is the marriage dowry from the brother of the wife to her husband, or, on the one hand, from the brothers of the chief's wives from various clans and on the other, from the sons of his sisters, i.e., from his heirs, to their sisters when his sons marry in a cross-cousin marriage. In this manner one clan becomes subordinate to another, and all lower clans become subordinate to the chief's clan and ultimately to the chief's family. The marriage tribute still exists on that level without any sort of para-governmental method of sanction. If a member of a gens fails to fulfill his obligation, there is no official fine or punishment, he merely loses face. The rendering of tribute is maintained merely by custom. Only on the level of a complete patriarchate does legal sanction in the form of official collection occur. Only here may one speak of enslavement. Tacitus speaks in this vein of the "slaves" of the Germans, "who only paid duty." Just as every citizen among the Trobrianders endeavors to present respectable marriage gifts to the chief, the leaders of the gentes among the Germans, the principes, lived in part from the "tributary gifts" of the fellow members of the tribe.

Tacitus emphasizes the particularly close relationship between the mother's brother and his nephew among the Germans. For instance, when hostages were demanded, the nephew (son of the sister) was considered more important than the son, since the nephew was a member of the immediate gens, while the son belonged to an outside gens. Through such parallels with the so thoroughly researched Trobrianders, we may draw rather certain conclusions as to the existence of other institutions not mentioned in connection with them, e.g., the existence of the marriage dowry or a related institution. So long as contrary data are *not* in evidence, the existence of such an exact parallel in gentile organizational forms among most of the more exactly observed tribes makes such an assumption not only permissible, but even mandatory.

When we consider the various implications discoverable in Morgan and Engels, as well as in the compilation of Krische, the assumption that the marriage dowry is to be found *not only* among the Trobrianders becomes even firmer.

THE OCCURRENCE OF THE MARRIAGE
DOWRY IN GENTILE SOCIETY

Engels reports of the Irish gens (sept) that until clan-held land
was transformed into a domain of the English king, the land was
common property of the gens, "so long as it had not already
been converted by the chiefs into their own private domains."
First of all, this indicates a two-sided process of development
leading to the patriarchate and to the enslavement of the
members of the gens: one is an exterior process, brought on by
outside tribes or peoples; and the other functions within the
clan. But how does the latter process arise? The insufficiency of
the material requires us to place those institutions with an identical tendency into one category even when they are to be found
among different tribes; the essential factor is that in all cases,
gentile organization and the brother-sister-sister's son relationship must have been reported. And that is indeed the case here.
Such pairing-marriage, as was discovered among the Trobrianders in the twentieth century, still existed among the Welsh
Celts in the eleventh century. If a marriage ended in divorce, the
wife divided the property, and the husband chose his share. If
the husband dissolved the marriage he was required to return
the dowry together with some other valuables to his wife. If the
wife dissolved the marriage she received less. Among the Trobrianders the dissolution of marriage is accompanied by the
cessation of dowry obligations. Thus the husband and his family
have an interest in maintaining the marriage, but not the family
of the wife. Among the Celts, since the wife supplied the dowry,
and it is not mentioned whether it was a one-time gift or a lasting obligation for her family, we may conclude that a marriage-
gift institution existed obligating the gens of the wife to the gens
of the husband.

According to Krische, Vogel reports that in the matriarchally
organized Nicobar Islands in the Indian Ocean south of the
Andamans, "Women are highly respected and girls have the
right to reject suitors." That of course can only be the case when

the woman brings material advantages to the man in marriage. In beginning father-right, where a wife is purchased, such a right is no longer accorded to women. Further: "Women enjoy full freedom, move about as freely as men, and as mothers they possess the respect and love of their children." Krische writes, "Vogel's report that the girls receive a dowry is to be interpreted that the young couples receive pigs, coconuts, and pandanus trees assigned by the mother's clan." Thus, an obvious dowry obligation on the part of the wife's gens to the family of the husband.

To what extent gentile organizations among the most varied peoples are in harmony with one another, even in details, is indicated by the report of Ratzel, Grosse, and Cunow on the matriarchal Mortlock Islanders of the Carolina Islands. The report permits conclusions about the occurrence of dowry even when it is not directly mentioned, or is merely indirectly implied. There too, just as among the Trobrianders, it is considered disgraceful to show that one has an intimate relationship with his wife. Further, also in analogy with the Trobrianders, the custom exists of what Ratzel calls the men's club-house, into which the girls move at maturity—the *bai,* without doubt similar to the *bukumatula* of the Trobrianders.

Le Bon reports of the Garos of Assam, north of Burma (East India) that earlier the highest authority in each clan was exercised by a woman. Now it is the *laskar,* a man, "who is ordinarily elected from the richest slave-owners, but who requires the approval of the women and remains subject to their council." An obvious transition to the patriarchate: there is a rich chief, but women remain an electoral force. Among the Garos there exists, according to Ratzel, an institution whereby the parents arrange the marriage contract for the bride, a custom admitting only two interpretations: either the bride is purchased by the man, in which case patriarchal purchase marriage is already dominant, or the parents of the woman, since they are obligated to render tribute to the man after marriage, must have an interest in her marriage, as they do in the Trobriands. In any case the dowry mechanism is present, which, judging from the other institutions, should scarcely deviate from that of the Trobrianders. But we shall not maintain that this is definitively the case.

Very important for our proof of the widespread occurrence of the dowry mechanism is a passage from Engels on the Greek gens: "At the time of their entry into history, the Greeks are on the threshold of civilization; between them and the American tribes, of whom we spoke above, lie almost two entire great periods of development. . . . The gens of the Greeks is therefore no longer the archaic gens of the Iroquois; the impress of group marriage is beginning to be a good deal blurred. Mother-right has given way to father-right. . . . After the introduction of father-right the property of a rich heiress would have passed to her husband and thus into another gens on her marriage, but the foundation of all gentile law was now violated and in such a case the girl was not only permitted but *ordered* to marry within the gens, in order that her property should be retained for the gens." (Engels, *Family,* p. 89) This is unmistakable: the wife brought a dowry into the marriage, and since her husband belonged to another gens in the period of full mother-right, the property was transferred from the gens of the wife to the gens of the man. Only father-right had the power, after it had been created by means of the dowry mechanism, to render this process harmless by breaking up clan exogamy, a process which henceforth would have worked to its disadvantage, as earlier it had worked to patriarchal advantage. We have seen that alongside this possibility of development the custom arose among other more fully patriarchal tribes that the male purchases his wife, whereby the dowry returns in her direction and the woman becomes totally enslaved: when she marries, she produces material advantages for her father.

THE MATRIMONIAL CLASSES
OF THE AUSTRALIAN ABORIGINE

Among the Trobrianders we have witnessed an institution of lawful matrimony in the form of cross-cousin marriage, which, in this tribe, is a means of compensating for the burden of the dowry paid by the brother (and his clan) to the spouse of his sister (and his family). His son must marry his niece (sister's daughter) in order for the dowry, at least in part, to return to him. We have further seen that this matrimonial institution, originally a system of tributary compensation, is transformed into a mechanism for accumulating riches in the budding patriarchal family of the chief, who enjoys the right of polygamy. It is no longer merely a mechanism for relieving pressure on him, it is already more: it is a mechanism for getting rich, insofar as he himself is a father and beginning patriarch. Therefore, when we encounter cross-cousin marriage in some other tribe, we may conclude that it also originally fulfilled the function of easing the tribute burden, and later was transformed into an enrichment mechanism.

The cross-cousin marriage institution can be perfectly derived from the matrimonial classes of the Australian Kamilaroi, described by Morgan in *Ancient Society*. A great deal of effort was required before it was possible to determine that the very peculiar and complicated system of Australian matrimonial classes was indeed a simple expression of the general institution of "lawful" cross-cousin marriage. Once we have established that this is indeed the case there can be no doubt, considering the other similarities between the organization of the Australians and the Trobrianders, that the dowry is present in some form from clan to clan. Otherwise the whole intricate order of matrimonial classes would be meaningless.

First we shall reproduce Morgan's portrayal. The Kamilaroi are divided into six gentes, which in turn are divided into two categories in regard to marriage:

A 1. Iguana (Duli), 2. Kangaroo (Murriira), 3. Opossum (Mute); B 4. Emu (Dinoun), 5. Coot (Bilba), 6. Black Snake (Nurai).

Originally it was forbidden for the three gentes to marry among one another because they were divisions of a prime gens.

Thus at first there were only two gentes. We shall call the later ones phratries instead of gentes in accordance with the Greek model. Along with the division of two prime gentes and six daughter gentes divided in two groups there is a division in matrimonial classes. Each of the prime gentes contains four matrimonial classes, thus eight in all, and they are divided according to sex into four male and four female divisions. The eight classes are:

MALE	FEMALE
1. Ippai	1. Ippata
2. Kumbo	2. Buta
3. Murri	3. Mata
4. Kubbi	4. Kapota

Each male and each female matrimonial class (1, 2, 3, and 4) contains a separation of corresponding brothers and sisters. Thus, Ippai and Ippata, Kumbo and Buta, Murri and Mata, Kubbi and Kapota are respectively brothers and sisters and are not allowed to marry. And they are also otherwise subject to restrictions regarding marriage, a fact completely contradicting clan organization, according to which each person from clan A should be able to marry each person from clan B. Mating is only permitted between:

Ippai   and Kapota
Kumbo and Mata
Murri   and Buta
Kubbi   and Ippata

Thus, three fourths are excluded (among which are to be found one fourth of the brothers or sisters, respectively), and only one fourth are available as object choice. The system becomes even more convoluted: the children remain in the maternal gens, since maternal succession is the rule, but inside the gens they move into a matrimonial class different from that of their mothers:

MALE	FEMALE		MALE	FEMALE
Ippai marries	Kapota	Their children are Murri	and Mata
Kumbo marries	Mata	Their children are Kubbi	and Kapota
Murri marries	Buta	Their children are Ippai	and Ippata
Kubbi marries	Ippata	Their children are Kumbo	and Buta

Following the descent we discover that in the female line Kapota is always the mother of Mata, while Mata is always the mother of Kapota; similarly, Ippata is the mother of Buta who is always the mother of Ippata. In the male classes the system is similar.

The Kamilaroi attribute the two original gentes to two primal mothers. The relationship of each child with a certain gens is also indicated by the laws governing marriage. Classes and prime gentes are structured as follows:

PRIME GENS I (Iguana, Kangaroo, Opossum), one primal mother.
CLASSES: Murri, Mata, Kubbi, and Kapota.

PRIME GENS II (Emu, Coot, Black Snake), one primal mother.
CLASSES: Kumbo, Buta, Ippai, and Ippata.

The gens is maintained by the fact that it encompasses all children of its female members in its membership. Morgan writes that it is very probable that originally only two male and two female classes were established, which were later divided into eight classes. We shall be able to corroborate this assumption of Morgan when we bring forward our hypothesis of the origin of exogamy. The fact that the three sub-gentes correspond respectively to the classes that they contain implies that they were originally unified gentes. There must be a meaning for the subdivision into eight classes, as well as for the marriage order which Morgan merely describes without explanation. He merely believes that the class system is earlier than the gens division; the division is a later product, supplanting the earlier system.

This explanation by Morgan is a necessary consequence of his assumption that the gens and the matrimonial sanctions within the gens were the products of a "natural selection." We are able to demonstrate that purely economic interests were responsible for the subdivision into matrimonial classes, just as other conditions brought about the division into four classes. The division into eight matrimonial classes, together with the further limiting of mating possibilities to one fourth of the tribal members of opposite gender was a product of the establishment of the economically disburdening cross-cousin marriage order. We shall see that the burden from which the cross-cousin marriage promised relief, namely the tribute obligation accompanying marriage, was actually a product of the division into four classes.

If we follow the sequence of descent together with the matrimonial order, it turns out that *it is always only sons of brothers who marry the daughters of sisters,* and never the daughters of brothers marrying the sons of sisters, and no other possibility exists. Thus, the complete system of cross-cousin marriage which can have only one purpose, the same purpose as among the Trobrianders: relief of the tribute obligation. Let us now examine this conclusion in reference to a table we derived from Morgan's descriptions. (See graph.)

Examining the individual classes, we see that a Buta woman is not only the daughter of Ippata; at the same time she is the sister's daughter of the Ippai and can only marry a Murri, who, at the same time, is the group son of her mother's brother. We can also see that Murri belongs to one of the three sub-gentes of the original gens, along with her mother and mother's brother. Similarly, Ippata, who marries her cousin Kubi (son of mother's brother), belongs to the same prime gens as her mother Buta and her mother's brother Kimbo. The same holds true for every woman of the Kapota or Mata group. Everywhere we examine a matrimonial class and its mating relationship to another class it is always the brother's son who marries the sister's daughter, and vice versa. According to this class system no other type of marriage is permissible except the cross-cousin marriage. In the next chapter we shall discuss its economic significance.

When the institution of the dowry acquires such an impor-

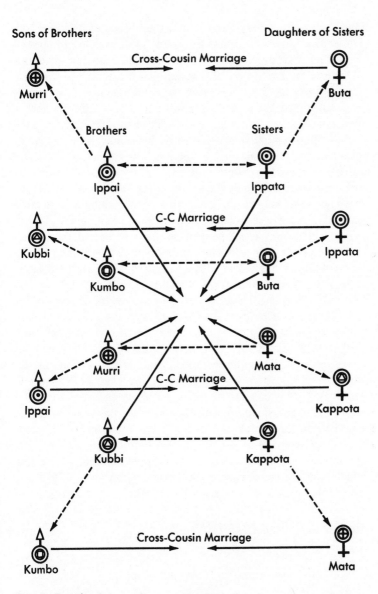

Fig. 5: Graph of Australian matrimonial classes as system of cross-cousin marriage.

tance, we become very interested in the history of its formation. The period in which marital ties were still loose, i.e., the period of pairing marriage, seems obviously allied with the economic institution of the dowry. However, pairing marriage was not present from the very beginning, and the marriage dowry must have developed out of more primitive forms, i.e., from a sort of tribute obligation. But who was required to deliver the tribute, and to whom? What was it that could have shaken the originally incestuous hordes, unaware of the meaning of paternity because pairings were not subject to norms and especially because the father's role in conception was unknown (as it is today among the Trobrianders), to the point that they created a system of such ominous consequence to themselves? Among the Trobrianders and among other peoples we have witnessed the institution of a tribute system, from clan to clan, or from tribe to tribe. Solely within a single clan with a primitive communist structure, tribute, no matter what form it might take, is meaningless and also does not occur. However, we encounter it in the form of the dowry inside a tribe from clan to clan with the purpose of obligating one clan to another, and ultimately of obligating all clans to the chief's family. What is the meaning of this phenomenon? At the moment we know no more than that this economic institution is related to the exogamy of the clan. If we wish to arrive at further conclusions, it is necessary to inquire into the origin of clan exogamy, which entails, at the same time, an inquiry into the prohibition of incest for offspring of the same primal mother. We might avoid this undertaking were we not occasioned by certain realities, which appear strange at first, but which later become coherent when examined more closely.

6) The Origin of Clan Division and of the Incest Taboo

VESTIGES OF PRIMEVAL TIMES

It has been recognized by most scholars studying the prehistory of human society that the question of clan division and the question of the incest taboo in the clan constitute the central problems of prehistoric development. There are a number of more or less plausible hypotheses which have been established in regard to these questions, and we shall later undertake a detailed study of those of Morgan–Engels and Freud. Usually they are characterized by an attempt to derive the prehistoric relationships either from presumed economic relationships of those distant times, or from the nature of human psychic drives. Freud was the first to have recognized that incest taboos imply the existence of original incest wishes. Thanks to the exact information supplied by Malinowski on the current conditions among the Trobrianders it is now possible to derive a hypothesis which answers a number of questions. We would not have constructed a new hypothesis had not certain current institutions among the Trobrianders impressed upon us their significance as vestiges of primeval times and thus permitted a reconstruction.

A hypothesis which attempts to explain the origin of the incest taboo must plausibly fulfill the condition of being materialist, i.e., the taboo must be perceivable as a necessary result of historical realities; a number of questions must be easily answerable; and the hypothesis must not stand in contradiction to the current organization but must basically reconstruct its previous historical stages. Thus, basic elements of the hypothesis must still be in evidence in the present situation.

Our assumption will only be able to claim general validity, then, when it is shown that it delivers a key to other questions besides the ones discussed here.

We derive our hypothesis from the following relationships among the Trobrianders:

1. The brother of the wife is her real provider and the "guardian" of her children. Except for the missing sexual relationship, we could speak of him as the actual spouse. He belongs to the same clan as she. (This is the case everywhere that clan-organization is in effect.)
2. It is his responsibility to render marriage tribute to a man who is a stranger and who has a sexual relationship with his sister.
3. The husband belongs to an alien clan and enjoys nothing

but advantages from his sexual relationship with the sister of the bread-winning brother.

4. Trobriand society is divided into four exogamous clans; these clans have different rank divisions—there are distinguished clans and less distinguished clans.

5. There is a legend to the effect that the primal mother came from a hole, bore two children, a brother and a sister, who lived together in an incestuous relationship. There is also a myth concerning the origin of the clan which states: "It is the rule that, originally, only one couple emerged from one such 'hole,' a brother and a sister; she to start the lineage, he to protect her and look after her affairs. Thus the rule is: one clan, one village, one portion of garden-land, one system of gardening and fishing magic, one pair of brother and sister ancestors, one rank and one pedigree." (Malinowski, p. 497)

The legend provides us with an image of a human society, derived from a brother-and-sister couple, primitive communist in structure, and sanctioning incest. This group is the later clan. At the present time the brother, even today the actual husband of the sister, were it not for the absent sexual relationship, becomes economically obligated to her alien spouse.

What led to this double obligation, the renouncing of sexual relations with the sister and the paying of tribute to her spouse? Let us consider a bit further: the spouse is a member of an outside clan, bearing, just like the clan of the brother, all the marks of an independent horde, originally organized according to mother-right (maternal line). Let us now apply the first part of our hypothesis, that the clans were not the product of a partition occurring in primitive society through exogamy, as is generally assumed; but, on the contrary, that one clan, originally a self-contained primal horde, forced the incest taboo on another clan which also had been self-contained, or rather, had prohibited sexual relations within its own group. The clans, unified at a later time, were thus originally distinct primal hordes. Why did one clan force this taboo upon another clan?

Let us further consider that the primal hordes were hunters and were unsettled, and were forced into a nomadic existence, particularly when natural catastrophes (the exact nature of which is unimportant here) occurred. In this case the young men were forced to go out in search of plunder, to lead an abstinent life, and to wander about for weeks, perhaps for months. Now, when such a horde of hunting men encountered another tribe, two things had to happen. The men of the alien tribe appropriated booty from the men of the group they had encountered, probably killing a number of them in battle; and goaded on especially by sexual abstinence, they took the women, the sisters of the assaulted men, in order to have sexual intercourse with them. If they remained victors it was easy for them to enslave the rest of the vanquished men, to deny them sexual relations with their own sister-wives, and to force them into performing some form of labor.

In the course of centuries, or of millennia, as mankind's numbers steadily increased and folk migrations became more frequent, such catastrophes had to occur more often, and as a consequence, the carrying away of women by force and the implementation of tribute from the brothers became customary. The struggle between primal hordes colliding with one another could not remain one-sided; the revenge of the ambushed on the victors, when the victors pulled out again (later blood revenge of the clan members), or later ambushes on the victor clan by a third clan with the same results must have carried such an insecurity into the life of the originally peacefully organized primal hordes that mutual fear led to a coalition of the hordes into tribes—with the carrying over of the matrilineal succession (clan division of the tribes)—and to a peaceful sanctioning of what had earlier been brought about by violent means: the introduction of exchange marriage from one clan to another. The original prohibition against sexual intercourse within a clan, forced by the victors from an outside clan, became a firm custom within the clan in the course of time. But the original situation whereby male relations of the women, their former husband-brothers, cared for them economically, remained, strengthened by the fact that advantage accrued to the recipient clan.

After the hordes (clans) had coalesced into tribes, exchange marriage (exogamy) had been introduced, and the form of economic support of women within the structure of a single clan had been retained, peace in human society was permitted to return. And since economic provision was based on mutuality, there would have been no further consequence, had not one clan always been originally the victor, and the other clan originally the vanquished. The victor clan was in a position to consider itself "superior," and derived certain economic advantages from this position. The victor clan could, for instance, ordain that its clan elder become the "chief," or leader in war for both clans (tribal chief), and that he enjoy certain privileges, such as receiving a larger share of the marriage dowry or tribute. Thus the right of the chief to polygamy was not necessarily in existence from the very beginning, it is very probably a product of the economic imbalance resulting in itself from the larger share of marriage dowry. The institution of the chief and the rank divisions in the clan are thus easily derivable from the relationship of victor to vanquished.

In summary:

1. Two peaceful primal hordes, living at some distance from one another, and organized according to principles of nature-right, primitive communism, and incest.

2. Economic or natural motives (change of hunting area) brought them into conflict with one another.

3. The men of one primal horde, of necessity abstinent during the period of wandering, attacked the other horde; prohibition of sexual intercourse was introduced in the vanquished clan (the external and ultimately economic origin of the incest taboo), and tribute obligation thrust upon the previous brother-spouse.

4. Revenge of the brothers, mutual annihilation, primal catastrophe: the onset of violence in a previously peaceful primitive society. Mutual fear between the men of the enemy hordes.

5. Reinstitution of peace through coalition and "treaty" regulation of the prior state of affairs; institution of exchange marriage with retention of economic advantages resulting from lasting sexual relationships (future institution of marriage).

6. Adherence to a symbol of the victory of one clan over the other in the form of rank division and common chief. This became the original motive force in the development from nature-right by way of mother-right or father-right.*

Among the Trobrianders we thus observe primal hordes peacefully organized into tribes, but splintered into exogamous clans, a system of tribute rendered by the brothers to their sisters' spouses, the chief's polygamy as a later result of an earlier imbalance of power, and the original maternal line of succession alongside the budding father-right. And we have already seen how class division and negative sexual morality result from this state of affairs.

Let us now examine the strength of our hypothesis in regard to other material and other tribes before we discuss objections and before we consider the Morgan–Engels and Freudian hypotheses on the origin of the incest taboo.

We have assumed that the endogamous tribes of primitive peoples, constituted in clans or gentes, in America as well as Europe, in Australia, India, and Africa, arose through the coalition of unrelated primal hordes, originally enemies to one another and later developing into the gentes—and not through an internal partition. This we concluded from the current situation among the Trobrianders, from which we derived all other conclusions.

a) Morgan and, after him, Engels concluded from the stone tools of the earlier Stone Age, which were discovered in excavations in all continents, that in the epoch of savagery in human history, as fishing developed and fire was discovered, folk migrations occurred quite generally. Morgan postulated for this period that a purely consanguineous family still existed, living in incest. Hunting and cannibalism characterized this phase, in which many Polynesians and Australians still live today. This is not as essential as Morgan's observation that the gens is constituted as a closely knit circle of blood relatives of the female line, which is distinguished from other gentes of the same tribe by its

---

* "Nature-right" could be aligned with the incestuous situation of the primal horde, mother-right with the exogamous clan organization.

own communal institutions of a social and religious nature. Engels postulated, following his view of the distribution of the original gentes into the tribal organization, that it is a matter of a "consolidation" through certain customs of the gentes. Is it not more probable that mythology and other unique characteristics of the gentes are an expression of their original state of being self-contained, rather than a later consolidation of a group which had split off inside the tribe? The unity of the gens is expressed in all its functions wherever we encounter them (maternal line of hereditary succession, common descent, communal ownership of land, clan solidarity, etc.), which distinguish it as a group from the other gentes of the same tribe. Among the Trobrianders the distinct origin of the gentes emerges as clearly as it does among the Iroquois, Romans, etc.

b) Morgan discovered among the Iroquois eight gentes, which derived themselves from various animals. Thus the tribal structure cannot have arisen through a division into gentes, but must have been formed through a coalition of gentes.

c) We observe the advancing process of assimilation of human organizational groups among the Indians as well as among the Romans. It emerges from the legend of the "foundation of Rome," writes Engels, "that the first settlement was established by a number of Latin gentes (one hundred, says the legend), who were united in a tribe; these were soon joined by a Sabellian tribe, also said to have numbered a hundred gentes, and lastly by a third tribe . . ." Engels himself mentions (Engels, *Family,* p. 109) that "very little was still primitive here except the gens. The tribes clearly bear the mark of their artificial composition, even though they are generally composed out of related elements and after the pattern of the old tribe, which was not made but grew." Engels attempts here to maintain the hypothesis of division, which would support Morgan's conception of the origin of exogamy from natural selection. However, we see that the already formed Iroquois evince a behavior at the time of Morgan's observation such as we have assumed for the clan-primal hordes: inwardly peaceful, outwardly warlike; struggle against enemy tribes, finally unification through peace treaty to larger formations with the institution of tribute. This contradicts the theory of division, which is not supported by any current material and is based only on the assumption that population growth and "natural selection" through exclusion of the blood relations brought about internal division together with exogamy. In another passage Morgan himself makes the statement, and Engels enters it into the context of his study, that among various Indian tribes with more than five or six gentes, three or four are united into a special group, "brotherhood," or phratry. Thus here again: after coalition, no partition.

The exact portrayal given by Morgan of the organization of the gens also speaks for its being original in nature: election of the sachem (leader in peace) and of the chief (leader in war), but never of the son of the chief belonging to an outside gens (usually it is the sister's son who is elected); rights of inheritance inside the gens; obligation to mutual protection; blood revenge obligation for all members of the gens when any one of their members is killed by a member of another gens, thus here the gentes become enemies of one another; the gens holding in its authority certain names which only it in the tribe may make use of; certain religious customs. Among the Seneca the tradition was that "bear" and "deer" were the two original gentes from which the others derived.

We also hear from Morgan that tribal names were more accidental in origin than intentionally chosen. It was often the case that tribes received their names from outside tribes; the Germans were first called "german" by the Celts. It remains the task of other studies to determine exactly to what degree, alongside the original coalition of primal clans, an inner partition also occurred. Among the Trobrianders we see, for instance, the tribes divided into clans which are not consanguineous, but the clans are divided again into remotely consanguineous sub-clans.

d) Among the Greeks, higher- and lower-ranking gentes have been observed, just as among the Trobrianders. Our derivation of rank division from the relationship of the original victor clan to the vanquished clan explains this with ease, but it is not clear how the gens, composed of members on an equal footing, could have developed subdivisions of varying rank. This would mean that the later tribe is identical with the original gens, a conclusion which stands in contradiction to the whole organization.

e) The most important evidence that the original clans were foreign to one another is to be found, aside from the tribute obligation of the brothers to the sisters' husbands, in the very curious custom of the courting of women by men, as it occurs not only among the Trobrianders in the form of *ulatile* and *katuyausi* expeditions, but also in other tribes.

Here is a portrayal of the custom which accompanies the courting of a bride among the Samoans.*

From his own observations Kubary very vividly portrays the courtship of a Samoan youth for his chosen one and her amorous response. In the evening at the end of a serene Samoan day young people of both sexes gather on the malae. A young warrior with a very well-groomed appearance stands in the company of a group of young girls. He stands erect and gesticulates with his raised arms so that his head shakes. He stamps with his feet, he kicks and retreats, he raises his arm as if he were armed with a spear, then again he swings his arm around as if he were about to smash an enemy with a club. Without doubt he is a warrior telling his pretty listeners of his exploits and his victories. His listeners are all eyes and ears. One sees what a strong impression his tale makes on the young girls, as they excitedly cheer him on. Suddenly he calls on fellow-tribesmen to join him in communal song. Our story teller is the lead singer, the others present constitute the chorus; however, the singing does not last very long. The warrior arises and positions himself in front of one of the comeliest virgins. She is shy; almost against her will she allows herself to be pushed by her girl friends and carried off into the open fields by the handsome dancer.

A sugarcane field is a safe hiding place for two lovers at night. No one will bother them here in the time of ghosts and spirits. Our couple knows this, and uncaring of possible

* Ploss-Bartels, "Brautwerbung und Brautstand," and "Das Weib in der Natur- und Menschenkunde" in *Geschlecht und Gesellschaft*, No. 13, p. 513.

eavesdroppers they speak. "You know, Lilomajava, that my
parents hate you, our only alternative is the *awanga*." A time
for the *awanga,* the elopement, is agreed upon, it is to take
place in the third night. On the beach of a neighboring
village, quiet reigns, but on the white sands dark figures are
moving about. A *toumalua,* the native travel canoe, is
pushed into the water. The dusky figures have disappeared,
an upright triangular sail is unfurled, and as it glides along
the shore it gradually disappears from view. Only when the
canoe is at a greater distance does the muffled sound of the
Triton horn reach us, a sound which accompanies the happy
couple along the coast, disturbing the natives in their sleep
while announcing to them this special event. The sound
hurries in advance of the couple to Palauli, where the lovers
hope to be out of reach of the parents' anger.

The next morning there is a disturbance in both villages.
The friends of the happy bridegroom run through the village
crying out: "*Awanga! Awanga!* The beautiful Tanetasi and
the brave Lilomajava are *awanga! Awanga!*" The proud
parents of the bride listen in a sullen rage to the public
announcement which seals the fate of their daughter. For a
time there is bad blood on all sides. The old fathers avoid
one another, and young men study their clubs and spears.
The main role, however, is played by the young couple.
After a few weeks everything is forgotten, and the parents
send their daughter a white mat as symbol of forgiveness.
The couple, who had remained away up to this very moment,
returns. The *feiainga* is celebrated, and the white mat,
bearing traces of the bride's celerity, is exchanged against
a part of the dowry. The other part is handed out when the
first child is born. If the couple does not marry out of love,
or if there are no difficulties standing in the way, then
everything is taken care of by the relatives. In earlier times
the *awanga* (bridal elopement) was quite normal in Samoa.

I think we may safely ignore the rather fitful poetic attempts
of the reporter. It is evident that the courting of the bride is not
a serious and urgent situation. Roles are distributed and played,
the villages confront one another in a state of playful animosity.

If these were not historical customs but, rather, current measures of violence, if the parents were really angry, the matter would look quite different. In actuality, everything transpires quite peacefully. At an earlier time bridal elopement was a normal occurrence. We may say that in prehistory it existed as a real carrying away by force (appearance of the suitor as savage warrior), and later as a custom that gradually loses more and more of itself, like a recurrent dream, which re-creates a truly traumatic experience and eventually subsides.

We now wish to add Malinowski's report on the *ulatile* expedition of the Trobriand youths. The lingering tones of the primeval custom of carrying women away by force are un-ambiguously audible:

> There are two forms of *ulatile* expedition to which the word applies in a somewhat technical sense. The first is a matter of necessity: a lover must visit his sweetheart in her own village. If, on one of the several occasions described in the previous section, two people from different communities have become strongly attracted by each other, they will arrange a meeting. As a rule the boy has some intimate friend in the girl's village, and this makes things easier, since this friend will help him. It is a matter of etiquette for the lover to adorn himself for the tryst, and this compels him to observe a certain measure of secrecy. He will not walk on the main road, but surreptitiously steal through the bush. "Like a sorcerer he will go; stop and listen; go sideways and push through the jungle; no one must see him." Thus one of my informants likened such *ulatile* to the clandestine expeditions of sorcerers* who, on their nocturnal expeditions, must not be seen by anybody.

* In the evil spirits and strange sorcerers which play such a great role in the emotional life and mythology of primitives, it is not difficult to recognize the violent acts of alien invaders. The invaders must have appeared as supernatural beings in the imaginations of people who had never seen strangers, and who had never even thought of the possibility of their existence. This is why, after the discovery of America, whites were honored by the natives at first as gods, before the whites had revealed their unequivocally capitalist nature.

As he approaches the village he has to be specially careful. In his own village such a passing intrigue, if discovered, would only arouse the jealousy of the accredited lover and start a minor quarrel. But an erotic poacher caught in another community might be seriously mishandled, not only by the jealous lover, but by all the other boys. He might also bring upon his sweetheart the reproaches of her regular lover. However, the main reason for secrecy is that it is enjoined by custom as a rule of the game. The two usually arrange to meet in the jungle near the girl's village. Sometimes the girl guides her lover to the chosen place by lighting a fire; sometimes they agree to imitate the call of a bird; sometimes she marks the way into the chosen spot of the jungle by tearing the leaves in a pattern or by placing leaves on the road.

Sometimes a group of boys, who have brought away specially pleasant memories of another community from some festive gathering, will decide to go there in a body, on a regular *ulatile* expedition. Here secrecy is necessary, too. For though such expeditions are customary and, in a way, lawful, they constitute an encroachment on the rights of two other groups, the ordinary sweethearts of the *ulatile* boys, and the youths of the other village. If caught by either party the adventurers would have to face a volley of abuse, or even of blows; for girls in the Trobriands can defend their rights by force, and the boys in each community regard their womenfolk as their own preserve. The adventurers would, therefore, usually steal out at night and put on their ornaments outside their village. But once on the main road, they become boisterous and defiant, for this is the proper behavior on such an occasion. There are some special bawdy songs, called *lo'uwa,* to which they keep time as they go along. (p. 265) [The following is an example of the songs:] Hoho! I awake from my sleep, I hear the festive beat of the drums, as they throb with dance music—attracting women with full-dress skirts, with festive skirts on their flanks. With his song on his mouth, with his small drum in his hand, his teeth blackened, Tokivina rhythmically treads in the village

of Wavivi, he walks in dancing rhythm through the village
of Wavivi. (p. 266)

Such songs, I am told, were also sung in olden days to
indicate that the party was neither on the warpath nor on a
sorcery expedition, nor bent on any other real mischief. As
they approach their goal they become quiet again, for they
must not be seen by the village youths. The girls, of course,
know when the expedition is drawing near, for everything
has been previously arranged in detail. The visitor most
familiar with the village creeps near and gives the agreed
signal. One by one the girls sneak out of the houses and
meet their lovers in the bush. Sometimes the girls are
already awaiting them at some pre-arranged meeting place
outside. Should this gathering of lovers be detected, a fight
might ensue, leading, in former times, even to war between
the two communities. (p. 267)

We observe certain contradictions here. On the one hand,
such "amorous expeditions" are a custom, in a certain sense
even "a good right." On the other hand, serious fights sometimes
break out between the *ulatile* youths and the native boys. The
contradiction can best be understood in the context of the previous discussion of the fundamental institutions of Trobriand
society. It is a vestige of prehistoric times in which men of one
primal horde invaded another primal horde.

Here we encounter a specimen of natural jealousy alongside
the full support of society for the institution of amorous expeditions. The clandestine activity seems more likely to be a custom
remaining from the predatory excursions of prehistory, rather
than an activity with a substantial motivation.

It is now appropriate to introduce a passage of Malinowski
concerning a very curious custom, still prevalent today in the
southern Trobriand Islands:

Now this communal weeding when practiced by women of
the villages of Okayaulo, Bwaga, Kumilabwaga, Louya,
Bwadela, or by the villages of Vakuta, gives the weeders a
curious privilege. If they perceive a stranger, a man from

any village but their own, passing within sight, they have the customary right to attack him, a right which by all accounts they exercise with zeal and energy.

The man is the fair game of the women for all that sexual violence, obscene cruelty, filthy pollution, and rough handling can do to him. Thus first they pull off and tear up his pubic leaf, the protection of his modesty and, to a native, the symbol of manly dignity. Then, by masturbatory practices and exhibitionism, they try to produce an erection in their victim and, when their manoeuvres have brought about the desired result, one of them squats over him and inserts his penis into her vagina. After the first ejaculation he may be treated in the same manner by another woman. Worse things are to follow. Some of the women will defecate and micturate all over his body, paying special attention to his face, which they pollute as thoroughly as they can. "A man will vomit, and vomit, and vomit," said a sympathetic informant. Sometimes these furies rub their genitals against his nose and mouth, and use his fingers and toes, in fact, any projecting part of his body, for lascivious purposes. The natives of the north are very much amused by this custom, which they despise or affect to despise. They love to enter into details, and to demonstrate by convincing mimicry. Local informants from the south confirmed this account in all essentials. They were by no means ashamed of their custom, regarding it rather as a sign of the general virility of the district, and passing on any possible opprobrium to the stranger-victims. Some of my local informants added that, at the *yausa,* as this custom is called, women would throw off their fibre skirts, and naked "like a band of *tauva'u* (evil spirits) pounce upon the man." He also added that hair would be torn from the man's head, and that he would be lacerated and beaten till he was too weak to get up and move away. (p. 274)

At the same time, I had a practical demonstration of the contrast between the way in which such a custom is represented by those who have it, and by those who do not. By the local men it was obviously caricatured as a shameful and savage habit; the men's derisive laughter and amused exaggerations were a clear indication of how superior they felt to the benighted heathen who practiced it. But the southern visitors, some of whom had come from Okayaulo and Bwadela, the home of the *yausa,* took, in a later conversation, a differing view, showing no embarrassment whatever. They told me boastfully that no stranger ever dared to enter their district at that time, that they themselves were the only people free to walk about, that their women were the best garden-weeders and the most powerful people on the island. (p. 278)

This custom impresses one as a vestige of women's self-defense in prehistory, as they learned in the course of time to defend themselves against invaders from alien tribes. The form their revenge takes is a mirror image of that which had befallen them; they took away from the man what they had to fear from him: they raped him. Inwardly peaceful, outwardly violent—such was the situation in prehistory. The solution was a merger of the enemy hordes into a peaceful tribe with a further differentiation into clans; this signified the restoration of tranquillity. But traces of violence in the form of rank division and in the form of marriage dowry remained. These traces were destined to lead to new violence.*

Let us briefly enumerate here a few other tribes among which these typical customs occur: marriage dowry, eating together at the marriage solemnization as a symbol of economic merger, and the ritual abduction of women. The fact that we receive reports from all areas, each with its own detail from the whole complex of rituals we observed fully functioning in the Trobriands, encourages the assumption that most people on the earth have undergone a similar fate in the struggle of enemy hordes, followed by a future peaceful settlement and merger.

* In his book *Psychoanalysis of Primitive Cultures,* Roheim describes the ritual of distribution among the Papuans of the Duau area. The ritual is basically in agreement with a similar ritual described by Malinowski. Furthermore, Roheim's report expands our knowledge of the psychic conflicts which accompany the rendering of marriage tribute.

Thus, the ubiquity of the incest taboo and the institution of marriage loses a great deal of its mystery.

Max Ebert, in Volume V of his *Reallexikon der Vorgeschichte,* has compiled a number of ethnological facts, from which we take the following:

> In the whole of southwest Asia the ritual exists whereby couples eat from a common bowl in the marriage ceremony. (p. 248)
>
> Old fables of the Chukchi tell of "abductions" of girls by men of other tribes, by spirits, eagles, whales, ravens, etc. Earlier it also occurred that a few young people would conspire to carry a young girl away by force, would bind her hands and feet, and take her to the house of a man wishing to have her as a wife. Not only men of outside families acted in this manner, even relatives and cousins did so if they had been rejected by the father or by the girl herself. After such an abduction had taken place the parents usually accepted another woman from the family of the abductor as recompense for their daughter. Marriages by elopement when the parents refuse permission are seldom. (Cited from Czaplicka, pp. 72 ff.)
>
> Among the Kamchatkans likewise the man must render service in order to earn a wife. . . . If he has received permission to take his bride, then a ceremony occurs where he must take possession of his bride by force. All the women of the village attempt to protect her from him. She is dressed in several heavy garments that are tightly drawn about her, giving her the appearance of a stuffed figure. The ceremony consists of his attempt to tear her clothes from her and then to touch her genitals with his hand. The other women defend the bride during the ceremony. (p. 251)
>
> In the Andaman Islands marriages among hunting tribes are organized by the older men and women. . . . Occasionally parents even give their small children in marriage. In all cases, parents take charge of the marriage arrangements for their children. But the parents of the young man

do not personally speak with the family of the girl; one or
more of their friends will attempt to function as mediator.
Since, from this moment on, the possibility of marriage is
being considered, the parents of the man avoid speaking
with the parents of the girl, and every communication
between them is transmitted by a third person. In this
manner food and other objects are sent to each other. The
recipient of such a present is always careful to send a return
present of similar value as soon as possible. If the marriage
takes place, then the parents move into a special relationship
to one another, a relationship requiring certain duties. In the
period between the onset of adolescence and marriage,
young men in the Andaman Islands live in a bachelors'
house. (p. 253)

The Koita and Motus tribes of southern New Guinea
have premarital customs similar to those of the Trobrianders,
and similar courtship and marriage customs. Presents, i.e.,
gifts of food, are exchanged by both families for many years.
(p. 253)

Among the Tillamook on the coast of Oregon in northwestern America . . . His relatives collected foodstuffs of
all kinds and also contributed money for the purchase of
the girl. The relatives of the girl promised certain presents
to her . . . After the marriage celebration the people were
served with berries, fish, and meat, and the bride's father
distributed other foods among the relatives of the young
man, which they then took home. (p. 255)

Among the Chukmas of southeast India the groom as
well as the bride are required to appear diffident during the
meal eaten together in the wedding ceremony. (p. 258)
(We are reminded of the self-consciousness of young
married couples in the Trobriands.)

Even today among the Wahabi tribes of the Njed, the
mountain plateau in central Arabia, relationships are maintained solely by marriages taking place between first cousins.
(Cited from E. A. Powell, *The World's Work,* 1923)

Among the Malit Eskimos of the Bering Strait, marriages
between first cousins frequently occur . . . with the thought

that the woman is closer to the man in this case. In an emergency, one believes, the woman would otherwise steal from the man and he would starve. In this case, however, the woman will take care of him. (Cited from Nelson, *The Eskimos About Bering Strait,* 1899, p. 291)

According to Sanderson, cross-cousin marriage occurs among the Wa-Yao, Ba-Ila, Ba-Kaonda, and Gilyaken.

THE MORGAN–ENGELS HYPOTHESIS ON EXOGAMY

In order to explain the prohibition on marriage in the same gens, Morgan and, after him, Engels assumed that in the law of exogamy and in the incest taboo the "principle of natural selection" was in operation. For Morgan, the prohibition of marriage even between collateral brother and sister constitutes "a good illustration of the operation of the principle of natural selection." Engels adds, "There can be no question that the tribes among whom inbreeding was restricted by this advance were bound to develop more quickly and more fully than those among whom marriage between brother and sister remained the rule and the law. How powerfully the influence of this advance made itself felt is seen in the institution which arose directly out of it and went far beyond it—the gens, which forms the basis of the social order of most, if not all, barbarian peoples of the earth. . . ." (*Family,* p. 34) And in discussing the matrimonial classes of the Kamilaroi, according to which brother and sister on the female side are not permitted to marry but second cousins are, Engels says, "What is significant is how the urge towards the prevention of inbreeding asserts itself again and again, feeling its way, however, quite instinctively, without clear consciousness of its aim." (p. 39)

Thus Morgan, like Engels, explains the division of the tribe in gentes as a result of a split in the originally consanguineous tribe. At the time they wrote, both authors were under the influence of the new Darwinian theory of natural selection, which they believed would account for the elimination of incest. Today, this conception is no longer tenable for the following reasons:

1. The harmfulness of incest has never been proved. In the Soviet Union sexual legislation has eliminated punishment for incest. In so doing it correctly took the position that a law prohibiting incest would be meaningless if incest is harmless. Incest has to do with natural selection only in the sense that pathological genetic characteristics might be added together if both brother and sister are unhealthy. But that is identical with the situation where two unrelated persons with the same genetic pathology have children. Furthermore, modern medical research is placing increasingly less value in the area of heredity, and relatively more value in the social factors in widely prevalent diseases, e.g., tuberculosis. To a similar degree the principle of natural selection is also losing its importance.

2. There is a precondition to the assumption of Morgan and Engels: primitive man must have been aware of the role of paternity in conception, and must have been able to judge the supposed harmfulness of incest for posterity and thus to place it in proper perspective. The former cannot have been the case, and Morgan himself is of the opinion in another passage, later confirmed by Malinowski's researches, that in view of the irregularity of sexual life in prehistory, paternity must have been unknown. Further, it is known that human beings lived in incest in the period of savagery for thousands of years without evidence of the slightest harm. There is no proof for the assumption that tribes developed better after the introduction of exogamy, and even if this were the case, the explanation might lie in the advantageous effect of the merger of two different tribes after a peace agreement, an event which might have occasioned a technical or cultural forward development.

3. The most important objection against the argument that exogamy derives from the principle of natural selection is to be found in the fact that primitive tribes could not have eliminated consanguinity even if they had subdivided into gentes. No matter how far such a tribe might have branched out in its brother/sister succession, all children still would have ultimately derived

from the consanguineous primal brother/sister couples. This has been overlooked by Morgan and Engels. It follows from this, however, that one must assume, even to uphold the hypothesis of natural selection, that two primal gentes, nonconsanguineous and completely foreign to one another, were the original bodies of the merger. The gens, therefore, would be an earlier social grouping than the tribe, which, from another side, supports our conception of the merger of gentes into tribes.

Taken together, these arguments would explain the origin of the incest taboo sociologically instead of biologically. Morgan made use of the theory of natural selection in his attempt to explain the complicated matrimonial classes of the Kamilaroi, which first had four divisions, then later eight. He also intended to explain the punaluan institution in reference to these matrimonial classes. They have the following sociological explanation:

Originally there were only four matrimonial classes, two male and two female, which could marry only in crosswise fashion. In a later division eight classes arose. We believe the latter division to be a result of the general introduction of the cross-cousin marriage, introduced with the intent of balancing tribute obligations, just as among the Trobrianders. Thus, as the obligation to render tribute emerged, not only must it have been related to a certain type of marriage order, it must have brought that order into being. The distribution into four classes was a natural result of the partition of two prime gentes into a female (sister's) class and a male (brother's) class, which married crosswise after the peace treaty and merger of the gentes. Thus, the punaluan family was the first phase of the family after merger, just as the consanguineous family was the last before the encounter of the two gentes. Brothers were obligated to render marriage dowry to their wives' husbands, or at least to give gifts related to the pairing. The victor tribe had secured certain advantages for itself according to our hypothesis, for example, special tribute for the communal chief or war leader, who belonged to the most "prominent" clan. This meant a one-sided burden for the originally defeated clan. The need for relief of this burden, as can only be guaranteed by cross-cousin marriage, must have emerged. The further division into eight classes, which is the complete system of compensatory pairings, was a result of this need for relief from the burden. The rest is concealed in darkness. However, as we have observed among the Trobrianders, the division into eight classes did not eliminate the imbalance in favor of the chief; indeed, perhaps it gave the first impetus to a redress of the losses which the division into eight classes had meant for him. The substantiation or refutation of this hypothesis is a matter for future research.

THE FREUDIAN HYPOTHESIS OF PRIMAL PARRICIDE

In his reconstruction of prehistoric conditions, Freud takes the Darwinian view that there are families among the apes who live in isolation from other groups, and whose leading male does not tolerate any other male. The "primal father," conceived according to the model of this ape leader, drove out all adolescent sons in the Freudian conception. The expelled brothers were eventually able to band together, kill the father, devour him, and thus put an end to the primal horde. Freud used here an observation of Atkinson that it frequently occurred that the lead stallion of a herd of horses came into conflict with other stallions as they roamed about. However, Freud also quotes Atkinson's opinion to the effect that the horde organization falls apart after the resulting struggle among the sons, a situation in which no new organization can come into existence. In contrast, Freud believes that a great many things owe their beginnings to this very slaying of the primal father: "social organization, moral restrictions and religion." (*Totem and Taboo,* p. 183) In order to find it plausible that religion and social order are the results of primal parricide, Freud believes, "we need only assume that the group of brothers banded together were dominated by the same contradictory feelings towards the father which we can demonstrate as the content of ambivalence of the father complex in all our children and in neurotics. They hated the father who stood so powerfully in the way of their sexual demands and their desire for power, but they also loved and admired him. After they had satisfied their hate by his removal and had carried out their wish for identification with him, the suppressed tender impulses had to assert themselves. This took place in the form of remorse . . . What the father's presence had formerly prevented they themselves now prohibited in the psychic situation of 'subsequent obedience' which we know so well from psychoanalysis. They undid their deed by declaring that the killing of the father substitute, the totem, was not allowed, and renounced the fruits of their deed by denying themselves the liberated women. Thus they created two fundamental taboos of totemism out of the sense of guilt of the son" (*ibid.*, p. 185), these being the prohibition against incest and against the killing of the totem animal. Freud considers the totem animal to be a "natural and appropriate substitute for the father."

A number of theories have since been based on the hypothesis of primal parricide. These have included not only the later work of Freud himself, but also the whole psychoanalytic ethnology developed by Roheim, Reik, and other Freudian pupils. Since the conceptions we have developed here contradict this hypothesis it is necessary to examine its basic elements more closely.

It appears to be a complete conception of prehistoric development, and possesses a certain plausibility at first because it takes well-known and thoroughly tested clinical results from analytic practice, applies them to primitive times, and explains, apparently without effort, the two most essential questions, totemism and the origin of the incest taboo. In spite of this it contains a number of unsupported assumptions.

1. The first assumption is that the primal horde had a powerful adult male as father of the entire group, living with several women, wives, daughters, and several sons. If the primal father, assuming that he existed, drove his sons out as they matured (an event that cannot have occurred merely at one time and at one place, but must have occurred frequently everywhere in the world in a typical fashion; and the event must have recurred for hundreds, perhaps for thousands, of years), then it cannot be understood how the primal hordes were able to reproduce, to

survive the struggle with nature, and to create civilization. Further: when did the expulsion of the sons take place? Sexual intercourse begins very early among primitives, long before puberty. Were children of the male sex who copulated driven out? The conclusion is obviously absurd.

If, with Roheim, we base our view on the saga of the father slain in prehistoric times, we must not overlook a fact that is clearly implied by the clan division, namely that the later father group was originally an alien group, against whom the later group of sons struggled, and not because of their relationship as sons, but because of the original animosity existing between the two unrelated hordes. This has nothing to do with incest. The Oedipus complex could only have arisen after the unification of the hordes, and after the formation of firmly entrenched families.

2. In addition, we have the assumption that the sons denied themselves sexual relations with their mothers and sisters; thus one group was without men, and the other group, as before, was without women. How was it possible that this group did not become extinct? If one wishes to hold to the view that the men took women from other groups, one loses the way in nebulous speculations, considering the sparse population of the world in those times. This way leads one astray.

3. Further assumptions that must also be correct if the hypothesis is to be upheld are (a) the assumption that the male is naturally violently jealous, and (b) the assumption that the emotions are biologically ambivalent. However, when we consider the widely spread custom of sexual festivals as they occurred among primitives, particularly as described by Malinowski in his account of the sexual life of the Trobrianders where jealousy has been extinguished, and further, the fact that violent jealousy in the form of its existence in our society first occurred as marriage ties came into being, and, moreover, that marriage is a later acquisition of human society, then the assumption of jealousy in savage man as it is postulated by Freud becomes doubtful. And ambivalence (limitation of sexual gratification, consequent emergence of hate-filled attitudes in regard to the inadequate environment) first has to be tested in connection with the social factors which bring it about. The experience of

psychoanalysis in dealing with mentally ill persons has clearly shown that ambivalence is perhaps present as a potential attitude in one capacity or another of the psychic apparatus, but what we witness in a sick patient is a case with a historical development brought about by the restriction of his sexual needs, a restriction which does not exist in primitive society. Hence, ambivalence is basically social in origin, depending on gratification of libidinous needs for its form and intensity. Therefore, as a social product, it cannot be considered the basis of human civilization. We have observed in the rites of mourning of the Trobrianders how a specific historical relationship of production creates ambivalence of emotions. If the relatives of the woman did not stand in an exploitative relationship to the spouse, they would have no reason to be ambivalent, and no need to conceal their hatred with strict rites of mourning. If ambivalence characterizes the psychic life of people in the twentieth century, then one must inquire into the sociological motives, and one must be careful not to apply the results indiscriminately to primitive peoples, who matured and lived under different conditions. We may be certain of these facts: because it knows the truth, the Trobriand child does not develop erroneous sexual theories; because it is able to satisfy its desires, it does not repress any sexual desires except for the incest wish; because the social atmosphere does not give boys a preferred position as it does in our society, young girls do not develop penis envy fixations or masculinity complexes. These things only begin as patriarchal violence and male hereditary privileges begin. Thus, we do not deny analytic findings, but we do not conceive of them as biological in origin. We consider them as historical formations, and we attempt to place them in proper perspective to the history of society.

4. The hypothesis that the sons deny themselves incest because of guilt feelings is based upon the other hypothesis, that emotions are *naturally* ambivalent. Morality is supposed to have emerged from this. It is a *petitio principii*. One of the assumptions made is the same as that which is to be proved. Feelings of guilt are already the expression of a moral reaction, and therefore cannot be used to explain the development of morality.

Freud interpreted the religious concept of the fall from grace, from which Jesus was to save the world, as an expression of a prehistoric act of murder. On the other hand, the biblical myth of Adam and Eve as well as the Catholic ideology of hereditary sin are revealed as basically myths of a sexual transgression, as conceptions of a sin against a sexual taboo. This does not exclude the possibility that the sexual transgression was accompanied by an act of murder. Our derivation of the incest prohibition implicitly contains the historical primal murder in the clash of two primal unrelated clans. Undoubtedly the first principles of morality derived from that clash. But in another sense, they are derived from sexual prohibitions that have nothing to do with the Oedipus complex, because the complex is historically younger than sexual repression, and as we have already mentioned, the later group of fathers was originally an alien horde of men. Thus the notion of primal parricide entails a mixing of two chronologically unrelated situations: a bloody struggle with men who were not the fathers, but from whose clan the future real fathers, who were not murdered, would emerge.

5. The Freudian hypothesis does not permit the possibility that incest occurred in prehistoric times. However, it has been proved mythologically and by direct observation that incest existed and lasted for thousands of years. Also, the fact that the father's role in conception was not understood, as is easily derived from the sexual life of primitive peoples, stands in contradiction to the Freudian view.*

6. The Freudian conception stands in contradiction to the typical sagas of the origin of the clans from two or more primal

---

* One might object with a certain degree of justification that ignorance of paternity is compatible with the state of promiscuity but that it is not compatible with monogamous pairing marriage. It would not be difficult, considering the behavior of the Trobrianders in regard to the paternity question, to conclude that knowledge of the role of paternity is repressed. The assumption of such a repression does not contradict the fact of ignorance in the state of promiscuity. It is certainly conceivable that, after the merger of the hordes, the affective rejection of the men who were strangers to the clan was so intense and so deep that no one wanted to recognize paternity. This theory, however, is first in need of thorough research. It is also questionable whether the acknowledgment of paternity was actually capable of damaging the matriarchal system of clan consanguinity.

mothers or primal brother-sister couples. It rests on the assumption of son–mother incest; in reality, brother–sister incest was crucial. The evidence for the existence of a primal father which Roheim wished to supply is always based on the existence of a totem animal. It is, however, first necessary to demonstrate that the totem animal was originally intended to represent the primal father. Neither the interpretation which holds that the sister is a substitute for the mother as the object of incestuous desires, nor the interpretation which holds that the totem was originally a father substitute, can be proved without reference to a historical context.

7. According to Freud, the taboo against incest should be understood in terms of the family; the taboo, however, dominates the whole clan; since the family is a much later formation, restriction according to whether one belongs to a father–mother–child group is a later product and is of secondary importance for the prehistoric period.

In summary we must say that the Freudian hypothesis contradicts a number of primitive society's basic institutions (two incestuous primal clans, incest taboo clan-wide, promiscuity and incest in the primal phase of development, priority of the matrilineal succession, etc.), and neglects the historical development of the family in its relation to the development of the economy to such an extent that the hypothesis becomes difficult to maintain.

Our discussion explains the prohibition against eating the totem animal and against continuing to live in incest as historical results of the prohibition against hunting and eating the characteristic animal of the hunting area and the prohibition against the clan's possessing their own women. These did not arise within the gens but were imposed on the one horde from the outside by the victorious group. In certain festivities of primitives where custom requires indiscriminate sexual intercourse and where the totem animal is eaten, we catch sight of an area where the old rules that once existed among two hordes break through once again and meet with clan sanction. The festivities are an expression of nostalgia for the organization of the incestuous primal horde, where there was more peace and the only obligation was the taking care of one's own clan. In particular these festivities break through the barrier of primitive pairing marriage, and occasionally even the incest barrier; thus, they are a relatively late formation in human society. Freud's view that the festivities of the totem meal are symbolic of primal parricide contradicts, even from Freud's standpoint, the fact that the incest barrier is broken at such festivals. Do the men, on a much higher level of social organization, permit themselves the very thing they had denied themselves on the totally un-civilized level of savagery? Did they then, as savages, have more feelings of guilt than they do now? And if so, why?

It is conceivable that further research will uncover the rela-tionship between the sagas of primal parricide and the clashes of unrelated primal hordes. Secondarily, the totem animal acquired the function of primal mother symbol, and later in the patri-archal organization, the function of primal father symbol. Thus, we believe that the Freudian conception of the totem as a first sketch of a religious concept is correct, not as an ideal cause of religion in general but as a description of processes in primitive society which, together with the need to explain natural phe-nomena, were able to form religious concepts. If, in the patri-archal epoch, man created gods in the image of the father, then in earlier times the model must have been the animal type he hunted, thoughts of which undoubtedly occupied him a great deal; or the model was the primal mother. The careful reader of Malinowski will discover that totemism is not nearly so impor-tant as other sexual and economic institutions. Ultimately, the *value* of an institution cannot be ignored if one wishes to under-stand correctly its relationship to the original organization. The task remains now to undertake a new and thorough study of totemism from the standpoint of matriarchal theory, whereby the previously undiscovered unconscious meanings of the various religious concepts and customs cannot be disregarded. Our critique is directed against the previous method of psycho-analytic research dealing with religious matters. It conjectures about the genesis of a religious phenomenon merely on the basis of its implicit meaning; thus, meaning and genesis are treated as identical. In order to comprehend genetically the irrational meaning of a hysterical symptom existing in the present, we must be able to place the meaning in the developmental history of the symptom, at the point where what is now irrational was thoroughly rational. Similarly, we must place the implicit meaning of a mythological or religious concept into the historical context of the social process, i.e., we must comprehend the significance of the religious idea in its socio-economic genesis and function. Thus the meaning of a given totem conception might well be the father conception, while its origin might be that of an animal of hunt, only later becoming the symbolic substitute for the father or the mother. This is a necessary deduction from the change in the historical function of the chief.

As he studied prehistory, Freud, like most ethnologists, saw only the fact which from the standpoint of matriarchal theory is confusing at first, that all organizations, even the most primitive, exhibit a chief and contain families. Another fact is obscured in this, the fact that the chief was not—wherever an advanced patriarchate was not yet in evidence—a ruler and patriarch in our sense, and that the family, in the beginning of history, does not exist in contradiction to the organization of the self-contained gentes. The family organization inside the gens obscured this fact from the eyes of most observers because they could not free themselves from the theory of the priority of the present family, and their line of thought was therefore unhistorical. The "chief" originally got on well with the maternal succession, and only at a later period did he move into contradiction to it as he became a patriarch. Similarly, monogamous family organization, in the process of gradual development, gets on well with the clan organization until, hand in hand with the changes in the chief's function, it moves into contradiction to the clan organization, and indeed becomes the destroyer of the clan. The ignoring of the Morgan–Engels theory, which has been so splendidly confirmed in its main points by Malinowski, has a concrete sociological implication. If one holds to the priority of the patriarchate and its family forms, then morality was always in existence, as part of man's nature.

However, the discoveries of Morgan show that everything is in a state of continual development and change. Negative sexual morality irrupted once in ancient society and will disappear in the future from human society. But what will take its place?

The Problem
of Sexual Economy

1) Historical Summary: An Overview

From earliest gentile society to the present capitalist state the distinctive phases of societal development have always exhibited two interacting processes. The first process, spanning from the stage of primitive economic communism to the capitalist state, has to do with the development of the instruments of production, with the expansion and increase of production, and with the correspondingly awakened human needs. Ultimately this process leads to a concentration of the ownership of production in the hands of a dominant social group, the capitalists. On the other hand, another process leads from natural sexual freedom, and from the gentile family based upon consanguinity, to the ideology of extramarital asceticism and permanent monogamous marriage. It moves along the lines of a continuous confinement, repression, and distortion of genital sexuality. If one begins at the terminal points of societal development, i.e., with the present forms of economic and sexual organization, and follows their development backward, one arrives finally at a point of confluence between economic and sexual organization; namely, one arrives at the point where private property and class division originate from the forms of sexual organization in gentile society, forms which, in the course of development, had enabled goods produced in primitive communist society to be accumulated in the family of the chief. We have observed how the first claims

of avarice and possessory interest flared up in the very beginnings of the present private economy, and how the first contradictions in the human community came into being, of which
Engels correctly notes,* "The first class opposition that appears
in history coincides with the development of the antagonism
between man and woman in monogamous marriage, and the first
class oppression coincides with that of the female sex by the
male [now we may say: with that of the clan of the female by
the clan of the male, W.R.]. Monogamous marriage was a great
historical step forward; nevertheless, together with slavery and
private wealth, it opens the period that has lasted until today in
which every step forward is also relatively a step backward, in
which prosperity and development for some is won through the
misery and frustration of others. It is the cellular form of civilized society, in which the nature of the oppositions and contradictions fully active in the society can already be studied."
(Engels, *Origin,* p. 58) And further (p. 60): "Thus, wherever
the monogamous family remains true to its historical origins and
clearly reveals the antagonism between the man and the woman
expressed in the man's exclusive supremacy, it exhibits in minia-
ture the same oppositions and contradictions as those in which
society has been moving, without power to resolve or overcome
them, ever since it split into classes at the beginning of civilization."

Thus the advance of technology was paralleled by a decline
in sexual culture. The natural ethics of primitive matriarchal
society, characterized by sexual freedom, were immeasurably
superior to the morality of the capitalist era. This can be seen
most clearly in the fact that antisocial sexual behavior (rape,
sexual murder, etc.) does not occur in the early societies. Any
mention of cultural or ethical progress remains empty talk so
long as this contrast in social development is not recognized, so
long as the "savage" is considered the prototype of an "un-
civilized" and therefore reprehensible human being. His sexual
culture is judged from the point of view of private enterprise
morality which equates "cultural" with "pure," i.e., asexual

* Engels, *Origin of the Family.*

(compare with fascist racial theories). Should monogamy be considered a step forward or a step backward? This formulation of the question is nonhistorical, nondialectical, abstract, and judgmental. Exploitation came into existence with the development of the means of production. Should exploitation, then, be considered a "step forward" or a "step backward"? If we attempt to answer the question in this form we will be led astray. We must inquire rather into the developmental tendencies of the society, and we are only able to determine whether the tendencies move in the direction of intensifying or of eliminating suffering. In the latter case, the subjective ingredient which is revolutionary theory performs a service by reaching to the wheel of history and turning it forward more rapidly.

Monogamy resulted from a concentration of wealth in the hands of one man, or as Engels describes it, from the need "to bequeath this wealth to the man's children and to no one else." The demand for female monogamy is a subsequent product of this relationship. If one traces the development of human society further back, beyond the point where the accumulation of wealth in one man's hands and monogamous marriage had their common origin, one is led to social organizations that are primarily characterized by and determined by sexuality, while production is almost entirely lacking in development and is based upon communal economy, or upon primitive communism.* This societal organization is intruded upon by a process consisting of a steadily increasing confinement and suppression of genital freedom. It first becomes apparent in the prohibition against sexual intercourse within the clan, i.e., the group of all maternally consanguineous relatives. Considered from the period of its conception, this process of sexual suppression is older than the class conflict between male and female; it is this process which first leads to class antagonism. Allusions to prehistoric conditions are discernible in mythology. They tell of elemental catastrophes

---

* Engels: "The lower the development of labor, and the more limited the amount of its products, and consequently the more limited also the wealth of the society, the more the social order is found to be dominated by kinship groups." (*Origin of the Family*, p. 5)

which threatened the economic existence of early man, and which brought about social movements from which the first impulse toward sexual restriction in the form of incest prohibition derived.* The growth of taboos and restrictions in respect to genitality moved hand in hand with the expansion of the material interests of certain groups in primitive society. The process as it occurs among the Trobrianders demonstrates that the interests in question are the interests of the chief's family against those of the clan. Prehistoric times are basically similar to our own in that the material conditions of the social system created certain legal and moral institutions, such as the incest prohibition within the clan, the marriage order, etc., which, because they ideologically infused every member of the society, were reproduced in the individual.

If we adhere to Morgan's classification of the development of human society in the stages of savagery, barbarism, and civilization, then the crucial turning point in the development from primitive communism to private property and interest in accumulation is to be found in the transition from savagery to barbarism. The turning point is primarily characterized by the dissolution of matriarchal society and the evolution of patriarchal violence. Chronologically the extent of human history before this moment is many times greater than the relatively brief span comprised by the period of private enterprise, which followed it. Since this turning point, social life has been characterized by the economic interests of the class constituted by the owners of the instruments of production, and by the conflicting interests of the oppressed class, while in previous society sexual interests had been predominant. If private enterprise and class division have characterized social structure since this turning point, previously the determining factor was the sexual partner-

---

* I am not able to deliver a professional verdict on the correctness of Hörbiger's theory of "glacial cosmogony." However, his explanation of the deluge legend, which has been discovered among most of the world's peoples and which he derives from actual cosmic catastrophes, is most assuredly deserving of our attention. His theory casts an entirely new light on the specific conditions of prehistoric society.

ship,* but, of course, the fact remains that even then the primitive relationships of production constituted the basis upon which the predominantly sexually oriented society could build. The interests of individuals were primarily sexual in nature, and they were gratified; the material demands were modest. Possessory interests and greed increased in proportion to the degree that sexual interests had to be suppressed. In a certain phase of human history the material conditions of life (at first the coalition of the primal hordes, later the preponderant force of the marriage dowry) brought about sexual restriction and consequent sexual repression. Psychic interests were then set free for a certain form of economic evolution, i.e., the private economy. The interests were those of greed and the desire to accumulate. They developed at the expense of the genital interests.†

We are now confronted with a question which is crucial for the history of sexual economy; namely, whether sexual restriction is a matter of the development of human society in general, or whether it is a matter of a specific economic and social stage of this development. The former explanation is assumed by Freud and most of his pupils, and even by a few Marxists (e.g., Salkind). On the basis of the present study we deny that sexual repression can be considered fundamental to the development of human society in general because, among other reasons, we recognize such an explanation as a mechanistic and undialectical interpretation, which can be refuted practically in the present and refuted historically through analysis of man's history. In

* "It soon becomes apparent that in the early stages of savagery, within certain prescribed limits, male and female groupings determined the nucleus of the social system. The marital rights and privileges arising within a group developed into a wondrous system which became the basis upon which society was constituted." (Morgan, *Ancient Society*).
† Thus it is incorrect when psychoanalytic ethnologists attribute the culture of such primitive peoples to their constellation of instincts, as when they speak of anal-sadistic culture. In reality, the altered structure of instincts was created by the social process, which first restricted genitality, and on a secondary level, brought about a strengthening of the non-genital partial drives. The desire for accumulation is first brought about by purely economic factors, but as it becomes anchored in psychic structure, it avails itself of the anal tendencies which were brought out by sexual restriction.

addition, the study of the relationship between the economic order and the sexual order has shown otherwise.

Because prior psychoanalytic research considered cultural processes primarily as a function of instinctual conflicts rather than as a function of social processes, it obscured a problem in its area of research which remains of incalculable importance. If we consider instinctual conflict as a result of a clash between primitive needs (hunger, sexual needs) and the conditions of existence (economy, natural influences, technology), then we are able not only to do justice to the dominant role that social circumstance plays but also to grasp at the same time the problem of the relationship between the socio-economic basis and the ideological superstructure of society, and thus to attain an entry into the understanding of the ideological process of a society, both in its conservative and its revolutionary form. This last section is devoted primarily to this question.

At first, however, it is necessary to direct some attention to the role of subjective factors in the history of the gratification of needs.

2) *The Gratification of Needs and Social Reality*

From early on, Engels had an inkling of the influence of sexuality on the composition and development of human society. If his opinions in this matter did not ultimately prevail, the reason is to be found in the fact that his conception of sexuality did not take into consideration the function of sexual pleasure, and concentrated solely on the reproductive functions of sexuality. Furthermore, the process of sexual repression and its economic background must have been unknown to him because of the level of psychological knowledge in his time. Engels, intending to integrate sexuality into the materialist conception of history as a factor influencing the formation of history, wrote in the preface of his work *The Origin of the Family:*

According to the materialistic conception, the determining factor in history is, in the final instance, the production and reproduction of the immediate essentials of life. This, again, is of a twofold character. On the one side, the production of the means of existence, of articles of food and clothing, dwellings, and of the tools necessary for that production; on the other side, the production of human beings themselves, the propagation of the species. The social organization under which the people of a particular epoch and a particular country live is determined by both kinds of production: by the stage of development of labor on the one hand and of the family on the other. (p. 5)

This point of view can now be amended. Mankind exists with two basic physiological needs, the need for nourishment and the sexual need, which, for purposes of gratification, exist in a state of mutual interaction. The exact manner in which society procures the gratification of these needs has been exhaustively treated in Marxist sociology. Since the need for nourishment is not subject to the sublimation which the sexual drive can undergo, but must simply be satisfied for better or for worse, it does not have the elaborate articulated role that the sexual drive attains in the composition of the psychic apparatus.

In a discussion of the needs whose gratification is useful to production, Marx in *Das Kapital* distinguishes between two sorts of needs, those which originate from the "stomach," and those which originate from the "imagination." Now, as psychoanalytic research has demonstrated, the needs of "imagination" as Marx described them have been revealed to be transpositions and the developmental offspring of the variable sex drives.

These subjective factors* never appear in the history of man and society as a need to reproduce, but rather as a need to eliminate sexual tension brought about by internal secretion and external attraction, i.e., as a desire for sexual gratification. The

* (*1934*) "Subjective factor" means, in today's political psychology, basically the average psychic structure of people in a given society. The structure itself is determined through the libidinous forces which brought it into being. (See my "What Is Class Consciousness?")

propagation of the species, which Engels in his book *The Origin of the Family* contrasts with the production of foodstuffs, is an objective result of the sexual drive but not a subjective one, in the sense that foodstuffs are subjectively produced for the purpose of satisfying the need for nourishment. Thus, a parallel to the production of foods does not exist. Sexuality does not occur as a reproductive function until a comparatively very late stage has been reached, i.e., after puberty, whereas the actual parallel to the gratification of the need for nourishment, i.e., the function of sexual gratification, appears immediately after birth, concomitant with the nourishment instinct. Only in this subjective sense, as a need to remove a certain tension through sexual pleasure, including its sublimated forms (spirit of invention, technical interest, scientific research), may we consider sexuality as a motivating factor in history, analogous to hunger.

Just as the nourishment instinct can be represented subjectively as hunger and objectively as a "tendency" whose function is to preserve the individual, the sexual drive can be seen subjectively as a need for a relaxing sexual gratification and objectively as a "tendency" whose function is to maintain the species. These "objective tendencies" are not the concrete realities; they are plain cumulative results. In reality it is as little meaningful to speak of a tendency whose function is to preserve the species as it is to speak of a tendency whose function is to preserve the individual. Both forms of preservation represent data in explanation of which the phrase "objective tendencies" is applied. In reality, their existence is secured by functions of the physiological apparatus: the tension in the stomach, announced on a psychic level as hunger, drives one (as in the biological "drive") to partake of food and thus maintains the individual; the tension in the sexual organs, particularly in the genitals, announced on a psychic level as a desire for sexual activity (desire for gratification, desire for pleasure), drives one to sexual activity in sexual intercourse and therefore maintains the species. In this process the extrapolation of "objective tendency" loses its meaning. Neither in the case of hunger nor in the case of sexual gratification does the individual entertain thoughts of self or species preservation. We must therefore ask:

1. What is the natural course of gratification of hunger and sexuality? (Physiology of metabolism, physiology of sexual organs, sexual psychology.)
2. How is society structured? Does it guarantee satisfaction of these basic needs or not; does it encourage or does it inhibit satisfaction? (Sociological treatment of needs.)
3. If society interferes with the satisfaction of these needs, instead of encouraging them, then what are the reasons? Which class or group in society is responsible? (Political economy and sociology.)

Thus, just as we are able to speak of an economy of the nutritional regimen, of the manner in which society enables a gratification of the nutritional needs of all its members, we must speak of an economy of sexuality: the form in which society regulates, encourages, or inhibits the gratification of the sexual drive. Just as there is an orderly or disorderly metabolism (the regimen of the nutritional instinct), there is an orderly or disorderly sexual regimen in individuals. Whether order or disorder prevails is a question of the manner in which society and its institutions behave in regard to the need for gratification. It is true for capitalist society that the majority of its members have a disorderly and uneconomic nourishment regimen forced upon them. It is equally true that they are forced to put up with an uneconomic sexual regimen. The task remains to investigate why and with which of its institutions society creates in different epochs its varying solutions to the needs of hunger and sexuality. Marx has given us an exhaustive sociological explanation of the disturbed nutritive regimen of the majority of our society's members: class division and exploitation. Similarly, certain relationships of production and corresponding interests of the ruling class are the cause of the disorderly sexual regimen and disturbed sexual economy of the majority of the members of class society in all its consequence.

Accordingly, we must distinguish between the sexual economy of the individual and the sexual economy established by society. The former is, aside from constitutional variations that exist between different individuals, primarily conditioned by the sexual economy of society. Whether we view the sexual regimen as orderly or disorderly is dependent on a clinical judgment we make according to the amount of tension neutralization characterizing the psychic apparatus of an average individual; furthermore, our judgment depends on attempts undertaken by the psychic apparatus to bring about the tension neutralization. In other writings* I have attempted to describe these characteristics: genital gratification in the sense of orgastic potency and a free-flowing performance of work (sublimation) as the main characteristics of an orderly sexual regimen; substitute sexual gratification, neurotic symptoms, compulsive work performance (performance according to the process of reaction formation) as the characteristics of the disorderly sexual regimen.

The form in which society organizes communal life determines the quantity and quality of tension relaxation in the psychic apparatus. If there are too few possibilities in society for sexual gratification and sublimation, if the psychic apparatus is so deformed by the influence of faulty education that it is not capable of utilizing the available possibilities, if the measure of displeasurable irritation due to lack and privation becomes too great, then the psychic apparatus begins to work with substitute mechanisms which have the goal of tension relaxation at any cost. The results then are neuroses, perversions, pathological changes in character, the antisocial phenomena of sexual life, and not least, disturbances in the capacity for work.

In opposition to the many sociologically "economist" conceptions of social processes, which equate the category "social base" solely with technology and natural resources, i.e., solely with the material conditions of existence, and attribute needs to the "superstructure of society," it cannot be overemphasized that economism has nothing in common with Marxism. In special reference to a study of the ideology of fascism, I must call into view the fact that Marx attributed the fundamental needs to the "base" of society. It is, of course, true that needs are constantly being altered by the process of production, and that new needs are being created, but that does not affect the

---

* "Der genitale und der neurotische Charakter," *Intern. Zeitschrift für Psychoanalyse*, 1929. See also *The Function of the Orgasm* and *Character Analysis*.

cardinal fact that basic needs as well as created needs are secondary elements within the base, that they are subjective factors in the making of history. Marx writes in *The German Ideology:* "The given data from which we begin are not arbitrary, and they are not dogmas, they are the authentic data from which one can only abstract in the imagination. They comprise *real individuals, their actions, and the material conditions of their lives, not only those prior conditions in which they found themselves but also those created by their actions.*" Hence, the sexual drive may be considered an element of the "base" even though it undergoes alteration in the social process, for it constitutes a very fundamental part of the "real individual" and determines his "actions" in a very crucial sense. Thus, the psychology and the physiology of instinctual behavior will take as their proper object of study, certain elements of the base in their mutual relationship with other elements of the base and with the social ideology of *the socialized individual.* To exclude the sexual drive (as subject and object of history) from sociological investigation would be tantamount to excluding food, clothing, and housing needs as matters proper for sociological investigation. And when one further considers that the productive factor, "labor power," is essentially a sublimated sexual energy, then it is no longer necessary to set forth further evidence as to the role of sex-economic data.

The tasks remaining are to develop a characterology and a theory of work-economy in the framework of sexual economy, and to determine clear pedagogical goals. These tasks can only be carried to completion by a society which has established a planned economy for the purpose of the orderly satisfying of the needs of *all* members of society. In capitalist society, considering the extent to which science is sex-moralistically biased and influenced by private enterprise interests, it is not even possible to expect a theoretical solution to the problems.

Since sexual misery is a phenomenon resulting from the normative regulation of sexual life as derived from the interests of the private economy, it is always found where sexual life is determined by considerations of lasting monogamous marriage; i.e., it is always to be found in a class society. The relationship between sexual oppression and the oppression of the immediate material life (food, housing, cultural needs) of the population is determined as follows. While material privation encompasses only the dominated class, sexual privation is a phenomenon which encompasses all ranks of class society, but which is also rooted in the material laws of class society. According to these laws even sexual privation has a different form among the oppressed class than it has among the possessing levels of society. The material privations of deficient nourishment and housing not only increase the sexual misery among the proletariat, but in addition, on top of the harsh restrictions of sexual legislation, they remove the possibility of those measures of relief which the owning classes can resort to at any time. If we now ask (in analogy to the question of the satisfaction of hunger) why capitalist society can find no other way to relate to the satisfaction of sexual needs than to refuse these needs, as, for instance, when the needs are pressed into the confines of monogamous marriage, or even totally suppressed until a certain age is reached, as occurs in childhood and adolescence—we shall then discover certain economic interests of this society at work. We see that it is only the private enterprise form of society which has an interest in sexual repression, and which requires it for the maintenance of two of its basic institutions, the permanent monogamous marriage and the patriarchal family. The fact that an extraordinary amount of sexual suffering, neurosis, perversion, sex murders, and limitation in the individual's capacity for work is thus brought about is a secondary result, not directly intended by the system but inseparable from it. The mental disturbances created in this fashion are the expression of disturbed sexual economy.* It is evident that so long as the dynamic of mental illness and character formation and its relationship with sexuality remained unrecognized, real research into the history of sexual economy could not be undertaken. The presence of the clinical discoveries of Freud was necessary. These discoveries themselves developed in the soil of the capitalist sexual order, which had first created neurosis and then the methods of research and treatment pertinent to it.

* See *The Function of the Orgasm*, and *Character Analysis*.

However, this sexual order had not always existed; it had developed out of other forms belonging to earlier stages of social development. If the present sexual order has exercised a significant influence on the development of society, particularly on its intellectual production, it still must be seen as itself a product of a specific social order of production and distribution of the means of existence.

In the history of mankind, the sexual order, existing in a certain relationship to the productive economic interests of society, was transformed from its natural state of affirmation and support of human sexual economy into a sexually denying and repressive order which induces a way of life inimical to sexual economy. This historical event unfolded in complete dependence on the transformation taking place from matriarchal to patriarchal society, and from primitive communist to private enterprise society. Sexual repression is unknown in natural society, just as it is absent in any natural organization of living beings. Private enterprise and the nascent patriarchate created all the economic interests which culminated in the social basis for sex-denying morality and the pursuant disturbed human sexual economy. Negative sexual morality draws its justification for existence as well as its contradications from the continuously developing phases of private and commodity economy. In capitalism, sex-denying morality establishes itself as an explicitly reactionary factor, becomes one of the main supports of the church, and in a certain sense, brings the oppressed class even sexually into a dependence on capital and its institutions. Also, by means of its influence on education, in and outside of the family from childhood on, it creates a psychic structure in the mass individual which is completely subordinated to the interests of the ruling class. Thus, our primary interest is not an academic or theoretical one, but rather a practical one: the standpoint of the proletarian revolution, against which negative sexual morality acts as an inhibiting factor. The bourgeois family becomes the most important ideological workshop of capitalism through the sexual repression it carries out, among other reasons, in order to reproduce itself ideologically. For this reason it is defended as the basis of the state by all bourgeois social politicians, and by sexual and cultural researchers, thus making more difficult the understanding of its reactionary role.

Reactionary scientists are more clearly aware of this role, which will be abolished in the social revolution, than have been revolutionaries up to the present time. It is a question of the conservative function of family ties. Here is an example that fits many cases:

> It is no mistake to characterize as among the reasons which led the Bolshevik "reform" of sexual legislation in its particular direction the desire to annihilate the force of parental authority, so odious to them. The principle of authority is renewed with every birth in the family, since, in obedience to the immutable course of nature, new human beings can only be created insofar as completely immature, physically and intellectually helpless beings are given to their parents, those fully mature human beings who then appear with inescapable necessity to the children as "authorities." This has the teleological implication that the immature child immediately begins to acquire the accomplishments of the preceding generations, supported by his trust in the authority of the parents; henceforth, this becomes the first and foremost basis for every real advance in civilization, which does not begin anew with each and every person but rather stands on earlier stages and from there moves to higher ones. Bolshevism wishes to strike and destroy this most intimate and powerful source of authority by destroying the family.*

The revolutionary movement which has shaken the world for a decade and a half will complete the process of decline in the patriarchal family which the economic decomposition of capitalism introduced. The decay of the family continues today primarily on an unconscious level; it is one of the symptoms of transformation in our social organization. The conscious and active influencing of this objective process of decomposition will

---

* Schmidt, "Der Oedipuskomplex der Psychoanalyse und die Ehegestaltung des Bolschewismus," *Nationalwirtschaft, Blätter für organischen Wirtschaftsbau,* Berlin, p. 20.

only then be possible when the sociological role of sexual oppression and of the sexual repression that afflicts all individuals is recognized as a totality and translated into the practice of sexual politics.

If the normative ordering of sexual life through the institutions of marriage and family is in dissolution because of objective forces, then the slogans "Sexual freedom," "Sex is a private matter," etc., are insufficient for comprehending or consciously influencing the restructuring of sexual life taking place independent of our wills and determined by the economic development. Chaos always results when a society fails to understand the social process to which it is subject and is therefore unable to direct it. The revolts occurring in the Middle Ages seemed chaotic because there was no theory of revolt at that time. For a citizen ignorant of sociology, social revolution means chaos because he is unable to grasp its meaning. For an informed revolutionary, civil war between the exploited and the exploiters means the grand commencement of a real ordering of the material life of society.

What is to follow when the normative regulation of sexual life through the institutions of marriage and family disappears? A bourgeois person would say in horror: sexual chaos. However, the history of sexual economy teaches one that the previous normative regulation, which led to fiasco everywhere and which really introduced sexual chaos, can make way for another system, one which is not moral-negative, but rather sex-economic-positive, and which can bring about real ordering of the sexual life. And this is, it must be said, not a "question for philosophy," but a question of historical process. The philosophical question is only whether one interprets history correctly or falsely, whether one recognizes the process or fearfully recoils and hides behind theories of the "ethical nature of man" or the "moral order."

We shall summarize here the findings which concern the laws of sexual economy as they have been developed in clinical and sociological study of the clash between instinctual need and social process:

1. The moral regulation of sexual life by private-enterprise

economy and bourgeois society is aided in its work by sexual inhibitions which are anchored in the individual from childhood on. These inhibitions create an irreconcilable contradiction: on the one hand, they bring about a sexual blockage due to the sexual repression and, thus, a sharpened sexual desire; on the other hand, they bring about a modification of the person's psychic structure with a diminished or completely disturbed capacity for gratification. This contradiction, which is a nonrectifiable conflict between tension and the ability to attain gratification, produces compensatory reactions of the sexual energy, in the form of neurosis, perversion and antisocial forms of sexual behavior.

2. In every individual the elimination of these contradictions is only possible through the prior elimination of moral sex inhibitions. These inhibitions are replaced by sex-economic principles, and by the self-direction of sex to the goal of sexual gratification, which, of course, will make moral regulation superfluous. In individuals this is attained by psychotherapeutic elimination of the sexual repression and the establishment of orgastic potency. Energy is withdrawn from antisocial and pathological tendencies when one's sex life is governed by sexual economy.

3. Sexual gratification does not stand in contradiction to the sublimation of sexual drives in the performance of work; on the contrary, the gratification is more like a precondition of the latter. The relationship between sexual gratification and sublimation is not mechanical in nature ("the more sexual repression, the more social production"), it is, rather, dialectical in nature: sexual energy can be sublimated to a certain level; if the deflection of energy is carried too far, the furtherance of sublimation is transformed into its opposite, into a disturbance in working capacity.

4. High cultures exist in which the repression of sexuality, particularly of genital sexuality, is absent—indeed, in which sexual affirmation and encouragement is the rule. Thus, sexual repression is not a precondition for cultural development and social order in general.

5. Sex-moralistic regulation of sexual life coincides with the rise of private-ownership interests at the beginning of class

society. The institutions of marriage and the family are in the service of these interests, and the demand for premarital and extramarital chastity is a reflection of these institutions.

6. A society organized around sexually affirmative principles is characterized by an absence, in any socially significant degree, of neurosis, perversion, antisocial sexual behavior and disturbances in the capacity to work. (This would be the ethnological proof that neurosis is an expression of disturbed sexual economy.)

7. A socially accommodated sexual gratification will automatically make sex benign within society; but, as a precondition, the negative sexual morality must be absent and an affirmative sex education from childhood on must be present.

8. Antisexual morality, fostered by the institutions of marriage and family, achieves the opposite (neurosis, perversion, antisocial sexual behavior) of its intentions which it says are of a socializing nature.

9. Affirmation and the sex-economic regulation of sexuality are characteristic of primitive communist society; the society characterized by commodity economy (private property, marriage, family) introduces sex-moralistic regulation and the corresponding suppression of childhood and adolescent sexuality.

10. The abolition of the commodity economy necessarily brings about the elimination of sexual morality and replaces it on a scientifically higher and technically more secure level with sex-economic regulation and support for sexual activity. The abolition of commodity economy is a precondition for the abolition of emotional disorder in individuals, and not least, it is basic for further increase in intellectual development.

3) Production and Reproduction of Sexual Morality

We have been able to follow directly the origin of sexual ideology in the genesis of certain basic elements of sex morality out of the economic interests of the chief and his family among the

Trobrianders. It remains to be seen whether this type of formation of social morality is universally valid or is validated only for certain elements of morality. Let us summarize the process of the formation of sexual ideology.

Until the encroachment of economic interests, sexual life is governed by the natural law of regulation to be found in the pleasure–nonpleasure principle. The natural regulatory principle crystallizes into social customs and practices, as for example, in the *ulatile* and *katuyausi,* which, instead of contradicting sexual gratification, serve to secure it. The rudiments of antisexual morality appear as the demand or claim of a group in society holding economic and political power over the other members of society. The demand is a measure to secure and increase the power of the group. Thus, the demand raised by the profiteer becomes the morality of those from whom the profit is taken. The group that has acquired dominance in society constitutes the production sphere of morality.

However, morality cannot be maintained solely by a single demand, claim or piece of legislation. Permanent restriction of the gratification of needs through external coercion would have the consequence that the new morality would be required to renew and impose itself continually. It would constantly encounter resistance in every member of society, and would therefore scarcely be able to maintain itself. In order to fully satisfy its economic purpose the sexual restriction must be more deeply anchored; it must begin to take effect in early childhood, when the resistance of the ego is easy to overcome. It must move from an external requirement by a social group to an internalized morality in all members of society. In what manner does this process occur? Through a modification in the psychic structure of the mass individual. This modification takes place in the sexual sphere assisted by fear of punitive measures. Fear of punishment for sexual transgression can only lead at last to an oppression of the sexual drive, once the latter is removed from consciousness, i.e., repressed, and opposing forces mobilized against it and securely integrated in the personality. The conflict originally existing between a sexual ego and an environment hostile to sexuality develops into a conflict between an ego which fears punishment and an ego with a conscious desire for sexual gratification, and finally develops into a (transitional) stable condition characterized by a moral ego which permanently holds down the repressed sexual impulses. The ego, previously existing in a state of pleasure affirmation, becomes forbidding and moral. The morality of society has reproduced itself in the individual. Sexual negation and sexual repression and thus the economic interests of the holders of power are secured in three ways: the morality of society is reproduced in all individuals subject to the same sexually repressive economic situation; these transformed individuals then influence their offspring according to their moral attitudes rather than their repressed needs; the economic situation continues in existence and continually reproduces the moral demands of the power-exercising class, so that the external social pressure continues.

Thus, production and reproduction of morality must be seen as distinct. The former appears as a "cultural" demand of the ruling group; the latter appears in all members of society as individual morality. The relationship between the economic basis and the ideological superstructure is therefore not a direct one. The formation of ideology takes place in many intermediate stages, which we can portray, somewhat schematically, as follows:

1. Specific development in productivity and corresponding relationships of production.
2. Specific economic interests of a social group or class.
3. Corresponding moral demands on the members of the society.
4. The effect of these demands on the needs of the mass individual, restriction of the satisfaction of needs, the production of social anxiety, etc.
5. Anchoring of the group's moral demands in the mass individual through the alteration of the modifiable needs, through changes in the psychic structure in the sense of the new morality: permanent reproduction through the internalization of the demands.
6. Inward acceptance of morality by the mass individual; the articulation of the ideology by the individual, and the

development (reproduction) of the ideology into social morality in the sum of the mass individuals.

This social morality, anchored in all individuals and reproducing itself permanently, has in this manner a reciprocal effect on the economic base in a conservative direction. The exploited person affirms the economic order which guarantees his exploitation; the sexually repressed person affirms even the sexual order which restricts his gratification and makes him ill, and he wards off any system that might correspond to his needs. In this manner morality carries out its socio-economic assignment.

Let us consider this matter with the aid of a very contemporary example: capital defends the maintenance of sexual repression with all means at its disposal. Even though the prohibition against abortion no longer serves its original purpose of producing an industrial reserve army, it is not repealed, owing to moral considerations. The birth rate in capitalist countries is continuously declining, but the rationalization processes in capitalism ensure that the reserve army remains ready. They combat propaganda for contraceptive devices and narrow the function of sexuality to reproduction; with all their might they fight against reform in the institution of marriage. As ever, they suppress adolescent sexuality with the assistance of the church, the school, the parents, and the housing scarcity. They are not able to cope with the problems of prostitution and venereal disease because the "morality" of decent women and girls would not permit it.

Society's sexual repression is therefore a reactionary issue of great importance. Society cannot do without its retarding effect on the social processes, because

1. It is a powerful prop of the church, which, with the assistance of sexual anxiety and guilt feelings, is deeply anchored in the exploited masses.
2. It is a prop of the institutions of family and marriage, which require a stunting of sexuality for their existence.
3. It requires children to obey their parents, and prepares for the later obedience of the adults to the authority of the state and capital by producing fear of authority in all individuals in society.
4. It lames the critical intellectual powers of the oppressed

masses. Sexual repression consumes a great deal of psychic energy that otherwise would be utilized in intellectual activity.

5. It damages the psychic ability of an immense number of people. It creates inhibition and cripples the power to rebel in materially oppressed individuals.

In sum, this represents nothing less than the ideological mooring of the dominant economic system in the psychic structure of the members of the oppressed class; in this manner political reaction is served. That is the sociological sense of the sexual repression in capitalism. It does not require a great deal of formal education but simply a little intellectual courage to recognize that the capitalist powers do not bring Christian belief, clothing, and "morality" to colonial people in the hope of advancing civilization, but they do so because they wish to implant the spirit of the submissive European in the individuals of that society, and to weaken and make them subservient through alcohol. The instilling of the capitalistic spirit in the psychic structures of the primitive peoples aims to make the overseer and the police club unnecessary. This is most easily attained by taming the revolutionary force which is harbored by satisfied sexuality.

Inasmuch as we were able to discover the sociological meaning of sexual repression and its capitalist function, it should not be difficult to find the contradictions which created it and will lead to its destruction. If on the one hand, sexual repression fortifies the institutions of marriage and family, it undermines them on the other hand through the sexual misery of marriage and family developing on this foundation. Sexual repression has the effect of making young people submissive to adults in a characterological sense, but at the same time, it brings about their sexual rebellion. This rebellion becomes a powerful force in the social movement when it becomes conscious and finds a nexus with the proletarian movement undermining capitalism. That the contradictions of sexual repression are seeking a resolution is apparent in the sexual crisis which has enveloped the capitalist countries with a steadily increasing strength since approximately the turn of the century. It fluctuates in its intensity according to the economic crises on which it is directly dependent. (There is an increase in the divorce rate in periods of economic crises.) The worsening of the material position of the masses not only loosens the marital and familial binds of sexuality, it stimulates a revolt related to sexual need, along with the revolt stemming from the need for food. That is the simplest explanation for the theory of "moral decline" in periods of crisis. It is characteristic for both capital and the church that in periods of economic crisis, they escalate not only material pressure on the masses but also reactionary pressure to the point of bloody terror even in sexual matters. The papal bull on Christian marriage at the end of 1930 must be considered in the context of the interrelationships between material and sexual rebellion. The same applies to the violent clash between Czechoslovak troops and members of a proletarian hiking club in May 1931, which was a result of the attorney general's prohibition of overnighting in tents without a marriage certificate. Many persons were wounded in the clash. It was the first time the sexual reaction had manifested itself in this crass form. This conflict is primarily latent at the moment, but there can be no doubt that a class-conscious sexual politics will force it to the surface, and in the framework of the revolutionary movement, will force it to a solution.

Thus, society's sexual oppression undermines itself by creating a permanently widening divergence between sexual tension and the outer opportunities of gratification as well as the inner capabilities for gratification. This process is accelerated by the programs of political education carried out by the revolutionary parties which loosen the bondage of the masses at another point. It is also accelerated by the growing concentration of the masses in larger and larger collective organizations, which promote the breakdown of the institutions of marriage and family. This is similar to the manner in which capitalist rationalization of the production process tends toward the economic destruction of the family. A new contradiction is produced here between the economic dissolution of the family in the masses and the necessity, from the standpoint of capital and the church, of maintaining the ideology of marriage and having it permanently reproduced in the new generations.

If the forces of political reaction understand the importance of sexual oppression as a factor in reaction and take steps to secure this oppression, a revolutionary party must then recognize the significance of sexual rebellion and support this rebellion against church and capital. And as the sexual legislation of the Soviet Union shows, the social revolution will eliminate sexual oppression.* It is able to do this because the private enterprise basis of sexual repression is progressively being destroyed. Marriage and family, as they are defined in private enterprise, cease to be socially necessary institutions. And with the disappearance of marriage and family the cardinal mechanism of sexual repression and authoritarian obedience also disappears. Sexual denial is once again transformed into sexual affirmation.

The original conditions of primitive communism return once more on a higher economic and cultural level as the sex-economic management of sexual relationships. They must return, since the motives which first eliminated this type of sexual regulation have passed away. Even if the old morality is capable of maintaining itself for a certain period of time in the new society as an "ideology without a base" it will not be able to reproduce itself in the mass individual, because young people will no longer be oppressed, neither socially and in the family, nor materially. Awareness of the sociological necessity of this process could only lead to a smoother and speedier development. Sexual science will withdraw from the service of sexual oppression and enter the service of sex-economic order. Sexual pedagogy will have the positive goal of sex-economic education, rather than the negative goal we have had up to now of moral sexual repression. The church will thereby lose its last support in the psychic structure of the mass individual. Planned socialist economy will finally fulfill the social function of bringing man into society. It will secure the gratification of biological needs that are multiplied in the process of becoming human, and of cultural needs that are developed through technology. The intellectual capabilities of the mass individual can now be immeasurably increased through the social institutions promoting the gratifica-

---

* The ascetic tendencies existing in the Soviet Union require a separate study.

tion of needs. In the process, those who preach the fixity of spirit and the moral nature of man will be brushed aside completely. Empty talk about culture will make room for the cultural and sexual awakening of those who create the wealth of society.

We are now confronted with a further task in the area of sexual politics of thoroughly eliminating, both on a theoretical and a practical level, the new contradictions in the sexual life of the Soviet Union.

POLITICIZING THE SEXUAL PROBLEM OF YOUTH

(1932)

"Politicizing the Sexual Problem of Youth" is the final chapter of *Der Sexuelle Kampf der Jugend,* completed in January 1932. This work was not printed until later that year because of the successful effort of certain Communist Party functionaries to block its publication through official party channels, though approval for such publication had been secured. Indeed, much of the controversy leading to Reich's expulsion from the German Communist Party flared around *Der Sexuelle Kampf der Jugend,* which, for the most part a brilliantly concise and frank discussion of sexual organs, diseases, perversions, and sexual misery, and well received in the youth organizations for which it was conceived, yet did not fail—as one reads here —to criticize Communist Party members and policies where they seemed at odds with the sexual revolution.—*L.B.*

We must be quite clear in our minds about the possibilities open to working youth in a capitalist society. Since the Young Communist League is adopting the clear political line of social revolution, it should aim at being the leader of youth in the field of sexual problems, too. And working youth would recognize it as such if only its approach to this question—this urgent and delicate question—were the right one of ruthless candor; if only they could feel that the YCL really understands their plight, and is defending their cause.

We must practice genuine self-criticism. We must ask ourselves why it is that, on this of all problems, we have until now been so mealy-mouthed, why we have not dared to consider the only opportunities open to working youth. As a first step, we must admit that on this question of sex we have behaved like the man asleep who keeps trying to chase a fly away by vainly flapping a hand in its direction.

It has been pointed out again and again in the revolutionary youth organizations that the "sex question" disturbs and impedes the struggle for revolution. And the conclusion has been drawn, again and again, that we must leave the sex question aside, because we have no time to deal with it and because we have more important things to do. But if the issue has come up again and again, more and more urgently, more and more pressingly, if, as a matter of fact, many youth organizations have collapsed, owing to the sexual difficulties of their members (a fact we must openly admit), then we must ask ourselves *why* the question is so disturbing, and we must not, just because it is disturbing, declare that we have no time for it and have more urgent things to do, that sex life is a private affair, etc. *Sex life is not a private affair if it preoccupies you, and in the form in which it has existed hitherto, it interferes with the political struggle.*

What other problem that causes similar difficulties would we dismiss in the same way? What would we say to such an attitude toward any other issue? We should rightly say that it was an evasive attitude. We should rightly condemn anyone who resorted to such excuses. We ought to be consistent with ourselves. Our view should be that for Bolsheviks there is no such thing as an insurmountable difficulty—and therefore, the attitude that I have described is a bourgeois and opportunist one.

When such problems arise they do not fall from the sky, but come out of the very real contradictions of our social system; and, as such, they demand an answer. We have found time in our class struggle to deal with sport, the theater, religion, the radio. Why are we not equally consistent when it comes to the sexual problem of youth? However, if we agree that we have been evading the issue, we must become clear about why this is so.

A superficial reason is the fact that by ignoring the problem of sex we hope to be able to devote ourselves entirely to revolutionary work, thus emphasizing the difference between us and the bourgeois types whose interest is centered on the problem of sex and who do nothing but chatter about it. This has led us into serious error. Many of us have wanted to dismiss sexuality altogether, as something inessential or even "bourgeois." We were wrong: that is the lesson of reality. We must solve the sex problem in a revolutionary way, by evolving a clear sexual-political theory; proceeding from it to a sexual-revolutionary praxis; and integrating both these in the proletarian movement as a whole. That, we are convinced, is the *right* way toward a definitive solution.

Many comrades justify their negative attitude by invoking Lenin's conversation with Clara Zetkin in which he sharply criticized the discussions and debates on sex taking place in workers' and youth associations and said that there were more important things to be done. We completely endorse the point of view which Lenin adopted at the time. He was attacking superficial, woolly chatter about sex which merely took people's minds off more essential things, and we, too, are against that. These "sex discussions" are generally nothing more than a substitute for sexual activity, intellectual masturbation of the most common kind. But we shall understand at once how the problem ought to be treated if, at the same time, we quote a second remark of Lenin's made in the course of the same conversation with Clara Zetkin: "Communism will not bring asceticism, but joy of life, power of life, and a satisfied love life will help to do that." If Communism is to bring about the enjoyment of sexual life, surely this has to be fought for.

The point of the matter, therefore, is this: we must not indulge in empty discussions about sex, but neither must we ignore the sex problem. Without talking about it we cannot solve it. What is left for us to do? We must talk about it *politically*. Then we shall be discussing it in the right way and taking the right action as a result. However, before we go into further detail and produce evidence to show that this is the only possible way out, we must still define the *deeper* reason for our avoidance of this question.

Where were we all brought up? Under what conditions did we grow up? We grew up in families, and were brought up under the capitalist system. The objection will be raised that there is a great difference between proletarian and bourgeois families. But it isn't as simple as that. We don't have to think for very long before coming up with a response; we need only consider some of the elements of our way of thinking and living.

Have we freed ourselves from the bourgeois ideology concerning property? Yes, to a considerable extent, for there is a marked difference between bourgeois and working-class families as regards property relations. Have we completely freed ourselves from religion? Here things are no longer as simple. There are many thousands of proletarian families that are religious. The further we penetrate into the petty-bourgeois proletariat, the more deep-seated we find religion to be. And what about sexual morality? Isn't it rooted in the very nature of the family—which proletarians, too, are forced to maintain, because of the conditions of life under capitalism?

Doesn't sexual oppression and the implanting of bourgeois morality form part and parcel of bourgeois marriage and the bourgeois family? Of course, the contradictions between the worker's way of life and bourgeois family morality are very great. The contradictions are different too in the middle and upper bourgeoisie. But bourgeois sexual morality nevertheless exists in the proletariat; and of all bourgeois ideologies it is the most deeply anchored because it is the most strongly implanted from earliest childhood. It is one of the bourgeoisie's strongest ideological props within the oppressed class.

We see all the time that even class-conscious youth find it very difficult to liberate themselves from this. Bourgeois sexual morality—whose most essential feature is that it does not view sexual life as natural, self-evident, and also connected with the particular social order of the time, but denies it and is afraid of it—is more deeply embedded in the very marrow of us Communists than we all realize. We should not allow ourselves to be deceived, either, by sexual showing-off, which is the counterpart of sexual timidity. This is simply the same bourgeois sexuality, with a different mathematical sign in front of it. Lenin was perfectly right, therefore, when he described the "glass of water" theory as a "good bourgeois theory."

What matters are the sexual deformations that every one of us bears inside himself as a result of sexual oppression and that are connected with unconscious repressed attitudes, so that in our sex life we are not quite masters of ourselves. These are the deeper reasons for our reluctance to deal openly and consistently with the problem of sex—the reasons why all of us without exception, even those who have the best insight into the problem, do not dare to include sexual liberation slogans in the rest of our propaganda. We must learn to understand why so many Communists get that funny smile and start pulling that special face as soon as sex is mentioned. We must seriously put an end to all that, however hard it will be for us to overcome our own inhibitions.

The further we reach into the unenlightened, non-class-conscious strata of youth, the greater the inhibitions we shall meet. But practice will show, as it has already shown in individual cases, that our work of bringing political knowledge to these young people—the political knowledge they need so badly —will be made easier to the extent that we succeed in overcoming their sexual inhibitions and moral prejudices. We shall be successful in our political work of enlightenment only if we propose an openly and clearly sex-affirming ideology in place of the hypocritical and negative ideology of the bourgeoisie. Many reactionary attitudes will come to grief on this front: first, because the Christian and National Socialist youth have no tenable argument against us; and secondly, and more important, because although they deny their sexuality, they also affirm it—in secret.

Let us now consider the question as it stands within the Young Communist League—using as our basis a discussion which took place at an evening of mass criticism of A. A. Bogdanov's *The First Girl,* held in Berlin on April 21, 1931. If we succeed in gaining a little clarity on this issue, it will make it easier for us to tackle other problems in the Fichte groups and in the Christian, petty-bourgeois and National Socialist youth groups.

A Red Scout, Comrade Hermann, said, among other things:

"There isn't a book in which the questions that affect the German youth are treated—the position of young men and girls in the proletarian organizations, in the youth movement in general, and questions of sexual relations of young people among themselves and with the responsible party officials. These questions naturally play an important role for us and they have to be discussed here. The question has been raised as to how the sexual difficulties of German youth can be overcome, and what we can try to do about it. I am sure there can be no overcoming of sexual difficulties for youth under the present system in any satisfactory sense. Because the greatest hangups for young people are economic; for example, if a girl wants to have a child but she hasn't got the money. Another thing is that most questions are still seen from the bourgeois point of view, even among ourselves, and moral bullying is still practiced not only by parents but even by party comrades, and is by no means a thing of the past. My own view is that an active Communist, an active party member, has very little time for love affairs and can't obtain one hundred percent satisfaction in this respect. Generally speaking we still have to get the girls into the movement and see to it that they really become comrades with equal rights. Girls are still too inhibited by their bourgeois upbringing; they still have too many feelings of inferiority to fight side by side with the men as we'd like them to. That is why we have to make them realize that they enjoy equal rights in the organization.

"Sex is always more of a problem for the girls. They feel these things much more than a young man, who goes with one girl one day and with another girl another day. The girls are always much more attached to a particular comrade; I'd say that was the norm, even if there are exceptions. I'm of the opinion that relations should be much healthier in this respect. Sexual tensions take up too much room in the lives of proletarian youth, who ought to regard the class struggle as their first task. These things are too much of a distraction. They really have lost us many a good comrade who's just got swallowed up and disappeared from sight. Useful people who could certainly have helped build the organization have let themselves be diverted from the struggle by all that personal stuff."

This young comrade put the problem in the right way on the most essential points. The sexual troubles of youth really can't be solved in a satisfactory way within the present system. But let us go further with our self-criticism. Let us examine the reason which the comrade gave for this, and see how we are still imprisoned in a bourgeois mentality in sexual matters, even when our political ideas are perfectly correct. The example he gives is that of a girl who for economic reasons can't satisfy her desire to have a child. This is doubtless true of many girls. But it is *not a central problem.*

Let us not deceive ourselves; very many girls think first and foremost of how they can have sexual intercourse *without* getting pregnant. Young people feel bad because they cannot cope with their turbulent sexuality as a result of material poverty and a lack of opportunities, of money and contraceptives. For the moment, then, let us leave psychological disturbances aside. And so I think Comrade Ernst was right, when he said:

> "Of course there is a big sex problem in Germany, as there is in all capitalist countries. It stems from the fact that young people live at home, because they can't get a place of their own to live. Many are unemployed, haven't the money to keep themselves and therefore can't live with whomever they want to live with. Many relationships which would be good under more or less secure material conditions simply break down, or can't even properly come into existence. Why? Simply because the necessary conditions are not available."

If we were to put the question of girls wanting to have babies at the top of the list, we are sidetracking the issue, even if the question does play some part. The typical bourgeois way of evading the problem of sex has been to put mother love and the desire for children on a pedestal and in that way to obscure everything else. It is a fact that the desire to have a child generally occurs only when the needs of the senses have been more or less satisfied. What young people are concerned about, to put it bluntly, isn't reproduction but contraception and sexual gratification at the time of their youthful ripening. They're concerned with *putting their love life in order.*

And the preconditions for this are totally lacking under capitalism. Housing construction is in the hands of real-estate speculators, who have a vested interest in mass poverty. Only the socialization of housing construction, the transfer of housing into public ownership, as is the case in the Soviet Union today, can solve this problem. The precondition is and remains the abolition of private ownership of real estate. But this can only be the result of a social revolution. Making the best contraceptives available to the young as soon as they wish to begin having sexual intercourse is a further fundamental precondition for an ordered and satisfactory sex life. But political reaction is just as sharply opposed to this, just as terroristic, as it is in every other area which the bourgeoisie considers important. The possibility of having an unwanted pregnancy terminated at a public clinic is another fundamental precondition. Hungry, wretched young people excluded from every kind of culture, hanging about the streets and the bars, are not capable of having an ordered, satisfying sex life because they are either sexually deprived—which isn't their fault but the fault of society—or sexually disturbed.

Since the cause of sexual disturbances and brutalization is bourgeois sexual oppression in the parental home and at school, what is needed to remove them is—once again—a complete reorganization of economic and social existence, in the sense that women become materially independent and free from the power of their husbands, and that parents lose the right to oppress and dominate their children. Yet another precondition for this is free public education of children and a complete change of outlook in the matter of infantile sexuality.

Comrade Hermann pointed out that moral bullying is practiced by party comrades as well as by parents. That is absolutely true. Many older comrades who have had to live in a marriage and a family are not behaving correctly toward youth. We have to admit to ourselves that this is a form of counter-revolutionary activity in our camp, and that in the last analysis it only serves the interests of the ruling class.

A great deal can be done in this field by organizing large-scale public debates between the young people and parents in which the young people, who dare not protest when they are alone at home or who fritter away their energies in futile squabbles with their parents, could bring out their problems and grievances in public at meetings controlled by the mass of youth and parents. We can be sure (for this has already been proved in practice) that parents will not be able to maintain for long in public the point of view they represent at home. And so the young people will come out victorious and new forces will be released for the youth organizations. And the parents, too, in many cases for the first time, will come into contact with the proletarian movement and will get their first clear view of themselves and their position. Now, is the sex problem of youth a politically important problem? We cannot deny it.

Comrade Hermann also said that an active party member has very little time for love affairs and can't obtain one hundred percent satisfaction in that respect. That is no doubt true, but put in this way it is incomplete and can lead to false generalizations. A Communist youth leader plays an immensely important part in the movement as a whole. He ought therefore to be an example for others, in matters of sexual behavior as well as in everything else. At the present time we are called upon to make great personal sacrifices and to subordinate our private lives to the class struggle. Yet in approaching this problem we must distinguish whom we are dealing with—with a young person who is completely class-conscious or one who is indifferent, with a bourgeois or with a proletarian who still thinks in a reactionary way about certain things.

But let us for the moment stay with the party official. It is quite true that our officials are terribly overloaded with urgent party work and have no time for "love affairs." In the proletarian youth movement there are three types of officials: first, the one that has no sex life at all and has dedicated all his energies to party work; then the second type who, without anyone hearing or seeing much of it, leads an ordered sexual life with some girl comrade and at the same time also devotes all his strength to the party; and, lastly, we have the third type who is constantly involved in conflict (which may be more or less acute) between his party duties and his love life. If we do not just glance in passing at these comrades but if we consider their careers as a whole, we shall find that the best official—that is to say, the one who not only does his work most thoroughly but also has the greatest staying power and sticks with the movement through thick and thin—is the one with an ordered love life. For him, sexuality has stopped being a problem. The first type is also a good official, but experience shows that often he can only last for a limited time. This is because he at first tries to drown his personal difficulties in work, but later he breaks down in one way or another and is lost to the movement. Medical and political experience of such party workers shows very clearly that the cause of the eventual breakdown is not only (or primarily) overwork, but rather, that the comrade concerned has been made unfit for the struggle by the difficulties of his sexuality— the difficulties of "private life" in conjunction with the great demands made on him by the party. One just can't survive a complete lack of a sex life without serious disturbances in the long run. We adopt this point of view not only for health reasons but also in the interests of revolutionary work, which is harmed by the continually high turnover rate of party workers. We have an interest in every party worker remaining fit for his task for the longest possible time, and one of the most important preconditions for this is a modicum of order in sexual matters.

Some people believe that by excluding sex altogether they gain strength. That is a fallacy. The fact is that if your sex life is too restricted, then your *working intensity,* at least, is bound to suffer; while if you have a sex life that is more or less satisfactory, then the freshness with which you tackle your work will more than make up for time lost on a "private life."

Of course there are times in party life—sometimes weeks, sometimes months—when the tasks are so great that comrades are obliged to restrict or sacrifice even the necessary minimum of sexual satisfaction. We have to reckon with this. However, this cannot be made the rule in ordinary times. And even in the periods I am talking of, some relief can be found for healthy comrades, in the sense that, given these circumstances, they can enter comradely relationships of shorter duration; this need not harm the permanent relationships provided the matter is discussed and settled quite openly. And so we see that we must not consider these questions abstractly but always in relation to the situation in which they occur.

A further point is to be made about the third type of party worker we have described. Comrades who are constantly involved in a conflict between party work and private life are usually those who have not rid themselves of an unnecessarily complicated bourgeois attitude toward sex. This is especially true of the women comrades; and in most cases some sort of sexual disturbance is also present. In such cases it isn't sexuality that makes difficulties for them; on the contrary, an existing sexual disturbance makes them suffer. Good advice is very precious in such instances, since very few people can afford to have their bourgeois deformations and sexual disturbances removed by prolonged psychological treatment. For the masses such treatment is impossible. But here, too, we must not fall into skepticism. We must realize that by creating a more open, freer sexual atmosphere within the organization, we can aid many of these comrades, as well, to find a way out of their difficulties and to do a better job for the party.

Comrade Hermann also said, and very rightly, that one of our most important tasks is to get the girls into the movement and see to it that they really become comrades with equal rights. But it was Comrade Lotte who, on the same occasion, hit the nail on the head when she said:

"What do things look like in practice inside the YCL?
It would be more to the point to say: How can we get more girls into the YCL? Because when there's a group of thirty-eight boys and only two girls, then everything looks quite different. Last night we held the first conference of Young Women Workers of Germany. The girls of the YCL met in Berlin last night and there were some wonderful girls among them. Of course, compared with the total number of women, far too few are organized, but once they're in, they work with much more staying-power and more enthusiasm than the boys. If we take a look inside the groups, the usual ratio is about twenty boys to two girls. Just because there are only two girls there, their position is pretty funny and complications certainly do arise. The boys go with other girls who aren't in the group and whom they can't immedi-

ately get to join the group, and in that way the boys often drop out too."

From all this we are bound to conclude the following:

1. It is more difficult to get girls to join the organization than boys.
2. The numerical ratio of girls to boys inside the organization is extremely harmful to our work, since the boys go with other girls and leave the organization.
3. The important practical question facing us is therefore this: How can we get more girls to join the organization so as to correct this state of affairs?

Comrade Lotte also discussed the reason why we cannot get the girls to join. She thought it was that our methods are not always such that a young person can feel at home among us for long. She said the Young Communists were trying to find new methods. One of the difficulties was that the papers read at meetings are too long, too learned and generally such that "nobody understands a word." She said very rightly: "If our methods were livelier, all relations would be improved, including the relationship between the boys and the girls. But first we must have methods which sweep the young people along, so that they get really involved in the cause. Delivering a political talk and then allowing five minutes for personal matters is doing things the wrong way round."

Let us now consider the first question: Why are girls more difficult to persuade to join the organization than boys? It is a well-known fact, and one which was mentioned on the evening in question, that girls prefer to go to dance halls. Comrade Lotte laid special emphasis on the point that correct methods must be found to attract girls away from the dance halls; she thought it was not enough to detail girls for this task, but that boys too should be used for this purpose. We may be sure that Comrade Lotte made no mistake there. She has overcome the reluctance to recognize the sexual needs of youth for what they are and to take them into account when trying to enliven our political work.

We must ask: Why would girls rather go to dance halls than to political groups? If we dismiss the whole question by calling the girls "bourgeois" or "unproletarian," we shall have achieved nothing. Still less if we regard them as backward, or worse still, if we despise them. Our failure until now has been due to our ignoring the fact that youth is more concerned with sexual worries than with political ones. We have made the mistake of pushing sexual matters aside as a "bourgeois affair." We have to learn to recognize that the sexual difficulties of youth are just as important to youth as are material difficulties. Both types of difficulty—the one directly, the other indirectly—are rooted in our capitalist society.

We must recognize that the lesser degree of political interest among girls is connected with the greater sexual oppression which they suffer from childhood as compared with boys. And we must draw the conclusion that sexual oppression is an important political issue. We must finally say out loud what every young comrade knows, namely, that an undetermined but large proportion of girls and boys join the youth organization for the same subjective reasons as those which take them to the dance halls—that is to say, in search of a sexual partner and a sex life. The fact that, in the end, most of them are prevented from having such a life by external or internal causes does not alter the fact that they are seeking one. We must not look at this through bourgeois eyes, and we must not be shocked and talk about brothels. As revolutionaries, we must unhesitantly and unambiguously place ourselves on the side of the facts. If it is true that sexuality is what preoccupies young people most and what sends them into the dance halls, then, we must act accordingly and get them inside our organization, sexual preoccupations and all.

Young people often (much more often than we believe, because after all they don't tell us and it isn't talked about openly) join the organization as much because of their sexual needs as because of an inarticulate political urge. A general subject of complaint in the youth movement is that many young comrades drift away from the organizations because they do not find there what they were looking for in the personal sense. Comrade Lotte said that girls and boys between their eighteenth and twenty-second year are no longer to be found in the YCL: "They aren't in the YCL, they aren't in the party. They are lost to us. We must find ways and means of holding their interest."

Other observations support this statement. Boys and girls come into the youth organization at fifteen or sixteen and drop out at eighteen or nineteen, and only a very small proportion reappear later in the party.

This is also connected with the way in which the day-to-day work of the YCL is done. The situation today is that a small number of party workers are overloaded with work almost to the point of collapse, while the majority only turn up for the May Day demonstration and do very little otherwise. We know that these inactive comrades are afraid of being overloaded with work like the others, that, as many of them say, they don't want to be squeezed dry like lemons. Here we are faced with an organizational problem of far-reaching importance: for the question of a *correct distribution of functions* is involved. And on this we have just one thing to say. When there are roughly as many girls as boys in the organization, and when these girls and boys have achieved a good comradely and sexual relationship with one another, then all of them will want to join in the work and it will be more readily possible to distribute the functions among everybody, and in that way to lessen the load on some and to get others more politically interested and involved. Official approval of sex life in the organization—that is to say, the opposite of the point of view which calls sexuality a private affair to be repressed wherever possible—can be helpful to us in a decisive way, even in the purely organizational sense.

If we do our work of political training energetically and fruitfully, we need no longer be afraid to offer recreation to the young comrades from time to time in forms which suit them. We still have to do a great deal of thinking about this. But we shall be successful only when we have completely eliminated mere hangers-on from our ranks.

There are two further things we must do. We must not only deliver our reports and lectures on economic, political and organizational matters in a livelier and more youthful way, as the comrade suggested. We must also take the essential problems of youth into account, and as an integral part of our cultural discussions we must schedule talks on sexual politics, starting from the purely personal questions that occupy youth and proceeding to the fundamental economic and social problems. In this way we shall stop the majority of our young comrades from either being bored or having to force themselves to listen to the talks, as is so often the case now. We shall then achieve what we are really aiming for: we shall create *an emotional and objective bond between youth and the cause of all the workers embodied in the Communist Party.* Young people— girls as well as boys, in all walks of life—will become deeply persuaded that the Communist youth movement and the Communist Party are the only ones to really understand their personal troubles, medically as well as socially; the only ones to offer them all possible assistance, by organizing sex-counselling services for youth and by creating a freer, healthier atmosphere more naturally suited to youth; the only ones to show them a way out of their predicament. This way out may not lead directly into paradise, but to the young comrades it will mean real fulfillment and a recognition of their innermost nature. It will mean a struggle against the ruling class, against church and school, against the bourgeois parental home, and political reaction—a struggle for the material and sexual liberation not only of youth, but of all those suffering material and sexual oppression, of the oppressed masses in general.

We shall then see young people streaming into the organization in masses. Our new worry will then be how to obtain the means and the organizational forces to organize these masses of young comrades properly, and to offer them the knowledge— political as well as sexual—for which they hunger.

But we shall solve that problem, too, provided we are not afraid of the attacks of the bourgeoisie and of the petty-bourgeois Social Democratic leaders who are certain to reproach us with "running brothels."

Are we going to stop making our propaganda in favor of the abolition of factory, real-estate and land ownership—are we going to hesitate to carry through their expropriation when the time comes—just because the bourgeoisie call us a pack of thieves and robbers? Most certainly not! In the same way, we should not let the accusation that we are "running brothels" stop us from using every possible means to carry through the sexual liberation of all workers.

We must finally stop trying to prove to the bourgeoisie that we too are "moral" citizens. On the contrary, we must fight "morality" as they understand it with every means in our possession; we must unmask it as a brothel morality in the truest sense of the word. We must eradicate it and replace it with a morality of our own, which, as this paper explains, will be on the side of an ordered and satisfying sexual life.

Only then shall we find the right way out of our difficulties; only then shall we take the right steps to prepare for the sexual liberation of youth. We must learn to speak as openly as Comrade Fritz spoke on that evening:

> "We sometimes see in the organization that when there's only one or a few girls in a group, then they are completely isolated and, as it were, used for purely spiritual purposes. I think it's very important, especially for girls, that they aren't just given theoretical or even practical work to do; it's very stimulating, both for boys and for girls, to be friendly with one another. Of course, there mustn't be any pressurizing— we'd have to take a very energetic stand against that—and we must also prevent the girl's being hurt by the party workers thinking that because they're doing important work and can only spare a few minutes for sex, they're entitled to be careless about personal matters. The fellow goes now with this girl, now with that, and that's all as far as he's concerned, he gives it no more thought. But a girl, especially if she's only just joined the group, may be marked for a long time by such an experience, and if a party worker she thought the world of at first has used her just to pass the time, she may suffer the same fate as Sanya in the book, and I believe that for many girls things have often gone the same way as for the "First Girl." We must make sure that the numerical ratio between boys and girls improves, so that there aren't just a few girls facing a large number of fellows. But when the number of girls and fellows in a cell is about the same, then we mustn't make bourgeois reproaches such

as, 'He goes with one girl one day and with another the next.' The girls stay in the cell, don't they? And so do the fellows, and it's purely a bourgeois prejudice if we insist that a fellow must absolutely continue to remain friendly with the same girl; we have a proletarian view of the world and for us such rules simply don't exist."

This comrade has posed the question and has answered it, too, in an absolutely correct way. The bourgeois demands "responsibility" from youth, and by that he means "sexual continence"; he says that sexuality must not be given "free rein," and by this he means extramarital sexual relations in general. Yet who, in reality, is more irresponsible—or more lecherous—than the bourgeois moralist? Who seduces girls, who uses them as objects, and who indulges in drinking and sex orgies? We do not want to seduce or force anybody; we do not want to reduce sex to the level of dirt. That is our kind of responsibility: we do want young men and girls to have a satisfying sex life. If you wish to call that "giving free rein to sexuality," then do.

Many of our young men and girls know exactly what the difference is between giving rein to a sick sexuality and to a healthy one. If in our cultural-political and sexual-political work we had taken more into account the views of boys and girls from the junior organizations and less the opinions of intellectual comrades with their much more complex sensibilities, we should long ago have found the right political approach to the sex problem of youth. This is certainly not to disparage the intellectual comrades. But we aren't the only ones to say it, and our intellectual comrades—students, doctors, teachers, lawyers, etc. —should be well aware themselves that they come from bourgeois homes. And often they bring along with them their sexual insecurity, bourgeois judgments, an overestimation of so-called platonic relations between the sexes, etc. As regards sexual ideology, they have suffered much greater deformation than simple workers. Many moral condemnations of the sexual life of young people have come precisely from those intellectual comrades who haven't succeeded in solving the problem for themselves.

To return to Comrade Fritz's remarks: he, too, is right in the way he interprets the central problem of the book *The First Girl.* Let us briefly discuss this question. What does the book describe, what are the problems it raises, and what solutions does it propose?

The First Girl is a brilliant description of the struggle of Russian youth against reaction and for the building of socialism. For this reason alone it deserves to be put in the hands of every young person. But it also treats centrally the problem of sex. It describes a Communist party cell which is extraordinarily enlivened by the first girl who joins it; it really blossoms for the first time. Although every line makes it clear that the cause of this "shot in the arm" is the sexual attraction that the girl radiates, this is not explicitly stated. But we may be sure that a sexually less attractive girl comrade, even though she worked as well as Sanya, would not have played the same role. In the cell described in the book, as in our own organization, the problem is a generalized one: *one* girl to *seven* boys. That can only end in trouble. At first the cells blossom, but then, when the girl makes friends among the boys, the disproportion begins to be disturbing. The girl starts leading what is called a "loose" sexual life. We can't prove it, but our medical experience tells us that her "sleeping around," her unselective acceptance of all sexual partners, is perhaps primarily due to a disturbance of her sexuality. The boy who has fallen particularly deeply in love with her becomes jealous. It would be quite wrong to try to ignore this fact: without being explicitly mentioned, it is clearly implicit in the whole relationship. It is no accident that it is precisely this boy that eventually shoots her. Other comrades in the cell are equally interested in the honor of the group, yet none of them— except just that one—picks up his gun in order to shoot her. Why did this unhappy ending have to come?

The boys in this particular cell were caught up in the bourgeois idea that venereal disease is a frightful disgrace and has to be treated in secret. They failed to see that the real harm done to the cell was due to the fact that there was only one girl and that many men were without a sexual partner, and also to the fact that neither the men nor the girl dared to tackle the sex problem, which was so immensely important to them, as energetically as they tackled the problem of political desertion; lastly, the boy who shot the girl was completely unaware of his jealousy as the final link in a chain of causes—a particularly dangerous form of ignorance. It is absolutely against the spirit of Marxism and Leninism to ignore facts just because the fact of the class struggle comes first. The relative value of facts has to be assessed correctly. Beside and apart from the fact that Communists are bound together by the common goal of revolution, jealousy, too, has to be recognized as a fact of human life, and its importance in a given situation has to be properly judged. We must not simply say that jealousy is "unproletarian" and therefore does not exist among us. Sanya would not have had to die and the cell's party work would not have been wrecked had the question been openly raised and discussed in Sanya's cell; had not all members of the cell suffered from that highly dangerous legacy of capitalism, a fear of sexual matters; had they not—and especially the girl—been sexually disturbed in some way; had they known how venereal disease could be avoided.

We must try to the utmost to free ourselves from the peculiarly bourgeois notion of "loose living," which is still too common among us. The essential fact for us must not be how often and with which comrade a boy or a girl has sexual intercourse, but solely and exclusively whether they are causing personal unhappiness or damaging the political work. To say it straight out, and in the spirit of Comrade Fritz's remarks: If boys and girls "go now with this comrade, now with that" and if this does no harm to party work, if relationships among the comrades in the group are strengthened as a result, if girls and boys stay in the group because of it and the work prospers, if the personal development of both comrades is undamaged, then it would be reactionary to oppose it just because we have a crazy petty-bourgeois idea of morality. "Going now with one, now with another" can in some cases be a good thing. It can be harmful in many others. The only thing to be done is to make young people just as clear-headed and responsible in these matters as the tasks of revolutionary work demand.

To begin with: it would be a good idea to make a list of all the phrases that are used in discussions on sexual questions to conceal sexual prudery and as a result, cloud things still further, instead of making them clearer. Here are some of the phrases: "spiritual love," "comradeship," "the sexes coming to know one another," "progression from sensual to personal love," "understanding one another," etc.

Whenever anybody gets up and uses these words and phrases without making themselves clear, whenever we feel that somebody is just beating around the bush in regard to sexual intercourse, then we must tell him with our customary Communist frankness that he should either keep his mouth shut if he doesn't know what he's talking about, or, if he's got something to say, he should say it clearly. Otherwise we'll never get to the end of it.

When somebody comes along and says, "We need all our strength for the proletarian revolution," we agree with him a thousand percent. But if he says, "There's no such thing as private life," or, "Your private life is your private affair," then we must ask him if he maintains this as a general rule. We must talk to him and try to convince him that not only the sexual problem of youth but the question of sex as a whole is something quite different *before* the revolution, *during* the revolution and *after* the revolutoin. We shall be able to prove to him that it is non-Marxist and bourgeois to generalize and to refuse to consider concrete facts.

Before the revolution the task of class-conscious Communist youth is to mobilize the mass of all youth for the revolution. During this phase the sex problem of youth is part of the general front of the proletarian movement. Before the revolution we cannot do much to help the mass of young people in sexual matters, but we must politicize the issue, and transform the secret or open sexual rebellion of youth into revolutionary struggle against the capitalist social order.

In time of revolution, when the old order is shattered and everything outdated sinks into oblivion, when we are standing knee-deep in the debris of a corrupt, predatory, cruel, rotten social system, we must not moralize if the sexual contradictions among the young are at first intensified. We must see the sexual revolution in the context of general historical change, we must place ourselves alongside youth, we must help youth so far as we are able, but more than anything else we must realize that we are living in a time of transition. To be put off by the confusions of such a transitional period, to take fright at the "crazy youngsters" and to fall back into bourgeois attitudes, such as asceticism and moralizing, attitudes which it is one of the tasks of the proletarian revolution to eradicate, means being left behind by historical events and standing in the way of progress.

After the revolution, when the people liberated from their exploiters can at last begin to build socialism, to transform the economy into a socialist one and to destroy the rotten remains of capitalism in every sphere, the question is once again entirely different. The workers' society is then faced with the important task of thinking about the future order of sexual life and preparing for it. This future order cannot and will not be other than, as Lenin put it, a full love-life yielding joy and strength. Little as we can say about the details of such a life, it is nevertheless certain that in the Communist society the sexual needs of human beings will once more come into their own. To the degree that working hours and working pressures are reduced as a result of socialist rationalization of work and increased productivity of labor, sexual life, side by side with cultural and sports activities and no longer corrupted by money and brutality, will once again take its place on a higher level in human society. And human beings will once again become capable of enjoying their sexuality, because private economy, which is the basis of sexual oppression and which makes people incapable of enjoyment and therefore sick or crazy in the true sense of the word, will drop away. We are not painting a picture of utopia. We can clearly see developments taking place in that direction today, fourteen years after the proletarian revolution in the Soviet Union. Evidence that socialism alone can bring about sexual liberation is on our side. Therefore under capitalism we must use all our energies to convince the oppressed masses of this truth, too, and mobilize them for a merciless struggle against everything that impedes such liberation. And in this mobilization, precisely because of the great material and sexual oppression, the authoritarian bondage in which they are held today and which creates a link between them all, young people will march in the front rank. We shall win them over to the cause of the revolution, we shall be assured of their enthusiasm, to the extent that we understand their sexual plight and can get across to them the only message which is compatible with complete responsibility and truthfulness today. The message is this:

In capitalist society there can be no sexual liberation of youth, no healthy, satisfying sex life; if you want to be rid of your sexual troubles, fight for socialism. Only through socialism can you achieve sexual *joie de vivre*. Pay no attention to the opinions of people who don't know anything about sex. Socialism will put an end to the power of those who gaze up toward heaven as they speak of love while they crush and destroy the sexuality of youth.

WHAT IS CLASS CONSCIOUSNESS?

(1934)

"What Is Class Consciousness?" was first published by Reich from exile in Denmark, in June 1934, as a pamphlet; it was then signed Ernst Parell, and it provides a critique of the Communist politics that had been overwhelmed the year previously by the National Socialism of Hitler.—*L.B.*

Preface

The central idea running through this essay may be described as follows:

Because of the exhausting struggle that revolutionaries the world over have had to wage on many fronts, they tend to see the lives of human beings only from the standpoint of their ideology, or to pay attention only to those facts of social life which are somehow, whether closely or remotely, related to their thinking and struggle. Yet the majority of the world's population, whose liberation from the yoke of capitalism is the object of that struggle, know little or nothing of their efforts, sufferings or intentions. They lead their subjugated existences more and more unconsciously, and in that way, serve as props for the rule of capital. Ask yourself how many of the forty million adult German citizens really care about the executions of the German revolutionaries that they read about in the newspapers, and how many of them remain more or less unmoved, and you will then grasp what this essay is trying to achieve: *a joining of the consciousness of the revolutionary avant-garde with the consciousness of the average citizen.*

We can only indicate a few possible starting points and throw up a few questions, which until now have been ignored by the working-class movement. Some of what we have to say may be incorrectly framed. Some may be actually wrong. Yet it is an undeniable fact that, psychologically speaking, the real life of human beings takes place on a different level from what the champions of the social revolution believe—and yet their mistaken belief is based, precisely, upon their most profound insights into social existence. In this lies one of the reasons for the failure to date of the working-class movement.

This essay should be read as an appeal by average, non-political men to the future leaders of the revolution—an appeal for a better understanding, with a little less insistence on a grasp of the "historical process"; for a more adequate articulation of their real problems and desires; for a less theoretical grasp of the "subjective factor" in history; and for a better practical understanding of what this factor represents in *the life of the masses.*

Ernst Parell
[Wilhelm Reich]
June 1934

1) Two Kinds
of Class Consciousness

Exposition

The following attempt to expose and clarify, from the standpoint of mass psychology, some of the difficulties that arise in connection with the reforming of the working-class movement suffers from many inherent faults. The practical circumstances and the living conditions in which we German refugees have to do our work are not easy. In the first place, our close contact with the masses has been lost, or is only partially established. The newspapers supply us with distorted information, contradict one another, and ignore questions of mass psychology, which in itself is a source of error. Libraries are not available, or only insufficiently accessible to exiles. The hard struggle for existence, and persecution by the authorities of the host countries, also leave their mark. The current splintering of organizations and of the discussions within the working-class movement makes the task still harder. Add to this the novelty of the whole subject of political psychology and you have reasons enough to exclude any possibility of producing a one hundred percent accurate, perfect study that might be translated directly into practical politics. We shall be glad if we succeed in pinpointing some important questions which have received no attention hitherto and in answering a few of them. Apart from that, we do not hope to do more than outline certain directions for our fellow fighters' initiative and for a critical reexamination of the intellectual methods and techniques at present employed by the revolutionary front.

The essay presented here is also a response to some questions that have been raised since the appearance of *The Mass Psychology of Fascism* and, in part, to certain criticisms that, in my opinion, suffer from the lack of a grasp of psychological problems such as is typical of many political economists.

Discussions with a variety of political groups have shown that any reply to the question What is class consciousness? must be preceded by a brief definition of the fundamental problems of the political situation as it is at this moment.

The severe defeat of the socialist movement in Germany is already exercising an adverse effect in other countries, and fascism is today rapidly gaining ground on the revolutionary movement everywhere.

Both the Second and Third Internationals have shown their inability to master the situation even theoretically, to say nothing of the practical side: the Second International, by its fundamentally bourgeois politics; the Third by its lack of self-criticism, the incorrigibility of its mistaken attitudes, and above all by its inability—due in part to lack of will—to eradicate bureaucracy in its own camp.

The Socialist Workers' Party and the International Communists want a "new International." Serious differences have arisen regarding the manner in which the new party is to be founded. Trotsky has already called for the founding of the Fourth International. The Socialist Workers' Party agrees in principle, but wants the new International to be the *result* of the workers' rallying together instead of, as Trotsky wants, creating the Fourth International first and rallying the workers around it.

The question we in the Sex-Pol movement are asking is this: Should an organization be founded at once, and should recruitment to it be based upon its declared program? Or should the program and the ideology be allowed time to penetrate the masses, and organizational steps be taken only later on a broader base? We have opted for the second method—believing that a "looser" preparatory organization offers many advantages, in that it avoids any premature setting of limits and the danger of sectarianism, gives better opportunities for permeating other organizations, and much else besides.

Our considered view of the prospects for further political development also supports this choice. The Sex-Pol working community believes that there are three main possibilities. First, there is the possibility of an unpredictable uprising in Germany in the near future. Since none of the existing organizations is even remotely prepared for this eventuality, none of them could control such a movement or lead it consciously to a conclusion. This possibility, however, is the least likely. Should it happen, the situation would be chaotic and the outcome extremely uncertain, but it would nevertheless be the best solution, and we should support and promote it in every way from the very start. Second, the working-class movement may need a few years before it rallies once more in terms of theory and organization. It will then form an *integrated* movement under good, highly trained, purposeful and determined leadership, will struggle for power in Germany, and will seize it within, say, the next *two* decades. This prospect is the most probable, but it requires energetic, unswerving and tireless preparation beginning today. Third, the last major possibility is that the rallying of the working-class movement under new, good and reliable leadership will not occur quickly enough or will fail to occur altogether; that international fascism will establish itself and consolidate its positions everywhere, especially by reason of its immanent skill in attracting children and youth; that it will acquire a permanent mass base, and will be helped by economic conjunctures, however marginal. In such a case the socialist movement must reckon with a long—a very long— period of economic, political and cultural barbarism lasting many decades. Its task then will be to *prove* that it was not mistaken *in principle* and that, in the last analysis, it was right *after all*. This prospect reveals the full extent of the responsibility we bear.

We propose, so far as conditions permit, to allow for the *first* possibility; to make the *second* the real target of our work, because it is the more likely one, and to concentrate all our efforts on bringing it about while doing everything within human power to avoid the *third*.

If, then, our aim is to create unity and striking power in the working class, and to bring about an alliance of all strata of the working population, we must begin by drawing a sharp dividing line between ourselves and those who talk a great deal about "unity" but, in practice, promote nothing but discord even though this may not be their real intention. Why is it that even now, after the German catastrophe, the forming of sectarian cliques continues undeterred? Why do things look so bleak in responsible circles both inside and outside Germany? Why do the old methods of sterile scholastic discussion and useless reciprocal recrimination refuse to disappear, refuse to yield to livelier, more effective methods better adapted to the reality of today?

We believe that this unhappy state of affairs is due to our clinging to old, worn-out, ossified dogmas, words, schemas and methods of discussion, and that this clinging is in turn due to the lack of *new* ways of posing problems, *new* ways of thinking and of seeing things with a completely fresh, uncorrupted eye. We are convinced that just one good new idea, just one effective new slogan would rally everyone except the completely hopeless addicts of debate, and would put an end to sterile talk. Anyone who feels "insulted" can take it that we mean him. The next task is to turn living Marxism into reality—first of all, in the way we see reality and discuss it.

This brings us to the question of the founding of a new international organization. If the congress convened for this purpose produced nothing but the old methods, slogans and ways of thinking and discussion, the organization would be stillborn. The expropriation of capital, the socialization of the means of production, the establishment of workers', peasants', soldiers' and employees' rule over the capitalists—these are old concepts and we know all this; we also know that we want true democracy for the working people and that the power is not seized in the voting booth but with arms. We know all this and much else. To proclaim it all once more and lay it down in a program would be of little value, for it has all been done before. The great question is why the people did not listen to us, why our organization fell victim to arteriosclerosis, why we allowed ourselves to be suffocated by our bureaucracy, why the masses indeed acted against their own interest in carrying Hitler to power. If we had the masses behind us today, we should not have to spend such an infinite amount of energy on the question of strategy and tactics, important as it may be.

Various groups in the movement today are using strategy and tactics *against one another*. What we must do above all, if we mean to achieve success, is to face these fundamental problems with completely new ideas, completely new methods of influencing the masses, with a completely new structure of both ideology and personnel.

We hardly need to supply detailed arguments to prove that we failed to speak the language of the broad masses—the nonpolitical or ideologically oppressed broad masses—who in the end assured the triumph of reaction. The masses did not understand our resolutions, or what we meant by socialism; they did not and still do not trust us. They read our papers out of a sense of duty, or not at all. Those who joined the movement had an inarticulate socialist feeling. But we were incapable of turning this feeling to advantage, and in the end it carried Hitler to power. The fact that we suffered our greatest defeat in getting hold of the broad masses, in inspiring the masses, is the fundamental cause of the many shortcomings, great and small, of the working-class movement: the rigid party loyalty of the Social Democrats, the resentment and sense of injury felt by many proletarian leaders, our addiction to empty debate and of the scholastic Marxism we practiced.

One element in the fundamental cause of the failure of socialism—only an element, but an important one, no longer to be ignored, no longer to be regarded as secondary—is the absence of an effective Marxist doctrine of political psychology. This does not merely mean that such a doctrine still remains to be created: it also means that the working class as a whole is extremely wary of psychological examination, of conscious practical psychology. This shortcoming of ours has become the greatest advantage of the class enemy, the mightiest weapon of fascism.

While we presented the masses with superb historical analyses and economic treatises on the contradictions of imperialism, Hitler stirred the deepest roots of their emotional being. As Marx would have put it, we left the praxis of the subjective factor to the idealists; we acted like mechanistic, economistic materialists. Am I exaggerating? Am I seeing the problem through the perspective of a narrow specialization?

Let us try to answer this question with the help of concrete examples, both important and apparently less important ones. We do not propose a panacea but only a small contribution which may be a start.

An effective policy, whose ultimate goal is the achievement of socialism and the establishment of the rule of labor over capital, must not only be based on a recognition of those movements and changes which occur objectively and independently of our will as a result of the development of the productive forces. This policy must also, simultaneously and on the same level, take account of what happens "in people's heads," i.e., in the psychical structures of the human beings who are subjected to these processes and who actually carry them out—people from different countries and cities, people of different occupations, ages and sexes.

The concept of class consciousness occupies a central place in the socialist movement and its politics. Great stress is placed upon the oppressed strata of the populations of all countries "becoming class-conscious" as the most urgent precondition of the revolutionary overthrow of the present social system. By this we obviously mean that human beings must undergo a certain change under the effect of economic and social processes so as to become capable of performing the social act of revolution. We know, too, that Lenin created the political vanguard and the revolutionary party in order to encourage this transformation in ordinary men and women—to accelerate and concentrate it, and mold it into a political force. In the vanguard, made up of the finest and most conscious fighters for socialism, the consciousness of the social situation—of the means necessary for mastering it, of the way forward to socialism—was to be concentrated at the approximate level to which the working masses would have to be raised if the task of revolution was to be successfully accomplished. This is no more and no less than a definition of the policy summed in the term "united front."

Two examples should in themselves suffice to show that we are far removed from a concrete understanding of what class consciousness actually is.

In a recently published brochure entitled *Neu Beginnen* (Starting Afresh), the demand is very rightly made for a "revolutionary party," for a leadership which is revolutionary in the full sense of the word; yet the existence of class consciousness in the proletariat is denied.

> The basis of all their [the Second and Third Internationals'] insights and actions is the belief in a revolutionary spontaneity immanent within the proletariat . . . But what if such revolutionary spontaneity exists only in the imagination of the Socialist Party leaders and not in reality? What if the proletariat is not at all driven toward the 'final socialist struggle from within itself,' that is to say by natural social forces? . . . Incapable of thinking otherwise than in terms of their dogmas and theories, they [the leaders] believe with truly religious fervor in spontaneous revolutionary forces . . . (p. 6)

The unparalleled heroism shown by the Austrian workers on February 12–16, 1934 proves that revolutionary spontaneity can very well exist without a consciousness of the "final socialist struggle." Revolutionary spontaneity and consciousness of the "final struggle" are two quite separate things.

We are told that the leadership must carry revolutionary consciousness into the masses. Undoubtedly it must. But—it is our turn to ask—what if we do not yet clearly know what we mean by revolutionary consciousness? In Germany there were, at the end, some thirty million *anticapitalist* workers, more than enough *in number* to make a social revolution; yet it was precisely with the help of the staunchest *anticapitalist* mentality that fascism came into power. Does an anticapitalist mentality qualify as class consciousness, or is it just the beginning of class consciousness, just a precondition for the birth of class consciousness? What is class consciousness, anyway?

Lenin created the concept of the vanguard, of the revolutionary party, as well as the organization itself whose purpose was to do what the masses themselves could not spontaneously achieve. "We have already said," wrote Lenin, "that the workers cannot, in fact, have a social-democratic consciousness. Such consciousness can only be brought in from outside. The history of all countries shows that the working class if left to itself is capable only of attaining a trade-unionist consciousness, i.e., of realizing the necessity for banding together in trade unions, waging a struggle against the entrepreneurs, demanding various forms of labor legislation from the government, etc."

In other words, the working class does derive a "consciousness" from its class situation—a consciousness, it is true, which is not sufficient to shake off the rule of capital (a tightly organized party is needed for this); but can it not be said that preliminary forms or elements of what is called class consciousness, or revolutionary consciousness, do, perhaps, exist after all? What is this consciousness? How can we define it? What does it look like in practice?

The denial of what might be called class consciousness or its elements, or of the preconditions for class consciousness, as a *spontaneous* formation within the oppressed class, is based on the fact that in this concrete form *it is not recognized*. This is what puts the leadership into a hopeless position, for however courageous, well trained and otherwise excellent the leaders may be, if the proletariat possesses nothing that might be called class consciousness, why then, no leadership on earth will succeed in giving it one. Anyway, what is this thing that is supposed to be carried into the masses? Highly specialized understanding of the social process and its contradictions? Complete knowledge of the laws of capitalist exploitation? Did the partisans in revolutionary Russia have such knowledge when they fought so splendidly, or did they, perhaps, not need it at all? Were they "class-conscious" workers and peasants or mere rebels? We raise these questions only to show that they lead nowhere.

Let us try to proceed from simple practice and experience.

A short while ago a great deal was being said within a certain political group about class consciousness and the need to "raise class consciousness on a mass scale." The listener was forced to ask himself, perhaps for the first time: What exactly are they talking about? What do they mean by what they call class consciousness? One of the people present, who had kept very quiet the whole time, asked a leading party official who had insisted with particular fervor on the need for developing class consciousness among the German proletariat whether he could name five concrete features of class consciousness and perhaps also five factors which impede its development. If one wanted to develop class consciousness it was surely necessary to know what it was that one wanted to develop and why it did not develop of its own accord under the pressures of material poverty. The question seemed logical. The party official was at first a little surprised, hesitated for an instant, and then declared confidently, "Why, hunger, of course!" "Is a hungry storm trooper class-conscious?" was the prompt counterquestion. Is a hungry thief class-conscious when he steals a sausage? Or an unemployed worker who accepts two marks for joining a reactionary demonstration? Or an adolescent who throws stones at the police? But if hunger, on which the CP had based its whole mass psychology, is not in itself an element of class consciousness, then what is? What is freedom? What are its concrete features? Wherein does socialist freedom differ from the national freedom which Hitler promises?

The answers until now have been extremely unsatisfactory. Has the left-wing press ever raised or answered questions of this kind? It has not. The notion that the oppressed class can carry a revolution through to a triumphant conclusion without leadership, and out of a spontaneously generated revolutionary will, is certainly false; but it is just as wrong to believe the opposite—that all that matters is the leadership because it has to *create* class consciousness.

No leadership could ever do so unless the beginnings of class consciousness were already present, unless class consciousness were already being formed spontaneously. But if a certain psychical situation in the masses exists, and has to be brought into harmony with the highly developed consciousness of the revolutionary leadership in order to create the subjective preconditions for a social revolution, then it is all the more essential to find an answer to the question: What is class consciousness? Should anyone object that the question is superfluous because our policy has always consisted in satisfying the workers' day-to-day demands, then we shall ask: Are we developing class consciousness if we insist on electric fans being installed on a shop floor? What if the Nazi shop steward does the same, and is perhaps a better speaker than our men? Will he have the workers on his side? Yes, he will. Where is the difference between the socialist and the fascist defense of "day-to-day interests," between our freedom slogans and the Nazi slogan of Strength Through Joy?

Do we mean the same thing when we speak of the class consciousness of a proletarian apprentice and that of a proletarian youth leader? It is said that the consciousness of the masses must be raised to the level of revolutionary class consciousness; if by this we mean the sophisticated understanding of historical processes which a revolutionary leader must possess, then our aim is utopian. Under capitalism it will never be possible, whatever propaganda methods we use, to instill such highly specialized knowledge in the broad masses who have to do the actual work of insurrection and revolution. When, at electoral meetings, we used simply to shout slogans, or if, as often happened at the Sports Palace in Berlin, a party official spent hours spouting learnedly about the finance politics of the bourgeoisie or the contradictions between the United States and Japan, the spontaneous enthusiasm of the masses was killed every time. By assuming that the masses were interested in objective economic analyses and had the intellectual equipment to follow them, we indeed killed what is rightly called the "class feeling" of the thousands-strong audience.

Revolutionary Marxist policy to date has presupposed the

existence of a ready-made class consciousness in the proletariat without being able to define it in concrete detail. It has projected its own, often incorrect idea of sociological processes into the consciousness of the oppressed class, thus making itself guilty, as someone recently pointed out, of "subjective idealism." And yet one could unambiguously sense the mass class consciousness at every Communist meeting, and its atmosphere could be clearly distinguished from that of other political meetings. In other words, there must be something like a class consciousness in the broad masses, and this consciousness is fundamentally different from that of the revolutionary leadership. To put it concretely, there are *two kinds* of class consciousness, *that of the leadership and that of the masses,* and the two have to be brought into harmony with one another. The leadership has no task more urgent, besides that of acquiring a precise understanding of the objective historical process, than to understand: (a) what are the progressive desires, ideas and thoughts which are latent in people of different social strata, occupations, age groups and sexes, and (b) what are the desires, fears, thoughts and ideas ("traditional bonds") which prevent the progressive desires, ideas, etc., from developing.

The class consciousness of the masses is neither ready-formed, as the CP leadership believed, nor is it completely absent or structured in a totally different way, as the Socialist Party leadership believed. It is present as a number of concrete elements, which in themselves do not yet constitute class consciousness (e.g., simple hunger), but which, *in conjunction with one another,* could become class consciousness. These elements are not present in pure form, but are permeated, mixed and interwoven with opposing psychical meanings and forces. A Hitler can go on being successful with his formula that the masses can be influenced like little children—that they simply give back to you what you put into them—only so long as the revolutionary party fails to fulfill its most important task, that of developing and distilling mass class consciousness from its present level to a higher one. There was no question of this being done in Germany.

The content of the revolutionary leader's class consciousness is not of a personal kind—when personal interests (ambition, etc.) are present, they inhibit his activity. The class consciousness of the masses, on the other hand (we are not speaking of the negligibly small minority of consciously revolutionary workers), is entirely personal.

The former is filled with the knowledge of the contradictions of the capitalist economic system, the immense possibilities of a socialist planned economy, the need for social revolution to establish a balance between the form of appropriation and the form of production, the progressive and retrograde forces of history, etc. The latter has no such far-reaching perspectives— it is concerned with the trivial problems of everyday life. The former covers the objective historical and socio-economic process, the outward conditions, both economic and social, to which men are subject in society. This process must be understood, it must be grasped and mastered if one wishes to become its master rather than its slave. For example, a planned economy is necessary in order to abolish the disastrous crises of capitalism and thus create a firm foundation for the lives of all working people. And creating such an economy requires, *inter alia,* a precise knowledge of U.S.–Japanese contradictions. But the latter type of consciousness lacks *all* interest in the U.S.–Japanese or British–American contradictions, or even in the development of productive forces; it is guided solely by the subjective reflections and effects of these objective facts in and upon an immense variety of trivial everyday matters; its content is an interest in food, clothing, fashion, family relations, the possibility of sexual satisfaction in the narrowest sense, in sexual play and entertainment in a wider sense, such as the cinema, the theater, amusement arcades, parks and dance halls, and also in such questions as the bringing up of children, the arrangement of living space, leisure activities, etc.

Being and the conditions of being are reflected, anchored and reproduced in the psychical structure of men and women at the same time that they form that structure. The objective process and the ways of inhibiting or encouraging and controlling it are accessible to us only through this psychical structure. We make and change the world only through the mind of man, through his will for work, his longing for happiness—in brief, through his psychical existence. The "Marxists" who have degenerated into "Economists" forgot this a long time ago. A global economic and political policy, if it means to create and secure international socialism (not National Socialism!), must find a point of contact with trivial, banal, primitive, simple everyday life, with the desires of the *broadest* masses of all countries and at all levels. *Only in this way can the objective sociological process become one with the subjective consciousness of men and women, abolishing the contradiction and the distance between the two.* The workers, who create wealth and the material basis of culture, must be shown the stage which culture and education have reached "at the top" and be taught to contrast it with the way *they themselves* live; they must be shown how *modest* they are and how they *make a virtue of their modesty,* even if this has sometimes actually been called a revolutionary virtue! Only when we succeed in merging these two kinds of consciousness, and only then, shall we leave behind us the philosophical inner-party debates on tactics, etc.; only then shall we break through to the living tactics of a living mass-movement, to a political activity truly linked with life. We are not exaggerating when we assert that the working-class movement could have saved itself an endless succession of sectarian and scholastic struggles, of factions and splinter groups—that it could have shortened the hard road toward that most *self-evident* of things, which is socialism—if it had drawn the material for its propaganda and tactics and policies not only from books, but, in the first place, from the life of the masses. One aspect of the situation today is that young people are, on the average, far ahead of their "leaders" on a number of questions; for example, it is necessary to speak "tactically" or "tactfully" with the leaders about things like sex, which the young understand as a matter of course. It ought to be the other way about: the leader should be the epitome of class consciousness of the first kind and should work toward developing the second kind.

Anyone familiar with the ideological struggles of the working-class movement will perhaps have followed us more or less readily thus far, and will probably have thought: "But this is nothing new—why the long discourse?" He will soon see that when we get down to brass tacks, many of those who are in general agreement with us will nevertheless hesitate, raise objections, have second thoughts, and invoke Marx and Lenin to oppose us. Before anyone so inclined reads any further, we recommend once more, as a test, that he should try to clarify in his own mind just five concrete elements of class consciousness and five obstacles to it.

The following statement will meet with a great deal of resistance on the part of those who regard class consciousness as a matter of ethics. Political reaction, with fascism and the church at its head, demands that the masses should renounce happiness here on earth; it demands chastity, obedience, self-denial, sacrifice for the nation, the people, the fatherland. The problem is not that the reactionaries demand this, but that the masses, by complying with these demands, are supporting the reactionaries and allowing them to enrich themselves and extend their power. The reactionaries take advantage of the guilt feelings of mass individuals, of their ingrained modesty, their tendency to suffer privation silently and willingly, sometimes even happily, and they take advantage of their identification with the glorious *Führer,* whose "love of the people" is for them a substitute for any real satisfaction of their needs. The revolutionary vanguard, through the conditions of their existence and the aims they pursue, are themselves subject to a similar ideology. But what is true of, shall we say, the youth leaders is in no way applicable to the youth they are supposed to lead. If one wants to lead the mass of the population into battle against capital, to develop their class consciousness, to bring them to the point of revolt, then one must recognize the principle of self-denial as harmful, lifeless, stupid and reactionary.

Socialism affirms that the productive forces of society are sufficiently developed to ensure a life corresponding to the average cultural level of society for the broadest masses of all countries. *Against the principle of self-denial preached by political reaction, we must set the principle of happiness and abundance on earth*. We need hardly point out that by this we do not mean bowling tournaments and beer drinking. The modesty of the "man in the street," which is his cardinal virtue in the eyes of fascism and the church, is his greatest fault from the socialist point of view and one of the many factors which impede his class consciousness. Any socialist political economist can prove that sufficient wealth exists in the world to provide a happy life for all workers. But we must prove this more thoroughly, more consistently, in greater detail than we generally do; we must bring all the meticulous care of scientific scholarship to bear upon demonstrating it.

The average worker in Germany or elsewhere was not interested in the Soviet Five-Year Plan as a revolutionary economic achievement in itself but only insofar as it meant increased satisfaction of the needs of workers. His thoughts went more or less like this: If socialism isn't going to mean anything but sacrifice, self-denial, poverty and privation for us, then we don't care whether such misery is called socialism or capitalism. Let socialist economy prove its excellence by satisfying our needs and keeping pace with their growth.

What I mean is that *heroism, which is a virtue in the leadership, is not transferable to the broad masses.* If the masses suffer privations in a period of revolution, they are entitled to demand definite proof that these privations are only a *passing phase* and thus differ from the privations suffered under capitalism.

This is one of the many difficulties which arise from the theory of "socialism in one country." We fully expect that this statement will meet with indignant denials; we shall doubtless be called "petty-bourgeois " and "epicurean." Yet Lenin promised the peasants that the landowners' lands would be distributed among them, although he was very well aware that land distribution encourages a "petty-bourgeois mentality." It was essentially on the strength of this slogan that he carried the revolution through, *with* the peasants and not *against* them. And in doing so he undoubtedly violated a lofty principle of socialist political theory, the principle of collectivism. The Hungarian revolutionaries of 1919, on the other hand, had lofty principles but no understanding of the subjective factor. *They knew the demands of history but not of the peasants.* They socialized the land at once and—they lost the revolution. Let this example suffice to

prove, in place of many others, that the ultimate aims of socialism can only be achieved by fulfilling the immediate aims of
mass individuals, by ensuring a much greater degree of satisfaction of their needs. Only then can revolutionary heroism
occur in the *broad masses*.

Few errors are as far-reaching as the view that "class consciousness" is an ethical concept. The ascetic view of revolution
has led only to complications and defeats.

We can easily test whether class consciousness is an ethical
or a nonethical, rational phenomenon by considering a few
examples.

If two human beings, A and B, are starving, one of them
may accept his fate, refuse to steal, and take to begging or die
of hunger, while the other may take the law into his own hands
in order to obtain food. A large part of the proletariat, often
called *Lumpenproletariat,* live according to the principles of B.
We must be clear about this, although we certainly do not share
the romantic admiration of the criminal underworld. Which of
the two types has more elements of class consciousness in him?
Stealing is *not yet* a sign of class consciousness; but a brief
moment of reflection shows, despite our inner moral resistance,
that the man who refuses to submit to law and steals when he is
hungry, that is to say, the man who manifests a will to live, has
more energy and fight in him than the one who lies down un-
protesting on the butcher's slab. We persist in believing that the
fundamental problem of a correct psychological doctrine is not
why a hungry man steals but the exact opposite: Why doesn't
he steal?

We have said that stealing is *not yet* class consciousness,
and we stick to that. A brick is not yet a house; but you use
bricks to build houses with—besides planks, mortar, glass and
(here I am thinking of the role of the party) engineers, stone-
masons, carpenters, etc.

We shall get nowhere if we regard class consciousness as an
ethical imperative, and if, in consequence, we try to outdo the
spokesmen of the bourgeoisie in condemning the sexuality of
youth, the wickedness of prostitutes and criminals and the im-
morality of thieves. But, you may ask, if we adopt the opposite

view, shall we not be harming the interests of the revolution? Couldn't political reaction turn our amoral conception of class consciousness into propaganda against us? Certainly it could and it will, but it does so anyway, however much we try to prove our unimpeachable morality—it does us no good, for it only drives the victims of capitalism into the arms of political reaction because they do not feel we understand them. Yet in the eyes of political reaction we are no better for all our morality. In its eyes we are thieves because we want to abolish private owner-ship of the means of production. Do we therefore want to abandon or conceal this fundamental intention? And is it not cited against us?

Everything, without exception, which today bears the name of morality and ethics serves the oppressors of working human-ity. We can prove both in theory and in practice that our new order of social life, *just because* it will be an amoral one, is capable of replacing the chaos of today by real order. Lenin's attitude to the question of proletarian ethics was unambiguously connected with the interests of the proletarian revolution. What-ever serves the revolution is ethical, whatever harms it is un-ethical. Let us try to formulate the question in another way. *Everything that contradicts the bourgeois order, everything that contains a germ of rebellion, can be regarded as an element of class consciousness; everything that creates or maintains a bond with the bourgeois order, that supports and reinforces it, is an impediment to class consciousness.*

When, during the November 1919 revolution, the masses were demonstrating in the Tiergarten in Berlin, most of the demonstrators took great care not to walk on the grass. This story, whether it is true or merely well invented, sums up an important aspect of the tragedy of the revolutionary movement: *the bourgeoisification of those who are to make the revolution.*

2) Some Concrete Elements of Class Consciousness and Some Elements Inhibiting It

We shall now try, without going very deeply into theoretical explanations, to describe certain ways of the behavior of average human beings, some of which work in favor of revolutionary consciousness, while others impede its development, i.e., are reactionary psychical attitudes. We are concerned here only with those psychical facts which are oriented either to the left or to the right, not with those which are politically indifferent and could benefit any political orientation—e.g., oratorical talent, critical ability, love of nature, etc. The examples which follow could be multiplied at will; these particular ones were established by me with the help of two young people.

In Juveniles (During and After Puberty)

Political parties of all hues have always struggled for possession of the young, not only because the young have a future before them (unlike most adults, who, as the witticism goes, "have a future behind them"). We are entitled, therefore, to begin by speaking of youth. Its capacity for enthusiasm and its readiness to take action, which, in turn, is the result of sexual maturation, make youth the most active age group. These qualities are not yet, in themselves, specifically oriented toward the right or left. The church, for example, has a larger number of juvenile followers than the left-wing parties. Yet it is not difficult to discern elements within the life experience of young people which drive them politically toward the left or right.

In every juvenile there is a tendency toward rebellion against authoritarian oppression, especially against the parents, who are usually the executors of the authority of the state. It is this rebellion, first and foremost, which usually draws the young into politically left-wing movements. It is always connected with a more or less conscious and more or less urgent desire for the realization of their sexual life. The more clearly developed the natural heterosexual inclinations of a juvenile are, the more open he will be to revolutionary ideas; the stronger the homosexual tendency within him and also the more repressed his awareness of sexuality in general, the more easily he will be drawn toward the right. Sexual inhibitions, fear of sexual activity and the guilt feelings which go with it, are always factors which push the young toward the political right, or, at the least, inhibit their revolutionary thinking.

Bondage to parents and the parental home is a grave, irreversible inhibiting element. (We shall call irreversible those psychical facts which can never become positive elements of class consciousness, and can therefore never be used by the revolutionary party in the interests of social revolution.) The only exceptions to this rule are the children of parents who already think in a revolutionary way. Parental bondage may have a positive effect in such a case; but in practice, it often leads to a reactionary mentality as a protest against the parents.

There is one particular need that moves young people more than any other, a need whose satisfaction would mean more than anything else to them, and yet which is not to be found in any manifesto or program for youth: the need for a place of their own to live. This need may be bracketed with antiparent rebellion as a positive element of class consciousness. Moreover, it is a desire which can never be satisfied by the kind of order that political reaction wants to establish or maintain. It is not opposed by any inhibiting factor; it is strong even among the most reactionary girls. The desire for life in a youth collective is a further positive element, but this is generally opposed by family bonds, "love of a home life," etc., which can be removed if the collective takes the place of home. The attraction of the dance hall operates powerfully in almost all juveniles. Unlike parental bondage, this is a reversible element, i.e., while it inhibits revolutionary consciousness under ordinary circumstances, it may strongly encourage it if the problem of the relationship between politics and private life is solved in a revolutionary way. A few exceptionally talented youth organizers in Germany have occasionally been successful in this respect.

Today, both the collective instinct and the attraction of the dance hall are of considerable advantage to the political reaction in Germany, which has *organized* these elements—the Christians in the form of *Kränzchen* (social gatherings), the Nazis, without doubt, in their collective youth associations.

The following report has been received from Germany:

> I talked recently with a seventeen-year-old schoolgirl from Berlin who was spending her holidays here. She attends school at Wilmersdorf and a few things which came out casually in our conversation will surely strike you as interesting.
>
> The boys and girls of the Hitler Youth (H.J.) and of the League of German Girls (B.d.M.) enjoy unheard-of freedom at school and at home, which naturally manifests itself, *inter alia,* in sexual activity and friendships.
>
> In the past, no girl of school grade would have dared to be seen with a boyfriend picking her up after classes. Today, boys (especially H.J. boys) wait outside the school in a crowd, and everybody accepts this as a matter of course. Everybody says that B.d.M. stands for *Bubi-drück-mich* (I-wanna-be-hugged). The Dahlem group of the B.d.M. had to be dissolved because six girls (under eighteen) became pregnant.
>
> Isn't it interesting to see how an attempt to organize the young can loosen the fetters of the parental home? These

examples are certainly symptomatic, as has been confirmed to me in the meantime.

It is not correct to say that these boys and girls "enjoy unheard-of freedom." Whoever says so cannot see the real relations, contradictions and needs involved. Even in the past, boys would come to the school door to fetch their girlfriends, if not, perhaps, at that particular school. Getting pregnant, having yourself picked up at school by a boyfriend, etc., appears as "sexual freedom" only in the light of petty-bourgeois morality. The freedom that the young people of Dahlem [a middle-class residential area of Berlin] are acquiring today has been taken for granted for a long, long time in Neukölln [a working-class area]. If we want to get an overall view, we must first see the deeply contradictory situation of the Hitler Youth: on the one hand, an extremely severe, authoritarian military training and segregation of the sexes, and on the other hand, destruction of family bondage through the collectivization of youth; the violent perturbation of family morality along with the insistence on rigid fascist family ideology. German revolutionaries must follow closely the development of these contradictions and explain them to the persons concerned.

In this specific case we must welcome the separation of the young from their homes; yet we must clearly analyze the contradiction between this separation and the official ideology of *Führer* and family. We must also realize that the young, who long to escape from the bonds of the parental home *into freedom and self-determination,* are in reality merely entering *another authoritarian relationship*—that of the labor service camp or the fascist organization—where they once again have to keep their mouths shut. It is precisely in the area of sexuality that these contradictions are most clearly revealed. To the extent that it is, however subjectively and inarticulately, revolutionary, the "freer behavior" described in the report corresponds to progressive tendencies in the Hitler Youth; but no really revolutionary social leadership would ever close down a group because a few of the girls happened to get pregnant. This means, as our correspondent naïvely fails to see, that the forms of behavior which he describes are not at all pleasing to the Nazi Party—indeed, are unacceptable to it. We must make it completely clear to these Hitler youths and girls that they are entitled to complete self-determination, and that it is the duty of society to provide for their needs, including first and foremost their sexual needs. If we regard what is happening today as sexual freedom, we are overlooking two things. First, that even this small degree of freedom is enough to make the state apparatus feel obliged to intervene; and secondly, that these are no more than mere glimmerings of freedom. There can be no question of freedom so long as the entire state and social ideology is against it; so long as girls and youths have nowhere to go when they wish to be left undisturbed, no contraceptives, and no understanding of the necessities and difficulties of sex life in general; so long as they are brought up in such a way that conflict is bound to accompany the start of their sexual life; so long as they cannot decide, together with their teachers, on the nature of their schooling and the manner of their preparation for the tasks of social life; so long as they have to study the dates of the births and deaths of the kings of Prussia, and not the history of the poor in the suburbs of Berlin and Hamburg, in Jüterbog and in the remotest country village.

It cannot be the ideal of youth to serve a *Führer* without ever uttering a word of criticism, or to die for capitalist interests disguised as the interests of the Fatherland. Their ideal would be to take possession of their own lives and make of them what they want. Youth must be responsible only to itself. Then, and only then, will the gulf between society and its youth disappear.

If youth understands the nature of the gulf which separates it from society today, it must by that token recognize itself as being oppressed: thus it becomes ripe for social revolution. If it can do away with the gulf, make social reality fit its own needs, and clear a path for its real, concrete, objective urge toward freedom, it becomes the executor of social revolution.

We cannot theoretically prove the necessity for social revolution to the youth of all countries and continents; we can only demonstrate this necessity by drawing attention to the needs and contradictions of youth. At the center of these needs and contradictions stands the immense problem of the sexual life of youth.

In a way that is contrary to the ideas usually held by political parties, our youth work teaches us that the average juvenile's insight into the class situation is very superficial and uncertain. Genuine insight is very rare, and is found only among intellectually precocious juveniles or those from revolutionary homes where they have never suffered oppression. Being an industrial apprentice tends to produce dull indifference rather than a revolutionary mentality. The apprentice mentality could become positive only in conjunction with other, more specific elements of class consciousness, e.g., the demand for satisfactory leisure activities. Hunger, too, contrary to the vulgar view, is in itself a demoralizing factor, leading to gangs, etc., rather than to class consciousness. You meet people who suffer hunger and other privations just as often, or even more often, in the Christian organizations or among the young storm troopers than in the YCL. Privation can become a powerful positive force if it is related to the desire for romantic experience, to sexual needs and to the child-parent relationship. But we must clearly realize that hunger by itself, when it does not demoralize, often drives young people into the arms of various bourgeois welfare organizations. Our experience shows that hunger has a far more revolutionizing effect on young people if it is accompanied by, for instance, the fear of being put in a home, which is easily recognizable as a class institution.

The juvenile tendency toward bondage to leaders and ideas is politically nonspecific; it can be exploited either way, and therefore easily becomes a harmful element unless the revolutionary party comes in first and channels it in the right direction.

Love of sport, the attraction of men in military uniforms (which please the girls, and vice versa), marching songs, etc., are generally, under the conditions obtaining in the proletarian movement today, antirevolutionary factors because the political reaction has far greater possibilities of satisfying the demands they create. Football, in particular, has a directly depoliticizing effect and encourages the reactionary tendencies of youth. Yet these tendencies are, in principle, reversible, i.e., they can be

used to the advantage of the left, provided we drop the economistic view of the all-powerful nature of pure hunger. The
extraordinarily high membership turnover of the revolutionary
youth organizations proves that the contradictions which I have
been describing have not been resolved. Revolutionary tendencies have not been properly developed, and the inhibiting
factors have not been adequately dealt with by the revolutionary
organizations, not so much because of absence of class feeling
in the young as because of the psychological shortcomings of
our party work. Only a tiny minority stay in the organization,
and even they only for a few years. I have no figures at my
disposal, but experience has shown that juveniles as well as
adult men and women in the millions from every walk of life
have, over the last decade, passed through the revolutionary
organizations without forming any lasting loyalty or bond to the
revolutionary cause. What drove them into our organizations?
Not uniforms, not material benefits, but solely their own inarticulate socialist convictions, their class feeling. Why did they
not stay? Because the organization failed to develop this feeling.
Why did they drift off into indifference or political reaction?
Because inside them they also had an antirevolutionary bourgeois structure which we failed to destroy. Why did we fail to
destroy it or fail to develop and encourage the positive elements?
Because we did not know what to destroy and what to encourage.

Simple "discipline" was not enough; neither were music and
marching, for the others were much better at these than we.
Slogans were useless, too, unless we could make them concrete,
for the others are better than we at political shouting. The only
thing that the revolutionary organization might have offered the
masses—and which, in reality, it failed to offer them—the only
thing that might have held the masses who came streaming to
us, and might have attracted the others, would have been to understand what these ignorant, oppressed coolies of capitalism,
longing for freedom and for authoritarian protection at the same
time, really desire without realizing it—to understand it, to put
it into words, to put it into their own language *for them,* to think

it out *for them*. But an organization that rejects all psychology as counter-revolutionary could not be equal to such a task.

In Women

Let us now try to give an approximate description of class consciousness in women.

Mere phrases, on the order of "integration into the production process" and "an end to dependence on men" and "winning control over one's own body" (and not much more was done than to repeat the phrases) have not gained much.

It is nonetheless perfectly true that the wish for economic independence, for independence from the male, and above all for sexual independence are the most important components of the class consciousness of women.

On the other hand, women's strong tendency toward bondage is reinforced by some characteristic fears: a fear of Soviet-style marriage legislation that would entail the loss of the husband as the provider; a fear of having no legally sanctioned sexual partner; and a fear of a free life in general. These are at least equally powerful inhibiting elements on the negative side.

In particular, a fear that the proposed collective upbringing of the children might "take them away" from their mothers has acted as a powerful brake on clear political thinking, even among Communist women—not at the party meetings, where they often speak in support of such proposals, but in private conflicts with their husbands at home. The same, of course, is true to a still greater extent of petty-bourgeois women.

We should have realized that rebellion against marriage as an economic bondage and a sexual restriction can become a valuable asset of the revolutionary movement only if we supply objective and truthful expositions of these thorny problems, which are at the very center of a woman's concerns.

Instead of which, our propagandists, none too clear about these things themselves, confused the issue by praising the Soviet marriage system on the one hand, and on the other, by welcoming the fact that marriages in the Soviet Union were again becoming more solid. The average woman's reaction to this could only be to say, "While you're making propaganda for the abolition of marriage and the family, women over there are still dependent on their husbands," or, conversely, "You just want to deliver us powerless into the hands of men."

Such contradictions require the most detailed scientific investigation by groups of professional psychologists and the most careful handling by the political organizations. After all, we were dealing not only with women workers in industry, who are more politically mature and more definitely left-wing by the very nature of their work (and whom, by the way, we also have totally failed to understand), but mostly with an overwhelming majority of housewives, domestic servants and homeworkers, small shopkeepers, shop assistants, etc. Experience teaches us that, for example, extramarital sex or the desire for it is a factor that could prove extremely effective in the struggle against reactionary influences. But it always goes hand in hand with a desire for security in marriage. Accordingly, we cannot develop it in the proper direction just by telling women that in the Soviet Union the traditional distinction between marital and extramarital sex has been abolished. Many women are revolutionary at work but reactionary at home. This is principally because their moral and cultural attitudes still outweigh their critical faculty and their economic and sexual interests.

The "women's rights" activities of various bourgeois organizations are founded on strong revolutionary impulses—some conscious (toward economic independence), some usually unconscious (toward sexual independence), but all directed toward changing the existing order of things. Only socialism can provide a practical answer to their questions. Yet the socialists do nothing to bring clarity into the ideological confusion of women. They do not explain to them that the things they want are mutually contradictory, that their aims are really socialist, though they cannot formulate them and so they have resorted to a form of sentimental revolt of the Pankhurst type. By talking about innumerable problems of everyday private life in the context of social life we could at least liven things up. Discussions would begin, and these discussions would be won by those with something to say—i.e., the socialists—if only they were not addicted to party debates on the orthodox pattern. The reactionaries would be completely defeated in any really objective argument.

At the end of 1933 a very curious and instructive movement occurred among some German women, which was a better example of this dialectic at work than anything that can be found in books. These women protested against their domestic bondage—a protest that could be revolutionary—yet they wanted to replace it by becoming "German fighters like Brunhilde," which in this particular form is a reactionary demand. We must clearly recognize that the ideology of motherhood, so energetically promoted by the Nazis, has an antisexual core which should be exposed. Being a mother is presented as the opposite of being a lover. Women want to be both. But they cannot find the way out of the contradiction created in them by capitalist morality. As a result, under the influence of political reaction, they deny themselves as sexual beings.

The women's rights movement, reactionary in its present form because it is directed against class feeling, is easily reversible because it militates for social change. In the case of women we find, once again, that actual hunger and an anxiety about feeding one's children only rarely lead to a revolutionary mentality. Far more often, this leads to a fear of politics in general, to opposition to the husband's or grown-up children's political activities, to dull-wittedness and prostitution. Such worries and fears could be turned into an effective driving force of class consciousness if combined in the right way with the other forces and counterforces involved.

It is very hard to say, for example, whether love of pretty clothes, make-up, etc., which today is a serious impediment to revolutionary thinking and feeling in women, might not have a reverse role to play. It is unlikely that a revolutionary organization will ever succeed in persuading the mass of women to adopt the austere appearance of Communist women. A way has to be found between bourgeois glamour and Communist asceticism, satisfying both the demands of the class struggle and the natural healthy vanity of women. Our political leaders should not dismiss such matters as being unworthy of their attention. We advise them to study the program whereby the political reaction manages to attract and hold German women.

The principal question confronting the women's movement is undoubtedly that of the future of the family and the raising of children. In the Sex-Pol movement in Germany we succeeded in winning over many women by explaining that socialism only proposes new forms for the continuation of a communal life of men, women and children, and that the so-called abolition of the family under Bolshevism means no more than the disengagement of the sexual interests from the economic ones.

The development of family ideology in Germany today deserves the closest attention, e.g., the contradiction between family life and service in the storm troops. Our future policy vis-à-vis women must derive from a close understanding of this ideology. And since prostitution will inevitably increase under the sexual and moral tendencies of fascism, proletarian policy must also include the winning of prostitutes to our cause.

A variety of events taking place in Germany can indicate whether class consciousness or the beginnings of class consciousness exists among the population, and in which way they tend. They supply hints of what the revolutionary leadership might usefully do. We have already mentioned the "Be Like Brunhild" movement, that inarticulate rebellion of women against the servitude of marriage and to the kitchen stove.

A little while ago, Goebbels was forced to speak out about a related question which is extremely embarrassing for the Nazis. After seizing power, they considerably tightened up existing laws on abortion and contraception, handed over the education of children to religious and military organizations, proclaimed the family as *the* basis of the nation and the state, launched the motto "A German woman doesn't smoke," condemned bobbed hair, reopened the brothels, excluded women from industry, restored various antediluvian privileges for men, etc. Thus the Nazis, consistent with their historical function, set off a process of extreme cultural reaction. It was only natural that many Nazi Party officials should carry out these measures exactly in the spirit in which they were meant. In one small town a soap company issued a poster showing a pretty girl with a packet of soap powder in her hand. The local Nazi boss promptly banned the poster because it offended the "moral sense" of the population. This and similar occurrences compelled Goebbels to launch an attack on "unauthorized moral judges and hypocritical apostles of chastity." He condemned "moral snooping" and those "whose dearest wish it is to set up vigilance committees in town and country." Such a system, he said, could only encourage informers and blackmailers. Women, he said, were already afraid to go out or enter a restaurant alone, spend an evening with a young man without a chaperone, wear jewelry or make-up; ". . . if they smoke a cigarette at home or at a party, that doesn't necessarily make them moral outlaws." National Socialism, he said, was not a pietist movement; the people should not be robbed of their *joie de vivre;* the aim was to achieve more life affirmation and less hypocrisy, more morality and fewer moralistic attitudes.

How are we to understand such statements? What is the lesson of this speech?

First: the average German woman must have reacted with lively indignation to the Nazi cultural policy, or else Goebbels would not have spoken as he did.

Second: the indignation must have been great, or else Goebbels, like Roehm on an earlier occasion, would not have had to intervene in a spirit contrary to the ideology of Nazism. The Nazi leaders are extremely skilled in mass psychology and would rather drop a part of their philosophy than risk the very basis of their power.

Third: in reality, Goebbels has nothing to say on this matter because he can neither understand nor surmount the contradiction between Nazism, which is intrinsically reactionary, and its supporters, who are intrinsically revolutionary—a contradiction which is evident in *all* spheres.

Fourth: we have here, in an impure and inarticulate form, an element of socialist class consciousness which we could develop if we were ourselves completely clear about the problem. We could reinforce the Nazi supporter's revolutionary mentality by making him aware of the reactionary consequences of Nazism; we could make the Socialist Party member aware of his petty-bourgeois inhibitions by the right kind of propaganda. As a general rule, we must relentlessly emphasize all contradictions, instead of treating the storm trooper *purely* as a reactionary and the Socialist Party member *purely* as a revolutionary who hasn't yet "seen the light."

Fifth: such a speech, pronounced by a Goebbels, must immediately reassure those Nazi supporters who had recently begun to doubt; it must gain new adherents and shake the confidence of opponents unless the insoluble nature of the whole problem of women's sexuality in the Third Reich is *concretely* demonstrated.

Why is the problem insoluble?

To reinforce the power of the family and to tie the woman to the kitchen stove, repressive measures such as those applied by some overzealous Nazi officials are necessary. But such measures completely contradict the "life affirmation" Goebbels preaches in his attempt to reduce the resulting dissatisfaction. Further: the very core and center of Nazi ideology is its morality (honor, purity, etc.). If an ordinary thinking man got up at a meeting and asked what the difference was between "morality" and "moralistic attitudes," the question would be bound to cause profound embarrassment (provided always that it was concretely phrased). If you stop a woman from going out with a young man, that's a moralistic attitude but not morality as demanded by National Socialism. Very well. But what if the young man kisses the woman? Or, worse still, what if he wants to have sexual intercourse with her? Is that part of *joie de vivre* or isn't it? If the Nazi functionary in the chair makes a concession at this point and actually allows the possibility of free love (which wouldn't surprise us in the least), the next question might well be: Wouldn't it weaken the role of marriage and the family if such things were openly allowed? And what would become of any children that might be born as a result? If our Nazi chairman now says that a child is a child just so long as the parents are Aryans, one might well ask whether there has to be a pregnancy every time people have sexual intercourse, and if not, what measures may be taken against it, etc. Such questions would start a lively public debate in a completely unpolitical form which would embarrass the Nazis a great deal more than a thousand illegal leaflets, for the simple reason that they would, without realizing it, be making propaganda on *our* behalf. No such thing as class consciousness? Why, it's to be found in every nook and cranny of everyday life. No use trying to develop the class consciousness of the masses—you'd land in jail? Just ask some of the questions that bother every Nazi, questions that the reaction can never answer, and you can stop worrying about class consciousness. The role of the vanguard in conditions of illegality? Why, this is it, right here! These are the concrete contents of proletarian democracy, not mere words or slogans about proletarian democracy which mean nothing to ninety out of every hundred people. Thousands of examples could be produced from all spheres of life to show that there isn't a single question which the Nazis could answer if it were well thought out and posed in a concrete and consistent manner—about religion, about trade unions, about relations between workers and employers, about the future of the bourgeoisie, etc.

The revolutionary leadership's most important task today is to point out the weaknesses of Nazism, and then to guide discussion among the masses so that it continues indefinitely without danger for anyone. The revolution can only develop out of the contradictions of life as lived today, not out of debates on the contradictions between the United States and Japan, or out of strike calls that cannot be implemented. Nor will it develop if we go on regarding every Nazi as a criminal and a sadist. What we have to do is to show up the contrast between their subjective aspirations and their inability to solve any objective problem.

We should not attach too much importance to proving that our views are one hundred percent correct and realizable. The correctness of a view is proved by practice. What matters is that we should see what is really happening and what the broad masses are interested in, and pinpoint the contradictions, etc. A theory cannot exist ready-made at the beginning of an action. It can only develop and shed its mistakes in the process of carrying out the action. This applies as well to the following sketch of the concrete elements which encourage or impede class consciousness in adult working men.

In Adult Working Men

Collective industrial work is undoubtedly the most important source of class feeling. Being a proletarian and working in a factory does not yet mean, however, that one is class-conscious. Nor does being a trade union member mean this, although both are essential preconditions of class consciousness. Proof of this is the fact that many German workers who previously belonged to a free trade union subscribe mechanically today to the Nazi trade union organization. When being organized has become part of the worker's flesh and blood, as is the case in Germany, consciousness of the *kind* of organization one joins is often reduced.

Nazi propaganda about the "honor" of work, the "equality" of worker and employer, the unity of the factory and of the nation, etc., can easily blind the average worker, especially if he has absorbed the Social Democratic doctrine of "industrial peace." Such a man is psychically so deformed that simply being told he is a "fully valid member of society" will make him feel better, especially if he is also given some kind of uniform to wear.

Any revolutionary who underestimates the material power of ideas is certain to fail. In our period of history it has proved stronger than the power of material poverty. Were this not so, the working class, not Hitler and Thyssen, would be in power today. The Nazis are very well aware how much they stand to gain when they woo the industrial workers. They know the precise amount of ideological poison they have to inject into the workers before labor legislation, such as that of January 1934, can become law. They are intelligent enough to know that they cannot pass such a law without virtually committing suicide, unless they have first made sure that the workers are ideologically subjugated to their own philosophy. Months of preliminary ideological work were necessary before Ley could produce his new labor law. If we do nothing but gaze in astonishment at the utter brutality of this law, which robs the workers of their last recourse, if we forget that we see it differently and feel about it differently from the worker who has been ideologically softened up, then in talking to him we shall express only our own thoughts and contradictions and not his. Our trade union work must also be preceded by ideological work—slow, carefully thought-out work—based on a precise knowledge of the areas in which the workers have been ideologically deformed. After all, a worker clearly senses when things are done against his interests—he has enough class consciousness for that—but he can also immediately summon up a whole range of thoughts and feelings to keep himself from realizing the full horror of the situation, which he knows he cannot control; and at that point he becomes the dupe of illusions. Hitler's gift of a sack of potatoes to every worker was ninety-nine percent ideology and only one percent practical value. The same is true of the recent tram-fare reductions, etc. A worker trained in the class struggle is not often deceived, but many, very many, have been ideologically softened up. Only a minority are trained. The majority, thanks to the free trade unions, have never known a strike. There is hardly a "dangerous" worker left in the factories. And so the average worker may have a correct sense of what is happening, but he is without leadership and is forced to fall back upon the hope that Hitler means well, after all, and that "he's doing something for us workers." He accepts the pittance without realizing that he is really the master and nobody has any presents to give him. Only a man who hasn't been crushed into complete submission by the thought that "a sack of potatoes is better than a kick in the pants" can feel angry because his employer, who is supposed to be his equal as a member of the nation, has an income a thousand times higher than his own.

If we ask what actually stops a worker from being roused to anger by the humiliating gift of a sack of potatoes, we shall find that the most important element is his *family responsibility*. We shall never develop class-conscious thinking in a worker if we simply invite him to strike (only the really stupid ones who don't know what goes in inside a worker's head do this), nor by urging him to join clandestine, heavily threatened trade unions he doesn't trust anyway. A revolutionary worker must first of all be a member of the Nazi trade union himself. He must show his workmates that he understands their deep, unexpressed worries, that, for example, he understands that they suppress their anger and refuse even to admit it to themselves because they are worried for their families. Millions of workers have problems like this, of which they are scarcely aware. Just as the major problem, besides wages, for the average young worker is the question of sex and of separate living quarters, so the question of family responsibilities (which we must not equate with the bourgeois ideology of the family) is the second major problem for the adult worker. If you tell such a man to go on strike, he won't understand what you want from him, and it's quite likely that he'll simply turn his back on you. But if you explain (we can only provide a rough schema of such an explanation here) that the reason why he refuses to give free rein to his anger at the insulting offer of a sack of potatoes is partly that he isn't quite sure whether Hitler is just a stooge of the employers or a real national leader who wants to do right by everyone, partly that he can't help being somewhat impressed by all the speeches and parades, but most of all because he has a family to support and it's safer to do as you are told, if you explain this and similar things, then you have understood the worker and he'll know it at once. And then you've proved yourself a true revolutionary because you've gained a supporter, if not for an immediate strike, then surely for a future one. If such isolated insights into mass psychology begin to multiply and to cover larger areas, the workers will soon realize that there are people who understand what worries them and what makes them angry, what holds them back and what drives them forward. That's the kind of thing we should put into our illegal leaflets! We'd have no trouble in distributing them, people would snatch them out of our hands, and those who produce the leaflets would lose the sense of futility which gnaws at them because they are obliged to repeat the same old clichés over and over again. They would acquire a sense of direct contact with reality. The propaganda of illusions would be replaced by reality, and the useless political shouting by an objective mastery of the situation.

Small occurrences often reveal more than great events. Let me quote such an occurrence to illustrate what I mean by class feeling and the factors which interfere with it. It will be seen that in this instance, as so often, bourgeois sexual ideology represents the inhibiting element. Some workers and peasants traveling in a slow train in Austria were chatting about work, politics, women, etc. A young worker, clearly a married man, was saying that all the laws were made for the rich and were rigged against the poor. I pricked up my ears to hear what else this class-conscious worker might have to say. He went on: "Take the marriage laws, for example. They say a man's entitled to beat his wife. Well, I tell you, only a rich man can beat his wife. If you're poor, you always get pulled in for it." Whether what he was saying is correct or not isn't the point. It is highly indicative of what goes on inside an average worker's head. As a poor man, he contrasts himself with a rich one and he senses the inequality: so far as that goes, he has the beginnings of a class-conscious mentality. But at the same time he would dearly love to be able to beat his wife *within the law!* And his class sense makes him feel at a disadvantage in this particular respect. Bourgeois sexual morality fights class consciousness in his mind. The right of sexual ownership which men enjoy in a class society, the power they wield over their wives and children, is one of the worst obstacles to the development of class consciousness in all members of a family. Everyone is demoralized by it, and the man, in particular, is securely tied by it to the bourgeois order, with the result that he secretly or openly fears the Soviet marriage system, daren't engage in political activities, etc.

This is not an ethical but a political problem and must be treated as a major issue of revolutionary propaganda and not, as hitherto, relegated to the back room of politics. We have here the most important and politically most effective area of a man's private life. It plays the same reactionary role for the proletariat as, say, the ideal of owning a bungalow or drawing a stipend plays for the petty bourgeoisie.

Other elements that work against the development of class consciousness are all-male clubs and the drinking-haunts habit, again comparable to the cult of small private property among the petty bourgeoisie. Only very few small owners are aware that the revolution would not, in the first instance, take their property from them. Career ambitions, identification with the enterprise (e.g., pride in the growth of a capitalist firm), the desire for permanent economic security and the prospect of a pension always act as impediments to class consciousness. The revolutionary party must offer a concrete answer to all these questions as they affect all social strata: What will the revolution do to my bungalow, my allotment, my evenings at the tavern, my bowling club, my position as lord and master of my wife and children, my pension rights, my firm that I'm so proud of?

We see now how wrong it is to try to delimit and determine in advance the place occupied, for instance, by sexual politics. Sexual politics isn't the only weapon against the political reaction, as some of us are wrongly accused of believing, nor is it a question of mere sexual reform. Rather, it enters into many concrete aspects of life, now as a positive element of class consciousness (e.g., in the young), now as an obstacle to its development (e.g., in married women). It is part and parcel of revolutionary work, where it must be closely linked with nonsexual issues related to economics or culture. It cannot be separated from those issues in political work any more than it is separate from them in life.

In Children

What are the elements of class consciousness and its impediments in children?

The organizing of a revolutionary children's movement has always been one of our party's weakest points. We are far from believing, as we are sometimes accused, that we know everything and can solve every problem all at once. But we have observed or discovered certain facts which require further attention, and all we ask of our comrades is that they refrain from purely destructive criticism, and instead of talking about Leninism, actually practice it by "always learning, learning and learning," by looking at everything and trying to see everything in a new light. I have already said that the proletarian party's policy for children has been too dry and rationalistic and therefore unsuitable for children, mostly because, apart from some individual children's group leaders of exceptional ability, the party has lacked any real knowledge of what children think and feel. Here again we can only provide an outline sketch, not a detailed schema; the whole question awaits objective study by qualified organizations.

Hunger, the condition of being physically undernourished, is a childhood experience which creates an unbridgeable gulf between poor and rich children, but is not in itself revolutionizing. It arouses hatred of property owners far less often than it provokes envy, servility and stealing, as, for instance, in the case of gangs of destitute children. If we tried to base our work among children simply upon hunger, we should find that such a basis was too narrow, for we want to reach many more children than those who are actually starving; moreover, poverty is never absolute but relative to whoever owns more. What matters, therefore, is how we handle the envy and submissiveness which develop out of constant privation and act as a brake on revolutionary feeling. Observations have shown that identification with older, class-conscious siblings or with parents is the strongest stimulus to revolutionary feeling in children, but this occurs only rarely. Just one revolutionary child brought up without religion can stir up an entire school, but unless this effect is properly organized, it will remain merely accidental. The texts which the party distributed to children in Germany had little effect because they put more emphasis on slogans that had to be learned by heart than on arousing the children's interest in real revolutionary problems and issues.

Anticipating objections from children's organization leaders on a local and national scale (objections that are never substantiated or based on practical experience), I must insist that the way to make children react most readily and actively to political questions is to discuss sexual problems, especially if one also succeeds in establishing a certain comradely relationship with the children. Sexual repression in the life of children is so directly felt by every child, while problems of class are, initially at least, so difficult for him to grasp, that the question of choice hardly arises here. Early information on sex, provided it is truthful, not only creates a very close bond with the person supplying it, not only removes the distrust that children generally feel for adults, but also provides the soundest basis for non-religious thinking and consequently for a class sense.

Here again, the difficulty lies not so much in children as in the adults who work with them. Starting with sexual information it is easy to go on to teach facts about capital and the church which a child would otherwise find difficult or impossible to assimilate. But in order to achieve success in this positive aspect of the work it is necessary to have a precise understanding of the child's inhibitions, which, later on in his life, will turn into reactionary bondage. You enter a peasant's cottage in the mountains; the parents are socialist sympathizers, yet as soon as a child is introduced to the stranger he is told, "Say good day to the gentleman," "Say thank you," etc., and so the child cringes and creeps and becomes "good."

Ideological struggle against what is known as "being good" should be one of the important tasks of the proletarian front. Unfortunately, a serious obstacle is created by the proletarian educators' own bourgeois deformation. Old wives' tales, bogeys and intimidations ("Wait till I fetch the policeman") are among the most powerful weapons of political reaction. Every proletarian father (with only rare exceptions) coming home from a day's coolie work at the factory takes out his frustration on his child. Here at least he wants to be the master; and being a master implies having someone to bully, if not the dog, then the child. Child-beating, of course, is part and parcel of this attitude. But it isn't enough to understand this, not enough to refrain from beating one's own children; what is needed is propaganda on the broadest international scale. Any mother seen beating her child in the street should be publicly challenged; such a measure, if carried out in an organized fashion, would soon engage everybody in a struggle for the child as a member of society, against the treatment of children as family chattels.

Some people would no doubt be in favor of "owning" children and, consequently, of having the right to beat them; but others, the overwhelming majority of whom know nothing whatsoever about communism, would be against the notion, and this would draw them directly into the class struggle, i.e., it would engage and activate them a thousand times more effectively and usefully than leaflets pushed under the door which would only be thrown unread into the wastepaper basket. Of course we cannot give all the details here, or issue precise instructions. Socialists in the capitalist countries must not wait to be told what to do; they must act out of their innermost sense of what is right and useful to our cause and of what is wrong and harmful to it. We should talk less about the need for initiative in the junior organizations and do more to pinpoint those areas of social life where such initiative could be applied. To do this we must thoroughly revise all our propaganda methods. We must replace paper wisdom with live issues; we must not be afraid of making mistakes—such fears lead to apathy—but must be prepared to make mistakes, if need be, and then correct them.

To return to the child. Sexual-economic research shows that an early and strict toilet training leads to the gravest character inhibitions in terms of activity. If we work on the cultural-political front under capitalism, if we concern ourselves with politics for children, we must—among other things—make the harmfulness of early toilet training widely known and discuss it in an objective way. The path that leads from such a subject to politics is shorter than some people care to think. Political reaction, in its role of defender of morals and discipline, will be quick to oppose us. But that is precisely what we want: we want to start discussions in which the population at large will participate with interest because the questions raised are difficult issues of everyday life. It will be the task of socialist psychoanalysis to assist the political organizations, guide the discussions, etc.

Another concrete example. Masturbation in young children and the threats of parents, teachers and clergymen on this subject have formed the subject of lively public debate for a long time. The CP leaders have failed to do anything about it partly because they themselves are caught up in bourgeois prejudices and partly because they are against so-called Freudianism, although this has nothing to do with the case, as Freud never adopted any position on this subject. Yet the crux of the matter is here, and nowhere so much as here. Should a child be brought up to be obedient or should it be lively and independent? These are class questions, not "individual" problems. The church is very well aware of this, for it does not balk at these "embarrassing" issues. For the church, infantile masturbation is *politics*. Of course we don't for one moment believe that the whole problem can be solved in one fell swoop, but we can at least open it up, we can start discussions on it, we can put a little life into our work.

Should anyone object that we are treading on dangerous ground and that some people may be put off by such a subject, we would suggest leaving that worry to experts well qualified to deal with it. No one can judge better than those of us who specialize in the problems of childhood how delicate, how disturbing, how urgent these problems are. They preoccupy *all* mothers, regardless of political affiliation, and *all* children. And the same is true of all other aspects of the party's policy for children—which we should view in terms of modern pedagogy applied to everyday practice. At the present moment, of course, our action has to be restricted to political discussion and ideological struggle. Let me say once more that I am fully aware how unwelcome the raising of these questions will be; but only by opening up these central problems of our existence can we hope to avoid early death from political arteriosclerosis.

We have mentioned only a few examples here. Should some pundit object that problems concerning the upbringing of children are still a matter of scientific controversy, I would reply: That is true, but solutions to these problems will not come out of the studies of learned men but only out of living, active struggle. We may be mistaken in some details; but remember that there is no controversy among the reactionaries about masturbation in young children: that they repress it is a *fact*. And it is likewise a fact that it is dangerous to interfere with infantile sexuality. Everything else remains to be seen.

I don't know whether the example which follows points to any direct practical conclusions. But I am sure that it teaches us to pay attention to the smallest details, to look for important things among all the unimportant ones and to distinguish typical, universal facts from untypical, individual ones. German children, like their parents, are going over en masse to Hitler; his principal method of wooing them is that of offering them war games and war stories. Our task therefore is to understand why such methods are successful and what it is that they do for the children. This isn't a matter of profound investigations but rather of simple observation and understanding of children. A group of little boys, six to ten years old, are playing at war in a city court-yard. One little boy is running round with a sword strapped to his side and a wooden gun in his hand, shooting at his playmates. I ask him whether he wants to kill his friends. He stops in his tracks, stares at me in astonishment and asks, "Kill them?" I say, "Why yes, of course, if you shoot you kill, didn't you know that?" "Well, I don't want to kill them at all." "Why do you run about with a sword and a gun, then?" "Because the sword is so shiny and long," he replies. I wasn't going to talk to him about pacifism and the complicated distinction between war and civil war; but I know from other experiences that although children have an unconscious desire to kill, they derive their enjoyment of war games not only from this desire but also from purely motor satisfaction, increased self-confidence due to holding a weapon, the rhythm of marching, etc. Should not such insights be used in our proletarian children's policy? Or is that utopian? I do not know; but these are certainly facts of life—children's life—and if we have not been successful with children it is surely because we failed to take the trouble to study such facts in all their multiplicity and to turn to advantage those that could be. These are extremely difficult problems, which defy immediate solution. But if we do not ventilate them, we shall never solve them in practice.

3) Bourgeois and Revolutionary Politics

"Politics" as Fetish

The Sex-Pol movement has to fight on many fronts. One of these concerns the tangled web of ideas in people's minds, ideas that are apparently quite meaningless if one asks the simplest questions about them. For example: "What is politics?"

Here is an occasion when one might ask it. We are trying to explain the fundamental principles of mass psychology as revealed by sexual economy, and somebody makes the following objection: "What you say may be very true and very useful, but aren't politics and the economic factor more important?" The audience, which has been listening to the report or lecture on mass psychology with great interest and approval, suddenly begins to doubt its own opinion, simply because of the curiously mesmerizing effect of the word "politics."

Often it happens that at this word even the speaker, who is meant to be putting the case for mass psychology, will retreat and say something to the effect that the relationship between politics and the practice of mass psychology "still remains to be examined."

The pundits of high politics and of the "economic factor" (who always think that this factor is being neglected, although in the newspapers and reviews you read about nothing else and never a word about mass psychology) are generally at a loss to explain what exactly "politics" is—a word that nevertheless

320

works like a fetish on ordinary mortals. We must always turn the most blinding searchlight on anything that smacks of fetishism. We must bombard such things with the most naïve questions, which, as we all know, are the most embarrassing ones and generally yield the most interesting results.

The political layman understands "politics" to mean, in the first place, diplomatic negotiations between representatives of great or small powers in which destinies of mankind are decided; of these he rightly says he understands nothing. Or else he sees politics as parliamentary deals concluded between friends and enemies alike, reciprocal swindling, spying, bestowing of favors, and decision-making in accordance with "the established rules of procedure." Of this, too, he understands nothing, but he is often repelled by it, and so he decides, with great relief, that "he wants to have nothing to do with politics." He fails to see the contradiction in the fact that the transactions he so rightly despises affect his own life, and that he is, in effect, leaving his life in the hands of people he considers to be a gang of crooks.

Politics may also mean wanting to win the masses of the population over to one's side. Anyone trained as a Marxist will realize at once that bourgeois politics must always be demagogical because it can only make promises which it cannot keep. Not so revolutionary politics, which can fulfill all the promises it makes to the masses and is therefore in principle undemagogical. Whenever it is or appears to be demagogical we may safely conclude that revolutionary principles have been abandoned.

Let us consider a typical passage of "political" writing of the kind which, in our experience, is thought of by the masses as "high politics." That is to say, it is not understood but regarded with great timidity and awe; if it produces a reaction, it is a passive one.

If one prefers the legalization of armaments to the armaments race, as England does, one has to admit that, together with such legalization, guarantees against any renewed breach of agreements must be provided. Such guarantees for the carrying out of a convention on disarmament should be discussed at the so-called disarmament conference in

Geneva. But Germany does not accept the condition
imposed by France. It remains silent on this subject in its
official communications and, in the Berlin talks with Eden,
the British Lord Privy Seal, it has so far refused to come to
Geneva. As a result, the Franco-British negotiations, as
already stated, have lost their object. The diplomatic
exchange of views outside the Geneva disarmament
conference has come to an end without yielding any result.
It is now for the disarmament conference to create, without
Germany, the required guarantees for peace. In this, France
is counting upon the co-operation of Great Britain.

    This is the content and meaning of the long French note
of April 17, which is a reply to the British note of March 28
and to Sir John Simon's *aide-mémoire* of April 10.

I have deliberately quoted this passage without reference to
its source so as not to hurt anyone's feelings. Anyone whom the
cap fits should wear it. Isn't that the only way to deal with the
tender sensibilities of politicians?

    Who is "Germany," who is "France"? What is a "diplomatic
exchange of views"? Is that really the content and meaning of
the French note? What relation does this "political note" bear to
the needs of the masses, their thoughts and feelings, the way they
live or merely vegetate? Why, none at all! Compare it with
Lenin's politics at the time of Brest-Litovsk. The smallest
famine-stricken child could understand the slogan "End the
war" but the adherents of "high politics" were against it.

    The broad masses, whose wishes and whose future are to be
guaranteed by revolutionary politics, think and talk differently.
Anyone who goes on speaking of Barthou's travels today without explaining—simply, clearly, intelligibly to everyone—the
reactionary swindle which is the real purpose of these trips, becomes an involuntary accomplice.

    If we look for the effect of high politics on the broad masses,
we shall see that, at the very most, it is aped in the form of beer-
hall politics by a few individuals. The vast majority tend always
to react passively, without interest, playing the role of mere
extras in the fairground show of "high politics." We must clearly

realize that this fairground show would come to a sudden end—
a very disagreeable one for the diplomats—if the extras were to
take up a more active attitude, if, in brief, they stopped being
nonpolitical.

If we forget even for a moment to ask ourselves the question: "What is happening among the masses?"—a question
absolutely fundamental to revolutionary politics—then we are
bound, whether we want to be or not, to get enmeshed in the
web of bourgeois politics or else to become nonpolitical. The
nonpolitical attitude of the broad masses is one of the political
reaction's main strengths. Another is the smoke screen with
which it surrounds its politics, so that even socialists are often
confused.

One of the revolutionary politician's most important tasks
is to sense and to discover the effect of backstage politics on the
masses. When in the summer of 1932 Hitler approached Hindenburg for the first time with the demand to appoint him Reich
chancellor, and when that demand was rejected following a
number of backstage intrigues, of which the people knew little
or nothing, Hitler appealed to his supporters with a fervent profession of faith in the "will of the people." The occasion for this
was provided by the Potempa case. Some storm troopers had
brutally murdered a Polish worker and had been sentenced to
death. Hitler interceded for them vociferously. The real motive
for this gesture was the snub he had received from Hindenburg.
In other words, when his feudal connections failed him, he
played the trump card of his mass base.

The masses had absolutely no idea of the game that was
being played with them. Rather, they felt themselves "understood" by Hitler in an upsurge of nationalistic identification.
Hitler's open support of the men who, out of a "sense of national
honor," had shot down a "Marxist dog," and his stand against
the hated government that had sentenced the murderers to
death, outweighed by far the effect of *erroneous* Communist
propaganda whose famous policy of "unmasking" consisted only
in calling the murderers murderers. An explanation, offered on a
mass scale, of the connection between Hindenburg's refusal and
Hitler's appeal to mass feeling would have been effective. But

the CP merely insisted that all reactionary parties are the same; it failed to grasp the real contradictions within the bourgeoisie; it had never learned to study and interpret the reactions of the masses on their own or the enemy's side. By doing nothing except to say that the murderers were indeed murderers, it placed itself, in the eyes both of the convinced followers of the Nazis and of those who, at that time, were only mildly sympathetic to them, on the side of the government which the masses loathed.

Why didn't Litvinov speak to the masses?

Revolutionary politics, in its content and the language it uses, is either an expression of the primitive, uneducated, life-centered character of the broad masses, or it is politics that merely calls itself revolutionary and is in effect reactionary and barren. Even where its position is correct in principle, it will not be understood by the masses and it will, therefore, objectively speaking, work against the revolution.

The world is on the threshold of a new murderous war. In Geneva, Barthou and Litvinov were thought of by their respective governments as champions of peace, with Germany as their opponent. A correct critique of Litvinov's statement from the international revolutionary standpoint has appeared so far only in Trotsky's paper *Nashe Slovo* (in the second week of June 1934). All other organizations of the proletariat seem to lack the faintest idea of what happened in Geneva. Not even this critique, however, asks itself the fundamental mass-psychological question: What do the speeches of the two statesmen mean to the average nonpolitical worker, employee or peasant in Germany, France, England or even in the Soviet Union? Does he feel that the power behind Litvinov is a workers' state? Does he detect any difference between Barthou's idea of peace and Litvinov's? Does he understand the fine distinction the Soviet government draws when it speaks of "imperialism as a whole" and of "special war parties"? Does the Russian worker realize that under the present set of alliances he is supposed to make common cause with French workers against German and English workers, and kill them if war breaks out?

How is an ordinary mortal to make sense of the following commentary by Bela Kun?

> We often oppose war *in general*. Communist editors sometimes find themselves in a difficulty over this point. "How can this be?" they ask, "the imperialists are plotting for war, yet here is Herriot visiting the Soviet Union and getting a good reception. How are we to explain this?" I have read some very bad articles about Herriot's visit. And in no article have we read what now, after Comrade Stalin's speech at the Seventeenth Party Congress, is completely clear—namely, that under imperialism there are always war parties. Imperialism as a whole, as an epoch, is in favor of war; but there are various war parties which are more active in promoting war. The present task is to concentrate our fire on that group of the bourgeoisie which represents the war parties and is most active in promoting war.
>
> Of course we must always emphasize that the groups of the bourgeoisie who today have donned a pacifist cloak or those who think that the time for war has not yet come will also be in favor of the war at the appropriate moment—will be just as much in favor of war against the Soviet Union as is the dominant war party. We must always emphasize this, but we must concentrate our fire principally on the war parties: in Japan, on the militarist-fascist clique of generals, feudal lords and industrial trust magnates, in Germany on the Hitler fascists, in Great Britain on the diehards, etc. (Bela Kun, "The Tasks of the Communist Press," *Rundschau* 33/1934, p. 1259).

And what of the *French* armaments industry?

A man who understands nothing about alliances and high politics might ask why Litvinov in Geneva didn't address the broad masses in every country who do not want war at any price? Why does he make alliances with imperialist governments, who do want war, but not with the masses? Why does he lend his support to the illusion—nourished precisely by the imperialist powers—that the League of Nations, which has long been dead, can actually prevent a war? Why doesn't he say straight out, in terms intelligible to everyone, that no League of Nations, no bourgeois government in the world can ever really prevent the war, but that only the concerted action of munitions and transport workers in all the capitalist countries can do it? Nonpolitical workers do not understand the foreign policy of the Soviet Union any better than they understand that of France. Yet this, of all things, would be the most important touchstone of a truly proletarian policy!

To be strict about it, we should not attempt to answer the question why the representative of a proletarian state has so completely forgotten the language of revolutionary diplomacy before we hear what the "only true leaders of the revolution" have to say about it. One thing is clear, however: a single word from Litvinov on the League of Nations rostrum, a word that flouted custom, diplomatic usage and League of Nations protocol, ignored all alliances and agreements, and was spoken directly to the munitions and transport workers, to mothers of future soldiers everywhere, would have done more to prevent war than twenty paper pacts. Does Litvinov really believe that he can prevent war by his policy? Wasn't Karl Liebknecht's refusal of credits in 1914 a thousand times more of a bulwark against war chauvinism than all the high-flown political arguments of the Social Democrats? But our proletarian revolutionary leaders are so much in awe of a diplomat, especially a Soviet one, that they no longer understand the language of the men and women they are meant to lead and they say that we are mad. And yet we say it again and again: the support of five or ten million future war victims is worth more than five hundred thousand bayonets, even Soviet ones! These words, which today are dismissed as madness, will be written in blood by the catastrophe to come.

There is only one salvation for the Soviet Union as a proletarian revolutionary state: to pit its own army, in alliance with the workers of the war and transport industries and the simple soldiers of all countries, against the capitalist governments and general staffs. If today the Soviet Union concludes alliances with the general staffs and the diplomats of capitalist countries, it does so only because of the collapse of the international revolutionary movement. Lenin always addressed the broad masses in his speeches and writings. This supplies the answer to our question: Can revolutionary politics ever beat bourgeois politics at its own game, by using its language, its tactics, its strategy, in short, by adopting *bourgeois* methods? No, never. It can only lose itself in the maze of politics, follow lamely in the wake of events, play the game *less well* than the bourgeois politicians. There is only one possibility: to cut through the Gordian knot of bourgeois politics, not by aping it but by attacking it with the fundamental principle of revolutionary politics: the principle of addressing the masses, ceaselessly, tirelessly, simply and clearly, of expressing the ideas of the masses, whether these have been thought out or not, of destroying the awe of the masses in the face of high politics, of refusing to take the swindle of high politics seriously, of mercilessly and relentlessly exposing it, of speaking the language of the masses, of adapting politics to the masses instead of vice versa, thereby democratizing it, simplifying it, making it accessible to everyone. Lenin's dictum that every cook ought to be capable of governing the state contains implicitly the fundamental thought of social democracy. "High politics" can exist only because the form, language and thought processes of revolutionary politics, for all their revolutionary contents, have adapted themselves to those of high politics— because, instead of addressing the masses, revolutionary politicians treat them like children. But the children must finally realize (and are actually recognizing it more and more) that they are being led by the nose.[1]

A Schema of Revolutionary Politics

If the social revolution is right in asserting that it can really solve the social problems of economics and culture in the spirit of

---

[1] The question of Soviet foreign policy and its connection with mass-psychological problems require detailed discussion elsewhere.

social democracy, the following political questions and principles must be posed:

1. What are the tactics used by bourgeois parties to win over the masses or to take them from other parties?
2. What are the motives that lead the masses to follow political groups or parties which can never fulfill their promises?
3. What are the needs of the masses at all levels?
4. Which of these needs are socially practicable and justified? Which are vitally essential?
5. Is the state of the world economy such that these needs can be satisfied by the overthrow of capitalist rule and the substitution of a planned economy for economic anarchy?
6. Do the masses know which social institutions impede the satisfaction of their needs, and why these obstructive institutions exist?
7. How can these institutions be removed and what should replace them?
8. What are the economic, social and mass-psychological preconditions necessary for the satisfaction of the needs of the broad masses?

Each of these questions points to the inexorable necessity for social revolution—each, without exception, in every single sphere of human life. In other words, mass-psychological work must not remain in the shadow of economic policy; quite on the contrary, economic policy must enter the service of a mass psychology which understands and guides the masses. The needs of men and women do not exist to serve economic policy—economic policy exists to satisfy these needs.

The Bourgeois Politics
of the German Communist Party

The experience of life in the German Communist Party shows that the only possible form of revolutionary politics, as outlined above, was lacking in Germany. When Communist leaders spoke for hours at the Sports Palace about the conflicting interests of the Great Powers and the economic background of the impending war, they were, without wanting to, imitating bourgeois politics. Our revolutionary politicians are too zealous in emulating the Paul Boncours. What makes them do this, and so lose any chance of success, is a question of the psychical structure of our revolutionary leaders. They will again feel sorely insulted when they read this. They will call it "Trotskyite counter-revolutionism." Nor is there any hope of convincing them that the politics they conduct are bourgeois in form and, consequently, also in objective reality. To anticipate their protests, we shall quote just one of many concrete examples to show that the German Communist Party has exchanged the revolutionary principle of politics for a bourgeois one.

In December 1932, the Social Democratic Party organized a demonstration in the Lustgarten. Communist organizations, in particular the *Kampfbünde* (Fighting Unions), joined the demonstration. They mingled with the mass of the Social Democratic demonstrators, and without any talk about U.S.–Japanese contradictions, they formed a united front. That was the will and language of the masses. The Communist Party leaders, who wanted a united front "only under Communist leadership," later reprimanded the party members concerned. The party orders had only been to line the streets and to "cheer" the demonstration. At the same time Torgler was secretly negotiating with the Social Democratic leaders about forming a united front. The masses *knew nothing* about these negotiations; the official line was that a united front led by the Social Democrats would be "counter-revolutionary." I personally took part at the time in a secret meeting on the forming of a united front between leading Communist and Social Democrat functionaries. No one in the party cells was supposed to know anything about it. *That is bourgeois politics.* The exact opposite would have been proletarian-revolutionary politics: the party should have instructed the Communists to support the Social Democrat demonstration and should have told the masses in the Lustgarten over loudspeakers that negotiations were in progress with the Social Democrats on the forming of a united front. That is what is properly called developing the ideology of the masses and giving expression to their wishes. Instead of this the party engaged in "high politics," "strategy" and "tactics"—without the masses, sometimes against the masses, keeping out everyone who wanted and practiced revolutionary politics.

The abolition of secret diplomacy is an old revolutionary principle. It is a self-evident one, for, if social revolution is the execution of the people's will against the owners of the means of production under the leadership of the industrial proletariat, there can be nothing left to keep secret. There should be nothing left that the masses ought not to hear: on the contrary, they must be able to know and check everything that happens.

Revolutionary Inner-Party Politics

If we survey the development of the politics of Communist parties since the death of Lenin, we find that the principle of constantly addressing the masses has been gradually lost, and that, with the increasing imitation of the forms of bourgeois politics inside and outside the party, bureaucratization has set in. Inner-party democracy has been replaced by backstage politics, mutual deception and the forming of cliques. This has completely undermined the strength of the revolutionary parties, although they comprised the best revolutionary elements.

When in October 1917 Lenin saw that the moment had come for popular insurrection, and when he met with opposition within the Bolshevik leadership, he remained faithful to his principle of revolutionary politics: he *addressed himself to the mass of party members*. He did not form a clique, he did not start any intrigues, he did not try to win by creating factions. Any exclusion of the masses from political deliberations and decisions is counter-revolutionary, irrespective of the subjective content involved. Revolutionary politics has nothing to conceal from the masses; it should reveal everything. Bourgeois politics cannot afford to reveal anything and so has to conceal everything. Backstage politics, wherever it may occur, is the distinguishing feature of political reaction.

It is immensely to the advantage of revolutionary sexual politics that it is constantly obliged to use the language of the masses and that the bourgeoisie can offer nothing that compares with it because a positive bourgeois sexual policy cannot exist. The revolutionary sexual politician therefore cannot degenerate into a bourgeois. There can be no such thing as secret diplomacy in the sphere of sexual politics. Sex-Pol must always speak to the masses or it will cease to exist.

4) How to Develop Class Consciousness with the Everyday Life of the Masses as a Starting Point

Leadership, the Party and the Masses

What I am about to say may be painful to hear. It concerns something that is harmful to the revolutionary movement but is an undeniable fact. Various revolutionary groups outbid one another in claiming to be the "sole," "true" heirs of "genuine Marxism and Leninism"; but if you look closely at the differences that separate them, you will find that in relation to the gigantic tasks to be performed they are very small. One group says the revolutionary party has to be there first; another wants to have the support of the masses before it will help to form a new International; the third proclaims itself constantly as "*the* working class" and the sole leader of the revolution without being even remotely so; the fourth has yet another view of its own on some question of detail, and so on. We have already suggested that such splintering is due to an incorrect or incomplete understanding of the major problems, and that the mutual abuse brings nobody forward a single step.

We look in vain in today's revolutionary debates for the following questions, or the answers to them: Why have all attempts to form a new revolutionary party been unsuccessful? Why has the old revolutionary organization failed to win over the masses despite its existing apparatus? Why, seventeen years after the Russian revolution, does the problem of the relationship between the leadership, the party and the masses still cause so many headaches? Doesn't it look as if somewhere there is an important error in the whole calculation? It is surely quite unconvincing to say that the catastrophe occurred because Stalin encouraged bureaucracy, or because the Social Democratic leadership had for decades suffered bourgeois degeneration, or because Hitler received funds from the industrialists. The fundamental question, again and again, is: Why did the industrial working class *accept* reformism and bureaucratism? It is the fundamental problem of the relationship between leadership, the party and the masses.

The founders of the Fourth International adopt the view—at least when you listen to their spokesmen and read their papers—that, first of all, it is necessary to create the revolutionary party, and *then* to win over the proletariat—only *then* will it be the turn of the petty bourgeoisie. I have no doubt that the actual leaders of the international communists condemn this method of posing the problem. One cannot call oneself a Marxist and separate the leadership, the party and the masses in this way. The relationship is (to use the exalted word just this once) a dialectical one; to put it in a nutshell, a revolutionary party cannot be made out of thin air, it can only form out of the masses and, in the first instance, out of the proletarian section of the masses. This presupposes that the founders of the party must speak the language of those masses out of which the party is to be formed. Yet the masses understand nothing of fine distinctions between various revolutionary tendencies and have no interest in them. A revolutionary party is formed not only by working out a set of ideas and a practice corresponding to reality, but also, in the first place, by dealing with problems of interest to various strata of the population. Then and only then will the broad masses supply the active members whom the party needs. This again has the reciprocal effect of improving the party's contact with the masses, and vice versa—party and masses raising one another up. Only through such a close fusion, accompanied simultaneously by a selection of leading cadres out of the mass, can a mass party come into being—i.e., a party which is not quantitatively but qualitatively determined and which genuinely leads the masses. The German CP organized "join the party" campaigns and accepted members without any selection. It was quantitatively a "mass party," but it collapsed, partly as a result of fluctuations in its membership and partly because of the lack of differentiation between trained party officials and mass members. We shall return to this question later in an article on organizational matters.

The German Sex-Pol group has always been guided by the realization that the leaders of a mass action can never survey all the details of that action but that the masses alone can never grasp the real meaning of a situation, formulate it and translate it into concerted action, and that in consequence, incessant contact is necessary between the leadership and the masses, with theory drawn from the life of the masses and returned to the masses as practice. We had learned from the experience of party life that party officials must not be mere executors of the leadership's decisions but mediators between the life of the masses and the leadership. To create such contact the Sex-Pol instituted so-called instruction evenings, whose purpose was not to instruct the party officials but to seek instruction from them. (We all remember the famous party conferences at which such initiatives were abruptly cut short.) There were no set subjects for discussion; the party officials and rank-and-file members were simply asked to describe the greatest difficulties they were having at that moment. This was in itself a guarantee that the problems discussed would be the most important ones *at that particular point*. We discussed the difficulty together, sometimes finding a solution that would be put to a practical test, sometimes postponing decision until more material was available. Real life *as lived* flowed out of these comradely discussions; we didn't have to rack our brains to invent theories, they suggested themselves of their own accord. Increasing participation and the liveliness of the discussions showed that the instruction evenings were an excellent idea. We learned that life refuses to be tricked; it has to be simply and energetically grasped. All we had to do was to let the ordinary members (many nonmembers were present, too) speak their minds. The only obstacles we met were psychological deformations due to false ideas implanted by bourgeois ideology, but these were disposed of by realistic, straight, undogmatic discussion. Our fourth instruction evening failed to take place; the official party representative refused to convene the members.

The Attitude of Sex-Pol to the "New Party"

The most urgent question facing the working-class movement in the process of reforming its ranks is: Should there be a new party or a revolutionary renewal of the Third International? Sex-Pol cannot fully support either alternative, for two reasons. In the first place we do not know which groups, organizations or circles will be the first to accept our view of the necessity for a revolutionary sexual policy. To judge by the behavior to date of the principal political organizations, the prospect in those organizations that do want a new International is no brighter than elsewhere. Yet this alone cannot be the decisive factor. Sexual politics is only a part, even if a central and essential one, of the general revolutionary front. It is important to know, therefore, which cadres will form the core of the regenerated workers' movement. So far, this has not been made clear in any sense. If we knew for certain that, say, today's rank-and-file members of the CP will form this core (for today's leadership certainly will not), there would be no sense in founding a new revolutionary party. Yet the revolutionary rank and file would not only have to override the old leadership (which shows not the slightest sign of genuine self-criticism) as it has done on many occasions in the past, but it would also have to actually remove it and replace it little by little with new leaders from its own midst. In the long run it is impossible to flout official decisions of the CP's Executive Committee—for instance, to refuse to proclaim a "revolutionary upsurge" or call for "mass strikes"— and at the same time to continue identifying the EC with the concept of a revolutionary party. Such behavior is politically confusing.

Today, more than ever before, the question as to who and what "the party" is needs to be made unequivocally clear. Is it the membership as a whole, or only the full-time apparatus, or only the EC? We know that even the best forces of social democracy are using the concept of "the party" as a fetish. Whether the unassailable unity of the party is a mighty force or a serious impediment to the revolutionary movement depends on the structure of the party, its policies at any given moment, its *objective* effects.

The hard core of the revolutionary movement—the industrial and transport workers—are today "still" not in the CP. The party is still doing all it can to win them over, but will power and subjective courage alone are not enough. You must have successes to show, and in order to achieve success you must know the best way of achieving it. It may be that this hard core will soon form the core of a new revolutionary organization but will not want to join the CP as it is today; they joined it in 1923 but later left it again, and it is necessary to understand why. The question of a new organization would then assume great importance, as it also would if a viable and permanent mass movement began to form, not among the Social Democratic industrial workers, but among the potentially revolutionary proletarian storm troopers.[2] Today, with everything in a state of ferment,

---

[2] The killing at Hitler's orders of the storm troopers' leaders—Röhm, Schleicher and others—on June 30, 1934, showed that the contradictions between revolutionary and reactionary trends in fascism described in *Mass Psychology of Fascism*—contradictions which, in fascist ideology, were presented as a unity—had become irreconcilable. I say this, not—as the "only true leaders of the revolution" do all the time—in order to prove that my analysis was correct, but for another reason. Shortly before the event, the Comintern had rejected with vehement abuse any attempt to view the Nazi Party as anything more than a servant of finance capital. (To be precise, the attempt consisted in seeing Nazism as a siphoning of the revolutionary energy of the masses to reactionary ends.) The Comintern then interpreted the killing, which removed the leadership of the left wing of the Nazi Party, as a confirmation of the "revolutionary upsurge" it had predicted! It is to be hoped that the history of the revolutionary movement will never see another instance of such ineptitude and superficiality. Those of us who took part in the inner-party struggles between 1929 and 1933 know that anyone who drew attention to the inarticulate revolutionary potential of the storm troopers was immediately accused of sabotage. This happened to anyone who mentioned the undeniable fact that large sections of the R.F. (Red Front) had joined the storm troops, or emphasized that the storm troops recruited their members among the working class and were only objectively, not subjectively, mere mercenaries of capital. The party did not like to hear such things; it saw only

we cannot foresee exactly what will happen. The question of a new party would never have come up if there had been the necessary opportunities within the CP for raising or discussing such questions and sounding out the chances of development. That was and is not the case. All we can do is follow closely

---

the reactionary function of fascism and not the revolutionary energies of its mass base; and as a result it lost the battle. Now, after the event, when the contradictions are obvious to everyone, it admits what it previously anathematized. Those who are "loyal to the party" will say: Well, that's better than nothing, you mustn't expect too much; after all, the Comintern is changing course in its estimation of fascism as well as on the question of a united front with the Social Democrats. Our answer to that is: *A leadership which is not ahead of the masses in understanding facts and processes, a leadership which does not foresee events, isn't a leadership but a brake on historical development.* When good Communists make such excuses for the leadership, they do it out of an unconscious fear of authority. Practical experience of party life has taught us that the average party official, unless he is defending a party decision, sees more and thinks better by himself, purely by instinct, than any official at the top. *Today there are new processes which have to be foreseen and predicted on the basis of present contradictions if one means to master the future instead of facing it completely unprepared.* For instance, there is a terrible risk that if the gigantic mass movements which are springing up in a number of countries (U.S.A., France) are not properly led and made conscious of their goal, they will peter out and will be followed by the bitterest disappointment and lethargy. It is just as possible that the growth of indignation and political insight among the masses will develop into a world-revolutionary situation. We are entitled to say that after the events of June 30, reinforced by Germany's grave economic disorganization, we might have dealt the decisive blow if only the Communist leadership in Germany had thoroughly prepared itself for such an opportunity since 1929, or at least since 1932. We should use the past not to make excuses but to learn. Today we need to understand the main lines of historical development, as well as the social factors which impede development, if we are to seize the initiative when the system breaks down. Until then, the broad masses of the world's population must come to feel, slowly but unshakably, that we Communists are the only ones who understand them. We must understand the masses, and not just the language of Barthou and Litvinov and our own daydreams. Such confidence cannot be created by sleight of hand; it must be a true, fervent confidence in us, in Communism, such that the "sole leaders" not only were unable to obtain in the space of ten years but actually undermined by their mistakes and lack of insight. The impending war will doubtless be the next enormous chance that will offer itself to the social revolution. We must not miss it as we missed the chances of July 20, 1932, of December 1933 and January 1934, and of June 30, 1934. But first the revolutionaries will have to get rid of their own blind faith in authority.

the process of revolutionary concentration and maturation which is taking place in all strata of the German population at present and infer the concrete situation as it is at any given moment.

If today's revolutionary cadres were primarily concerned not with defending their own organizations but with rallying revolutionary energies, the organization would be supple enough to respond promptly and correctly to the masses. Instead of mechanically calling for strikes, it would be able to help the storm trooper, the youth leader, the women's organizer in their acute difficulties by offering explanations and solutions, and so gain their confidence and eventually their allegiance. The dreary, scholastic, inhibiting aspect of *all* the existing organizations, the thing that so repels the masses, is that each of them believes itself to be the God-given leader of the future revolution and for this reason tries to denigrate every other organization as counter-revolutionary. Such vain arrogance and childish conceit cannot be attacked often or energetically enough. Sex-Pol must make quite sure that it does not regard itself, as constituted today, as the leader of the sexual-political wing of the revolution. Ultimate leadership is not a claim and certainly not a right; it is the result of a process. Whoever succeeds best in grasping the world's events, making them intelligible to the broad masses —especially the nonpolitical ones—and advancing the process of revolutionary ferment will eventually assume leadership. To assert leadership in the revolution is not a merit, a quality or a claim; it is a heavy responsibility; it is a *result,* and therefore it cannot be achieved by words or tricks. Today, in a world situation that is so confused and complex, so little understood, and capable of so many different outcomes, he who proclaims himself most loudly as the sole, true, one hundred percent obvious leader of the revolution that is yet to come will be the first to sink silently into oblivion when the moment comes to speak *with justification* of a revolutionary upsurge.

The following are further points of importance for the rebuilding of the revolutionary movement. In the nation as a whole the really class-conscious proletariat forms a small minority. Even if it is the rightful leader, it still needs allies. German comrades are always telling us that there is every reason for optimism because good revolutionaries are finding each other once more, discussing and working together and advising one another. That is doubtless very important, but it is not yet a reason for optimism. What matters in the first place is whether these good revolutionaries are really in touch with the broad, unorganized masses; whether, in order to enter into such contact, they really listen to the language, the thinking, the contradictions of these broad nonpolitical or politically misled masses; whether they can understand that language, translate it into the language of the revolution and give it back in clear, class-conscious form. These cadres will remain a general staff without an army unless they encourage party officials to become part of the broad masses in order to understand *exactly* what the nonpolitical or politically misled masses have on their minds.

Sectarianism becomes impossible if the party members are no longer merely the executors of the leadership and its decisions but a vital mediator between the leadership and the masses. The task of the leadership is not "to carry the Communist program to the masses" or "to make the masses into class-conscious militants"; its most important task, besides studying the objective historical process, consists in *developing* the revolutionary instincts *which are already there;* and in developing these instincts simultaneously in the proletariat, the petty bourgeoisie and the peasantry.

In today's revolutionary press almost nothing but party jargon is to be found. There is hardly ever any sign of comprehension of the contradictions facing the various strata of the population. Yet, such a dialogue with the broad masses—both in terms of language and of subject matter—should fill at least three-quarters of every newspaper; the remaining quarter is enough for reiterating the fundamental principles of Marxism.

To put it differently, until we have learned to present difficult theories in simple language intelligible to everyone, until the masses have reached the point where they begin to be interested in these theories, we must constantly say the same thing twice in different ways: in Marxist language and the language of the broad masses, who are the only people that matter. Without their sympathy and active support for the cause of the revolution we shall always remain miserable word-slingers.

When these questions are discussed, we in Sex-Pol are often

asked to provide ready-made recipes. This in itself shows how little the fundamental task of a revolutionary Marxist—that of being capable of independent thought and action—has been understood. One can only give examples to illustrate specific principles, but something which is correct in one case may be wrong in another. Let me give a few examples to clarify my meaning.

Folk Songs and Folk Dances as Sources of Revolutionary Feeling

Lenin taught, rightly, that the revolutionary must be able to feel at home in every sphere of life. We might add that he must be able to develop the specific revolutionary tendency inherent in every sphere of life.

If we think of proletarian theater and "red cabarets," we are bound to recognize that apart from a few exceptions, it has simply been a case of mechanically transposing political and trade union slogans to the old art form, e.g., superimposing a revolutionary statement on a bourgeois-type song. The revolutionary artist's most important task is to do precisely what Sex-Pol has learned to do in its own sphere—namely, to develop specific revolutionary tendencies and forms out of the available material *as it exists under capitalism.*

This does not require much "science," but it does require an uninhibited, free, relaxed and, in short, revolutionary view of life. The CP instituted the "red cabarets" in order to attract more people, including nonpoliticals, to its meetings, and the method worked very well. It was found that the more artistic, rhythmical and popular were the numbers presented, the more striking was their effect. This effect was reduced if the numbers were old bourgeois ones with a revolutionary slogan slapped on as an afterthought. Now, it isn't possible to organize enough red cabarets to bring the entire population to party meetings. From this it follows that revolutionary art, revolutionary feeling, revolutionary rhythms, revolutionary melodies have to be carried to the places where the masses live, work, suffer or just wait. This can certainly be done in countries which are still democratic or only semifascist, but it can even be achieved in completely fascist countries by using special stratagems. Revolutionary musicians, dancers, singers, etc., need only the simplest means to form groups including youths, girls, older children and even adults; like street singers, they must go into the courtyards, the market places—in short, wherever the executors of the future revolution habitually gather. By performing good folk music, folk dances and folk songs, which the revolution can take over because they are intrinsically anticapitalist and therefore are, or can be, adapted to the feelings of the oppressed, they can create and spread that atmosphere which we so badly need to turn the broad masses into sympathizers of the revolution.

A bureaucrat will make all kinds of objections to this proposal; he may even say that it creates a "distraction" from the class struggle, which is "the most important thing." I do not know whether the proposal involves concrete problems, or what these problems are; whoever expects ready-made recipes will never accomplish anything. But in principle—and never mind the form—what we of the Sex-Pol group say is true: we must attach the masses to us by *feeling*. And attachment by feeling means *trust,* like the trust a child has in his mother, who protects and guides him; it means being understood down to one's most secret worries and wishes, including, first and foremost, the most secret thing of all: sexuality.

Revolutionary Scientific Work

Working for the masses also covers scientific research and the questioning of bourgeois science in all its branches, not only political economy. Bourgeois science dominates the formation of ideology in our society, and this domination is the more powerful the nearer the particular branch of science approaches life. We need only think of sexual-political literature (race doctrine). From this it clearly follows that the neglect of revolutionary scientific work in countries with a high level of culture is bound to reduce our opportunities of influencing the masses. It will also increase our difficulties in constructing a new social order after the victory of the social revolution. By solving the problem of revolutionary scientific work we shall at the same time solve a large part of the problem of the intellectuals.

Once more the reconstruction of the revolutionary movement must begin with an honest look at the way in which revolutionary scientific work has been conducted to date. Here we can only deal with broad outlines. Let us consider just a few important facts. Marxism has been treated as a philosophy for its own sake, mostly in the form of endless debates on "accident and necessity" which no ordinary mortal can understand. Kurt Sauerland's well-known book on dialectical materialism was a classic example of this approach, a combination of philosophical formalism and party opportunism. Scientific research in the natural sciences lay fallow, and in the social sciences the situation was hardly better. We were not up to the standard of the bourgeois scholars. Except for a few good contributions, even the review *Unter dem Banner des Marxismus,* whose purpose was to cultivate and develop Marxist science, was paralyzed by formal language and abstract dialectics. It never stimulated discussions or effectively intervened in the controversies of bourgeois science. It did nothing but protect its revolutionary loyalty. This raises a question of principle. A revolutionary should not think that he has discharged his task on the scientific front by accusing his opponents of overlooking the theory of the class struggle, or by declaring his loyalty to the revolution in every third sentence. This is in no way a substitute for objective argument.

First of all, we need to take a close look at the situation and structure of bourgeois science in general. It is broken up into a hundred thousand individualistic fragments, serving either the careerism of the lower stratum of scientists or the private obsessions of the higher stratum. Within the same technical field, one scientist cannot understand another. Bourgeois science is academic not only in its language but also in its choice of subjects (compare the number of detailed papers on the structure of brain tissue in chronic alcoholics with that of papers on the social conditions which cause alcoholism). And the closer the subject studied is to real life, the more remote from life is bourgeois science, the more grotesque the theories it produces, the more abstract the discussions around these theories. For this reason a science like, say, mathematics is the most free from the influences of bourgeois thinking, while, say, research into tuberculosis has not yet got to the point of thoroughly studying the effect of poor food and housing on the human lungs. Of psychiatry, the home of the wildest idiocies of all, let it be said only that this science, whose purpose should be to define the fundamental principles of psychical hygiene, operates as a specially designed tool to render this impossible. These examples may suffice to show why Marxist science needs to compete on the terrain of purely technical knowledge so as to become objectively superior to bourgeois science and also to attract the young intellectuals and scientists, whom we shall urgently need after the revolution.

Marxist science cannot be developed simply by sticking the slogan of class struggle onto science like a label: it can only be developed from the questions, problems and findings of individual branches of science itself. It must be objectively demonstrated *where* bourgeois science has failed, *why* it has failed, *where* and *how* the bourgeois world view is an impediment to knowledge, etc. Then, after this has been done, really, objectively done, one has a right to call oneself a Marxist scientist and, as such, to investigate the relationship between individual sciences and the economic class struggle.

The above views are not empty assertions—they are firmly based on the experience of the development of sex economy. We shall use this special example, therefore, to elucidate a further question of the scientific controversy between the proletariat and the bourgeoisie which, in accordance with the principles of revolutionary politics, leads to a more general problem.

Anyone familiar with the dissensions inside the world of bourgeois science realizes the hopelessness of any attempt to defeat by argument an opponent's false views. Freud discovered that psychical disturbances are consequences of sexual repression. The lunatic asylums, psychiatric clinics and welfare hostels of the capitalist countries are bursting with the products of bourgeois sexual economy. A humorist worked out a little while ago that judging by the increase in the number of the mentally sick in the United States, two hundred and fifty years from now there will only be mentally sick people left. That is not at all as improbable as it sounds. Until a few years ago one could still hope that Freud's revolutionary discoveries might conquer the psychiatric profession and the question of the prophylaxis of neuroses come under urgent consideration. That would have been the first step toward a dialogue between the Marxist and bourgeois views in this field, without the word "Marxism" having to be expressly mentioned from the start. But what actually happened was that psychiatry remained quite untouched, persisted in the nonsensical view of "degenerative predisposition" as the cause of psychical disease, and even in some places won over a part of the psychoanalytical movement. A leading psychoanalyst declared a short while ago that there was no need to bother with prophylaxis of neuroses; it was quite enough to practice individual therapy. The reason is obvious: the question of prophylaxis of neuroses leads to the wider question of the bourgeois sexual order and challenges the very existence of religion and morality. To launch a "Marxist" attack on Freud's errors by "unmasking" him as a "reactionary" would be idiotic. But by objectively demonstrating the areas where Freud is a scientist of genius and where he is an old-hat bourgeois philosopher, one could perform useful Marxist revolutionary work.

Is there any hope, then, that scientific discussions will decide the struggle in the scientific field in favor of revolution? No, that can never happen. This does not mean that we should henceforth reject all discussion: on the contrary, we must promote discussions and try to acquire leading positions in all scientific organizations based on the objective value of our work. We must learn from discussion why and where the bourgeois scientists go wrong in their thinking and ignore essential facts. Only in this way can we ourselves become better trained. But the real struggle is waged elsewhere. To stay with the example of sex: no bourgeois psychiatrist of average mentality will ever accept the view that neuroses, psychoses, addictions, etc., are consequences of the appalling sexual economy of the masses. The broad masses, on the other hand, are extremely interested in these problems, if only because they are a source of serious suffering for them and because the narrow-mindedness of the psychiatrists—those administrators of the capitalist sexual order —and the psychical misery resulting from it affect them personally and directly. I am sure that the average working-class youth has a better understanding of the relationship between repressed sexuality and psychical depression or loss of working capacity than most average psychiatrists throughout the world.

We can safely say that once the masses are leading a sexually satisfied, healthy life, the question whether mental illness is an expression of a disturbed sexual economy will decide itself even in the minds of the champions of bourgeois morality in the Marxist camp—the doctors, educators and others—who, as a result of their bourgeois deformations, reject psychoanalysis because they fail to understand it. The principle of always turning to the masses, always addressing the masses in an intelligible fashion, applies here too, in the sacred sphere of supposedly unassailable science. Sex-Pol owed its popularity, and the sympathy it received, to broad strata of the German and Austrian population, not to any organization, for it had none; not to any power, for it had none; it owed it solely to its basic principle of making the question of sexual health *a public issue*. That is why even the party bureaucracy is powerless against Sex-Pol, and will remain so.

What is so eminently true of Sex-Pol applies also to every branch of medical or other science—for instance, tuberculosis research. But revolutionary scientists must not disseminate false, bourgeois ideas among the masses, thus only helping the reaction. They must first work out the principles of a dialectical, materialist approach in their particular field and, only then, put these principles before the masses. It is clearly far better to say nothing at all than to preach the bourgeois notion, while shouting "Long live the revolution," that sexual intercourse is bad for the young.

The masses have a magnificent instinct for the truth, but this instinct is frustrated when the revolutionary organization offers them nothing, and the bourgeois charlatans will offer everything from table-levitating to the miraculous spring at Lourdes.

The Fear of Revolution

The Communist revolutionary movement wants the same as the petty-bourgeois pacifist movement: the abolition of wars and the establishment of peace on earth. The revolutionaries hold the view, rightly, that this goal is attainable only through a forcible overthrow of the rule of capital, e.g., by the transformation of an imperialist war into a civil war. The pacifists reject civil war as just another example of the use of violence. They refuse to recognize that by this rejection they are upholding a system that gives rise to wars.

The broad nonpolitical masses look upon Communists as "men of violence." Moreover, the view of the broad masses is *decisive*. The masses fear violence, want peace and quiet, and for that reason will have nothing to do with Communism. At present, nonetheless, the masses are encouraging the very thing they want to abolish.

Communist propaganda to date has proposed the theory of violence and opposed that of pacifism in an absolute and mechanistic way. That is why a considerable proportion of Social Democrats failed to join the Communist movement. The theory of the seizure of power by violence cannot be abandoned, but neither can the broad masses be directly won over to it.

One of the major strengths of the National Socialist movement has been that, besides the illusion of a "German revolution," they promised the masses a *nonviolent* seizure of power. In that way, quite unconsciously, of course, it appealed to both the revolutionary and the pacifistic wishes of the masses.

In order to resolve this contradiction it is necessary to pose two questions: First, what do the masses feel about violence? Experience shows that they are pacifistic and afraid of violence.

The second question is: What is the relationship between the use of violence (which we know to be necessary) and the masses' attitude toward it? The answer to both questions is, and can only be, the same. *The larger the mass base of the revolutionary movement, the less violence will be required,* and the more, also, will the masses lose their fear of revolution. The increasing degree of influence of the revolutionary movement inside the army and the state apparatus has the same effect. For this reason the Russian revolution had only a minimum of casualties. It was the imperialist intervention that caused the blood bath. By then it was historically clear and obvious to everyone that the blame lay with the imperialists and the White Guard.

However, the size of the mass base will depend on the extent to which the revolutionary party can grasp the language of all the working strata of the population and is able to articulate their desires and revolutionary ideas. This is where one needs a conscious mass-psychological praxis.

Possibly, at this point, "a principled opponent" will object that the Russian revolution succeeded—as one so often hears—without the aid of sexual politics and mass psychology. Our immediate answer would be that the Russian peasants were not bourgeoisified as Americans are; that the Russian proletariat are not identical with the British working class, and that, moreover, the Russian revolution was led by Lenin, who was the greatest mass psychologist of all time.

To return to the question of the mass base of the revolution, let us consider a second, still more concrete example.

*The Cop as Stand-in for the State
and as an Individual*

The ordinary German cop has always been full of curious contradictions. In a logical development of its "social fascism" theory, the Communist press has incessantly complained of "police violence," "police mobs," etc. The party's anger at the police is perfectly understandable, for the police attacked and broke up every demonstration. But however justifiable its action may be, a revolutionary leadership has no right to give in to anger or other feelings of affect. It should not ignore the fact that without the sympathy and active help of a large part (indeed the majority) of the police, an insurrection cannot succeed except with an immense loss of life. The same is true of the army.

The Communist leadership should not for a moment forget that the policeman and the soldier are sons of proletarians, peasants, employees, etc. Instead of raging against them, it should ask itself what goes on in the mind of the average policeman or soldier to make him turn his back so dramatically on his own class.

I don't know if the sketch that follows comes near the truth. It may not. But think of a mounted police captain armed and helmeted, riding high above the crowd on the street; and then imagine him at home, in the midst of his proletarian family circle, as brother, husband or father; imagine him in bed, or in his underpants! In the street, he is the "representative of the state." Little working-class girls involuntarily act ingratiatingly toward him; for haven't their mothers told them they will go get the policeman if they are "naughty," that is, if they disobey, or perhaps play with their genitals? So, of course, the policeman sees himself as the custodian of order and it makes him feel very grand. That is the reactionary element in him. At home and in the barracks, he is the underpaid, depersonalized, eternally subservient stooge of capitalism: a contradiction which, with many other similar ones, is decisive for the revolutionary struggle.

The majority of the Prussian cops were until recently Social Democrats. During the weeks in which Hitler came to power, many of them helped Communists and Socialists to escape the persecution of the S.S. A consistent, reasonable, understanding use of reactionary propaganda could have fairly easily resolved the policeman's psychical contradiction. But let me say it again: we offer no recipes, only a method of viewing various problems.

Here is an example of how *not* to do things. When the von Papen government was formed in July 1932, one of its first actions was to stop women from visiting the police barracks, which had previously been allowed. The resulting attitude was somewhat rebellious. Those of us who worked in the "lower" organizations heard from many sides that the mood of the younger cops was more or less as follows: "We've put up with a great deal without protest—reduced wages, longer working hours, and so on. But we're damned if we'll let them take the girls away too." Sex-Pol immediately informed the Central Committee and advised it to take account of this mood, and to come out publicly in support of this particular interest of the police. The C.C. wouldn't hear of it. They said it had "nothing to do with the class struggle." We also found that in cases where cops had attended the Sex-Pol medical-advice centers their hostility toward the working-class movement was considerably reduced. But no one paid attention to such facts. Admittedly they do not belong to "high-level" politics. Yet they show quite unequivocally that a direct approach to various strata of the population must be based not on abstract political issues, but on the actual needs and preoccupations of the masses.

If we remain deaf to the small, seemingly incidental and secondary phenomena of the life of the masses, the masses will never believe that we will understand them after we have seized power.

A friend of the Sex-Pol movement picked up two apprentices while traveling by car on a country road. The talk quickly turned to politics. The boys were real proletarian lads, not yet of voting age, with a vaguely socialist outlook, but, as they said, without any interest in politics. They left all that kind of stuff to their honored Social Democratic Premier, and would gladly surrender their right to vote, too, in exchange for the pretty girls they met on their travels. Our friend assured us that these were certainly not depraved vagabonds, but healthy, average working-class boys. Anyone who has no ear, no understanding and no will to learn from such things is a hopeless case.

In Austria, soldiers from working-class and peasant families have just killed hundreds of their class comrades and razed their homes to the ground. Nowhere was the question asked: How is such a thing possible, and what can we do about it? Yet, on this question, and on the answer to it, depends nothing more nor less than the "high-level" strategical question of whether, and how, insurrections and street fighting are possible, given the present level of military equipment in the hands of the state.

Instead of hurling abuse at each other's heads and calling one another "traitors of the working class," which leads nowhere because no one is better than the next man, those who call themselves the leaders of the proletariat would do better to ask such questions, and to try to understand these soldiers; then they would learn how to influence the army and the police.

The Development of a Revolutionary State Policy from the People's Needs

When a representative of Sex-Pol met with Wilhelm Pieck, the representative of the party's Central Committee, for a discussion in 1932, Pieck said that the views expounded in *The Imposition of Sexual Morality* contradicted those of the party and of Marxism.

Asked to explain, he said, "Your starting point is consumption, ours is production; therefore, you are not Marxists." The Sex-Pol spokesman asked whether human needs arose out of production or whether, on the contrary, production was there to satisfy human needs. Pieck failed to understand this question. Only two years later did the distinction become clear: economistic communism developed its entire work and propaganda solely from the objective aspect of social existence, from the progress of the productive forces, from economic contradictions between states, the superiority of the Soviet planned economy over capitalist anarchy, etc., and it then "tied the politics of state into the small daily needs." But this tie-in was an utter fiasco. Sex-Pol, on the other hand, aroused maximum interest, even among the most politically confused people at every level, by developing the necessities of the social revolution out of subjective needs, and by basing all political issues on the "whether" and the "how" of satisfying the needs of the masses. Herein lies not only the fundamental difference between living revolutionary work and dogmatic, scholastic "Marxism," but also the reason why even the best party officials, once they get stuck in "high state politics," fail to understand what Sex-Pol is all about.

Some Comintern officials, of course, are aware that something is missing from their work. Yet they cannot find the concrete point at which state politics and mass needs come together. For example, Manuilsky in his speech entitled "The Revolutionary Crisis is Maturing" delivered at the Seventeenth Party Congress of the C.P.S.U. (quoted from *Rundschau,* No. 16, p. 586) said:

Let us take our Communist Youth International. The Communist Youth International has, over a period of years under the guidance of the Comintern, raised a splendid generation of young Bolsheviks who have more than once proved their boundless devotion to the cause of Communism. But it has not proved capable of penetrating deep into the masses of working youth. The Social Democrats haven't got this youth either. The youth in the capitalist countries belong to the millions-strong sports organizations created by the bourgeoisie, by its military staffs and by its priests. In Germany, a certain group of unemployed youth has gone into the fascist barracks. But the members of the Young Communist League have not quite understood this lesson. In Germany they fought the fascists courageously. In a number of countries they are doing quite good work in the army, and are getting long sentences of imprisonment for it, yet it no more occurs to them to join, say, a Catholic sports organization, where tens of thousands of young workers meet, than it would occur to the Pope to join the League of Atheists in hopes of making propaganda for Catholicism. (*Laughter.*) But members of the YCL and Communists are not bound by prestige considerations as the Vicar of Christ is. Communist and YCL organizations must be always on the move, they must be present wherever workers are present, they must be in the sports organizations, in such leisure-time organizations as the *Dopolavoro* in

Italy, in the labor service camps, but above all they must be in the factories.

All this is perfectly correct, but the most important thing is lacking. When a member of the YCL works inside a Christian youth organization, the economico-political analyses of the CP's Central Committee are of absolutely no use to him in attracting the interest of his young Christian colleagues. He has got to know what he should talk about and what solutions Communism has to offer, not so much to problems of political economy as to the special problems of Catholic youth. From this starting point he can go on, very gradually, to show how a planned economy would serve as a basis for solving personal problems. And so we may say that Sex-Pol agrees with Manuilsky in principle, so far as the inner-organizational work of Communists is concerned, but it differs profoundly from him on the concrete questions of the actual interests of average young men and women, Christian or otherwise, and the crucial personal problems that should serve as the starting point for the work of the YCL propagandist.[3] The same applies to every formalistic notion of the Comintern leaders.

They are always saying, quite rightly, that work concerning the masses is necessary, but at the same time they reject the *concrete contents* of such necessary work, especially if these contents are personal and removed from "high politics." They see the personal and the political as opposite poles instead of recognizing the dialectical relationship between them. Not only are some personal problems (such as the question of sexual partners or of separate dwellings for young people) among the most typical social problems, but one could go so far as to say that politics is nothing more than the praxis of the needs and interests of the different strata and age groups of society.

To sum up very briefly: the difference between revolutionary and bourgeois politics is that the former sets out to serve the needs of the masses, whereas the latter is wholly founded on the

[3] See *The Sexual Struggle of Youth*. This book was banned by the German Communist Party, while young people at all levels snatched it up with the utmost eagerness.

structural, historically conditioned inability of the masses to formulate their needs.

Anyone who has worked in Communist cells knows how even party members feel about "high politics." The political lecture was part and parcel of the weekly meeting. The speaker would hold forth about bourgeois politics—some would do it better, some less well—and all the others would listen with more or less interest, but always passively. Discussion would spring up, as a rule, only in cells where intellectuals or old, well-trained party members who actually enjoyed discussing "high politics" formed the majority. In the last few months before Hitler's seizure of power it happened more and more frequently that proletarian comrades, quite unfamiliar with "high politics" but aware that something had to be done, interrupted the dull political lecture to say something like: "You've been telling us for years what the bourgeois wants and what the bourgeois does, now tell us what *we* ought to do, what *our* politics ought to be." The speakers did not know what to say. When the success of Sex-Pol speakers began to be talked about in various branches, and it was said that Sex-Pol speakers could get the most un-educated members of the masses and the party interested in politics by starting with personal issues and proceeding to politi-cal ones, the party began asking for Sex-Pol speakers because they wanted to get the "nonpoliticals" to their group evenings. The party's work with women and youth was failing every-where because the same method of talking about the "political situation" was used everywhere and people everywhere were equally bored. But the Sex-Pol speakers were trained to inquire first of all into the personal worries of women, young people, the unemployed, etc. They would propose "nonpolitical" subjects, such as "How should I educate my child?" or "Boys and girls in our organization." Every discussion of these issues relating to everyday life aroused great interest and lively participation on the part of the audience and always led to the great political questions, which, when presented in the old form, stifled any revolutionary feeling. Instead of going in for "high politics" and talking about "how to tie in the day-to-day problems" and then virtually excluding such problems from the discussion, the Sex-

Pol proceeded systematically, always beginning with personal issues and ending up with, say, the Hitler-Brüning political setup. The official party representatives attacked our method as "counter-revolutionary diversionism." Yet they kept sending for us to come to Oranienburg, Jüterbog, Dresden, Frankfurt, Steglitz, Stettin, etc., to "bring in the nonpoliticals." In large factories, where the employees were widely contaminated by National Socialism and had been out of touch with the red trade unions for years, the Sex-Pol persuaded dozens of people to come to meetings, revived the work of the Communist cells, got women and juveniles interested, etc. The movement was too young and too weak; at first it was reluctantly tolerated and later it was banned by the party leadership; all it could do was to gather experience. Its method, which was attacked as a reactionary diversion from politics, was in reality the true method of revolutionary propaganda. This was proved by the fact that the "nonpoliticals" always became interested in politics in the end.

No revolutionary organization will ever be victorious without the revolutionary politicization of the masses, who are simply not interested in high politics in the old form. The so-called revolutionary campaigns to which the masses responded with a greater or lesser degree of indifference were attempts to "mobilize" the masses by the force of example. In the majority of cases these attempts failed completely.

The experience of Sex-Pol work in Germany can be applied to all fields of revolutionary politics. The sluggish masses cannot be politicized by example alone, still less by psychologically false appeals on the lines of "To the Toilers of the World," etc. If the masses are to become politically active, they must begin by asking themselves the fundamental question of revolutionary politics: "What is it we want? How do we get it?" If it is true—as we don't doubt that it is—that the social revolution will make a reality of the idea of social democracy, so that the entire population will participate in politics (not in the bourgeois game of diplomacy but in revolutionary politics), and that it will not only "draw" the masses into the work of organizing social life but actually place the main part of that work in the hands of the masses—if all this is true, the fundamental principles of work with the masses which we have only cursorily sketched here with the help of a few examples become an inescapable necessity. These examples make no claim to being universally applicable; they only suggest ways of dealing with the question of whether and how the latent energy of the masses can be roused to active life.

Taking Control of What Is Rightfully One's Own

It is clear that there can never be a leadership capable of surveying and directing *all* the problems and tasks thrown up by social life. Only a bourgeois dictatorship can do this because it takes no account of the needs of the masses, and because it actually depends on the apparent lack of demands and the political apathy of the masses. Under capitalism today labor has been socialized for a long time; only the appropriation of the products of labor is private.

One of the social revolution's promises is that it will socialize large factories, i.e., place them under the self-management of the workers. We know the difficulties that the Soviet Union had with such self-management at the beginning and is still having today. Revolutionary work in factories can be successful only if it arouses the workers' *objective* interest in production and proceeds from there. But workers today have no interest in production as such, certainly not in its present form. In order to acquire a revolutionary interest in production they must think of it as their own property *now,* under capitalism. Workers in factories must be made aware that their labor makes these factories theirs by right, and only theirs; that this right, which the capitalists at the moment still claim for themselves, leads to many duties; that, in order to be one's own master, one has to know something about industrial management, organization, etc. Our propaganda must make it clear that it is the workers, not the present owners of capital and the means of production, who are the real masters of the factory. In terms of mass psychology it makes an enormous difference whether one says, "We are going to expropriate the large capitalists," or "We are taking our property into our rightful control." In the first case, the average nonpolitical or politically deformed industrial worker will react with a sense of guilt and a certain inhibition, as though he were seizing someone else's property. In the second case, he becomes conscious of his legitimate ownership, which is based on his labor, and the bourgeois view of the "sacred" nature of private property will lose its power over him. The problem is not that the ruling class disseminates and defends its ideology; the problem is why the masses accept it.

Is it beyond the powers of a revolutionary organization to explain to the workers that they are the rightful owners of the factories they work in, and that they should start thinking about their responsibilities *as of now?* Just as the petty-bourgeois and proletarian women in the Sex-Pol groups were anxious to learn *now* what the best way was of bringing up children, organizing housework, etc., whether it was a good idea to set up collective kitchens on every floor of a tenement building, etc., so, in the same way, workers in factories must start *now* to prepare for the take-over of these factories. They must learn to think for themselves, they must train themselves to look out for everything that will be needed and to think of how it should be organized. The Soviet experience can help them in this process. But it cannot save them the work they must do themselves, for our conditions and possibilities are completely different. Without any doubt, this is the only way in which workers can be given an interest in the social revolution—not by learned lectures on the political situation and the Five-Year Plan. The actual take-over of power in factories must be preceded by concrete preparation for this take-over *in the mind.* The same applies to every youth organization, every sports organization, every military group. This, and only this, deserves to be called "arousing class consciousness."

The revolutionary party leadership has and can have no other task than that of working on these preliminary stages of revolutionary social democracy, guiding the preparations, making its own superior knowledge available. Drawn into concrete work in this way, every worker will feel he is the real master of his factory and will no longer see the entrepreneur as an employer but as the exploiter of his own labor power. A revolutionary leader should know what surplus value is, and a worker should know exactly how much profit for the entrepreneur he is producing with his labor. *That is class consciousness.* Then he will strike, not just out of a sense of solidarity, not just because the shop steward tells him to, but *in his own interest,* and no trade union leader will be able to deceive him ever again. He will fight for his own interests—more than that, he will force the strike upon his weak-kneed trade union leaders and will sack them if they let him down. Until now, revolutionary propaganda has consisted, in substance, only of negative criticism. It must learn to be constructive, anticipatory and positive as well.

Exactly the same principle of *becoming conscious* through tackling concrete problems applies to youth of every social class and stratum. Working-class youth will take part in concrete trade union work. Others will concern themselves with organizing their personal lives, dealing with their parental conflicts, solving the problems of a sexual partner and housing. In this way they will create new forms of social life (at first only in the mind), then they will argue and eventually fight for these new forms; nothing will stop them. Talks on the political situation or even about the "sexual problem of youth" are useless. That is control from above. Youth must begin *as of now* to organize its own life in every field. At first, in doing this, the young people cannot pay much attention to the authorities or the police, nor should we expect them to; they should go right ahead and do what they think right and what they believe they can accomplish. They will realize soon enough that they are rigidly fenced in on all sides, that the system makes it impossible to organize even the simplest and most obvious things in the life of young people; thus their own practice will show them the nature of revolutionary politics and revolutionary necessity. If the capitalist authorities interfere with their efforts to obtain contraceptives, or, for instance, to organize cooperatives, if they interfere with threats, then with arrests, finally with heavy sentences, then and only then will young people feel acutely where and how they are oppressed; then they will learn to fight, not in a vacuum, not for the sake of slogans brought in from outside, but against the harsh reality of life under capitalism. That is how the young

Czechs learned to fight when the police attacked their camping grounds, where they were leading the sexual life they wanted to lead. They fought for their rights in the streets—bare fists against the power of the state. In Germany today, people camping together have to produce their marriage licenses; German youth so far has accepted the ban, reluctantly but without protest, still hoping to find ways of circumventing it. Their awareness that they have a right to run their own lives as they see fit will inevitably drive them, too, to fight for it. All they need is a little support, an organization, a party which understands them, helps them, speaks on their behalf.

Conclusions

The class consciousness of the masses is not a knowledge of the historical or economic laws that govern the existence of the human being, but it is

1. knowledge of one's own vital necessities in all spheres;
2. knowledge of ways and possibilities of satisfying them;
3. knowledge of the obstacles that a social system based on private property puts in the way of their satisfaction;
4. knowledge of one's own inhibitions and fears that prevent one from clearly realizing one's needs and the obstacles to their satisfaction ("the enemy within" is a particularly true image of the psychical inhibitions of the oppressed individual);
5. knowledge that mass unity makes an invincible force against the power of oppressors.

The class consciousness of the revolutionary leadership (the revolutionary party) is nothing more than knowledge plus the ability to articulate on behalf of the masses what they cannot express themselves. The revolutionary liberation from capitalism is the final act that will grow spontaneously from the fully developed class consciousness of the masses once the revolutionary leadership has understood the masses in every aspect of their life.

REFORMING
THE LABOR
MOVEMENT

Points
for Discussion

What follows is a summary of some changes in our method of proceeding. They seem to be needed if we judge by the past errors.

PRELIMINARY

It is not possible to go into particular cases. What is needed is to become clear about our basic outlook and analysis. This, in turn, is applied in particular cases. If correct in fundamentals you will not have errors in specific applications. But suppose your basic outlook and method are wrong. In this case even a correct decision in specific cases will be an accident. The chance for error will be immense.

Making Judgments about Political Events

1. *Two* questions need to be asked in thinking about *every* development: (a) Does this case display a trend that is reactionary or revolutionary? (b) Do the people involved believe it has a socialist or a capitalist aim? (The objective and the sub-

jective are for the most part not closely matched. For instance, objectively the S.A. troops are counter-revolutionary. Subjectively they are revolutionary.)

2. If the tasks that need doing are to be done rightly, you must ask in deciding each judgment and policy:
—What's happening in the various strata of the masses?
—What favors us there? What opposes us?
—What is the broad, unpolitical or miseducated masses' perception of the political events?
—How do these masses perceive and feel about the revolutionary movement?

3. Every development is contradictory. It has elements which favor and which retard the revolution (for example, the reactionary and the revolutionary elements within Fascism). *Foresight* is possible only when
—the contradictions are understood;
—the different possible courses for further development are explored.

4. The social process contains progressive but also retrograde or retrogressive forces. (For example, in the Hitler Youth, sexual freedom is progressive, and trust in authority is retrogressive.) Revolutionary work consists of the understanding of both, and the aiding of the revolutionary tendencies.

5. Human needs do not exist for the sake of the economy. Rather, the economy exists for the sake of those needs.

6. The police, and others whom one flinches from as foes, should be pictured in their undershorts. And so with every feared authority.

Methods of Proceeding

7. To win the masses by means of manipulating and spellbinding—let us leave all that to the political reactionaries. The revolutionary movement does not want to spellbind. It should rather disclose processes to the masses. It should locate and

articulate their unexpressed and their unformulated needs. (The theory of the inevitable revolutionary upswing—that's an example of spellbinding.)

8. Secret negotiations is the politics of reaction. The politics of revolution is to turn always to the masses, and to root out secret negotiations. (For example, Litvinov's speech to the last session of the disarmament conference.)

9. If you read your own wants back into the masses, and you do not judge the *real* situation *independently* of your own wants, then the most directly met wants will remain unfulfilled. (Projection of the situation in a small circle onto the masses.)

10. The attitude called "economism" only leads to mistakes. Not the machine, but man, makes history. He uses machines for that end. The economy as such never enters directly into consciousness. There are many intermediary stages and also contradictions (for example, the worker who is Christian, the Nazi woman who is poor).

11. Possibly when the masses revolt against the material and sexual misery, it seems a problem-free development. Is this why it always is an incomprehensible problem when the masses *act against* their own interests ("irrational conduct")? Examples of the latter: the woman who welcomes marriage though it may be her cage; the worker who ignores the facts of exploitation when his job horizon appears clear; the adolescent who comes out on behalf of sexual repression.

12. Class consciousness is not something to be taught to the masses like lessons in school—as a set of doctrines. Rather, it is to be elicited, drawn out of the masses' own experience. The discovery of the politics of all human needs.

13. Demonstrate clearly that when the proletariat acts in its own interests, it represents at the same time the interests of all employed persons. Head off any conflict between the proletariat and the middle classes, for the industrial proletariat in high capitalism is numerically in the minority; and it is bourgeoisified too.

14. Better to employ no leaflets (or other actions) than to employ poor ones. Be sure to avoid anything that will disappoint and discourage the masses! Your will and your intention are not decisive. Decisive is how the masses react! (As distinguished from occasions when the people decide.) Instead, build confidence by all that you undertake. For instance: admit to not knowing something.

15. Do not exhort the masses to undertake more than they can carry out. A slow advance! Mostly, work by adopting the long view. Yet, catch hold of the advantage in every sudden turn of events!

16. The destiny of the revolution will always be ruled upon by the broad unpolitical masses. Therefore, and responsively, discover the politics that underlie private life. Politicize the trivial doings, wherever folks gather. In the dance hall, the movie house, the grocery store, the bedroom, the tavern, the betting office! The energy of the revolution is collected in the little things of everyday!

17. Always think internationally. Never just nationally ("We Germans aren't interested in the popular front in France, or the Saar question, or the Chinese revolution").

The Party—We Are It

18. Class consciousness comes in two forms. That of the masses is different from that of the leadership. (Examples of the former kind: the needs of adolescents, such as the need for their own living accommodations; the factory worker's refusal to accept a cut in his pay; the fury of the S.A. people when they were disarmed. Examples of the other kind: a knowledge of how the mechanism of crisis takes its course; a technical understanding of the socialist economic plans; an understanding of imperialist contradictions and armaments races throughout the world, combined with the most attentive empathy with the needs of the masses.)

19. The political force of an organization or movement is ultimately determined not by its will or its program, but by its mass base, i.e., by what elements of the mass come in to join it. Hence the same fate should not lie in store for the revolutionary leadership as it did for Goebbels, who could brush off the massacre of June 30, 1934, since he was the representative of no mass base by which he could be held accountable and which might have made him come down on the "right" side.

20. A crucial question: In what ways am I, a revolutionist, hampered by bourgeois, religious or moral habits? In what ways, therefore, am I crippled in my revolutionary work? At what points do I, too, tend to trust in authority?

21. The least we should expect is that the revolutionary leadership will act, not only subjectively but also objectively, in the revolutionary interest.

22. Where mistakes are made, it is imperative that corrections be carried through not only at the lower level but also at the higher level.

23. The political line must be submitted constantly to the control of the base. (Inner-party discussion.)

24. It is wrong to launch political steps silently, and often in secrecy. This only sows confusion and breeds incompetence. For every political step, a full accounting ought to be stated to the members of the party. The failures that occur should be the occasion for true self-criticism, which doesn't merely distribute blame mechanically to the lower levels of the party ("The decisions of the Xth Party Congress have not been carried out properly").

25. In this connection, the problem of the leadership has to be raised. There must be renewal of the personnel at the middle and upper levels of functionary cadres. Whoever acts and does so ignorantly . . . whoever proves reluctant to act . . . is not prepared to lead—and the pressure of the masses should lead him to admit it!

26. It is essential to find and prepare *in advance* the means

which will avert the bureaucratization of a living revolutionary organization. Why does the ordinary worker so readily turn into a mandarin when he is appointed a functionary? The best tell-tale warning: the sex-ethical attitude toward the willingness of young people to marry.

27. How are we to detect the future turncoat, the police spy, the renegade, unreliable type in a decisive moment, even before he realizes or is aware of it? (Vanity, ingratiating manner, soft-pedaling his position in debate, exceeding friendliness, or forced and abstract display of the revolutionary viewpoint, etc.)

28. What are the recognizable signs of the firm revolutionist? (Outwardly simple bearing, capacity for direct contact with people, simple straightforward conduct in sexual matters, absence of phrase-making, of course an emotional but above all a reasoned conviction favoring socialism, no mandarin tendencies when entrusted with tasks, absence of patriarchal attitude toward women and children.)

29. Composition of the party in the process of its building: quality, not quantity at the core! A core (the party), plus the matrix of sympathizing masses (formerly the simple party card-holders). A testing procedure before the admission of others.

30. No overburdening of the functionaries! Absolutely provide them with free time! Don't be indifferent to the private life; instead, aid in its right ordering! Always have substitutes prepared and ready to step in. Work allocated in tolerable proportions. Meetings brief and to the point! Criticism sought if pointed; critical carping *stringently rejected!* First always understand the point of view of the other! Avoid the "scattershot" approach, and intermittent "campaigning"; rather prove what is most fundamental and urgent, until the action is wrapped up as though by itself.

31. No needless heroism! Do not be proud of martyrdom, but conserve your resources! There's no art or fame in serving a sentence. But it can take the greatest art to avoid serving a sentence. Don't brag about "proletarian solidarity." Rather, really do practice solidarity (think of how it faltered in the case of the "Rote Hilfe").

32. Personal conflicts and relationships often disturb the political work! (For example, a wife who is self-centered and hampers the husband; or vice-versa.) Learn how not to reject the personal, but to politicize it.

33. In our thinking, we must learn to go through changes. This is to be distinguished from lacking convictions. Our adherence to organization and to transmitted ideas can get in the way of seeing the living reality, and we must learn to recognize that. (The revolutionary organization, and our conscious solidarity in it, are the bases for the individual's revolutionary work. Yet where the organization becomes an unconscious substitute for a homeland and family, the sharp focus on reality can be obscured.)

34. Also with regard to inner-party issues, always turn to the open court which is the party (this, of course, in times of legality). Inner-party secret proceedings are harmful. Anyone who must hide his opinion is not one of us. The same applies to anyone who subordinates the revolutionary cause to the service of tactics rather than the reverse.

35. To develop one's own initiative means quite unequivocally to gaze upon life steadily and to draw the consequences.

Index

369

ABOUT THE EDITOR

LEE BAXANDALL was an editor of *Studies on the Left,*
the pioneering historical and theoretical journal of the New Left.
He has written theater scripts and poems, and translated
Bertolt Brecht and Peter Weiss. Born and raised in Oshkosh,
Wisconsin, he now lives in New York City. He was
New York reviewer for *Encore* and is a contributing editor
for *Performance* magazine, and has published essays and
reviews in many other periodicals, including *The Drama Review,*
Partisan Review, Les temps modernes, The Radical Therapist,
Journal of Aesthetics and Art Criticism, The Nation
and *Liberation.* He compiled and edited the books
Marxism and Aesthetics: A Bibliography and *Radical*
Perspectives in the Arts.

BERTELL OLLMAN, who wrote the introduction,
is a professor in the Department of Politics at New York
University and recently published a book, *Alienation:*
Marx's Conception of Man in Capitalist Society.
In 1971 he was a senior research fellow at the Research
Institute on Communist Affairs and a visiting professor
in the Department of Sociology, both at Columbia University.
Mr. Ollman is a long-time student of psychoanalysis and
is currently working on several books on Marx's method
and the Marxist theory of class consciousness.